Randy Manning

GOLF

A Turn-of-the-Century Treasury

Mel Shapiro
Warren Dohn
Leonard Berger

GOLF

A Turn-of-the-Century Treasury

CASTLE

Golf

A Turn-of-the-Century Treasury

Manufactured in the United States of America

ISBN 1-55521-121-6

The Castle logo is registered in the United States Patent and Trademark Office

86 87 88 89 9 8 7 6 5 4 3 2 1

CONTENTS

1

A New Golf Alphabet

A NEW GOLF ALPHABET.

By Carrie Foote Weeks.

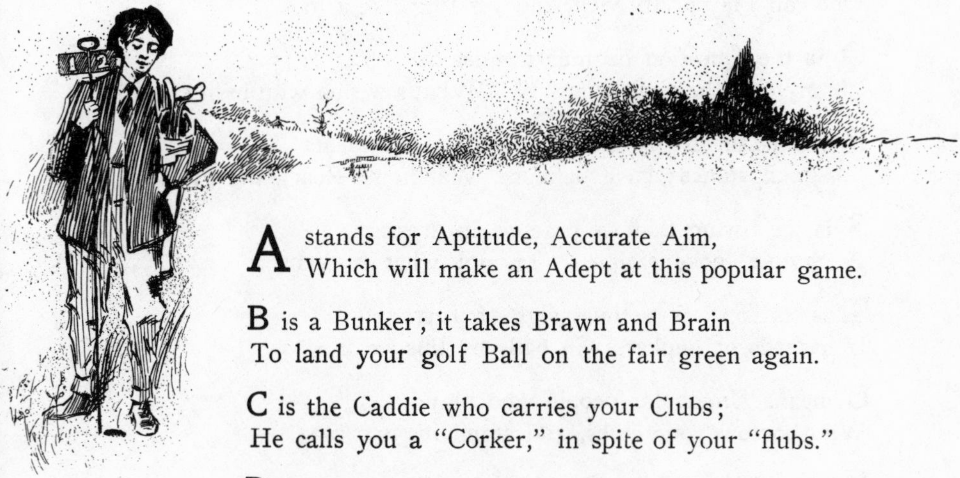

A stands for Aptitude, Accurate Aim,
Which will make an Adept at this popular game.

B is a Bunker; it takes Brawn and Brain
To land your golf Ball on the fair green again.

C is the Caddie who carries your Clubs;
He calls you a "Corker," in spite of your "flubs."

D is the Driver you use at the tee;
The dirt which you Dig, and that other "big D——"

E is the Energy ever displayed
When Engaged in a round with a pretty young maid.

F is a Foursome, a Foozle, and "Fore"—
If your Form in the first F is bad, you're a bore.

G stands for Grip; the professional's Grasp;
And the Green which you reach, if you conquer this clasp.

H is the Hole, not as deep as a well;
And sometimes it's Heaven, and oftener H— ?

I can be Iron, or mashie, or cleek,
You know best yourself which Iron you seek.

J is a Jerk. If your ball finds a cup,
To play with a Jerk often sweeps it right up.

K is to "Keep your eye on the ball;"
If we follow this rule, there is hope for us all.

L stands for Links, and for "Like as we Lie,"
Which is different from "Lie as we Like," by-the-bye.

M stands for Medal play, also for Match,
At both you are beaten if you play at scratch.

N is a Niblick, respected by all;
For it is a good friend in Need, to a ball.

O stands for Oxygen, Ozone, and Odds,
Which golfers accept as gifts of the Gods.

P is "to Press;" "Don't" makes a good rule,
One can Play pretty well, and yet Putt like a fool.

Q is the Question beginners must ask:
"Is my club the right length?" "What's wrong with my grasp?"

R stands for Reply made by old golfers keen:
"A good stance; have patience. Watch me Reach the green."

S is the Swing that we practice in dreams.
A Stymie looks simple. 'Tis not what it seems.

T is to Top. Sometimes sign of Terror;
If hazards or bunkers win balls by this error.

U means Unpopular people who play,
Who borrow your clubs, and stand in your way.

V is the Virtue of one Scotch high-ball,
To lengthen your golf yarns, and drives, in the Fall.

W is a Wrist shot, Whippy and free;
Those who do it well, good golfers must be.

X might stand now for "great eXpectations,"
Day dreams of golfers, in all ranks and stations.

Y is Yesterday; a word hardly known.
It's this Year, and new heroes sit on the throne.

Z stands for Zenith. The golfer whose fame
Touches this point can die, saying, "I've played the game."

2

Golf

SCRIBNER'S MAGAZINE

VOL. XVII MAY 1895 No. 5

GOLF

By Henry E. Howland

ILLUSTRATIONS BY A. B. FROST

THE origin of the royal and ancient game of Golf is lost in obscurity. Whether it was an evolution from the kindred games of Kolf, Hockey, or Jeu de Mail, whether developed in Scotland or carried thither from Holland, may never be definitely ascertained.

Its record is woven into Scottish history, legislation, and literature from the beginning of recorded time. More than four hundred years ago it was a popular game in Scotland, and archery, the necessary training for the soldier, so languished in competition with it that, by the stern ordinance of Parliament and royal decree, it was proclaimed "that the fut ball and golf be utterly cryit doun and nocht usit." But although forbidden to the people, it was a favorite royal pastime. King James played it with Bothwell in 1553, and the royal accounts show that he had money on the game; Queen Mary played it after the death of Darnley, perhaps as a solace in her widowhood; James VI., an early protectionist, laid a heavy tariff on golf balls from Holland, and gave a monopoly of ball-making at four shillings each ball to a favorite. The great Marquis of Montrose played at St. Andrews and Leith Links, and was lavish in his expenditure for golf-balls, clubs, and caddies. The news of the Irish Rebellion came to Charles I. while playing a match at Leith. James II., when Duke of York, won a foursome, with an Edinburgh shoemaker as a partner, against two Englishmen; the shoemaker built a house in the Canongate with his share of the stakes, and, in order to commemorate the origin of his fortunes, placed on its walls as escutcheon a hand dexter grasping a club, with the motto, "Far and Sure." John Porteous, of the "Heart of Midlothian," Duncan Forbes, of Culloden, who turned the tide of Prince Charlie's fortunes in 1745, were adepts at the game, and Covenanters in their sermons, poets, philosophers, and novelists have paid their tribute to the royal sport.

With lingering feet it crossed the Grampian Hills in the wake of his somewhat sportive Majesty James VI. of Scotland, and made its home at Blackheath, where it maintained a precarious existence under the care of Scottish Londoners, until the establishment of the famous clubs of Banbury, Westward Ho, Wimbledon, and Hoylake, when, with a suddenness unexplainable, and an unparalleled popular favor, it extended all over England; since then it has spread to the uttermost parts of the earth.

The nurseries for golf in the United States are many and varied, and are increasing so fast that the tale outruns the telling. The first one, established at Yonkers on the Hudson, some five years ago, by Mr. John Reid (of course a Scotchman), bears the name of St. Andrews, in honor of the Royal and Ancient Golf Club of the East Neuk of Fife, in

Stymie or not stymie?

the shadow of "Auld Reekie," the clustering point for the great mass of golfing history and tradition. It is an inland course of stone-wall hazards, rocky pastures bordered by ploughed fields and woods, and is prolific in those little hollows known as cuppy lies; the Saw Mill River meanders in its front, and a fine view of the Palisades from its highest teeing ground makes it an attractive spot for tired city men to whom it is accessible for an afternoon's sport.

The links of the Shinnecock Hills Golf Club, established three years since by Mr. Edward S. Mead, with Willie Dunn as its keeper, is a golfing Eden. The great rolling sand-hills, covered with short stiff grass, lying between Peconic Bay on the north and Shinnecock Bay on the south, with the ocean beyond, are picturesque in their beauty, and since the resolution of matter from chaos have been waiting for the spiked shoe of the golfer. The hazards are mainly artificial; there are some stretches of sand, railroad embankment, and deep roads, that are tests of skill and temper; the breezy freshness of the air, the glory of the boundless expanse of downs and water, and the splendor of the sunsets, make a perfect setting for the beauty of good golfing.

Newport is a well-to-do club with a large investment in land and a tasteful club-house now in course of construction. From its site the whole course is visible, and the panorama of Narragansett Bay, with the fleet of yachts lying at anchor on one side, and of the ocean on the other, is most pleasing. It is a course of nine holes, with turf of the true golfing quality, stone wall, and artificial hazards — and a tricky

The St. Andrews Club, Yonkers, N. Y.

Leg Wrappings.

quality to its putting greens which require careful approaches to save many extra strokes. Its members are enthusiastic sportsmen, who are not diverted by the giddy attractions of that favorite resort from the serious work required of a good golfer.

The Tuxedo Club has its links partly in Tuxedo Park and partly outside of it, about ten minutes' walk from the club-house. The Ramapo Hills rise abruptly a few hundred yards on either side of the course, the curve of the valley at either end making a beautiful nest, which is traversed by the Ramapo River and its tributary, the Tuxedo Brook.

There are nine holes in the course, which crosses Tuxedo Brook four times and furnishes great variety in its hazards of hills, stone walls, railroad embankments lined with blast furnace slag, apple-trees, and a combination of terrors in front of what is known as Devil's Hole, consisting of brook, bowlders, and road, which has spoiled many a score. The course is known as a "sporting links," where straight, long drives are the only hope for preserving the temper, and the hazards are such that they make glad the heart of man when surmounted, but to the beginner, are outer darkness where is weeping and gnashing of teeth.

The game was first introduced into New England by the Messrs. Hunnewell, who laid out a course on their estate at Wellesley. Since then golf clubs have sprung up as if by magic in the neighborhood of the modern Athens, a full list of which, with their characteristics, would exceed the limits of this article.

A player who has done a round at the Country Club of Brookline will have passed over various points of

Shinnecock Hills Golf Club.

Willie Dunn's Shop at Shinnecock.

avenue, steeple-chase course, race-track, polo-fields, and pigeon-shooting grounds; he will have come triumphantly through a purgatorial stone-wall jump, a sand-bunker and bastion, a water-jump, and finally a vast gravel-pit or crater, which has made many a golfing heart quail, and whose depths the great Campbell himself (the Scotch professional keeper) has not disdained to explore. As in the case of the embankments at Shinnecock, it requires but a true drive or a fair cleek shot to negotiate it; but the moral effect of these hazards is such that the true drive or the fair cleek is problematical. Stone walls, trees, ploughed fields, fences, and chasms, however, present excellent sporting requirements on a course, for variety is the spice of golf. It is difficult to picture a prettier sight on a fine golfing morning, than this course with its red-coated players, the shepherd, his dog, and his flock, in a lovely setting of undulating land, fine trees, old-fashioned colonial club-house, race-track and polo-field.

The course at the Essex County Club of Manchester-by-the-Sea, consists of eleven holes, all visible from the piazza of its pretty club-house. The hazards are nearly all natural, consisting of fences, barns, roadways, a broad valley of cleared land filled in with sand and traversed by a winding brook, which is also met and crossed at other points. The teeing-grounds and putting-greens have been made with great care, and the course will always be a popular one.

At Pride's Crossing is a private course of nine holes, laid out over the estates of several of its members. The green is mostly lawn and pleasure grounds, extending along the front of handsome summer-houses, the whole by the gifts of nature exceedingly attractive, with nothing formidable save the impossibility of driving a ball accurately through parlors and kitchens—some amateurs, however, have essayed it to the discomfiture of the ladies and servants—and a trying bit of corn-field, which yielded a far more valuable crop of lost golf balls in the harvest-time of 1894, than of corn.

The Myopia Hunt Club of Wenham, famous in polo and hunting annals, is an admirable golfing land, with good distances, natural hazards, commanding extensive views of the adjoining country, which is dotted with fine residences and covers, where the whistle of the quail tickles the sportsman's ear, and the music of the kennelled hounds testifies to the varied sports of its members. At the last hole is a pond in whose depths lies a hidden treasure of golf-balls, and over whose surface has been wafted many a smothered and unsmothered curse. The story is told of one enthusiastic tyro who drove two or three balls into the water, and sent his caddie to the club-house for a fresh supply ; then, opening the box, he drove the whole dozen into the placid pond. Such exhibitions are common to the game, and a great relief to the surcharged heart.

The Weston Golf Club has among its officers General C. J. Paine, who, when not holding the tiller of an unconquered yacht, does not disdain the cleek and the mashie, and ex-Governor William E. Russell, an enthusiastic golfer, who has laid aside the cares of state to compete in tournaments.

The Rockaway Hunting Club, of Cedarhurst, Long Island, is a prominent club, and has a fine seaside links of nine holes. The members are enthusiastic golfers and the play is constant through the year. The hazards are sunken roads, high cedar-tree hedges and ravines. The tasteful club-house, recently completed, is well patronized both in winter and summer.

A good lie.

Enthusiasm.

In addition to these may be mentioned the Nahant Club, which has received less than all others of the gifts of nature and art, but is frequented by players who make up for its defects by their enthusiasm ; the Dedham Polo Club, the Cambridge Golf Club, and the Kebo Valley Club at Bar Harbor, the Warren Farm Golf Club, the Westchester Country Club, the Staten Island, Meadowbrook, Philadelphia Country Club, Morristown, Morris County,

The Golf Links at Tuxedo.

Tacoma Golf Club, Tacoma, Wash., and Chicago Clubs, all of which have fostered the interests of the game.

It has been played for twenty years in Canada, the Royal Montreal Golf Club being the pioneer. The course commands a fine view of the city and the St. Lawrence with the Belœil Mountain and the Vermont hills in the distance.

The course of the Quebec Golf Club is over the Plains of Abraham, and is full of historic interest. The scenery is unequalled in its grandeur, the St. Lawrence lying far below and the beautiful Isle of Orleans not far distant.

There are important and well-established clubs also at Toronto, Kingston, and Ottawa, and the number is rapidly increasing throughout the Dominion.

To prevent the friction and the uncertain results which necessarily follow from having a number of clubs each offer prizes for so-called championships, a National Association has been formed to give authority to certain meetings where, each year, the amateur and professional championships shall be played for, as in England and Scotland, the amateur championship being well guarded from professional play, while the "open" events will admit amateurs and professionals alike.

There is no Anglomania about this game in America—it has its own inherent charm. To the novice it seems the simplest of all sports, but to the expert the most complicated; to him it is "a thing of beauty and a joy forever." The scoffer who speaks with a contempt not born of familiarity, or views it with assumed indifference, may assert that the game, with its system of strokes and score, will restore the unhealthy atmosphere of the croquet ground; that it will try the souls of the clergy and become the undoing of parishioners. "It is simply driving a quinine pill over a cow pasture." He may watch with a pitying and ill-disguised contempt the frantic efforts of stout elderly gentlemen to extricate a ball from a hazard, and say, as an old farmer did, who leaned over the fence and smiled placidly at a perspiring banker, "Don't you think you are pretty big for that little marble?"—yet he cannot stay its triumphant progress.

Jeers at the paraphernalia of the game have some justification. Red coats are not becoming to the American landscape, and on a warm July day are fairly distressing; the various wrappings with which some men adorn their legs, as for defence against whin gorse and "fog," which we have not, are suggestive of ornament rather than utility, and excite laughter in the cynical observer; but such criticism is the veriest dalliance. From the moment one of the Phil-

The Drive.

istines essays a stroke, and by accident makes a fair drive from a tee, his conversion is assured, he has gone through all the phases, and learned "to endure, then pity, then embrace;" the game then becomes dangerously near being interesting; henceforth he will strive persistently, in season and out of season, to show "the golf that is in him;" he will regret the neglected opportunities of his youth, and the disease which has no microbe and no cure is chronic and seated on him for life. Henceforward he will adopt the motto of the Hittormissit Club, "Drive it if you can, club it if you will, kick it if you must."

The game illustrates the analytical and philosophical character of the Scotch mind. In it muscle and mind, hand, ball and eye, each play a part, and all must be in perfect accord. Some of its fascinations lie in its difficulties—there are twenty-two different rules to remember in making a drive; some golfers write them on their wristbands, others have them repeated by their caddies at the beginning of their stroke; one enthusiast, after painfully obtaining the proper position, had himself built into a frame, which thereafter was carried about to each teeing ground, that he might be sure of his form. The loose, slashing style known as the St. Andrew's swing, in which the player seems to twist his body into an imitation of the Laocoön, and then suddenly to uncoil, is the perfection of art. It is a swing and not a hit; the ball is met

Uncertain Arithmetic.

at a certain point and swept away with apparent abandon, the driver following the ball, and finishing with a swing over the shoulder in what is almost a complete circle. A jerk is an abomination; the true motion requires a gradual acceleration of speed, with muscles flexible, save that the lower hand should have a tight grip on the stick—a swing like "an auld wife cutting hay;" if this does not convey the idea, "Eh, man, just take and throw your club at the ba'." Oh! the careless ease of that swing and the beautiful far-reaching results that follow! But be not deceived, over-confident beginner, wise in your own conceit; a topped ball that rolls harmlessly a few yards, or some practical agriculture with perhaps a broken driver, or a wrench that follows a fruitless blow, will be your reward, if you venture to imitate that dashing, insolent, fearless stroke, which seems so easy because it is the very perfection of art and crown of skill. It is but the fruit of a life spent club in hand, for the best golfer, like the oyster, is caught young.

The recognized styles of the drive are as varied as the players, a fact attributed by golfers to the errors of greatness, easy to imitate, but dangerous without the genius to turn them to good account. An admirer of a famous Scotch champion declared, as a result of patient and anxious observation at the end of a round, that the great player had every fault at golf that he himself had been taught to avoid; genius, however, is not trammelled by rules, and the greatest

The Brookline, Mass., Country Club.

Essex County (Mass.) Club Entrance—Smoking-room.

players have always adapted their game to their anatomical configuration.

In addition to the recognized styles of famous golfers there are swings of diverse and wonderful grotesqueness—the "Pig-tail" style, the "Headsman," the "Pendulum," the "Recoil," the "Hammerhurling," the "Double-jointed," the "Surprise," and the "Disappointment"—whose respective names are in a measure their explanation, the last-named not being applicable to the state of mind of the player, as one might suppose, but to that of the spectator, who finds that a faulty style in the beginning of a swing may often result in as clean a stroke as one could wish. These styles have been characteristic of famous golfers, and with all of them the ball starts low-flying from the club, skims like a swallow's rise as the initial velocity begins to diminish, continues in its career for two hundred yards, and drops to the ground as gently as a bird alights.

But who shall tell of the unrecognized styles, the hooking, slicing, heeling, toeing, foozling of the would-be golfer in his game of eternal hope and everlasting despair, of bright anticipation tempered by experience, playing as if he owned the green instead of using it, cutting out divots of turf, ploughing the waste places, larding the lean earth as he walks along, plunging down the escarpments of a hazard, and keeping the recording angel busy during his sojourn there, driving into those in front, and passed on the green by succeeding players—

> "While those behind cry forward
> And those before cry back."

Let kindly forgetfulness draw a veil over this stage of his career.

The drive, however, as many insist, is but the prelude, and, therefore, the least important of the shots. It passes

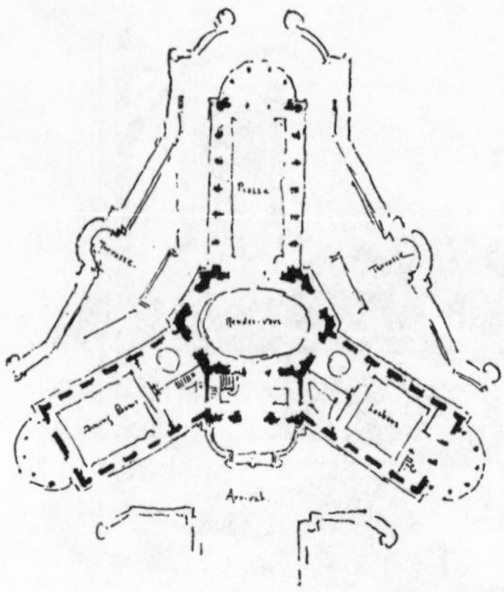

WHITNEY WARREN, ARCH.

One of the Façades of the Newport Golf Club-house.

The distinctive feature of this Club-house, as shown by the plan, is that it is divided into three parts. One is given over to the dining-room, kitchen, and servants' quarters; another to dressing and locker-rooms; and the third to the social or general club features—the three wings being joined by an elliptical hall—the rendezvous.

many a pitfall, reduces the dangers that lurk in cuppy lies, bastion bunkers, pit bunkers, and hazards, but the approach shots in playing "through the green" are a test of skill, nerve, and temper, and cut a greater figure in the score than the drive from the teeing-ground. The term "approach shot," in its common acceptation, conveys the idea of a stroke played with the iron with something less than the full swing, and involves differences in distance, elevation, and style. Then comes in the nice judgment as to three-quarter shots, half-shots, and wrist shots to cover the distance, the straight forward stroke, or the cut in making any of these; then must you choose whether to run the ball up along the ground and risk the irregularities of turf and soil, or loft with accurate judgment, and pitch the ball dead on to the elevation, so reaching the putting-green where you would be. To see a finished artist at this work is a sight that lingers long in the memory—his glance to measure the distance and assure himself of the direction, the momentary rest of the club behind the ball, the knuckling over of the body toward the hole, the cross-cutting downward stroke with its clean blow, and then the triumph as the ball pitches with its reverse "English" on to the ground far short of the distance the unpractised eye would have measured, and grips into the earth as if with inanimate intent to save the player any unnecessary trouble in holeing out. Even though one may know nothing of its difficulties by experience, he grasps intuitively an enlarged idea of the merits of the game; but to a player the success of such a shot, made with a clear purpose, gives the same exquisite thrill of ecstasy as a two-lengths lead in a boat-race or the strike of a three-pound trout. On the putting-green the work seems easier—indeed, a scoffing onlooker once said he could hole the ball with his umbrella, and did; but there is as much nicety of judgment, accuracy of eye, and delicacy of execution in this stage as in any other part of the game. The approach putt brings you near the hole; then should come a careful survey of the ground with objects to guide the eye on the line, which will be facilitated by diligent practice on the drawing-room carpet; a rest of the putter for a moment behind the ball, near the right foot, the forearm resting against the leg, a following pendulum-like swing of the club, without a jerk, and the ball will roll as if in a groove to its appointed resting-place.

It would be wise for a tyro not to watch a professional match until he has made a trial himself. "Can you play the violin?" a boy was asked. "I don't know," he replied, "I never tried;" and the novice at golf, to whom it all looks so easy, would probably make the same answer. When from actual experience he has learned its difficulties, when modesty and humility have entered into his soul, when he has tired his brain with diagrams and rules in books of instruction, with their nice distinction between an upward swing and a lift, and a downward swing and a hit, and complicated formulæ for every kind of club or iron in every kind of lie on the course, when he has had burned into his memory, as with a red-hot cleek, the five injunctions of the golfer's Koran, "Slow back;" "Keep your eye on the ball;" "Don't aim too long;" "Aim to pitch to the left of the hole," and "Be up"—then let him with meek heart and due reverence follow Willie Dunn and Willie Campbell in a match-play over a round of eigh-

On the green.

Chicago Golf Club.

Farmhouse used as club-house—lost ball in the meadow.

teen holes, and take an object-lesson in the art which he has labored so painfully and fruitlessly to acquire ; then will his respect for skill, patience in play, judgment in the selection of the proper club, and nerve in critical moments, rise proportionately to the descent of his own self-conceit ; and his vaulting ambition for a record as a golfer will receive a spur that may help him to acquire it.

The game is too young in America to have developed players of remarkable note, though creditable records have been made ; but coming years may cast the halo of championships on heads now young that shall link their names with Allan Robertson, old Tom Morris, Anderson, the Parks, Dunns, Piries, Straths, and Kirks of a previous generation who made history in the golfing world, and with that of "poor young Tommy," as he is always affectionately called, the son of the famous old keeper at St. Andrews, whose play was so incomparable that, although he died at the early age of twenty-four, he was the most formidable golfer of his time. At twenty he had three times won in succession the championship belt, and to his golfing career the motto "Capite et supereminet omnes" was universally accorded.

It is one of the traditions of these great players at St. Andrews, that it was their guiding principle never to make a bad shot, an easy theory to enunciate, but the great army of amateurs who with heart-breaking efforts have striven to

"Four strokes at the bunker and not over yet."

rise to that standard, and the record of their topped balls, broken clubs, misses and foozles at critical stages in a match, can bear witness to the difficulty of reducing it satisfactorily to practice. The merit of these fine golfers was that their play was sure—as they played to-day so they would play to-morrow; there was nothing unequal in them, no wavering, no unexpected breaking down at a moment when the championship might depend upon a single stroke. They have been known to play ninety consecutive holes without one bad shot or one stroke made otherwise than as it was intended; and it was this dead level of steadiness under all chances of hazards and bad lies, and all conditions of cold, wet, wind, or snow, as in young Tom Morris's last famous match before his death, that placed them in the front rank of golfers.

Fore !

The true golfer is critical of lucky strokes or flukes; in his estimation they are as discreditable as bad ones; certainty and precision is his standard, and his comment in broad Scotch, the real golf language, after a bad shot by a good player, calculated to draw applause from ignorant bystanders, would probably be "My, but yon was a lucky yin, bad play—didna desairve it." George Glennie, a famous player whose purism was proverbial, once in a "foursome" drove his ball into a burn; his partner wading in with boots and stockings, took the ball on the wing with his niblic, as it floated down, and laid it dead at the hole. "Well, what about that stroke?" said his partner to the sage, who had preserved unyielding silence. "No golf at a'"—then, in a soliloquy, as he advanced to the teeing-ground, "just monkey's tricks."

The game can be played in company or alone. Robinson Crusoe on his island, with his man Friday as a caddie, could have realized the golfer's dream of perfect happiness—a fine day, a good course, and a clear green; if Henry VIII. had cultivated the more delicate emotions by taking to the links of the Knuckle Club, he might have saved his body from the gout and his name from the contempt of posterity; he might have dismissed the sittings of the Divorce Court and gone to play a foursome with Cromwell, Wolsey, and the papal legate; and all the abbey lands which fell to the nobles would have been converted into golfing greens by the fiat of the royal golfer. He might with Francis have established a record on the Field of the Cloth of Gold. Such a game would have cemented their friendship, for the man with a keen love of golfing in his heart is more than the devotee of an idle sport, he is a man of spiritual perceptions and keen sympathies. As a teacher of self-discipline the game is invaluable. The player is always trying to get the better of the game, and, as Allan Robertson said, "The game is aye fechtin' against ye."

The fascinations of golf can only be learned by experience. It is difficult to explain them. It has its humorous and its serious side. It can be begun

Playing as if he owned the green.

as soon as you can walk, and once begun it is continued as long as you can see. The very nature of the exercise gives length of days. Freedom of movement, swing of shoulder, and that suppleness of which the glory had departed, all return to the enthusiast. He has a confidence in his own ability which is sublime, because it is justified by performance, and that self-control which chafes the ordinary adversary.

His sense of the ultimate purpose and the true proportions of his existence is unruffled, whether he views life from the exaltation of a two-hundred yard drive on to the hill, or the lowest heel-mark in the deepest sand-pit on the course; while the feelings of momentary success or depression which so possess the souls of weaker men, pass over him with no more influence than the flight of birds. His soul is so wrapped in the harmony of earth and sky and the glory of the game, that no buffets of fortune can come at him.

This is what makes it a tonic to the

Wasted time.

pliment to call a man a "dour" player, it seems to be recognized that the characteristic of all language in golf should be its brevity. The difficulty of contending with an uncertain temper in others is nothing as compared with ruling our own, and the dust and bad language that rise from the depths of a bunker emphasize the truth of the words of Holy Writ, "He that ruleth his own spirit is greater than he that taketh a city;" but yet it is certain that he who hath not lost his temper can never play golf.

Golfers as a rule are an exceptionally honest race of men, but uncertain arithmetic is occasionally encountered on the green. "I aim to tell the truth," said one; "Well, you are a very bad shot," was the reply, and there is often an area of low veracity about a bunker. Accuracy is a cardinal virtue in the game, and a kindly judgment may attribute such errors to forgetfulness; but as the chief pleasure is to beat your own record for your own satisfaction, and as this form of deception makes real progress continually more difficult, for the discount is always in

nerves, while the temper goes through a personally conducted tour, beginning with impatience and ending with complete equanimity. Egotism is powerless to excuse a fault, for that can lie only with the player himself. He cannot vent his fury upon his opponent, even though a tree opportunely situated may land a ball on the green, while his own flies hopelessly into the woods; for the game is born in the purple of equable temper and courtesy, and the golfer's expletives must be directed against his own lack of skill, or lies, or hazards, and the luck and vengeance must light, and often do, on the unoffending clubs, even to their utter extermination. To the language with which every golf course is strewn, differing more in form than in substance, from the "Tut, tut, tut" of the ecclesiastic to the more sulphurous exclamation of the layman, the divine quality of forgiveness must be extended; but as it is a com-

Temper.

your path, the man of treacherous memory gets small comfort out of his duplicity.

With the development of the game comes the development of the caddie, who is one of its principal adjuncts. In America he is still the small boy with no special peculiarities to distinguish him from others. In Scotland he is as much of an institution as the player himself. He has grown up on the links, and is the guide, counsellor, and friend of the player, whose clubs he carries. One of his principal qualifications there is that he should be able to conceal his contempt for your game. He is ready with advice, reproof, criticism, and sympathy, always interested, ready at critical times with the appropriate club, and, if need be, with the appropriate comment. He is anxious for the success of his side as if he were one of the players. His caustic remarks are borne with equanimity, and his contemptuous criticisms with the submission they deserve.

A clean miss.

A foozle.

The relation of the fairer part of creation to golf varies between that of a "golfer's widow" and that of a champion. Singleness of thought, concentration of purpose, quietude of manner, are essential in the game, and the expert golfer, whose tender mercies are ever cruel, will unhesitatingly cry "Fore" to the flutter of a golf cape or the tinkle of light feminine conversation, so distracting by reason of the natural gallantry of man. In the words of a promising young golfer, who found it hard to decide between flirtation and playing the game, "It's all very pleasant, but it isn't business." But the sincerity of their enthusiasm is so apparent, and their adaptability to the nicer points of the game so great that there are few clubs now where they are not firmly established, and where a man who has finished a hard day's play cannot take pleasure in an aftermath of tea and blandishments.

Health, happiness, and "a spirit with a' the world content," lie on the golfing ground. The game is a leveller of rank and station. King and commoner, noble and peasant, played on equal terms in days gone by, and rich and poor, clever and dull, are "like as they lie" when matched in skill.

"There's naething like a ticht-gude-gowing mautch to soop yer brain clear o' troubles and trials." It is so fostered by companionship and wrapped about with the joys of friendship, that he who

Topped.

has his soul's friend for his golfing mate is on fortune's cap the very button. With such company, when the November wind streams down the course, whipping out our little clouds of breath into streamers, we can stride over our eighteen holes with the keen joy of living that comes at intervals to the tired worker. And then, oh! weary soul, what joys await the faithful! The putting off of mud-caked shoes, the brisk plunge or shower-bath, and the warm glow thereafter; the immaculate shirt-front that crackles at your touch, the glad joy of dinner and the utter relaxation of content, "with just a wee drappie of guid Scotch to follow."

The poet, scorning the material things of life and the pursuit of wealth, sings thus:

"But thou, O silent mother, wise, immortal,
To whom our toil is laughter, take, Divine One,
This vanity away, and to thy lover
Give what is needful,
A stanch heart, nobly calm, averse to evil,
The purer sky to breathe, the sea, the mountain,
A well-born gentle friend, his spirit's brother,
Ever beside him."

Mr. Santayana should go a-golfing.

3

Golfing 'round the Hub— Boston

Golfing 'round the Hub

BY GEORGE H. SARGENT.

SO firm a hold has the Scotch game taken upon the people of Boston and its vicinity, that within a radius of twelve miles from the Boston City Hall, no less than twenty-nine links may be found, comprising in their circuit every variety of hazard known to man. An imaginary round would take one over courses varying from five to eighteen holes in length, and over many kinds of turf, from unkempt raggedness to velvety green. The Boston golfer who starts out on a round of the Hub has many miles of golf ahead of him, and he surely will not lack for variety; yet if all the courses were made into putting greens for one gigantic links the most noticeable thing that would strike the Brobdingnagian golfer who essayed the round would be the preponderance of short holes.

The golf clubs of the Boston district almost encircle the city, the only break being where the waters of the harbor separate the promontory of Winthrop on the northwest from the long arm of Nantasket which runs up toward it from the southeast.

The natural starting point of a golfing pilgrimage about Boston would be one or the other of these two points. Whichever it be, the golfer will start with a voyage. A pleasant half-hour's sail down the harbor brings one to Hull, where, on a high bluff known as Telegraph Hill, is a sign which proclaims to the world of summer visitors that here the Hull Golf Club lives and moves and has its being. Like several other golf clubs, this grew out of a yachting organization, the members of the Hull Yacht Club having taken up the game on other courses, and become so interested that a course of their own became an imperative necessity. So the Hull Golf Club was organized and links laid out on this point, not far from the yacht-club house. While the course is new and rough, it affords the yachtsmen an opportunity to combine the pleasures of yachting with golfing; and the club boasts a unique hazard in the form of a government fortification

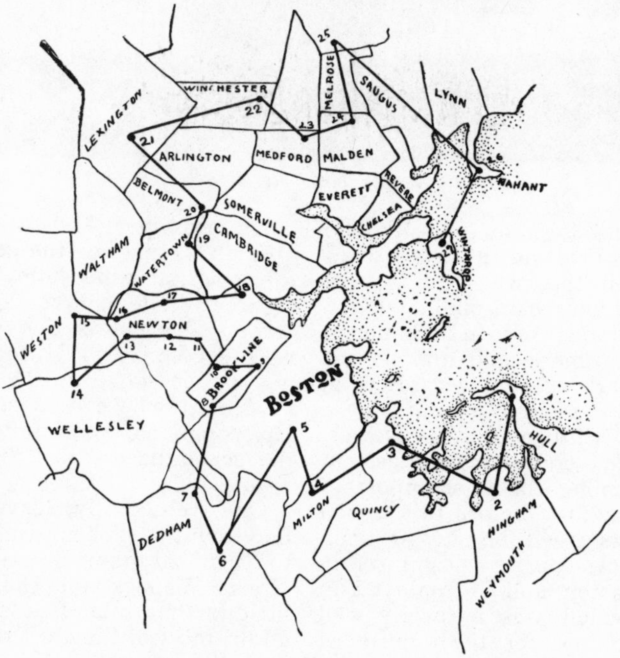

erected for the defence of Boston Harbor in the late war with Spain. From the ninth green of the course, the last hole, may be seen the ocean-going traffic of Boston, as the ships and steamers pass out the main channel, close by the frowning headland. The course abounds in short holes, and has a total length of 2,429 yards. But as the Hull Yacht Club has recently consolidated with the Massachusetts Yacht Club, and the latter organization brings an increased membership, more funds for the improvement of a pretty little course will be available another year.

From Hull, across an arm of the harbor, is another short and pleasant sail to the little course of the Crow Point Golf Club in old Hingham. This, like the Hull, is a new club, and there is a keen rivalry between the two, leading to a series of interesting team-matches when the summer colonists invade both places.

Leaving this course and making his way up the south shore toward Boston, the next to be visited is that of the Wollaston Golf Club, at Norfolk Downs, in Quincy. This club is rapidly assuming a place among the most important in New England, for before this season ends the members will be playing upon an eighteen-hole course. Organized in 1896, the Wollaston Golf Club played on leased land which was naturally well adapted to golfing, for the quality of the turf is much like that of the Myopia links, wearing well and healing readily. Last year this was noted as one of the best-kept courses in New England. Wollaston has a pre eminent claim to possessing "links," for its situation at Norfolk Downs is upon actual "downs" or "links" like those which gave the word to golf language as a synonym for "course." Last fall the club membership had reached such proportions and the club's position in the golfing world was so well established that a tract of some seventy acres was secured by outright purchase; and nine additional holes were laid out this spring to make a full course by joining with the old one. It is the intention to lay out nine more holes next year, when the club will give up its lease of the land covered by the original nine holes and have an eighteen-hole course, all on its own acres. The course is over beautifully-rolling country in Milton and Quincy, not so very far from the original Merry Mount where Wollaston's roistering Episcopalians were taken captive by the scandalized Miles Standish, before 1630.

OVER THE POND AT ALLSTON.

One reluctantly leaves Wollaston's fine turf and its beautiful surroundings to turn to other golfing fields. The Hoosic Whisick Golf Club in Milton, a little farther inland, is largely a family affair, most of the club members being

Bostonians of leisure, who make their summer homes in this charming village, away from the sound of locomotives. Scenery is not a necessary concomitant of golf, but the views from parts of this course are superb. The course itself is somewhat short, but it has some "sporty" hazards; and in spite of the varying lengths of the holes, from 120 to 390 yards, it was here that Alex. Findlay, the professional, made his famous record of twenty consecutive holes in exactly four strokes each, a record which is believed to be unique.

From Milton the golfing pilgrim goes directly into Boston, for a round upon the public links in Franklin Park. In October, 1896, acceding to an increasing demand, the more readily, perhaps, because two members of the Board of Park Commissioners were golfers, the city of Boston established a public course—the second in the United States. Willie Campbell laid out what was then the longest nine-hole course in the country, on a tract of some sixty acres, uncrossed by roads or paths, in what is known as the Country Park section of Franklin Park. Campbell has been retained ever since as professional and greenkeeper, and here he gives lessons to hundreds of beginners who crowd the course—often uncomfortably—in pleasant spring and fall weather. The Park links are indeed the beginner's delight. Here he may cut divots to his heart's content, and freely does he avail himself of the privilege. The course is nearly two miles in circuit, and has only one short hole—120 yards—while there are holes of 498 and 542 yards, giving splendid opportunity for practice with the brassy. There are two streams and a narrow pond to be crossed, but as yet no artificial hazards have been provided. Players on the course must secure permits from the Park Commission, and a charge of fifteen cents a round, or two rounds for twenty-five cents, is made.

SEAWARD FROM THE SIXTH TEE, HULL.

On public holidays and on Saturday afternoons in summer the links are closed, for experience has shown that there are yet many Park visitors who know nothing of the game, and, therefore, fear nothing from standing fifty yards in front of the duffer, whose ball may fly anywhere should he be fortunate enough to hit it. One golfer who played at the Park tells of a choleric old gentleman who persisted in walking directly in the line of play on the long hole. "Fore!" shouted in stentorian tones, had no effect upon him. So the player waited until the old gentleman was well ahead, and then, with a cry of "Look out!" he drove the ball, which landed almost at the visitor's feet. The old man walked on, and, after another wait, the player repeated the experience. On the third stroke the old gentleman turned, and declared he would have the golfer arrested if he persisted in driving that ball at his head. The golfer explained, as well as he could, that he was trying to make that hole in five, and he merely wished his rights. "That's all right," exclaimed the old man fiercely, "but don't you dare hit me!" Obviously, with such people on the course, play on the public links becomes less and less pleasant as one becomes proficient, and Campbell notes that each season a new crop of golfers come up. Those who play one season learn enough of the game to appreciate the advantages of less crowded links, and join some of the clubs near at hand. So firmly has golf become established as a public institution in Boston, however, that better accommodations for public golfers, including the erection of a club-house and work-rooms for the professional, are only a question of time.

From the public course the way of the golfing pilgrim leads southward into Dedham, where two golf courses may be found. The Norfolk Golf Club was organized in the spring of 1897, and a course of nine holes laid out near Islington station of the New England Railroad. Most of it was old pasture land, on which the turf was close and hard, requiring little to be done on the fair green. There are ponds and, of course, stone walls, but these may be made into useful hazards. The links run over a picturesque country, with a splendid view of the lowlands in the distance. So well has the club prospered since its organization that the Bostonians who compose most of its membership contemplate extensive improvements.

Dedham's other golf organization—the Dedham Golf Club—is an outgrowth of the Dedham Polo Club, to which many of its members belong. The bold riders whose prowess is known at Narragansett Pier, Meadowbrook and Brooklyn, took up the game some three years ago, and secured a tract of land, on which a short course of nine holes was laid out and a club-house erected. It lies along the upper waters of the historic Charles River, and the roll of the surface of the country is admirably adapted to the game, while there are hazards of ravines, woods bordering the course, streams, a road, and the omnipresent stone walls. Dedham is improving, however, and as the golfers of the aristocratic old town grew in experience, the terraced "table cloth" greens gave way to broad ones, where putting could be done under less artificial conditions.

ALLSTON OVERLOOKING THE CHARLES RIVER.

Golf thrives in Dedham, for there is also a short private course on the

THE COMMONWEALTH GOLF CLUB, CHESTNUT HILL, NEWTON.

handsome estate of Hon. Samuel Warren at "Karlstein," and with the Dedham Boat Club, the Dedham Polo Club and the Norfolk Hunt Club, all composed largely of the same people, the Dedham Golf Club was an absolute necessity to complete the quartet of sporting organizations.

"Playing to the next hole," as the sporting writers say in all their accounts

TELEGRAPH HILL.—THE LINKS OF THE HULL GOLF CLUB.

of golf matches, the drive, to continue the simile, is toward the fountain-head of golf in this part of the country, to "The Country Club," in Brookline. Not the Brookline Country Club, nor the Country Club of Brookline, but "The Country Club," for this organization of Boston's wealthiest classes, who are devoted to country life, has the right to its title by being the first "country club" in America. Its race meetings have long been famous, and some years ago it had a polo team which won on many a hard-fought field. All the best features of country sport have been fostered by this organization, and it was but natural that it should be one of the first clubs in America to take up golf. The game had been played by some of the members abroad, and on a private course which was laid out on the Hunnewell estate in Wellesley, the first golf course in New England.

In the spring of 1893 a course of nine holes was laid out on The Country Club grounds by Willie Campbell. Although well-nigh perfect in affording good lies through the green, and having excellent teeing grounds and putting greens, the necessity of maintaining a race-track and steeplechase course over parts of which the golfers must play has hitherto kept The Country Club from having an ideal links.

J. G. THORP, RUNNER-UP, CHAMPIONSHIP '96.

So popular did the game become that last year $42,000 was paid for the Baker estate adjoining the club property, and nine additional holes were put in, giving the members an eighteen-hole course to play over this season. The total playing length is about 5,200 yards. Among the hazards on the old course, some of which have been criticized by the golfing experts, are "an avenue, steeplechase course, race track, polo fields, pigeon-shooting grounds, stone-wall jump, sand bunker and bastion, a water jump, and a vast gravel-pit or crater." These are the hazards, by the way, which Mr. Sutphen, in Gordon G. Smith's "World of Golf," credits to the Baltimore Country Club. Most of The Country Club members would cheerfully resign them to the Baltimore Country Club, or any other organization that wants them, although they do not seriously bother the expert manipulator of the cleek or the true driver.

Golf in America owes much to The Country Club. Many a New England course can claim this as its parent organization, for wherever The Country Club members have gone to spend their summers, they have taken the game with them, and distributed greens and teeing grounds all along the north and south shores of Massachusetts Bay, and carried them inland to the mountains.

More than this, it was a leader in golf in The Country Club, who, when the two so-called "national championships" were held at Shinnecock and Newport, saw the necessity of a governing body for the game in this country. No club could occupy the position here which the Royal and Ancient Golf Club of St. Andrews held with relation to the sport abroad, and so Mr. Laurence Curtis, with the late Mr. Theodore Havemeyer and others, brought about the organization of the United States Golf Association. One of the early golfers of The Country Club, Mr. W. B. Thomas, had just been elected to the presidency of this organization, succeeding Mr. Curtis, who took the place of the late lamented Mr. Havemeyer, the first president. If golf is indebted to The Country Club for its advancement, it has paid the debt in kind; for while not all The Country Club members are interested in racing, or polo, or shooting, golf is a game in which young and old, men and women, may play with equal zest. Golf has proved a financial tonic to more than one country club in America.

Two courses of limited extent, within the town of Brookline, form the next links in this golfing round. The Warren Farm Golf Club is an offshoot of The Country Golf Club, always providing for overflow meetings, so to speak, on Saturdays and holidays, while its regular players find this six-hole course more convenient of access than the larger course of The Country Club.

The other, the Chestnut Hill Golf Club, is largely social, but has links running, as its name implies, over the slopes of Chestnut Hill. It joins to a succession of rather unfair greens, an ample variety of hazards, including trees and brambles, to meet the requirements of those who demand a more than "sporty" course.

Chestnut Hill is on the edge of Newton, formerly called "the Garden City," but which might now be called "the Golfing City," for it has no less than five golf courses. Time will come, and that probably soon, when a consolidation must take place, for some of these golf courses are on building lots too valuable to be given up to the sport of a limited number of players. At present the difficulty in the way of consolidation lies in the fact that members of each course prefer the narrower limits of a course near home, to a larger field which is less easy of access. It seemed, when Newton had only four clubs, that the golfing proclivities of her citizens were well provided for, but last year another club was organized, and this year may see yet another. The latest is the Commonwealth Golf Club, situated near Commonwealth avenue, that artery of blue blood which continues through Newton after leaving Boston. Mr. Dana Estes, the publisher, was at the head of this organization, and after one season of success, it has decided to enlarge and improve its course, on which is already a handsome club-house, from which every teeing ground and putting green in its nine-hole course is visible.

Newton Center comes next in order, and here the home of the golf club of that name is a scene of activity in summer, when the nine-hole course is thronged with players. The erratic player goes into three figures with certainty, for the lies are often appalling, and even Alex. Findlay, who said he could get around any nine-hole course in 50, failed to do better than 57 the first time he played on the Newton Center links. He has since done it in 44, as has also the Rev. E. M. Noyes, who holds the club championship, although most

LAURENCE CURTIS (COUNTRY CLUB),
EX-PRESIDENT UNITED STATES GOLF ASS'N.

W. B. THOMAS (COUNTRY CLUB),
PRESIDENT UNITED STATES GOLF ASS'N.

THE FIRST TEE AT OAKLEY COUNTRY CLUB.

of the members look upon Mr. Noyes's score as an inspiration.

In many respects the Newton Golf Club course is like a private course, as most of it is laid out on land which has been loaned to the club by wealthy men who are members. The course was a short one, but this spring it was lengthened to about 2,520 yards, and considerable was done in cutting down trees which, however pleasing to the eye, did not add to the enjoyment of the play-

THE CLUB HOUSE, OAKLEY COUNTRY CLUB.

ers. Nature has done her part well toward providing a good course, and the opportunities have been improved so that the club limit of membership, 150, was reached last year.

Leaving Newton on the southwest to play over into the adjoining town of Wellesley, the golfing pilgrim reaches the course of the Wellesley Hills Golf Club, laid out three years ago. It is now nine holes, but the land adjoining the links is looked upon with regard to its possibilities for making an eighteen-hole course when the club is a little older. The turf, like that in the "Country Churchyard," "heaves in many a moldering heap," but with time and money good golf links have been built on many a less promising foundation.

Before leaving Wellesley mention must be made of the Wellesley College Golf Club, the only known organization where golf is compulsory. Here the young ladies of the college find it a part of the prescribed physical training, under the direction of Miss Harriet Randall, the accomplished athletic director.

Adjoining Wellesley is Weston, where the Weston Golf Club, one of the oldest in the neighborhood of Boston, numbers among its founders General Charles J. Paine, who can handle a golf club, as well as the tiller of an unconquered yacht. Here, too, the late Governor William E. Russell frequently played. Weston maintains a club team which plays many matches with other clubs in the Boston district, and generally acquits itself with credit.

From Weston the line leads back through Newton into Boston once more. Across the Charles River, in Newton, is the course of the Woodland Golf Club, at Auburndale, where a great hotel is headquarters not only for the golfers, but for bicycle clubs, tally-ho parties and other sportsmen who come out from the city. A short course and hazardous, is this, but it is well kept, and it had a representative at the last national amateur championship.

"THE COUNTRY CLUB," IN BROOKLINE. THE FIFTH GREEN, LOOKING ACROSS THE POLO GROUNDS.

In Newton, too, is the nine-hole course of the Braeburn Golf Club, with an excellent variety of hazards, the natural features being admirably utilized. Here, too, the members gaze upon an adjoining tract of land and plan a possible arrangement of nine additional holes. The course of the Braeburn Club is well kept, and its open tournaments are always popular.

The Allston Golf Club, which has a nine-hole course within the city limits of Boston, is even more easy of access from the business district of the city than the public links in Franklin Park. Commonwealth Avenue street cars, which run directly by the course, bring golfers out from the famous subway in twenty minutes. The course is on land owned by an express company, the perambulating horses of which often form tantalizingly movable hazards. Despite its uncertainty of tenure, the club has a little club-house, and extensive improvements on the land have been made. The feature of the Allston course is its famous pond, 100 yards wide, over which a player must drive unless he prefers to work his way with a mashie through an apple orchard. The pond is fed by springs and drained by evaporation. Caddies declare that it is bottomless, but players aver that its bottom is paved with at least a million golf balls. A steep bluff furnishes admirable opportunity for practicing lofting shots, and a water-main zigzagging across the course contributes variety to the hazards. Yet the ease of access makes up for many shortcomings, and the club is one of the most popular in the Boston district.

Crossing the Charles River into Cambridge, the golfer next comes to the links of the Harvard Golf Club. This was established a few years ago as the Cambridge Golf Club, and in 1896 furnished the runner-up in the national amateur tournament in the person of Mr. J. G. Thorp, who was beaten only by the redoubtable Whigham. Last year the club was reorganized as the Harvard Golf Club. Under this title it is now a flourishing organization, with a nine-hole course in Watertown, just across the Cambridge line. Here the students indulge in a great deal of informal match-play, and here the Harvard team practiced for the intercollegiate championship, which they won at Ardsley last fall. In addition to the Harvard students and members of the team, there are members who retained their interest in the old club. It was for playing on these links on Sunday that the first Sunday golfers were arrested in this country; and as they were students in college, they preferred to pay their fines and avoid notoriety rather than, as advised by eminent counsel, take the case to a higher court.

The club which was responsible for the change in fortunes of the Cambridge Golf Club was the Oakley Country Club, organized and incorporated last year by some of the leading golfers of the University City. This club acquired the famous old Pratt estate in Cambridge and Belmont, with a colonial mansion erected in 1742 by a descendant of a Huguenot exile from France. On these grounds an eighteen-hole course was laid out, with a preponderance of short holes. The old mansion, with its oval ball-room and its fine two-story hall, with balcony and winding stairways, was converted into a club-house, and proved to be admirably suited to the purpose. The links have fine turf, and while their improvement has but just been fairly started, they have proved exceeding popular. Here, as the course is partly in Belmont and partly in Cambridge, Sunday golf players may keep on that part of the course on which the ban does not rest, and escape the blue laws.

Somehow, golf has not taken as deep root in the northern suburbs of Boston as on the south and west, although there is good turf. Probably this is for the reason that the vacant land in the immediate northern suburbs is largely near the level of tide-water. On this side of Boston the clubs are farther from the city, yet there are several within the twelve-mile radius. One of the most active of these is the Lexington Golf Club, which has a nine-hole course in that historic town. Truly the "red-coats," who were repelled so bravely in the early days of the Revolution, have now taken the town, and the "rebels" have laid down their arms and taken up golf clubs. The course has excellent turf and plenty of hazards, although the application of dynamite to some of them would improve the chance of low scoring.

To the east of Lexington there lies the golfing ground of the Winchester Golf Club, a flourishing organization formed in 1897, and having a club-house and links on Woodside Road in Winchester. The greens are excellent, and the teeing grounds are better than in most clubs of limited membership, but local rules are still necessary to provide for balls in hoof-marks and cart-tracks.

Still farther east is the Medford Golf Club, with a course of varying length. Five holes is the number generally played, but there are extra teeing grounds and putting greens, by which a nine-hole course, partly over rough ground, is possible. Most of the members prefer to make nine holes by playing twice around and combining two holes on the second round, rather than essay the task of mowing "fog" and "bent" by playing the extra holes. Changes made in the course last year, however, give the club a nine-hole course which will be in fair condition by the end of this year, with good distances and fairly satisfactory greens.

On the east of Medford is Malden, which has a golf club born last year, with a course several years old. The course was laid out on the private grounds of Hon. E. S. Converse, the philanthropist, and after being kept private for three years, the use of the grounds was generously given to the young men and women of Malden society, on condition that a club be formed. The condition was not hard to comply with, and was soon met by the organization of the Pine Banks Golf Club, where devotees of cleek and mashie may prepare themselves for play on longer courses.

North of Malden the Wakefield Golf Club has just been reorganized after a trying year, in which the course suffered somewhat from neglect. Under the new conditions there is a good prospect that Wakefield will take its proper place among the golfing suburbs of Boston.

Nahant, which is a summer home of wealthy Bostonians, and which has been facetiously termed "Cold Roast Boston," has a golf club, for which nature has done little more than provide room for the course. The Nahant Golf Club is an outgrowth of the Nahant Club, where the social activity of the members finds a larger field than the sporting side. This club shares with the Royal Minchinhampton Golf Club, of England, the honor of having as a trophy a swallow which was killed by a driven golf ball. The ex-president of the United States Golf Association is authority for the authenticity of this remarkable shot, which demonstrates the unerring accuracy of the drives made by Nahant Club members, one of whom is United States Senator Lodge.

NEWTON CENTRE GOLF CLUB-HOUSE.

"Home," in this round of the Boston links, takes one to the Court Park Golf Club of Winthrop, on an arm which runs down into Boston Harbor toward Nantasket, the starting point. One of the most picturesque places on the Massachusetts coast, near Boston, the course can be reached by a short sail from the city, and the links provide sport for many summer visitors. One round may satisfy the golfing pilgrim, but he who lingers late, and, after his round of all the Boston courses, sits on the deck of the little steamer, bound for Boston, and watches the flashing beacons of the har-

"THE COUNTRY CLUB" IN BROOKLINE.

bor, and the city lights twinkling afar, while the rising moon makes a broad furrow of silver on the rippling water, will feel that the pilgrimage is worth the making, and that the round ends fittingly.

While these are the golf courses of Boston and its immediate vicinity, mention must be made of other courses where the Boston golfers play, or the golfing round the Hub is not complete. Most prominent among these are the links of the Essex County Club and the Myopia Hunt Club. The former, at Manchester-by-the-Sea, are widely known as the scene of the national women's championship of 1897. Here, in the summer time, many tournaments are held, and the course is especially popular with the women of Boston society. On the nine holes of this course there is a good variety of hazards, and the up-

THE NEWTON GOLF CLUB-HOUSE.

keep, under the direction of Mr. J. Lloyd, winner of the open championship two years ago, is not surpassed in New England. The Myopia Hunt Club, at Hamilton, where the open championship was held last year, then had only a nine-hole course, with nine additional holes under way. These were opened for play in the last of the tournaments last fall, and the members now have one of the best full courses in the East. On the links the members of the aristocratic summer colony of Boston may be found any day in summer with driver and putter; and, while half an hour's ride from Boston by train, the surpassing quality of the turf and the natural attractiveness of the links cause them to be opened early and closed late in the season.

THE BRAEBURN CLUB-HOUSE.

FIRST TEE, BRAEBURN.

Another popular course near Boston, just outside of the twelve-mile limit, is that of the Concord Golf Club, which in its first two or three years was famous for its team-play, and now for its almost universal informal match-play.

Old Salem has a good course where golfers of that old seaport indulge in the Scotch sport; and along the north shore, near the "reef of Norman's Woe," is the course of the Magnolia Golf Club, much patronized in summer by Boston players. Others find golf on the south shore, at Scituate, or in historic old Plymouth, where a short nine-hole course affords them opportunity to play "the only game."

Team matches, where so many clubs are found, are common, as might be expected, and there has been a Neighborhood Golf Cup competed for by Concord, Lexington, Salem and the Vesper Country Club of Lowell for several years. In Newton, last year, a trophy was offered by President Andrew B. Cobb, of the Newton Golf Club, to be competed for by the golf clubs of Newton.

The need of a district association of Boston golf clubs, similar to the Metropolitan Golf Association in New York, is apparent, and it is almost certain that such an association will come in due season. In the meantime, golf

FORTY ACRES OF BRAEBURN FROM THE FIFTH TEE.

THE WOLLASTON GOLF CLUB.—APPROACH TO THE SEVENTH GREEN.

interest grows constantly in and around Boston, and enthusiasts look forward to the coming of that happy day when every man may sit on his own putting green, and Boston players shall hold all the golf championships.

This purview of the conditions of the circle of the courses round the Hub brings into focus the extent of the golfing ardor that has been developed with the earnestness that characterizes the New Englander in all his undertakings.

THE CLUB-HOUSE, NINTH GREEN AND FIRST TEE, WOLLASTON.

4

A Gossip on Golf

A GOSSIP ON GOLF.

By Horace G. Hutchinson, Author of the Badminton "Golf."

TEN or twelve years ago a lighthearted lady following a very great golf match round the St. Andrew's links of Scotland dared to observe to her grave male companion:

"How funny it seems, being so solemn over a *game*."

"It's not a game," came the reply in the shocked tone in which it seemed to him natural to rebuke such irreverence. "It's not a game; it's a study."

The remark of this light-hearted lady was but the expression of that spirit of slight veneration for that "grand old manner" in which our forefathers pursued the Royal and Ancient Game in the dignified habiliments of high hats, knee-breeches and swallow-tailed coats.

When a nation borrows from another an art, a sport, a pastime—anything of which the nature is progressive—the borrower generally takes up the novelty at the point to which the lender has brought it, and modifies it according to its national characteristics. Thus England, a jovial, cricketing nation, in assimilating the game of Scotland, a serious, golfing nation, did not fail to modify it by the influence of English cricketing joviality.

A second borrower has come on the scene. America, taking her golf from England rather than from Scotland, at a stage of its development at which the traditions of the old kind were already modified, has grafted upon it her own characteristics.

Comparing infinitely little things with infinitely big ones, I see a strong analogy between my personal position at the time I took up golf, and that of the States, in respect of golf, at the present date. For I had not the chance of learning the game at any of the great Scottish centers (there were no great centers, in those days, that were not Scottish), and they were immensely far, by the British measurement of distance, from Westward Ho, the nursery of my golf. There were at Westward Ho, none of the classic models, available to me, on which youth should form its style; for in learning golf it is particularly true that example is better than precept, and it is likely to puzzle the American beginner, as in days past it often has puzzled the English beginner, to find how wide the difference is apt to be between the teachings of example and the teachings of precept. When, now and again, it happened to us to see one of the classic models, we found him violating all those maxims of "Slow back," "Don't press," and the rest, that had been impressed upon us from the date of our earliest studies in golf. It was only a later wisdom that showed us that the violation and the contradiction were apparent rather than real; that the "slowness" of the back swing was truly only a relative "slowness"—relative to the pace of the downward swing; that "Don't press" did not mean "don't hit hard," but "don't try to hit harder than you can."

When one is a boy it appears inevitable that one's style of learning should be imitative, and to be a boy and to have good golfing models before one's eyes is the ideal condition of the tyro.

In the absence of all teachers, you must condescend to learn from a book. It is not impossible, if you will only apply your mind to it. One of the best and freest and strongest styles known to the writer is that of a man who began golf after he was grown up, with no "coach," but with a book to teach him. He studied this book—it was not a big one—and worked with it at his swing for a week *before he began to try to hit the ball at all.* This was a very wise and very self-controlled young man, and the secret of his singular success is beyond doubt to be read in the italics. No doubt he had a dull week, but he had much better times ever after than the beginner who persists in caving in the ball's head.

I played golf a good many years ago in the United States, when probably I was the only man that did. The game was over an improvised course at the Meadowbrook Club on Long Island—not an ideal links, but quite as good as many of the "best inland links" in England. Far better, in all likelihood, nowadays are those links of the Shinnecock Hills, St. Andrew's, Morristown, Newport and others. But it is only on soil where the turf is of the right royal sandy nature, with crisp, short grass, that the game can be played in its perfection. All the good links-ground of the old country is made by alluvial deposit, aided by the sand blown up off the beach and washed up by the waves.

The Meadowbrookites of that day were kind enough to say that they thought golf seemed "a very good Sunday game." Nowadays it appears that some Americans think it quite good enough for some of the week-days. Considering all the clubs that are springing up all over the country it is impossible that there should be a sufficient supply of good professional teachers. One fears that it is inevitable that the golfer should have to resort to the book.* The membership of those clubs we may perhaps roughly estimate, on a very moderate average, at some two hundred or three hundred each, say two hundred thousand in all; and to this figure must be added a large number, an immensely large number, of players not attached to any club.

The American tyro who takes up golf after reaching years of discretion does not start from quite the same point as his British compeer. The latter almost inevitably grafts his budding golf on a stock of cricketing experience. The former, as a rule, will not have this experience. He will begin with a relatively open mind. There is much in his favor in this attitude. The cricketer is handicapped by the past use of a bat—a slogging weapon (whereby let us not be thought to speak disdainfully of the great game of cricket)—a weapon which he clutches with the right hand while his eye is kept hopefully forward, not bent on the ball, but projected whither he proposes to smite that ball. The youth of America is not brought up so universally on one game. A great deal of base-ball, a little polo, a little tennis and lawn-tennis are his occasional lessons; all aiding no doubt in the harmonious movement of hand and eye, but none of them, except perhaps the first,

* Mr. Hutchinson, no doubt from motives of modesty, does not mention two books which should be in the hands of every serious golfer, viz., the volume entitled "Golf," in the Badminton Library, and "Hints on Golf."—ED.

directly teaching that right-hand grip of a weapon wielded by the two hands which is a stumbling block in the path of the English cricketer commencing golf.

Polo is of all games the one which most resembles golf in its style of stroke. The club must be swung back with comparative slowness, and the forward stroke must be carried well through. As illustrative of the affinity between the strokes of golf and polo it may be noticed that the Peat brothers, noted polo players, quickly acquired considerable skill with the driver as soon as they took up golf. We generally find that the Englishman who comes to golf with his original cricketing vices strongly possessing him, strikes the golf-ball better with an iron than a wooden club, because the former is more like a bat. For that very reason it is not the best kind of club to begin with, if the learner desires to acquire the proper golfing swing; and the American tyro will not have this special temptation of the Englishman to begin with the iron club.

Equally fatal both to Englishman and American is the tendency to look forward, whither the ball should go. The British and the Columbian eye, equally, must be kept fast on the ball until the latter has been struck—this is imperative. Neither must the right hand of either nation be allowed to become the "predominant partner" in the golfing stroke. The functions of the right hand should be analogous to those of the House of Lords—to correct the too erratic vigor of the stroke whose main energy is wielded by the left. All beginners have a tendency to sway the body away from the ball as they raise the club. This, however, is all wrong. The body should not sway; it may, and should, turn from the hips, the shoulders swinging round as if the backbone were their pivot (this, of course, is not an anatomically correct description), but the whole body must not be allowed to sway away.

Smoothness is the quality to aim at in the swing. Remember to let the arms go out to their full length at once as you withdraw the club-head from the ball, and, similarly, follow on after the ball, when struck, with arms well outstretched (or outflung rather, by the energy of the stroke), for in this way you will make your club-head travel longest on the ball's line of flight. This is important both for length of drive and accuracy. If you are slicing or pulling the ball, so that it describes a curve, out of the vertical plane, in its flight, you may be sure that your club-head at the moment of meeting the ball is not traveling in the line of flight which you wish the ball to take. Recognition of the cause of the evil will help you to cure it.

Stand with your knees slightly bent and your legs moderately wide apart, so as to give you a firm hold of the ground, with the ball nearer the left foot than the right and about at such distance from you that when you lay the heel of the club to the ball its shaft reaches to your left knee as you stand upright. Grip the club firmly in the palm of the left hand, lightly in the fingers of the right, and then swing up quietly, remembering the instructions as to the direction of the swing and the mode of turning the body, keeping your eye on the part of the ball which you want to hit, the while, and increasing the rate of the swing so that the club-head shall be traveling with its greatest velocity at the moment that it meets the ball.

Just now there is so great a demand for golf-clubs in England that the trade is hard put to it to supply them in sufficient numbers and good quality; and the sapient club-maker is apt to reflect that the beginner has not the knowledge to discriminate between a good club and a bad one, and, moreover, that his performances will be very little affected by the character of the instrument he uses. It is very likely that America, in the initial stages of her golf, will be deemed by the club-makers a fair field for the planting out of crooked shafts and green heads. When the States have got their golf into something like organized order, Americans will probably reflect that the importation of clubs from England is rather analogous to the importation of Welsh coal by a Newcastle man, for the great bulk of the hickory used in the making of shafts comes originally from America.

America already has its National Golf Association, and thereby has already solved a problem in golfing matters which has vexed the soul of very many English golfers for a long while, has been the occasion of much public correspondence, of a good deal of heart-burning, and is now no nearer its solution than on the day of its first being propounded. Scotland naturally looks with some jealousy on the rather intemperate zeal with which England has "taken up" her national game. She resents the slight alterations and modifications of rules which England wishes to introduce. If England chooses to play golf on places to which the rules of Scottish golf are not quite applicable, that is not Scotland's fault, but England's misfortune. Thus Scotland is apt to argue. And between the desire of one set of English golfers to adhere to the old traditions, and the desire of another set for rules which shall be applicable universally, nothing is done; there is no headquarters to which moot questions can be referred, no central authority. It is a felt want, though it is very possible that no central authority is better than an injudicious central authority whose decisions might not carry weight. The States are fortunate to have settled this matter satisfactorily and without friction.

Under the authority of the association the question of the superiority of tournament or competition by score as the best test of golf in such a contest will be ultimately settled. Other things being equal, all that remains to be said is in favor of the tournament plan, in which men play matches by holes—the original way of playing the game. But other things are so often unequal—such as the hazard of the draw, which often lets one man in easily, while two others of the strongest fall to Kilkenny-cat work on each other in the first round. The method which we in England call "the American tournament" suggests itself as most obviously appropriate—that method by which each competitor plays all the rest, and the winner of most matches wins the palm. Unfortunately, its propriety is only apparent, for a round of golf takes half a day, virtually, and in a year of three hundred and sixty-five days too many of them would be occupied, on this plan, in finding out the champion. Moreover, a round of eighteen holes is short enough for an adequate comparison of men's mettle. So what is to be done? We in Great Britain have no decided answer to send over, for we play our amateur championship by tournament. You ought to explain, when you say "by tournament" that you do not mean every man against every other, but, by drawing your opponent, playing by holes—our open championship by score. By tournament, in the English sense, we mean a competition by holes in which the players are drawn against each other at the start. The winners of the first round engage in mutual contest in the second, and so on until all have been beaten save one, who survives as victor of the tournament. In order to modify the inequalities of fortune often felt by those who enter for the tournament, it has been proposed that, for one day or two days, competitors shall play scoring rounds, and that those whose scores fall beneath a certain figure shall then play off, tournament fashion, for the ultimate glory.

Then there is the "bogey" plan, wherein a certain bogey or imaginary score is fixed, for each hole, by the committee which regulates the competition; and the competitors fight this bogey score, hole by hole. The victor is he who is fewest holes "down" or most holes "up" to the bogey. The worst feature of the bogey method is its name. Scottish golfers cannot get over that: it is so shocking to the grand old traditions; it smacks almost of levity, and, remotely, of profanity. But the bogey plan, nevertheless, has much to recommend it; it obviates all unfairness and many of the objections urged against the decision by score, which, after all, is not the game of golf but a mere means for comparing the play of a number of golfers in a single round.

One can but refer to these various modes of competition: it is wiser to decline the invidious task of deciding their rival merits. Bogey, though he has a bad name, has much to recommend him. In Great Britain we are too conservative to embrace him heartily; it may be that a democracy may see its way to his reception with due honor.

It is not one of the least merits of this Royal and Ancient Game that two players of very unequal caliber can make a mutually interesting match together. It is not here as with those games, like tennis and racquets, in which one player's stroke depends on that of the opponent. Where players are so unequal at those other games that immensely long odds have to be given, there is little fun for either side. But at golf, each pursues the slightly uneven tenor of his way unaffected—in any direct manner—by the other's doings. By strokes given at certain holes, or by certain holes of vantage given before starting, an equality of result can be produced from the most unequal play. Still a match in which the players are well paired, without odds, is the most enjoyable, and the learner should always try to play with those who are more advanced than he, for thus he will himself advance the quicker. Pleasant matches are those foursomes in which a first-class player on either side is in partnership with a player of inferior class. The latter has then the satisfaction of feeling that he is aiding and abetting the great performances of his partner, and at the same time inevitably learning the lessons which will enable him, in days to come, to rival them.

But he must not expect those days too soon. The learning of golf is a slow and tedious process at the best; though illumined by many bright flashes of hope, the clouds of despair darken it at least in equal number. The exasperating thing is that the secret seems always to be escaping you; for a day, perhaps for a week, you may surprise and delight yourself by playing your iron to the general admiration. You think you have acquired the stroke of beauty as a joy for ever: the next day it may have utterly gone from you. The consolation is that it will return. At a certain, tolerably advanced, stage of your education you are likely to find yourself playing your iron well one day, your driver well the next, and your putter well the third. "Oh," you keep on explaining, "if only I could catch a day on which I could play all three!" But that glad day does not hasten to arrive: you will know the sickness of hope deferred again and again, before it comes to you; and when at length it comes, it passes. You have to catch that day again and again before you can make certain of repeating its success, and even then the best success is so merely relative—so infinitely less than the success which you can achieve as you con the strokes over in your armchair; the ideal is so very far removed from the actual. And it is the glory of golf that this great gulf between hope and achievement exists in the game or the finished player no less than in the game of the merest tyro. Nay more, the gulf only grows the wider as knowledge of the game increases.

The neophyte of this cult has no notion of the subtleties and secrets that it contains. To him it is a matter of hitting the ball — and it will go. He knows nothing of playing the drive with a "pull," when the wind is from the right front, with a slight "slice" when the wind is from the left, in order that in either case the ball at the end of its flight may find the wind assisting it. He does not even know the thrill of sensuous delight that quivers through the fingers from the lofting shot nicely cut to fall dead on its alighting. Even such a simple secret as cutting the ball with a brassey to make it rise quickly over a steep bank straight in front is utterly beyond his ken. It is fully as much as can be hoped for him if he have some remote comprehension of the methods of hitting the ball with a soaring flight when the wind is behind him, and of sending it low-skimming, like swallows when rain is coming, in the face of the adverse breeze. For him most of these subtle delights do not exist; he has not yet come to his inheritance of them. And no golfer yet has ever entered so fully into such an inheritance as to exhaust it. After a quarter of a century of assiduous golf in many lands, the Sphinx still startles one by showing herself in a new aspect, with new subtleties, unsuspected before, which one lights on wholly by accident. It seems that she will never yield up all her secrets. "Age cannot wither, nor custom stale her infinite variety."

And from this panegyric of the great game, which to some—but not to those who know it—perhaps will seem too unmeasured, may be inferred the writer's diagnosis of the terrible mania for golf which is besetting all our intelligent classes. We borrowed golf from Scotland, as we borrowed whisky, not because it is Scottish, but because it is good. The sole form of flattery that America bestows on England is that sincerest form of flattery, the imitative. It may be that she has borrowed golf from us, because it is "quite English, you know"; but she will continue to use the loan, not because it is quite English, but because it is quite good. The most irreconcilable cricket, baseball, polo, or tennis player must admit that it is a fine thing to have discovered a game of great and varied excellence, which is played in the midst of the most delightful surroundings, and which will provide you with an inexhaustible interest from the time that you are becoming too old for the more violent games until the long-deferred day of your death. For long-deferred it cannot fail to be, and of the many sections that have reason to bless the game of golf, surely the life assurance companies should bless it with the most grateful fervor. One cannot altogether ignore this aspect, though one may sympathize with the sourest scorn of the Scotsman for the Englishman who "plays golf for exercise." That the game provides charming and healthful exercise is a detail the more in its favor, but that any man should name this as the essential reason for which he follows a pastime so glorious in itself must be an idea forever loathsome to the mind of the rightly constituted golfer. Such a notion can only be the possession of the man who has never approached the shrine with sufficient piety to win from the Sibyl a single word of response.

5

Golf Round and About the Quaker City

Photo by T. C. Turner.

THE PHILADELPHIA COUNTRY CLUB'S CLUB-HOUSE.

GOLF ROUND AND ABOUT THE QUAKER CITY.

BY HANSON HISS.

JUST nine years ago last April the royal and ancient game of golf was introduced into the City of Brotherly Love, and from a standpoint of athletics and outdoor recreation, it brought in its train a revolution deep, lasting and far-reaching. Men who for reasons corporeal couldn't play football, wouldn't play tennis, and abominated croquet, were quick to see the advantages of the royal and ancient game and play it with the determination of enthusiasts. Mothers and daughters deserted balls and teas within the city limits and successfully courted other balls and tees on the rolling hills and grassy knolls of Philadelphia's beautiful suburbs, until now, in the present year of grace, it is safe to assert that in no section of the United States has the game a stronger hold or deeper root.

Distinctively a game for the gentle

Photo by T. C. Turner.

THE SIXTH GREEN, PHILADELPHIA COUNTRY CLUB.

folk and popular alike with both sexes, it furnishes almost exclusive outdoor amusement for the upper-tendom of that most exclusive city. Ten years since the game was as absolutely unknown from Devon to the Delaware as the childhood of Rameses II, but to-day not to be able to discourse learnedly on the very science of golf is to acknowledge oneself far back in the athletic darkness of croquet, battledoor and shuttlecock, or grace hoops, and certainly on the outskirts of that charmed circle, to whom a proper place of residence is more potent than all the laws of the Medes and Persians.

With a radius of twenty miles, Father of golf will question for a moment that the game has come to stay. As a matter of fact, to quote the father of golf in the United States, it is a game which exactly suits Philadelphia and Philadelphians. Neither boisterous nor effeminate, requiring alike consummate skill and hard muscles, and temptingly holding out almost boundless possibilities for fine playing and headwork, it naturally appeals to the people of that section.

There are few games of like nature at which whole families may play with varying degrees of skill and proficiency. As a matter of fact, golf alone may lay claim to this unique and most important distinction. And in Philadelphia there

Photo by T. C. Turner.

THE FIFTH GREEN, ARONIMINK COURSE.

Penn, from his lofty perch on the tower of the public buildings, surveys the homes of thousands of enthusiastic golfers. Not only men and women who can play the game if they want to, nor those who play golf when the spirit moves them, and both classes are sinners equally deep-dyed from the viewpoint of your genuine golfer, but devotees of the linked green to whom golf is as the very breath of their nostrils, and who talk, write, and almost dream of their favorite pastime.

Many of these golfers are members of one club or another, from The Devon, seventeen miles by rail from the city, to The Philadelphia Cricket Club, on beautiful Wissahickon Heights, or The Belfield Club, within sight of the Mint. No one knowing aught of Philadelphia or

are whole families who enter heart and soul into the game. Those of A. J. Cassatt and Clement A. Griscom, both of the Merion Club, are cases in point. Instances may be given *ad libitum* where father, son and daughter are earnest and consistent golfers.

All told there are thirteen golf courses in the vicinity of the City of Father Penn, and of these five are on private estates. The links at "Lynwood," on the handsome country seat of Mr. Joseph B. Kenley, enjoy the honor of being the pioneer course in Pennsylvania. Other private links are on the estates of Mr. Howard M. Sill, Mr. T. Harvey Dougherty, Mr. Clement A. Griscom, and Mr. Henry P. Dixon.

Were it possible to further increase the interest in golf in Philadelphia and vicinity, the approaching contest for the Woman's Championship of the United States, which will be held on the links of the Philadelphia Country Club, at Bala, will serve that purpose. The city will be the Mecca for women golfers from every city and State, and it is quite probable that many of the crack players will meet their Greek in the membership of the Woman's Golf Association of Philadelphia.

It is but meet and proper, since the championship is to be decided in Philadelphia, that the links at Bala should have been selected. This club is probably the best known in Philadelphia, and is certainly the most complete in all respects. Not only is the club-house most convenient and accessible, but its position is seclusion to the last degree. The far-off scream of the locomotive whistle may occasionally be heard, but its distant echo only serves to accentuate the club's retired position.

From the porches of the club-house one may look over a wide expanse of fertile country and varying landscape. A few peaceful farm-houses half hidden in the trees, waving fields of grain and green pasture, all go to make up a scene restful and soothing.

The club-house is by no means a modern building. It looks more like one of the fine old Colonial mansions which dot Loudon and Fauquier counties, Virginia, and the Maryland side of the Potomac, than the home of a club presided over by "the hero of a hundred parades," General Edward de V. Morrell, and having for its Vice-President Mr. J. Dundas Lippincott, and Mr. Charles H. Townsend as Secretary, and Mr. Joseph W. Paul, Jr., as its Treasurer.

The golf course is a most difficult one to successfully negotiate, owing to the numerous hills which, while neither too steep nor too high, demand both skill and strength. The bunkers, as a rule, are artificial, though a few are natural, and the soil is chiefly clay. Since the course was laid out improvement upon improvement has been made, the most recent change, and probably the most important, having been made this spring. The present excellent course is largely due to the kindly and persistent genius of Mr. George D. Fowle, one of the most ardent golfers in the city and until recently President of the Golf Association of Philadelphia.

Last year the club had two most excellent golf teams. The first consisted of Messrs. J. Wilmer Biddle, George T. Newhall, Isaac T. Starr, Lynford Biddle, Louis A. Biddle, David H. Biddle, and Alan D. Wilson. In the second team were Messrs. Benjamin C. Allen, William P. Smith, Lynford Biddle, S. L. Bodine, Louis S. Fiske, and A. Sydney Carpenter. It is probable that this will also be the personnel of the team this year. With four Biddles in the two teams, and the Chairman of the Golf Committee a Biddle, the club's champions for golfing honors are truly representative of Philadelphia.

Photo by Rolfe.

ON THE MERION COURSE.

Through the tireless energy of a half score of self-sacrificing and public-spirited golfers, the ancient Scottish game has reached a high state of organization in Philadelphia. Indeed, in some things Philadelphia has anticipated the National Association, notably so in organization, for so long ago as 1897 there was formed the Golf Association of Philadelphia, the object of which, as stated in the by-laws, is "To promote interest in the game of golf in the city of Philadelphia and vicinity, and to regulate all contests between its members." The association only admits to membership regularly organized golf clubs having the exclusive use of a nine-hole course. At the present time the following clubs form the association: Philadelphia Cricket Club, of Wissahickon Heights; Philadelphia Country Club, of Bala; Merion Cricket Club, of Haverford; Aronimink Golf Club, of West Philadelphia, and Huntingdon Valley Country Club, of Rydal.

Each of these clubs appoints two representatives, who arrange a schedule of interclub contests and decide on prizes and trophies to be awarded.

The result of these matches decides the Association Championship. Last year the palm was won by the Huntington Valley team. The games are divided into two sessions, one extending from the latter part of April until the latter part of June, the other from the first week in September until late in November. During the months of July and August the several players are widely dispersed and are upholding the honor of their beloved State in many fields and pastures new.

The officers of the association, elected last January to serve until the birth of the twentieth century, are: Mr. Samuel Y. Heebner, of the Philadelphia Cricket Club, President; Percy C. Medaira, of the Huntingdon Valley Country Club, Vice-President, and Alan H. Harris, of the Philadelphia Cricket Club, Secretary-Treasurer. The value of this association to the golfers of Philadelphia is obvious. It creates a friendly but well-sustained rivalry between all clubs, and has been the direct cause of good golf in Philadelphia.

But the men are not alone in the matter of organized golf. Shortly after the formation of the "Golf Association of Philadelphia" the women golfers formed the Woman's Golf Association of Philadelphia upon much the same lines as the senior organization, the by-laws stating that its object is to promote interclub competition and to govern all contests between its members. The organization is more or less of a wheel within a wheel. The same clubs belong to both, and both are governed by the same rules and regulations. The chief and in fact only difference, lies in the fact that women, and women alone, are allowed to compete for the Association Championship.

Women's tournaments are held every Thursday from April to November, barring, for reasons aforesaid, the months of July and August. In addition to

Photo by T. C. Turner.

CLUB-HOUSE, HUNTINGDON VALLEY COUNTRY CLUB.

these weekly matches, the association holds monthly handicap contests for the annual cup, mixed foursome and inter-team matches.

Miss Edith Burt, President of the association, is also the leading spirit in the golf department of the Philadelphia Country Club, and is a most expert player. Indeed, the fine players numbered in the membership of the organization is legion. Some of the most prominent are: Mrs. Charles A. Potter, Miss M. Maule, Mrs. Walter M. Gorham, Miss Starr, Mrs. G. Lee Knight, Miss Hood, and Miss Supplee, from the Philadelphia Cricket Club; Miss Davids, Miss Burt, Mrs. S. C. Price, Miss Steel, and Miss Berwind, from the Philadelphia Country Club; Mrs. Samuel Bettle, Miss Griscom, Miss E. E. Cassatt, Mrs. Charlton Yarnall, Mrs. E.V. Dougherty, and Miss K. K. Cassatt, from the Merion Club; Mrs. Bradford Knight, Miss Knight, Mrs. H. Soulmin, and Miss Hannis, from the Aronimink Club; Mrs. Caleb F. Fox, Mrs. J. S. Patterson, Miss Starr, Miss Margaretta Hutchinson, and Miss Martha Lippincott, from the Huntingdon Valley Club.

In no part of the United States can one find a better specimen of womankind than the Philadelphia woman golfer. Full-blooded and firm of flesh, well-rounded and muscular, with a firm, strong, honest grip, she is indeed fair and good to look upon, and presents a most promising augury for the future of the Keystone State. If the Quaker City woman golfer is a fair specimen of the much-decried new woman, would there were more of them.

The Devon Golf Club enjoys the distinction of a paradox. It has no club-house, yet it is housed in one of the most extensive and costly buildings in the country. Indeed, the club, *per se*, is a condition unto itself. Called into life by the first fragrant breath of early spring, and flourishing in apparently perennial vigor all summer, it fades and dies away on the first approach of early winter, and is as unlike its kindred organizations who worship at the same athletic shrine as it very well could be.

Photo by A. W. Tillinghast.

THE BELFIELD CLUB-HOUSE.

The links of the club are alike beautiful and well laid out. It is a nine-hole course and covers an area of somewhat over forty acres.

Some of the Devon bunkers are artificial and some are natural, but all are trying and difficult. The course is flanked on all sides by long lush grass, the presence of which has caused the downfall of many an excellent player from courses not so difficult and soul-trying.

It is possible to make the course in 38 or 39, but few members, however, can do it inside of 42 or 43, and 46 is a fairer average.

Time was when the Aronimink Golf Club was an integral part of the Belmont Cricket Club, that time-honored and laurel-crowned association, with a brilliant record of twenty-seven successful years.

Golf was not played by the Belmonters until the spring of 1896, but when

Photo by T. C. Turner.

APPROACH TO NINTH HOLE, HUNTINGDON VALLEY.

the game was introduced by Mr. Harrison Townsend, Mr. Clarence H. Clarke, Jr., Dr. T. A. Davis, and a few other enthusiastic devotees of the sport, the club forthwith began to make up for lost time. But there always has been and always will be a certain rivalry, more or less friendly, between different branches of sport in the same club, and the Belmont was no exception to this long-established rule. The feeling finally reached a point where the golfers thought it best to withdraw, and, accordingly, the Belmont Golf Association was formed, with Mr. Harrison Townsend, President; Mr. Clarence H. Clarke, Jr., Vice-President, and Mr. Arthur B. Huey, Secretary-Treasurer. But this

Photo by T. C. Turner.

THE NINTH GREEN, BELFIELD.

name in time gave place to that of the Aronimink Golf Club, and as such is a member of the association.

It must not be supposed, however, that there is any feeling other than the most friendly between the golf club and its distinguished parent. On the contrary, the members of the Aronimink are chiefly members of the Belmont Cricket Club as well.

The club-house is located at the end of Chester Avenue, near the Forty-ninth Street Station of the Pennsylvania Railroad, and but ten minutes' ride from Broad Street Station, and it is said was erected in 1652. It is a venerable-looking old mansion, roomy, spacious and deep-windowed, and is picturesque in the extreme. The greatest care is taken with the grounds, and the members feel that they are hard to rival. The course is in plain view from the club-house, and is located among the hills, almost within sight of the built-up section of the city. The first tee is but a stone's throw from the club-house, just across the road. The first hole is 257 yards. As the links progress they grow more and more difficult. The second hole increases to 441 yards, and then come fences, wild and tangled shrubbery and long grass galore, until the wire-edge of the most wildly hilarious golfer's enthusiasm is worn off before "Hoodoo Hollow," that Waterloo of nine out of ten golfers, is reached.

When this apparently unsurmountable difficulty is passed, and the elevated ground reached, new trouble arises, or rather descends, for there is a steep incline, which calls for the utmost care in stroke. No. 4 is but 158 yards long, and far to the right is the much-coveted green with the creek down below. No. 7, or "Round Top," is very similar to No. 4, and No. 8 is the famous "Pons Asinorum," before which many a good player's pride has been humbled.

The Aronimink Club is famous for its many fine women players, and this reputation is well deserved. Miss Laura Knight's record of 132 for eighteen holes is yet to be beaten. Mrs. Stephen Russell is also an enthusiastic player, as are also Mrs. Harrison Townsend, Miss K. G. Trumbull, Mrs. Eugene L. Ellison, and Miss Eleanor Geopp. The basis for handicapping is "scratch," and "scratch" is 170. The par of greens is 84.

Photo by Rolfe.

APPROACH TO FOURTH GREEN, PHILADELPHIA CRICKET CLUB.

It is said that good cricket players are almost invariably good golf players, and in no case is this more clearly proven than in that of the Philadelphia Cricket Club on Wissahickon Heights, three minutes' walk from the station, on the Chestnut Hill Branch of the Pennsylvania Railroad. The Philadelphia is one of the oldest clubs in the country, and is certainly one of the best known, having been organized February 10, 1854.

As is the case with most of the Philadelphia clubs, the men and women have separate golf departments, but, unlike their rivals on the links, the number of women who play nearly equals that of the men. In all there are 216 golfers in the club. The course is of nine holes and 2,424 yards, and is most difficult. As a nine-hole course it is far and away the best in the vicinity of Philadelphia. The soil is of clay, and the bunkers are chiefly artificial. No. 1 starts near the club-house, and the tee is 243 yards. No. 2 is the longest, with a stretch of 469 yards. Mr. Samuel Y. Heebner, President of the Golf Association of Philadelphia, is the most active member in the golf department. Other prominent players are Mr. Charles A. Potter, Mr. Alan H. Harris, Mr. Joseph H. Patterson, Mr. Herbert M. Forrest, Mr. William Findley Brown, Mr. David Biddle, Mr. A. H. Smith, Mr. Marion K. Wright, Mr. F. H. Bohlan, and Dr. Charles Claxton. The records are held by Mr. Charles A. Potter, who made eighteen holes in 83, on July 17, 1897, and Mr. J. Wilmer Biddle, who made thirty-six holes in 180, on September 11, 1897.

In common with every other Philadelphia club where golf is played, the club has many brilliant women players. Mrs. Walter M. Gorham, who made 123 over an eighteen-hole course, is probably the best player. Other enthusiastic golfers are Mrs. Wilbur Hamilton, Mrs. G. Lee Knight, Miss Elsie Supplee, Miss Corinne Mock, Mrs. Herman Lewis, Miss Starr, and Miss Ellen Hood.

The Merion, the third, but by no means the least important, of the famous triumvirate of Philadelphia cricket clubs, is located at Haverford, and not at or very near the beautiful suburb of Merion, as many strangers erroneously believe. Eight miles from Broad Street Station, and a mile back from the railroad, it is one of the most complete clubs in the country. It has long since lost its distinctive cricket character, and is now quite as famous for its corps of expert golfers. The club was organized in 1865, and golf was introduced in 1895, and the club now has nearly 300 players, the majority of whom play regularly.

There are nine holes in its course, and for the present the links will remain that size, the club not willing, as the Chairman of the Golf Committee stated, to spoil a good nine-hole course in order to make a poor eighteen-hole one.

As is customary, the first hole of the course begins near the club-house, is 373 yards long, and is appropriately called the "Cross Roads," as it ends at the intersection of Black Rock Road and Fisher's Road. The other holes are the "Gully," "The Beach Tree," "Long," with its stretch of 473 yards; "Oak Tree," "Hill Top," "Coon Trap," "Terrace," and "Home." The length of the course is 2,833 yards. The best record for eighteen holes by a member in competition is held by Mr. Charles S. Farnum, with a total of 91. Miss F. E. Cassatt holds the woman's record for eighteen holes at 123. Miss Catherine Cassatt, Mrs. Charles S. Farnum, and Mrs. Edward V. Dougherty are also excellent players.

Photo by Rolfe.

ON THE MERION COURSE.

The Huntingdon Valley Country Club achieved the distinguished honor last year of capturing the championship honors of the Golf Association of Philadelphia, and, judging from the personnel of this year's team, bid fair to hold the coveted pennant. This club is a most precocious infant, as not until the second Monday in June will it celebrate its second birthday. The grounds are located at Rydal, thirteen miles from Philadelphia, on the New York Division of the Philadelphia and Reading Railroad, and are complete and well planned. As is customary in Quakerdom, there are separate golf departments for the sexes.

The Belfield Club, on Thorp Lane, Germantown, near Wistar Station, six miles from Philadelphia, was organized in 1870, and now has nearly 150 golf members, many of whom are experts. The golf course has been well laid out and is now one of the finest in the country. It is a nine-hole course, and is remarkable for the great quantity of timber.

Golf was not in the schedule of the Athletic Association of the University of Pennsylvania until March last, when a golf club with a large initial membership was formed. As a rule, the University men who excel in lacrosse are also excellent golf players, and a majority of the members of "Pennsy's" lacrosse team are now enthusiastic golfers.

Definite arrangements have been made with the Philadelphia Cricket Club whereby all members of the club will have the privileges of the latter's nine-hole course at Wissahickon Heights. It has been agreed that the members of the University Golf Club shall be allowed the use of the course two days each week, while those members alone who shall from time to time constitute the first and second 'Varsity teams, not to exceed ten in number in all, shall have the privilege of playing over the course at all times, including Saturdays and holidays.

Owing to the overcrowded condition of the Wissahickon course the Board of Governors of the Philadelphia Cricket Club decided that it would be impossible for all of the University players to play each day in the week, especially on Saturdays and legal holidays. It is felt that this action will have a tendency to make the competition for the two teams more spirited.

Be it said, in concluding this brief account of "Golf Round and About the Quaker City," that in no section of this or any other country is the ancient game more played or better played. Men and women alike enter the arena to excel, and they do excel. There is a healthy, friendly, and ever-increasing rivalry not only between the several clubs, but between individual members of the same club.

Golfing enthusiasts in sections of the country where the game is played may study with profit the conditions which hold in the City of Brotherly Love.

Photo by T. C. Turner.

THE ARONIMINK CLUB HOUSE, ORIGINALLY ERECTED 1652.

6

Modern Golf Clubs and Modern Methods

MODERN GOLF CLUBS AND MODERN METHODS

By Horace Hutchinson

THE golfer is essentially a hero-worshipper; and not only is he a hero-worshipper, but he has faith in the methods of heroes, a faith that is touching. He has at the same time a sublime confidence, although hitherto latent, in his own abilities for heroic achievement; he has not a doubt that, adopting the methods of heroes, he will join the demigods on Olympian heights. Which means, to put it into the language suited to the comprehension of the golfer, that every golfer has an inextinguishable faith that if he has his clubs made on the pattern of Harry Vardon, and can get just his crook of the elbow and overlapping grip, he will be just as fine a player. Why should he not? Anatomically there is not much difference between himself and a champion; hitting the ball is an affair of hand and eye; both he and the champion have the same number of hands and eyes; why should not one hit it as well as another? Why not — provided both use similar weapons?

H. Vardon,
Open Champion, U. S. A.

The result of this faith—which is universal, even if not universally admitted—is that so soon as a man plays himself into the happy position of champion, or of eminence at all famous, he becomes at once, to a host of pious followers, an occasion of that most sincere form of flattery which expresses itself in imitation. There is a residuum, of course, of the stiff-necked fellows that follow their own counsels, unaffected though champions come and champions go. They stick to their old fashions.

Generally they are of the unamiable generation that quarrel about the rules of golf, for they not only stick to their opinion, which is right and proper, but also believe it to be of value and expect others to adopt it, which is absurd.

Leaving them, let us consider the case of the more amiable, the pliant, the believers. We find in each generation that the great man was able to stamp with his own individuality the golf club of his time. Thus Allan Robertson, when courses were exceedingly narrow, so that the "sure" was of more value in comparison with the "far" than it is now, played with light, easily-wielded clubs, and played gently and swung quietly, with them. He set the mode of his generation.

J. H. Taylor,
Open Champion,
Great Britain.

There followed him young Tommy Morris. He was a slasher; by temperament not "douse" nor canny, after Allan Robertson's pattern, but a bold spirit, trying for long flights, long carries. He made the golf club of the general more formidable, perhaps more supple, somewhat heavier, and he hit parlous hard with it.

The St. Andrews' green was beginning to widen out a little in his day. His bold methods justified themselves, as used by him. Some of his followers they brought to perdition. Young Tommy died in his zenith, and this means that his influence held its power longer than it would have done had his force been seen to wane or be menaced by the power of a rising rival.

Between the day of young Tommy and the day of the late Mr. F. G. Tait, no other influence at St. Andrews was so great as young Tommy's memory; and in most of that interval St. Andrews was setting the tune to all the golfing world.

The first man to do mighty things with clubs markedly different from those used by young Tommy was Harry Vardon. Harry Vardon won his first championship with clubs a good deal lighter and a good deal shorter than the commonly—though tacitly—recognized standard.

The modern golfer was as pious in imitation as the golfer of the Morris period. At once the world began with one accord to lighten and shorten its clubs, nor did it seem to shorten its drives in doing so.

For a long while Andrew Kirkaldy, the sort of sturdy person who holds to his own opinion, denied that Vardon's reputation was fully earned, but about that time he uttered the remarkable dictum that "the lighter the club the longer the drive."

Such a statement as that has at least the merit of bringing the question into a form in which it can be criticized. It puts the issues plainly. Now, as it is stated, it is not too much to say of this axiom that it is stark nonsense and the precise opposite to the truth. To the meanest capacity it is apparent, even if he cannot put the obvious fact into a form that explains it, that, other things being equal, the heavier the club the longer will be the drive. That is truth. But it is also truth that other things are not always equal.

Presuming (a big presumption, perhaps), that your club head is going in the right direction when it meets the ball, the strength of the blow that it deals the ball is determined by the momentum of the striking body — that is to say, by the weight multiplied by the velocity.

To get the greatest possible momentum is the problem. If the weight of the club be increased to that of an iron crowbar the velocity with which the ordinary human hands can move it is so reduced that the result of multiplying the great weight by the tiny pace comes out at much less than the result of the multiplication of the pace and weight of a normal club, and similarly the momentum that human hands can give a walking cane is nothing like what they can give the normal club, because, although the pace is so great at which it can be moved, the weight, by which the pace has to be multiplied, is quite inconsiderable.

So it is pretty clear that virtue lies in an Aristotelian mean; the best results will be gained from the club with which a man can get the greatest momentum; it must not sacrifice so much to weight that he can get no pace into it, nor so much to pace as to have no weight.

The Late Mr. F. G. Tate,
And the Amateur Championship Cup of Great Britain.

The clubs with which Vardon won the championship were light, they were short, but they had a good deal of spring. The effect of this was that many copied them, in the hope of imitating his results, to what end they only know. Mr. Tait, great player that he was, held out against the fashion; his clubs were always long and heavy, and he used them with singular control, as it seemed, always appearing to play well within himself, as we say, and to have a fund of force in reserve.

Our latest English champion is Taylor; and Taylor won his last championship in extraordinary scores, with certainly the most marvelous weapons with which man has brought miracles to pass since the days when Samson wielded the

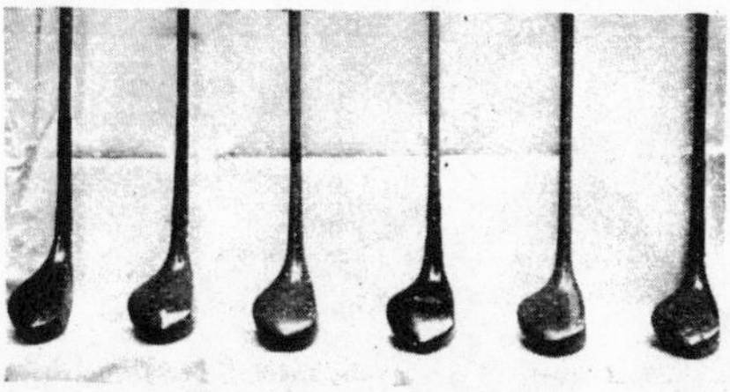

1 2 3 4 5 6

1, Straight-Faced Driver; 2, Bulger Driver; 3, Fork-Spliced Driver; 4, Socket Driver; 5, Single-Piece Driver; 6, Vardon Driver. Nos. 1, 2 and 6 are Scared Clubs.

1 2 3 4 5

1, Cleek; 2, Jigger or Lofting Cleek; 3, Vardon Mid-Iron 4, Ordinary Mid-Iron; 5, Park Goose-Neck Putter.

1 2 3 4

1, Centra-ject Mashie; 2, Taylor Mashie; 3, Ordinary Approaching Mashie; 4, Concave Mashie.

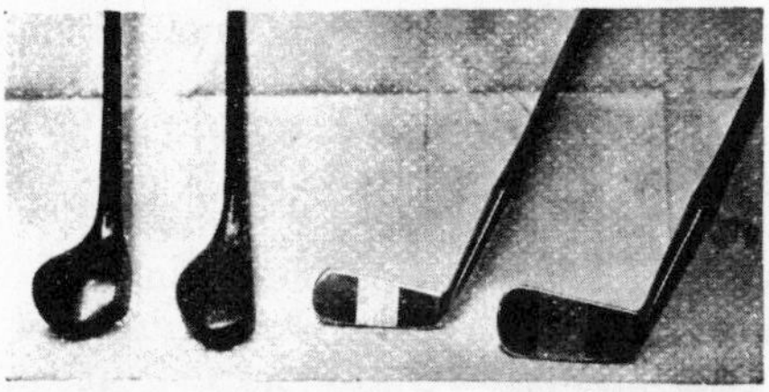

1 2 3 4

1, Bulger Driver; 2, Straight-Faced Driver; 3, Ordinary Putting Cleek; Deep-Faced Putter.

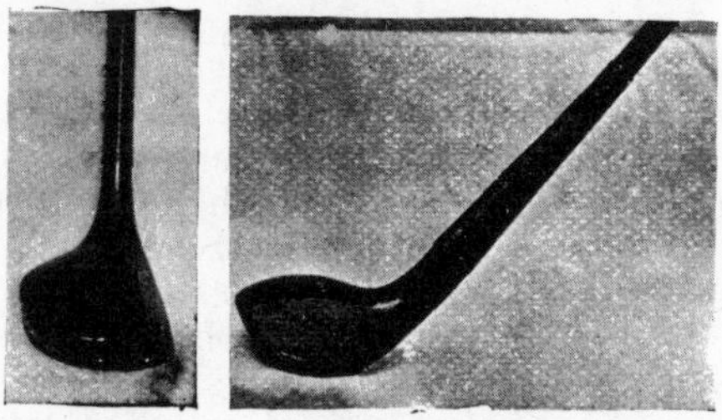

1 2

1, Brassy Niblick, End View; 2, Brassy Niblick, Side View.

1 2 3

1, Modern Spoon; 2, Brassy Niblick; 3, Bulger Driver.

donkey's jawbone. They are short, shorter than Vardon's, they are light, lighter than Vardon's, and their shafts are as stiff as pokers. How it is possible for man to get the length of ball that Taylor drives with them must ever remain a mystery. Taylor himself asserts that if there be any spring in the shaft of the club it is impossible to use the wrists properly in the stroke, impossible to time the use of the wrists properly.

Vardon, since winning his first championship, has rather increased the weight of his clubs, so that his length of drive puzzles us less than it used to do; but Taylor's clubs, light, short and perfectly stiff, feel as if they might do for putters, but as drivers are impossible. His latest championship play is too recent for us to see the effect of those weapons on the general style of driving clubs, but there it little doubt that not a few will copy them.

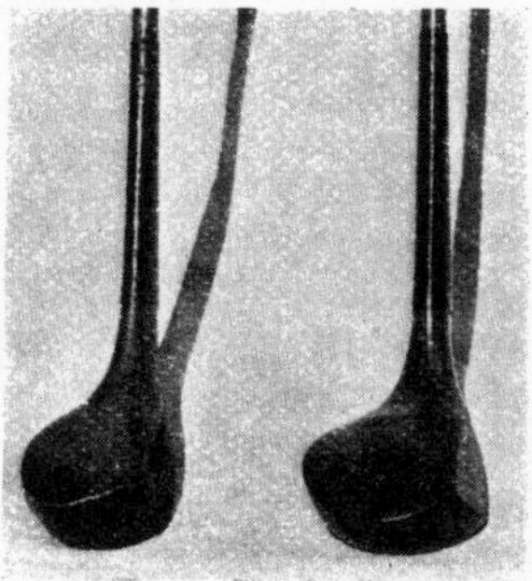

1 2

1, Brassy; 2, Modern Spoon.

For a man of Taylor's sturdy build, strength of wrist and shortness of swing, it is likely enough that they may be the ideal things; but the ordinary mortal will probably want a club that will do more of the work by itself. Taylor's ball has not quite the length of carry of Vardon's, but it has a better run, and when they play together the two are seldom far apart after the tee-shot.

For the rest the new and rising school does not seem to have any very novel ideas about its clubs. Mr. Hilton, the British amateur champion, plays with clubs of quite the ordinary measure. Mr. Maxwell, the young player who perhaps has shown finest form of the new school, plays with a driver that seems but a small thing in the hands of a man of his physique, and Mr. Bramston, a very long hitter, uses a very modest and short club.

On the whole, the weaver's beam is not in vogue, and when people begin to know more widely the little clubs with which Taylor plays so well, the normal size and weight of the club probably will be further reduced. That, however, is matter of prophecy—a hazardous departure from the safe and narrow course of fact.

Taylor's great strength is in his approach play. His methods he has explained in full detail in *"The Book of Golf and Golfers."* Copies of his own mashie have had a large sale.

Park, who is undoubtedly a very fine putter, has adopted a style of iron putter with a neck so bent that the blade lies behind the line of the shaft. The merit of this is that the weight lies in front of the blade, and thus helps the blade to go straight through, when the ball is struck —an obvious merit.

Mr. R. Maxwell Driving.

J. H. Taylor, Putting.

The merit of Taylor's mashie is not as particular as this, the club being merely a very well balanced, ordinary mashie with a sufficiently large blade and sufficient but not excessive loft. Both these points are important in a mashie. Sufficient loft is necessary in order to get loft and a fairly dead pitch on the ball, but excessive loft, though once in a while it may pitch the ball marvelously dead, calls for great accuracy in striking the ball exactly on the right spot of the blade; and further, it is not possible to get the length of shot, that is sometimes useful, from a club greatly lofted.

For a like reason it is well to have sufficient breadth of blade. If the blade be too small and niblick-like the difficulty of accurate hitting is increased. Sayers, the noted North Berwick professional, put this pointedly and well when he said: "You do not need to be so careful with them"—with the big bladed as with the small bladed mashie, he meant; there is not the same chance of that hitting of the ball on the socket which the Fairlie clubs were specially devised to obviate.

The golfer is not a very rational animal. If he would only consider that his aim should be to find out the weapons that will make the game most easy for him he would modify them a good deal; but very

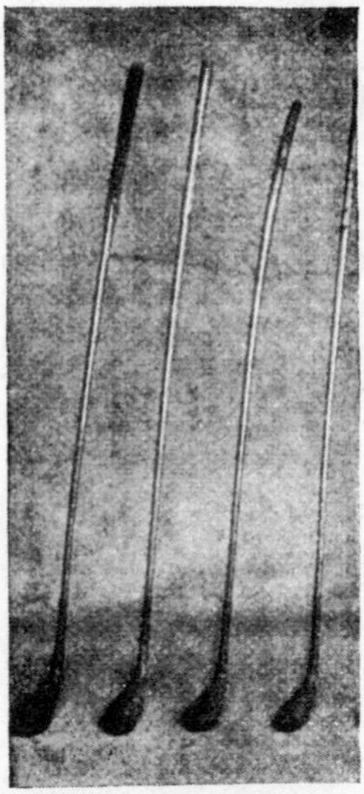

From "The Book of Golf and Golfers." by Courtesy of Longmans, Green & Co.

Set of Old Clubs.

few have the grasp of first principles that is required to make them face the problems of the game in this fashion.

Our good friend to whom so many a weary legend attaches, Allan Robertson, was a great exponent of the "baffy" spoon—that is to say, a short-shafted wooden club, with a face much laid back. It performed the functions that the modern gets out of his cleek or his driving iron, throwing the ball high and letting it fall pretty dead. It could be played with a full or a half swing.

Just now I find a great many, especially of the English players, using what is practically the same club, under the name of a Toby. Probably they regard it as a new invention. It does not require the skill or the force to play the Toby well that is required for the accurate and strong play with the cleek and iron. They are clubs particularly suited for women at golf.

Women seldom have the strength required for really first-class iron play. On the whole, one is rather disposed to commend the use of the Toby or the baffy spoon to the large class that find a difficulty in playing the irons and driving mashies, but it has the highest sanction, Mr. Hilton, the amateur champion, affecting half-shots with the brassy.

From "The Book of Golf and Golfers," by Courtesy of Longmans, Green & Co.

Set of Hugh Philip Clubs.

The weak point about these wooden substitutes for the more generally recognized irons, is that they fail when the lie is bad. They do not help in cutting the ball out of evil places, as the iron blade will cut it out.

On the other hand, there is this to say, that they are not nearly as severe on the good turf of the links, taking one stroke with another. The iron, cutting out a solid big divot, does now and again less harm than the wooden club which just scruffs away the top of the turf, for the simple reason that if the solid turf be replaced there is a fair chance of its growing again, unless the soil be very dry indeed, whereas there is nothing to replace at all after the scruffy stroke with the wooden spoon.

Taking the rough with the smooth, there is no doubt that the wood is less severe on the turf than is the iron.

I have referred to the bent-necked putter. Lately I have seen a putter that seems a very good one—one that might best be described as a wooden putter made of aluminium. The meaning of this is, of course, that the head is made in the shape of the head of a wooden putter, but

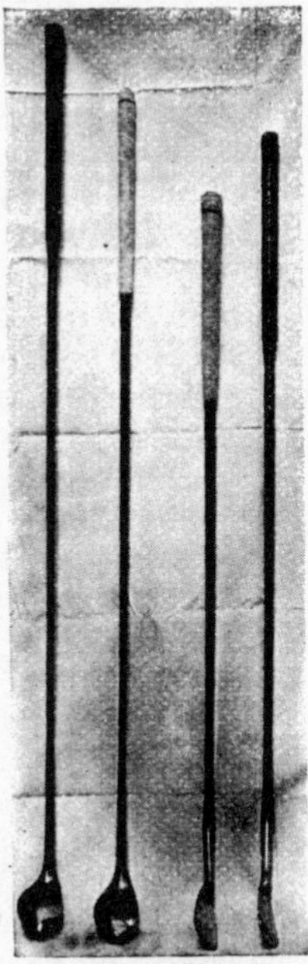

1 2 3 4

1, Ordinary Driver: 2, Vardon Driver 3, Taylor Mashie 4, Ordinary Mashie.

Mr. John Ball, Jr., at Rushes Hole.

that the material used for it is aluminium.

It has not been hidden from the insight of the observant golfer that the wooden putter is a better tool for running the ball up over rough ground, and for playing the longer approach putts, than the iron putter. The latter seems to keep the ball running closer to the ground, so that it is more liable to kicks and unkindly treatment from inequalities of the ground. The iron putter appears to better advantage for the short putts on the smooth greens. Moreover, the wooden putter has this disadvantage, that with the weight massed as it is more or less at one spot behind the point of impact, the difference of the run given to the ball by hitting it on this exactly right point of impact from the run given by a stroke deviating from the correct point of impact ever so little is very great, far greater than in the case of the iron putter, which is homogeneous all over its head: a quality of great moment.

The same is the case with the aluminium-headed putter, which has no lead in it, with no massing of the weight at any one point. It is homogeneous. And while it keeps this merit of the ordinary metal-headed putter, it has also the merit of its wooden model, in that it sends the ball running over rough ground with the same freedom as the wood itself.

Of new inventions likely to become popular in the immediate future, this aluminium-headed putter takes the first prize, according to the humble judgment of the present scribe.

India-rubber grips to clubs are fairly popular; but they do not serve you well in wet weather, becoming as slippery as eels. Aluminium cases, with rubber or wood filling and facing, for driving clubs, are adopted by a few, but any deviation from the exactly right point of impact has more effect on the ball when they are used than with the ordinary clubs. The black vulcanized fiber, sometimes used instead of horn, is certainly an improvement on that brittle substance, and a couple of screws, to fasten it, better than the wooden pegs. Therewith we have fairly exhausted this brief account of many inventions.

For the photographs of the late Mr. F. G. Tait and of Mr. John Ball, Jr., I am indebted to the kindness of Mr. Walter Stone. For those of Mr. Maxwell and Harry Vardon, to Mr. W. H. Fowler.

Vardon Making Iron Shot for a 140-Yard Hole.

7

The Women's Championship

Copyright. Photo by T. C. Turner.

MISS UNDERHILL AT FINISH OF SWING.

LUNCHEON ON THE LAWN.

THE WOMEN'S CHAMPIONSHIP.

(AND OTHER GOLF AT BALA.)

BY CHARLES TURNER.

FAIRER than Scotland in its fairest moods, richer than the Riviera in seductive spring, more glorious than the sea-skirted margins of our fair summer land, are the rolling hills of Bala when the first touch of autumn pencils the landscape and the Greek-like votaries of golf gather within the borders of the Country Club for their Olympiad.

Indeed, the paradoxes and puzzles which the calmer atmosphere of the study have made palpable as the distinguishing characteristics of the Women's Golfing Championship of 1899, were, to a large extent, hidden on the links of Bala by the brilliancy of the company and of the surroundings, the play and pulse of life, and the panoply of battle.

On the field and in the glamour of the play, it did not seem so remarkable as it does to-day that Miss Beatrix Hoyt, the knight errant of golf in a hundred fights, should go down before the sturdy onslaught of Mrs. Caleb F. Fox, who was to follow up that victory by vanquishing, with equal ease, that scarcely less noted paladin, Miss Anna Sands, and to be herself put *hors de combat* by a figurative David in the comparatively slim person of Miss Ruth Underhill. So natural, indeed, that one almost lost sight of the fact that the ultimate triumph was accomplished by one round of golf so poor that the two left in the field, when all else were disarmed, would, had they played similar golf three days before, have scarcely earned the right to be in the tourney at all.

Whereby hangs a moral, that the very magnetic volatility which is the charm of our sisters and our cousins and our aunts, which makes them a delight to the eye and a refreshment to the soul of man, is a heavy handicap when the physical battle and the nervous tension waxes long and fierce.

Let me not be writ down, for these words, a deprecator of the glorious privileges which have come to our womanhood through golf, or as a detractor. Nay, rather otherwise. May the day be far off when golf shall rob them of their subtile and distinguishing femininity, or detract one iota from its delicate, inexpressible, and irresistible power.

Yet, facts are facts, and it is the duty of a chronicler to set them down, even though he incur the risk of a hasty and undeserved verdict, and of being "a crusty old fogy." It is a fact that the player's supreme effort, which created the champion and the challenger, was excelled by ten of the sixteen players in the qualifying round, and equaled by all the other six, as a glance at the following table proves:

Miss Underhill, Nassau Country Club, in finals,	101
Add 6 for last hole not played	6—107
Mrs. Fox, Huntingdon Valley Country Club..	102
Add 7 for last hole not played................	7—109

Whereas in the qualifying round the following scores were made:

Miss Beatrix Hoyt, Shinnecock Hills Golf Club—									
Out......................	6	9	5	5	4	5	6	6	6—52
In......................	6	7	5	4	5	4	5	5	4—45— 97
Miss Frances C. Griscom, Merion Cricket Club—									
Out......................	6	7	4	6	4	6	6	7	6—52
In......................	7	5	6	3	6	5	5	6	5—48—100
Miss Jane H. Swords, Morris County Golf Club—									
Out......................	6	7	4	4	4	5	6	7	9—52
In......................	6	7	8	4	6	5	7	6	5—54—106
Miss Marion Oliver, Albany Country Club—									
Out......................	6	7	5	6	4	5	6	6	8—53
In......................	6	9	5	5	6	6	7	6	4—54—107
Miss Florence McNeeley, Merion Cricket Club—									
Out......................	8	9	5	6	4	5	6	5	7—55
In......................	7	6	8	3	6	6	5	6	5—52—107
Miss May Barron, Ardsley—									
Out......................	8	9	5	5	5	6	6	6	8—58
In......................	5	7	6	4	6	5	8	4	4—49—107
Mrs. J. Franklin McFadden, Philadelphia Country Club—									
Out......................	6	7	4	7	4	7	5	7	8—55
In......................	6	8	7	3	7	6	5	6	4—52—107

Nor can it be said that the competitors were novices, flustered by the novel position of finding themselves for the first time in the critical position of the observed of all observers. Miss Underhill had twice passed through the championship ordeal, to say nothing of

MISS BEATRIX HOYT DRIVING FROM THIRD TEE.

Miss Anna Sands, Newport Golf Club—									
Out......................	6	7	5	6	4	6	7	5	6—53
In......................	5	6	5	4	5	6	6	5	6—48—101
Mrs. A. De Witt Cochrane, Ardsley Club—									
Out......................	5	8	4	6	4	7	6	5	7—52
In......................	5	7	6	5	5	5	7	5	6—53—105
Mrs. Caleb F. Fox, Huntingdon Valley Country C.—									
Out......................	6	8	4	5	4	5	6	5	7—50
In......................	6	6	6	4	5	6	7	6	7—53—103
Miss Elsie F. Cassett, Merion Cricket Club—									
Out......................	6	7	5	5	6	5	5	6	7—52
In......................	6	7	6	5	5	7	5	5	5—51—103
Miss Pauline Mackay, Oakley Country Club—									
Out......................	7	8	5	5	3	5	6	7	7—53
In......................	6	5	7	4	5	6	5	6	7—51—104
Miss Alice L. Day, Morris County Golf Club—									
Out......................	7	7	4	5	4	5	7	8	7—54
In......................	5	6	7	5	6	6	6	5	5—51—105
Miss Ruth Underhill, Nassau Country Club—									
Out......................	6	8	5	5	5	5	6	7	7—54
In......................	6	7	5	3	6	5	7	6	6—51—105
Miss Genevieve Hecker, Wee Burn Golf Club—									
Out......................	6	7	5	5	4	7	4	7	6—51
In......................	6	5	6	4	4	6	9	5	9—54—105
Miss G. M. Bishop, Brooklyn Country Club—									
Out......................	5	8	6	5	5	8	5	6	7—55
In......................	6	8	5	4	5	5	6	5	7—51—106

minor campaigns, and Mrs. Fox is not new to the championship tourney and had had preliminary experience of a very varied nature; moreover, she was playing on links where even the very stones may be said to be her familiars.

All the conditions surrounding the championship were conducive to the best results. The Philadelphia Country Club House is a restful place. The members of it are sympathetic and hospitable. The management was perfect throughout the week, the weather was all that could be desired, and the links have no superior throughout the country for women's play.

Indeed, though based on the links of

Muirfield, in Scotland, the links of Bala bear the impress of the influence of the women who form a considerable proportion of its players. They are very compact, lying, as it were, in a ring fence. The holes and tees are in close proximity; it is, in most cases, indeed, from the finish on one green to the teeing ground of the next, but a few yards. The climbs are by no means steep, the ground is by no means rocky or difficult, the greens are perfect, and the entire distance is by no means exhausting.

Expectation ran high that, with all these favoring circumstances and with the large increase in the number of available players, the entry would be large and the contest keen. Nor were expectations belied, for the entries were three times as great as those for the competition of 1896, more than double those of 1897, and one-third larger than those of last year.

Amongst the entrants, too, were the pick of the players. Undeterred by the presence of the apparently invincible champion, Miss Hoyt, they came from far and near, Chicago, Pittsfield and Cincinnati each sending contingents, and all the Eastern clubs bevies. Indeed, it may be said that, with the exception of Miss Maud K. Wetmore, of Newport, the runner-up of last year, and Mrs. Chatfield-Taylor, of Chicago, all who might be fairly expected were there.

There was work and a-plenty in front of all those who entered, and glory and honor enough, as well as pleasure, to those who might not reach the highest places, for though Tuesday would dash the hopes of all but the highest sixteen to be possible champions of the U. S. A., yet on Wednesday there was open to them the scarce less coveted honor of winning the Philadelphia Woman's Golf Association trophy, for competition by the next sixteen, or the Consolation Cup, presented by the Philadelphia Country Club, open to all entrants, to say nothing of the pleasure of selecting one's own partner and playing in the Mixed Foursome Handicaps.

Expectation a-tiptoe was not disappointed when, on Tuesday, October 10th, seventy-four of the seventy-nine entrants tripped, blithe as a May morning, from the club-house to first tee, and it became apparent that neither the champion nor her last year's rival had lost their cunning, and had met for the first time others of their peers.

THE GALLERY AT THE START OF THE FINALS.

It soon became evident that, taken on the whole, the play was of a higher order than heretofore, so high, indeed, that whilst the trials were still in progress it set the patriarchs of the game to considering whether the test would not ere long require to be strengthened, or, more properly speaking, lengthened, a conclusion strongly supported by the closeness of the finish of the first two sixteens. The first sixteen's scores ranged from 97 to 107, and they were the chosen ones to whom the blue ribbon alone could fall. But seven of the next sixteen were within one stroke of the gate (108), four were within two strokes (109), and five within three strokes (110). There might well be doubt in the minds of those who have the lawmaking whether present conditions effect its purpose—equal opportunities for all and privileges for none.

However, to leave this problematical question for the more definite one of fact, Miss Beatrix Hoyt justified again her extraordinary capacity by winning the gold medal for the lowest score, though closely pressed by a general excellence never before attained.

From this point on our interest in the main revolves around the chosen sixteen, for it is only they whom we shall meet in the central play, and they in the main have established reputations. After Miss Hoyt came such noted players as Miss Frances C. Griscom, who bettered her last year's form by seven strokes, followed closely by Miss Anna Sands, who tied with Miss Griscom in the play of 1896 and got up to the semi-finals, Miss Elsie Cassett, champion of the Woman's Golf League of Philadelphia, Mrs. Franklin McFadden, who holds the record of 93 strokes over the Bala course (a score, by the bye, which she did not come within 14 strokes of in the qualifyinground), Mrs. Caleb F. Fox, who qualified at Ardsley last year.

Indeed, our interest will diminish below the sixteen point, because it will center around the contests, and those only, in which the semi-finalist, Mrs. Fox, and Miss Underhill played, and we shall have entertainment enough. Even in watching the drawing there will be an example of the wondrous luck which seems to follow in streaks and to frustrate all the laws of equal opportunities and flout chance. Take the drawings of the two ultimate competitors and see in how marked a degree the one was favored and the other left. Mrs. Fox first drew Miss Hoyt, the champion; secondly, she drew Miss Sands, a mere shade less formidable than the champion; thirdly, she drew Miss Marion Oliver, of Albany, without doubt the most promising player in the contest.

On the other hand, Miss Underhill drew first Miss Jane Swords; secondly, Miss Pauline Mackay, and thirdly, Miss Cassett, only being called up for her supreme effort in the finals. Of course, this is the fortune of war, and I am not complaining. I am merely pointing out the puzzles and paradoxes inseparable from the wisest and best-intended arrangements.

The "told you so's" and "of courses" and the prophets of the ex-champion's "walk over" received a rude shock early on the second day of the contest, when it was seen that from the start Miss Hoyt was not playing up to her first day's form; whether it was overconfidence or misjudgment, the fact was palpable. From the first hole which Mrs. Fox took to the last, there was the same laxity on the green, and to putting of the most extraordinary weakness, Miss Hoyt, like Findlay S. Douglas, owed her defeat. Of course, it would be absurd to dethrone her from the position of an extraordinary golfer, but it "was not one of her days."

The events of the second day heightened the interest. The official queen was dead, but there was an interregnum. It was not yet possible to say "Live the queen"; that event was yet separated from accomplishment by a wondrous vista of possibilities.

That it was the interest and duty of a faithful chronicler to follow the rising star of Mrs. Fox on the third day was self evident, because she was drawn against Miss Sands and thereby hung much. Could she maintain her position yet once more against a foewoman worthy of Miss Hoyt's steel? The answer came with startling assurance. She could and she did, but only after such a battle royal as is seldom seen. Misfortune at first dogged Miss Sands like a shadow, and at the ninth hole her opponent was 5 up; yet with a recuperative power beyond calculation she brought the game even on the eighteenth hole; two extra holes had to be played, and on the twentieth she missed a foot putt and succumbed.

Here was the unexpected, indeed: two of the most formidable opponents felled. The next was to be Miss Marion Oliver, who came unheralded, but not unprepared, for it may without exaggeration be said that Miss Oliver gave Mrs. Fox the game of the week. Indeed, it was without doubt the nearness of her

Photos by T. C. Turner.

MISS UNDERHILL.

MRS. FOX.

1. PUTTING.
2. APPROACH SHOT.
3. APPROACH SHOT.
4. DRIVING.

almost accomplished triumph which disconcerted the nerve of the youthful aspirant from Albany, and cost her the loss of a victory that will assuredly come her way ere many moons. Seldom has there been seen on any links such work as hers with the wooden clubs, work by which she held Mrs. Fox down "five" on the eleventh hole, and kept the match dormy 4. Then perhaps the event of the week came to pass, and Mrs. Fox pulled herself, by the supreme effort of winning four holes straight and the extra one to boot, again to victory and to the finals, up to which point Miss Underhill had been quietly working through a far less trying series of games.

Undoubtedly Miss Underhill was the surprise of the competition, not so much because she was a dark horse as because the public eye was riveted on Mrs. Fox, whose drawings were so phenomenally sensational. Had this eclipse not obscured Miss Underhill the public would much earlier have recognized her possibilities, not only from her past form, but from her present play.

As to her past, it would have been remembered that had it not been for the execrable weather which marred the qualifying round away in 1897 she would then have got into the fold, and that last year, at Ardsley, she had exhibited the highest form of generalship and skill in a sensational match with Madeline Boardman, of the Essex County Country Club, when, though 4 down at the thirteenth hole, she brought the game square at the eighteenth, and won out on the second extra hole.

Since then her public form has been sustained in a three days' open tournament at Lakewood in May, this year, when she was first in a large field.

To those who saw her play on Wednesday in the first match, when she easily disposed of Miss Janet H. Swords by 3 up and 2 to play, or on Thursday, when she won from Miss Pauline Mackay by the same score, she exhibited all her usual characteristics. She played on both days with great judgment and coolness. The deliberation of her address had not diminished, whilst it would have been impossible for the length of her back swing to have increased. That has always been a highly notable feature of her play. There was the same pendulous see-saw of the brassie, and the unique, almost croquet-like attitude in her putts. Yet it was not until after she had made the score of the tournament, 47 on the out holes, in her game against Miss Elsie Cassett, that her position and prospects attracted attention.

Of course, there is this to be said in extenuation of the public's attitude, that Miss Cassett was the first really formidable of her three opponents. Not only was Miss Cassett the champion of the Women's Philadelphia Golf League, but she had two days before (on the Wednesday) beaten Miss Frances C. Griscom (who, at Ardsley last year, put Miss Underhill out of the championship) by 3 up and 2 to play, and had followed that victory on Thursday by winning from Mrs. A. De Witt Cochrane with a score of 7 up and 6 to play.

Whether it was that Miss Cassett was really off her form, as the best are most likely to be, or whether she was irritated into the fidgets by Miss Underhill's deliberation of "address," or what not, the fact remains that, in going out, Miss Underhill made 5 holes to Miss Cassett's 1. At the tenth hole she was 5 up, and that she won out by 5 up and 4 to play.

Saturday brought the end of the great contest, when Mrs. Fox paid the penalty of the fierce assaults which luck or fate had put upon her in the three previous days. She lost, but it was a loss attributable more to exhaustion than to lack of capacity. Nay, she made a fighting finish of the finest sort up to the very end, being, whilst yet there were two holes to play, only "one down," and although the total scores by strokes of neither contestant was equal to their play in the preliminary round, nor to that of the finals in the Consolation Cup contest by "the next sixteen," the reason thereof was palpable.

And so, under perfect Indian summer skies, amidst the best of good fellowships, and of congratulations to all concerned in the management of many arduous contests running contemporaneously, the woman's championship of 1899 passed into history.

And now, in conclusion, let me add a few words (which I am provoked to do by a sniff of contempt which I detect in the air) in favor of that supplementary golf, which is so pleasant and needful an adjunct to the strain of the morning's contests for the blue ribbon. The Philistine may scoff at these contests as "side shows"; it is his fashion; but the fact, to take one instance only, that in the Mixed Foursome handicap, restricted to women who had entered the championship contest and to such male colleagues as each for herself might select, forty-four women entered, is a pretty conclusive indication that the supplementary play fills an essential want.

Indeed, so long as the number of entrants for the championship continues to increase, and the number is thinned down after the first day to sixteen, supplementary play is but bare justice. Many of those who failed to qualify failed by an insignificant number of strokes; in all particulars they rank equal to the chosen. They have come to the trysting place, where there is skill and enthusiasm galore, where greens are perfection, and it would be next to cruelty to deprive them of such an opportunity to appease their golfing hunger, and maybe in supplementary victories deaden the smart of less successful efforts in the championship.

Take a case in point. Miss Hoyt won the gold medal for the lowest score in the qualifying round on Tuesday, yet next day, doubtless to her astonishment, and maybe to her mortification, lost her match to Mrs. Fox. Had there been no other golf she must have gone off with her smart unhealed, or stayed an idle spectator. But, having the opportunity on Thursday to select a running mate in the open foursomes, she chose Roderick Terry, Jr., the Yale golfer, and won the very handsome prize for the lowest gross score, the pair having rounded the course in 88—nine strokes less than her single-handed round—a result, of course, as was the case in all the other foursome scores, of the presence at the driving tee of the greater strength of the male member of the duet.

What applies to Miss Hoyt, who had the consolation of one honor and the satisfaction of one try, applies with more force to the sixty other matrons and maidens whom the qualifying round shut out inconsolable and unsatisfied.

Besides, we are not all golf fiends; there are others, and may their tribe increase, who are happiest when, combined with the exhibition and the practice of high skill, there is that social intercourse and flow of soul which the very tension of the central competition forbids, but the minor contests encourage; and if there be any at future tournaments whose soul rebels against the diversion of the lesser golf, may they live up to their high principles, and take themselves off ere the merry time of unrestrained good golf, good temper and good times begins. They are marplots and "they never will be missed."

MR. GEO. D. FOWLE. MISS OLIVER. MRS. FOX.

HOMEWARD BOUND.

8
Winter Golf in Southern Sunshine

WINTER GOLF IN SOUTHERN SUNSHINE

BY JOHN DUNCAN DUNN.

IN a brilliant address recently delivered at Dundee by that good golfer, Scotch fellow-countryman, and busy statesman, the Hon. A. J. Balfour, he pointed out in well-chosen phrases the excellent virtues of golf as a pastime, and especially dwelt on the happy dispensation of nature that wherever golf can best be played there is some of the finest scenery and some of the best air to be enjoyed anywhere, not only on seaside links, where the ocean itself supplies an object of perpetual and ever-varying interest, but on the best inland links with which he was acquainted. When the honorable gentleman, in the fortune of war, is relieved of some of his arduous occupations, and visits our shores in friendly rivalry (and no golfer would be more welcome), he will have no reason to modify his views, if he visit, as I did last winter, the golf links of the South.

The first problem which would face the illustrious golfer would naturally be, "What is the South, and where shall I begin?" The answer to this would be, in the New Englander's proverbial method, another question. "When will you begin?" On this depends everything.

We will assume that the normal conditions of the summer season have been left behind, that the Northern season, say north of Lakewood, has been closed, and that the golfer, like myself, is in quest of fresh fields and pastures new. Whither shall he go and how?

As to the first question, I shall speak unhesitatingly. Paraphrasing an almost national phrase, I shall say, "Go South, young man, go South," but I should have to extend its application, and say, "Go South, *all* you, either young or old, who, from force of circumstances, require or desire to avoid the rigors of the Northern winter."

As to the second question, "How shall I go?" I am divided in my advice. There are two courses open, to go direct to the farthest South and work up with the Spring through Florida, Georgia, South and North Carolina, ending at Virginia Hot Springs or Richmond, or *vice versa*, begin in Virginia and work down. I went direct by a Clyde line steamer from New York to Jacksonville, Fla., on the 3d of January last year, just after having had two weeks' skating, and in a few days was luxuriating in tropical seas. Then I could have turned northward and met the zone of happy medium winter lingering in the lap of autumn, at Hot Springs, Virginia. I question whether, so early in the season, it would not have been wiser to have gone down by steamer to Norfolk, and at Old Point Comfort made my entry into Southern golf from its most northern links at Hampton Roads, thence working southward with the season. But I did not; and though personally I have no reason to regret the somewhat roundabout route I took, I mention the alternative for the benefit of those who may follow, where there is winter golf in Southern sunshine.

And here let me turn aside yet once more, to affirm, with the emphasis born of experience, that for air, scenery, society, and especially for hotels, those who patronize their own South and eschew the south of France for winter golf, gain much and lose nothing. I have tried them both and I know.

I think I have said that Virginia Hot Springs would be, for some reasons, and especially for golfers, desirable as a good first halting place southward, or a good ending to a Northern tour.

Its attractions as a health resort are so well known that it would be almost an impertinence for me to dwell upon them. It is as a golfing and sporting social center that I have to consider it, and really the fun I found there was so fast and furious that I had hardly time to eat or sleep.

Golf, of course, claimed my premier interest; and good golf, too, can be played, for the plateau is 2,500 feet above sea level, the turf throughout is excellent, and the incentives to play are numerous. But the incentives to turn from golf to other diversions are perhaps more numerous and certainly enticing, if you happen to be chaperoned by so good an all-round sportsman as was my host and friend, Mr. A. A. C. Beauclerk.

One little incident in which I bore quite an unexpected part will always remain a pleasant memory of Hot Springs, and that was the cake-walk. It was my first acquaintance with this typical Southern recreation, and I enjoyed it immensely, so much so that my friend, Mr. Sterry, in a spirit of mischief, induced me to don my kilts and join in the procession with my bagpipes, a relic of the days when I was a member of the well-known London Scottish. Of course this added fuel to the fire, and the faces of the negroes, when the judges unanimously awarded me the cake, were a study. Of course I declined the soft impeachment, but the incident culminated a right merry night.

Most certainly the next stop which I would advise would be Asheville, N. C., the center of a long-famous hunting and fishing country, which, like good wine, needs no bush, and attractive beyond usual from its proximity to Biltmore, the Vanderbilt estate, of which I had heard much before ever I set foot on American soil. A climate that will produce a Biltmore is ideal for the home of golf links, and so the Swannanoa Country Club have found it. In the lap of the hills, yet within two miles of the city, its cozy clubhouse and ample balconies invite even the invalid to the enjoyment of the game, for from them most of the greens on the course

HOT SPRINGS, VA.—A. A. C. BEAUCLERK IN FOREGROUND.

AT THE HOT SPRINGS, VA.

can be watched. From which let not my golfing reader jump at the conclusion that the course is an easy one. Far from it! Its rolling hills and water-courses, its trees and hazards, will provide as sporty a course as a player can desire, yet over excellent turf, too. Nor should I omit to give its meed of praise to the interpretation which all alike put upon the hackneyed phrase, "Visitors are welcome," for on links, in hotel and at private homes, that one word "welcome" is characteristic of the South. I have never seen the equal to the hos-

A MATCH WITH THE AUTHOR AT SWANNANOA, ASHEVILLE, N. C.

pitality of the Southerner. The Battery Park Hotel was my abiding place at Asheville, and if *Falstaff* had had the good fortune to have been the guest of host McKissick, he would never needed to have put his rights into a query, "Shall I not take mine ease in mine inn?" It would never have been written, for he could not have been anything else than at his ease there. I was more than at ease, and my sojourn was one of the happiest weeks of my life.

Columbia made a too short demand on me. Its nine-hole course, overlooking a beautiful river and rolling country, is more of a residential resort than a tourist's, but a morning on its links is enjoyable and its club house is singularly wellplaced, for from it all but two of the greens can be seen at a glance.

LAST HOLE SWANNANOA, ASHEVILLE, N. C.

Another of my stopping places on the borderland of the South was that popular winter resort Aiken, on the South Coast and Georgia Railroad, nineteen miles from Augusta. I had heard beforehand the names of two of its contests. Their names alone were seductive enough to make me desire to see the course over which the Southern Cross Cup and the Palmetto Handicap were played. I found it all my expectation had imagined; but there is a fly in the most perfect amber, and here I made my first acquaintance with those features of necessity, clay putting-greens sixty feet in diameter and perfectly level, with the circumference banked and sodded and regularly sprinkled and rolled. I had heard of such greens in India and Egypt, but I had never played over them. The course is on a high-rolling sandy ridge, along the side of a dense wood. It is a very diversified tract of land, with an abundance of natural hazards. Golf has done great things for Aiken. Many Northerners have bought land and built homes in the neighborhood, and fully avail themselves of the pleasures of the Palmetto Golf Club.

A little further on, on my way to Charleston, I paid a short visit, all too short, to the Pine Forest Golf Club at Summerville. The name of the club is certainly not a mere catchword, for the forests abound in the long-leaf pine, which yields a health-giving odor that more than justifies the title. Indeed, Summerville may be said to be dedicated to the pine, for the legend of the town is "Esto pinus sacra." The soil over which the course runs is sandy and so exceedingly porous that it dries up like magic after rain. It was rather a surprise to find on this soil sodded putting-greens, and it speaks well for the interest in golf that the club should have gone to so large an expense as this must have necessitated, but it pays, as the numerous visitors at the Pine Forest Inn testify.

Of course, I could not leave out of my itinerary Hot Springs, N. C., for many reasons, one of which was the pressing invitation of my friend and fellow golf enthusiast, Mr. T. D. Green, of the Mountain Park Hotel. Amidst the superb scenery of Hot Springs, in a gully between the Lover's Leap Mountains on the one side and the Big Smoky range on the other, nestle the links of the Wana Luna Golf Club. Of course it is bisected by a river—every valley seems to have that—and in this case the French Broad is the river, which, by-the-bye, is not broad at all. It is one of the features which have to be negotiated, however, and I use the word "one" of the features because there is another running the whole length of the links, in the shape of a very formal, and, to a golfer, formidable avenue of maples; and as everything must huddle close together in these narrow valleys there is a line of railroad, too, which adds its modicum of trouble. But, really, amidst such scenery and over such good pasture and with the comforts of a cheerful little clubhouse, the time flies all too quickly for details to be troublesome.

The borderland wayside links may fitly end at Thomasville, in the extreme southwest of Georgia, where one can almost imagine that he feels the tang of the Mexican Gulf. Everything about the Country Club of Thomasville betokens taste and judgment, and from the moment you pass through the rustic woodwork arch of its grounds till you leave, there is a sense of luxury and comfort. The home of the club is in Glen Arvern Park, three hundred acres of high ground surrounded by as well-wooded and diversified a country as ever delighted the eye of a sportsman and golfer. I found its well-sodded greens and well-turfed course throughout a continuous delight. It did not seem possible that there could be such climatic conditions as those which, in the summerlike parlors of the Piny Woods Hotel, I read of in the North. Fortunate are the golfers of a land where they can so dodge the seasons. Yet I was still only on the borderland, for I had not yet entered Florida.

FIRST TEE, RICHMOND COUNTRY CLUB, COLUMBIA, S. C.

It is not part of my necessities, fortunately, to have to plead the cause of Florida as a winter resort. She needs none beyond the hosts, ever increasing, who, year by year, settle within her borders and luxuriate in her balm of Gilead, but, as a golfer who has imagined that in the pine woods of southern England he has long enjoyed the idealic in winter, let me own that I have lived unknowingly in the house of bondage. I never knew what winter golf in idealic winter was until I made the acquaintance of Florida.

And as the climate is, so are the opportunities for indulging in my favorite pastime. Everything in the evolution of the State has tended to prepare it for golf—seashores that tempt one to design links every few miles, hotels that beggar the splendor of the Arabian Nights and baffle imagination in its wildest flights, visitors galore from every State in the Union, of every age, hungering for just the gentle exercise, entirely within their control as to speed, that golf provides, social instincts that cluster round the clubbable charm that golf makes for so abundantly, and communication from the North by rail and water, than which none in the wide, wide world can be better.

There is only one embarrassment, and that is, in what order shall I make my Florida circuit, not where shall I begin, for nature and commercial enterprise have settled that point. Jacksonville is the beginning, without any question, but then it is also the parting of the ways, and the question immediately meets the golfer, when he tears himself away from the starting-place, which finger-post shall he follow? One pointer reads, "Follow me," and on it is inscribed, "The East Coast Golf Clubs," with the witchery of St. Augustine as its first enticement. On the other tablet is inscribed, "The Plant or Western Golf Association," with world-famed Tampa as its goal, where my father, Thomas Dunn, is now in full golfing control.

Fortunately I can take them both, so that my conclusion is only one of postponing the blandishments of the other, and so I draw lots and The Plant or West Coast comes out of the hat, and then I settle down to the antecedent pleasures of Jacksonville, where I find, in the company of a numerous residential membership, most excellent entertainment on the links of the Florida Country Club and most excellent fare at the St. James. The grounds are very conveniently reached by an electric car system, which covers the three miles from the city and deposits you at the club gates. Golf has some antiquity, comparatively, at Jacksonville, for the present club was preceded by an older association, the St. John's Golf Club, and is in its new organization some four years old, a sufficient time to have allowed the Bermuda grass to have mastered the problem of turf. "Visitors are welcome" here, too, and I found that that phrase had lost none of its full Southern meaning at Jacksonville.

HOT SPRINGS, N. C. T. D. GREEN, PUTTING.

I had scarcely left Jacksonville an hour before I was welcomed open-armed by my old summer host of the Lake Champlain Hotel, whom I had last seen there when I had the honor to play the

AT MAGNOLIA SPRINGS, FLA.

"pipes" before the illustrious President of the United States. But one hotel in the North is all insufficient for Mr. Seavey, and so soon as he departs from the Northern woods he hies him to Magnolia Springs, on the St. John's River, where, he says, with the facetiousness of a golfer, he goes that he may entertain "Colonel Bogey, looking young and confident at 41." The change of climate is good for the ubiquitous "Colonel," for I can testify that, although the links are good and my play not below the average, I had a hard tussle to come as near as I wished to his record.

Trending westward yet a little further, I cried halt at Kissimmee, that euphonious name of a club on the banks of a lake with the singularly discordant name (in print, at least) of Tohopekaliga. The

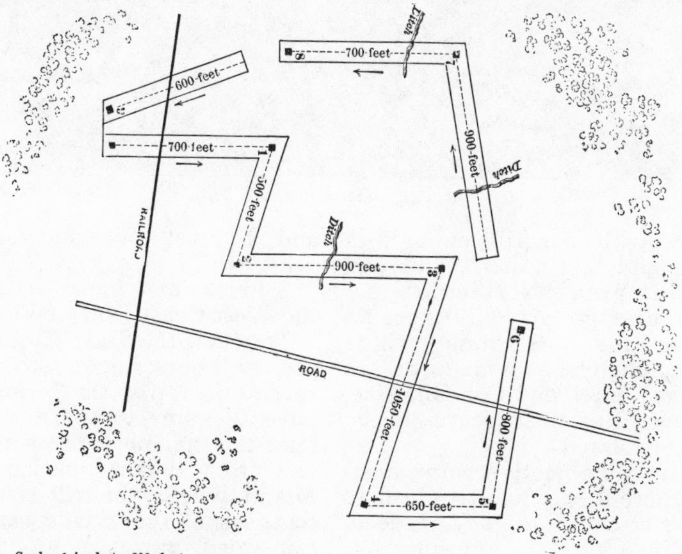

Scale, 1 inch to 800 feet.

THE LINKS AT TAMPA, FLA.

discord goes no further than the name, for a more delightful situation than the links on its cypress- and myrtle-covered banks can scarcely be conceived. It is an excellent course, and has been the cause of excellence in others; for here, I was informed, was discovered, or at least first observed, almost accidentally, the value of a Japanese clover, which is now better known as "Bermuda grass," and the use of which has transformed so many links from sands to pasture.

The Kissimmee course is wholly a natural one, with hazards enough in sandy ridge and lake and streams and wood to satisfy even a Northerner.

At Kissimmee golfers will meet an old friend in Dudley S. Phinny, whose acquaintance many have made at the Cayuga Lake Hotel, and Col. Gillespie, widely known, but unsuspectingly by many, as "Trilobite."

Tampa was my objective point westward, and there it is difficult indeed to confine one's attention to golf. Indeed, it is first difficult to do anything but wonder at the wonders which enterprise and skill and artistic taste have worked, and before you have recovered from this, you are launched into such a galaxy of competitive pastimes afloat and ashore, by day and by night, that it becomes difficult for you to disentangle yourself. In the end, of course, golf triumphs and carries you off a prisoner to the tee, where you find a course to set all your Scotch blood tingling, a course as near to the Scotch ideal as it is possible to make in the South. Nothing has been spared in money or advice to procure this result, and I must say success has been achieved.

ON THE ORMOND LINKS, FLA.

And so in a blaze of triumph ends the West Coast Golf of Florida.

To reach the East Coast links there are two courses open: to retrace your way to the top of the Λ again, or, if you have the time to spare, still better, to take the steamer across to Key West, and from thence another steamer to Miami, where you will strike the most southern of the East Coast links, and can work upwards along the three hundred odd miles of seashore to

A TYPICAL ORMOND GREEN.

St. Augustine, and I can assure you that you will find resting and playing places on the way to satisfy all your expectations, be they never so high.

The course at Miami, on Biscayne Bay, is one of nine courses controlled by that great benefactor to golf in the South, "The Florida East Coast Golf Club."

A DRIVE-OFF AT MIAMI, FLA.

By the arrangement which this corporation has made all its courses are part of an interchangeable system, and by the outlay they have made and the encouragement they have given to the sport, they have riveted golf to the soil.

The course at Miami, although part of the Royal Palm Hotel domain, is not part of its immediate surrounding. It is, in fact, nearly two miles from the hotel, but then its approach is either over an excellent shell road or alternately by boat up the Miami, and when you have mastered the mystery of what you think at first is an artificial abomination, but speedily recognize as a necessity, the box tee, you will find good sport at Miami. A word to the novice on the box tee: If you are inclined to sclaff leave your pet driver at home.

Northward, but no great way, and you come to that delightful fascination, Palm Beach, and its twin hotels, the Royal Ponciana and the Palm Beach Inn, on the shores of Lake Worth and of the ocean. It is not for me to paint the lily and adorn the rose, even if I were able, and I must repress the desire even to attempt to portray Palm Beach. I am not precluded from recommending it, however, and this I can freely and gratefully do. It is wonderful what has been done to overcome the difficulties which the tropics present for a golf course that will satisfy a critic from the temperate zone; but when I mention that the whole magnificent lawn over which the Palm Beach course runs has had to be coaxed into existence, and that to keep it in condition it is piped throughout with a tap every fifty feet, I have mentioned only some of the difficulties which have been overcome. The result is a good course, through the greens over the Bermuda grass especially so, but do not attempt to loft onto the putting greens, for if you do your ball will bound off; approach by running up, and then you will discover why, for the place you putt on in Florida is not a green; it is just as gray and hard as a rock. I was told at Palm Beach that there was an intention to try cocoanut matting on the tees, and it is probable it would be successful. It seems a curious combination, but then we must remember that they play cricket outdoors on it in Australia, and find it an excellent substitute for grass between the wickets. Whatever golfing difficulties you may find at Palm Beach, you may be very sure of overcoming, for Arthur Fenn is the instructor, and when that has been said all has been said that is necessary.

ARTHUR FENN AND ALEX H. FINDLEY AT ROYAL PONCIANA, FLA.

And should you tire of golf for a time there is boating and cycling and fishing from the pier, the like of which I never saw, and you can see your fishing at Palm Beach. The water is as clear as crystal, and every movement of the finny denizens of the deep as apparent as if their native element did not exist.

The last stage but one on the northering tour is Ormond-on-the-Halifax, where the seashore is as hard as a road, and when the wind is right you can coast seventeen miles on a bicycle. When you have arrived at the end of your jaunt, however, you had better have a pull with Boreas powerful enough for him to reverse the wind, or your journey back will not be "all violets," as the cockney says. You will find easier work on the links, notwithstanding its marsh hazard, its ditches, and the railroad. Do not miss Ormond, however, for it is a restful, healthful resort, where you can possess your soul in more patience and enjoy golf free from many of the counter-attractions that impinge so largely upon one's leisure at some of the other resorts we have passed and the gay center we are fast approaching, St. Augustine.

St. Augustine deserves a chapter entirely to itself. Indeed, if I were to attempt to do justice to it in all its phases it would require more space than I have had allotted to me for the whole subject of Golf in the South. Fortunately for my readers, other pens have depicted, with a brilliance I do not claim, its many historical and picturesque allurements. To me it had, however, one special appeal; for it was here that a mere handful of my compatriot Highlanders brushed aside three times their number of Spaniards of other days, and as I lingered on the scene I could almost fancy I heard the skirl of their pipes. Spain has left the mark of its occupation deep on St. Augustine, however. Spanish coats-of-arms crop up in every quarter, and the very names of its Alhambra-like hotels, the Ponce de Leon and Alcazar, confirm the legend of their occupation. Nor does the name alone suggest it; the gorgeous flowers and fountains, the music and mantilla, are of the land of the Sun and breathe the romance of Spain and the further Orient, from which Spain received her impress in so many things.

Even when one comes to the links the illusion is maintained, for part of the course of the St. Augustine Golf Club is laid out in the grounds of the old Spanish fort, and its moat forms one of the troubles the golfer has to overcome, and cedars, coexistent probably with Spanish rule, add their torments. It is a good course, nevertheless; a remark which may be made with equal justice of the other course, that of the Country Club of St. Augustine, which I must not pass without a word about its unique tee on the top of a tower built of coquina, or pulverized shells. As the drive from it is over about 100 yards of water, it is the source of a good deal of fun, although a man who has missed his drive from it may be apt to give it another name.

FIRST TEE, ST. AUGUSTINE, FLORIDA COUNTRY CLUB.

The golf links of St. Augustine have formidable competitors in the other pastimes and diversions of this famous social center. I can testify that golf

ORMOND-ON-THE-HALIFAX, FLA.

is an excellent corrective and tonic to an indulgence in them, which cannot be avoided.

Had time permitted I should have much liked to have wound up my Southern trip on the links of Old Point Comfort, or gone on to Richmond, Va., and enjoyed a few days play over the links of the Jefferson Hotel Co., on the Lakeside Country Club, where from January to May golf is in high season. Both are pleasure deferred, and my many golfing friends who have been there assure me that Richmond is where I should both begin and end my Golf in the South.

9

How to Get Out of Trouble in Golf

Painted for OUTING by Jas. L. Weston.

TO BE OR NOT TO BE?

OUTING.

VOL. XXXII. AUGUST, 1898. No. 5.

Photo by T. C. Turner. GETTING OUT OF LONG GRASS.

HOW TO GET OUT OF TROUBLE IN GOLF.

BY WILLIE TUCKER, INSTRUCTOR, ST. ANDREW'S GOLF CLUB.

A SCOTCH proverb says, "He who plays with a thistle must expect to get pricked," and he who plays golf must expect to get into trouble. Indeed, a golfer's life is one continuous series of problems, "How to get out of trouble." Trouble he will have, willy-nilly. This may at the first blush seem a somewhat dispiriting view to take of so fascinating a game, but it is the very variety of the points of the game, ever occurring yet scarcely ever duplicated, that give it its unique position. It is this that renders it so exhilarating to the devotee, both mentally and physically.

I have not especially in my mind the troubles which beset beginners, for the reason that no amount of precept has for the beginner half the value of a very small quantity of example, and nowhere except upon the links can anything really worth learning be taught. Even there, however, there are troubles special to golf besetting the beginner. The main of these is not so much in the acquisition of the knowledge of how to perform this or that motion, as it is in overcoming the habits of childhood or youth acquired in the wielding of the baseball bat, the cricket bat or the polo stick. The novitiate who comes to golf from any of these field sports has tendencies and instinctive habits of holding the club and striking the ball that are indeed hard to eradicate; they are habits that have become second nature; they have become imbedded, as it were, in the bone, and nothing but the most determined and long-continued efforts can eradicate these very troublesome tendencies.

When, however, these have been overcome on the links, there yet remains a crop of troubles upon which hypothetical and written advice is nearly as valuable as example, for the reason that the experience gained in early play enables the novitiate to understand what is written, an impossibility in the very earliest stages of the game. Just as it is useless to explain higher arithmetic to a pupil who has never heard of the multiplication table, so it is useless to expect a pupil who has never held a club in his hands to comprehend terms relating to "slicing," "drawing," "following on." Yet the bulk of the instructors who have favored the world with their practical hints flood their writings with what, to the beginner, must be jargon. I propose these observations only for those who have, by practice on the links, discovered how much there is yet to learn, and what an infinite variety of trouble and pleasure lies before them.

USE THE NIBLICK WHEN IN THIS DILEMMA.

Let me illustrate: We will suppose that a player is fairly experienced in all the lesser minutiæ of the game; that he has command of his club; that he can drive with accuracy and put with fair precision, and that he can traverse a course of eighteen holes in, say, one hundred strokes. Still, giving all these qualifications in, there will only be thirty-six strokes—two strokes for each hole, the drive-off and the holing—which may be counted upon with anything like certainty. He may be able to drive with fair accuracy an estimated number of yards from each tee and *put* an estimated number of feet on each green, but, between the anchorage of the tee and the port of the green, what uncertainties will arise? Ah, there's the rub! The power of the wind may be misjudged, or its direction miscalculated; he may drive too high, and his ball fall without an inch of *run* in it, or he may drive too low, and a long run may take it into the much-dreaded long grass. It may strike an unseen tree-limb, or get into the intricacies of a stone wall; it may glide into a ditch or fly off at a tangent and overshoot the aimed-at mark. All these and a thousand other posers will meet the golfer, golf he never so wisely.

The main purpose of all advice to the golfer must, therefore, be "how to get out of trouble," what club to use under certain general conditions, why to use it, what it will effect, what it will not effect, and the method of getting the most out of the club and of the player's physique. This is the burden of these notes from one who has been in more trouble on the links than falls to the lot of the ordinary amateur.

The clubs forming a set vary very much with the experience of the player, but they are roughly divisible into two classes: Those mainly used for driving long distances, the driver, the brassey, the cleek and the iron. The other class of clubs, the mashie, the niblick and the putter, are mainly used for the shorter distances, approaching on the green. I will treat of each club separately.

UNDER THE FACE OF A STEEP BUNKER

The Driver is used for the first stroke from the teeing ground. The object is to gain as great a distance as can be accomplished. Of course, the distance attained varies with the skill of the player. A fair stroke should carry 180 yards. It is also used through the green, and in the hands of an expert is often given preference to the brassey. The reason the driver is more powerful than any other club comprising the set is that the face is filed perfectly flat, with a slight bulge, and the weight is more compact and central behind the ball, giving the ball longer carry, quicker flight, and in the majority of cases a run of twenty or thirty yards after it touches ground, but this depends entirely upon how the ball is struck.

In teeing do not tee high unless the wind favors you, as one invariably gets the ball in the air with the result that you get less carry and no run, and when you have a good lie through the green it becomes much easier to pick the ball up, but if you use yourself to a high tee

A JERK SHOT WITH THE BRASSEY.

when driving off, you invariably top your shot through the green.

Downhill with Driver.—If you have a hanging lie and distance, take your driver, providing your lie is good; care should be taken to get your position correct, the ball being about the center. The club should be gripped firmly with both hands, and the face turned in a trifle to counteract a slice. Do not take more than a three-quarter swing. In swinging your club your weight should fall upon the left foot the moment the club comes in contact with the ball; hold your club a little shorter than usual, and follow through with decision.

Uphill with Driver.—If you have an uphill lie the correct position in this instance is: Have the ball about the center, hold your club firm and shorter than usual, take a three-quarter swing with your weight on the *right* foot, and *don't press* or pull back.

The Brassey.—Next to the driver the most formidable club. It will easily cover 165 yards. It should be used through the green if your lie is a little cupped, or lying upon bare ground or dirt, or if the distance is less than you would have to use the driver for.

The face of the brassey being spooned, and the weight being more distributed on the sole by the brass plate, give the ball a tendency to carry high in the air, with no run. If your ball *is cupped* stand with your *right* foot a little in advance, with the weight on the left. The ball should be about the center. Take a full swing, hitting ground and ball *at the same time.* Be sure you tighten your grip when coming in contact with the ball, and let your arm follow through as much as possible.

The Mashie and Niblick.—The mashie is the next important club, being used to loft a ball over stone walls, fences, or to play a stimie, and often used for long grass. But the main object of the mashie is for the approach to the hole. The mashie will pitch a ball high, so that it will stay within a few feet of where it falls, allowing better judgment when you have a bunker, rough ground, or a hazard quite close to the green, and a hazard beyond the hole.

If your ball is located near a stone wall, a straight-cut shot could be employed, in order to raise the ball over the wall very quickly. The ball should be a trifle in front of the left foot, the right foot well in advance; the face of the mashie is laid back, and the club

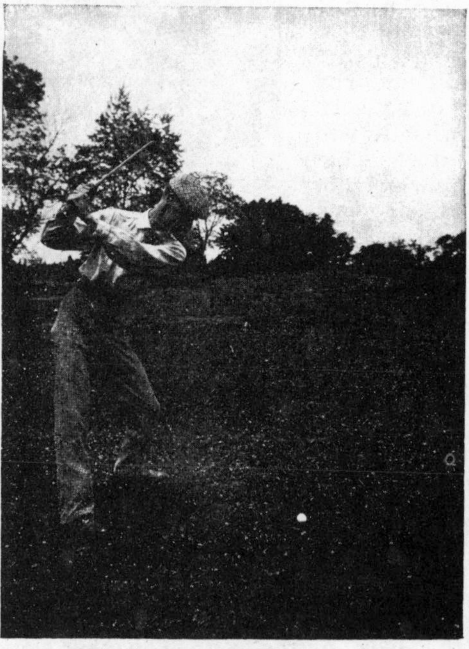

UPHILL WITH DRIVER.

gripped tightly in both hands; a half (½) swing is necessary. The main object of this shot is to raise your ball over the obstacle.

If your ball is located near a bunker, or any position requiring strength to manipulate the shot from any obstruction, do not use your mashie. It may not only twist your shaft but will probably break it; but when in such a dilemma use your niblick and do not try and get far, but play yourself safe, with the probabilities of getting away clean your next shot well toward the hole, as the case may be. If under the face of *a steep bunker*, and lying bad, do not attempt to get over, but play back with your niblick, then using your mashie or mid-iron, according as the distance may be to get on the green.

The Cleek.—The cleek, which is the favorite club of the beginner, should be used if the distance is less than you would use the brassey for, say 145 yards, or your lie is cupped. Should the green be open, a long, low running ball can be had from such a lie, but should a bunker or hazard be situated at 120 or 130 yards, take your mid-iron and play short, for if you do not succeed in getting your cleek shot away well, it will go just far enough to find the bunker.

DOWNHILL WITH DRIVER

THE ORDINARY IRON, OR MID-IRON.

The half shot with the cleek is a very fine shot to play against a wind for 100 or 120 yards in preference to a full iron shot. The cleek will keep the ball low and straight, but with the iron the ball gets too high and it is at the mercy of the wind, and will probably take you 30 or 40 yards out of your course. The driving mashie, mashie iron, mashie cleek and driving iron could be used with equal effect as the cleek. It is far better, if you have a heavy lie and a hazard to negotiate, to take your mid-iron in preference to the cleek.

The Ordinary Iron, or Mid-iron, as it is termed, is, in the majority of cases, the most difficult club to manipulate with accuracy. There are three different shots, or rather distances.

"The running approach" should be used from a distance of about 50 feet or so from the hole, and should be played with the knees bent. Take a short grip of the club with the wrists fairly stiff and follow on as though the club and hands were one. The ball should be a trifle nearer your right foot and you should swing as far back as the cut shows.

The idea of this shot is, providing the ground is clear of all obstructions, to pitch a low ball a little more than half the distance you require to go; it should then run the remaining distance to the hole. It is far easier for the novice to regulate distance and direction by this shot than to pitch a ball on to an open green with a mashie.

The Half-Shot with Mid-iron is without doubt the most uncertain, or, rather, the most difficult shot. It should be used for about 100 yards from the hole when your shot requires to be lofted, and when there is no bunker within 50 feet of the hole, as from the mid-iron there is often a run.

See that you have lots of ground when you have to pitch over a hazard with a half mid-iron shot. Take a firm grip with both hands and let your left knee bend in toward your right; take a half swing and try and work your shoulders and the club at the same time. Follow through and be sure you do not jerk your swing.

THE MASHIE WILL PITCH A BALL HIGH.

Getting Out of a Bunker.—A niblick should be used for this shot and should be gripped short and firm; the face of the niblick should be a little on the slant and the weight should be on the right foot; play with a half or three-quarter swing and take the ground about two inches under the ball. Do not attempt to get on the green; the player's only aim in this case should be to get over the bunker.

It is far better policy to play your ball 10 yards back on to the fair green at the loss of one stroke, when it might cost you three or four to get 10 yards over the bunker, in addition to losing your temper, when it will appear twice its height.

In getting out of a bunker, or long grass, hold your niblick light with both hands; take a firm three-quarter swing and aim two inches behind the ball, imbedding your niblick in the sand, the face of your niblick a little on the slant.

When the ball has found its way into high grass, and is also nestling near a rock, the player's aim is to secure correct position. See that the ball is in line with the right foot; use a niblick, and grip it pretty firmly in both hands; an upright swing would be in order, and the club should be brought down in a vertical position, hitting the ball and the ground together; this is termed a "jerk shot." This is a hazard, and the player is not allowed to put the club behind the ball.

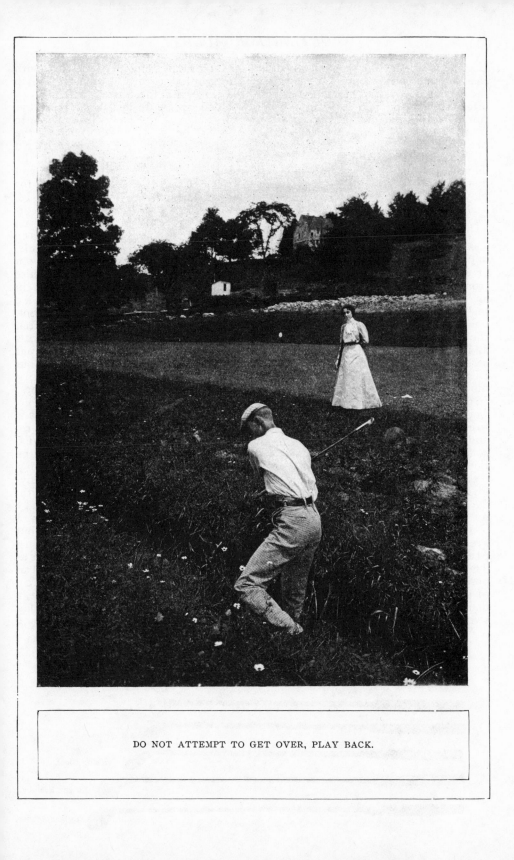

DO NOT ATTEMPT TO GET OVER, PLAY BACK.

Beginners are inclined to stand behind the ball, and consequently do not bring the niblick down straight enough, which often results in their missing everything, and possibly the breaking of the club. This is a difficult shot to play.

PLAYING A STIMIE.

Approaching to the Hole Out of Long Grass.—If a player is confronted with an obstacle just before he reaches the green, and, as is the case in some instances, his ball has found its way into long grass, and a rock is in front of the ball, the best thing for him to do, instead of playing on the green, is to play back. The correct position is to grip the niblick very firmly in both hands, and, taking a three-quarter (¾) swing, hit as firm as possible.

Playing a Stimie. — Use a mashie, and aim from the point of the club, with the right foot greatly in advance. Grip the club with the fingers and make a decided stroke. In this shot it is always advisable to play to the left-hand side of the hole. If you have two for the hole, never attempt to negotiate the stimie, for if you should miss the hole in taking the stimie shot, it very often happens that you put yourself out of holing altogetber.

The Putting Cleek is the most reliable club to use on the putting green, anywhere within twenty feet or so of the hole, but for a long put, such as is termed an approach put, it is better judgment to use a wooden putter. The man who can play with accuracy his approach put is a hard antagonist to meet.

A SET OF CLUBS.

10

American Balls and British Golfers

AMERICAN BALLS AND BRITISH GOLFERS

By HORACE HUTCHINSON

THE reception of the American—that is to say the rubber filled—golf ball in Great Britain has been curious as a spectacle. It has afforded a pleasant object lesson in human nature, and it has been interesting and instructive too, in its purely golfing results. Personally, I have perhaps had exceptional opportunities for enjoying the spectacle, because it so happened that by a friend's good offices I was given a thoroughly good trial of the balls as far back as October, 1901, and have played with hardly any other kind of ball ever since. That is as much as to say that I had a six-months' start with the balls over nearly all my fellow countrymen; I knew quite well what they were—their merits and their demerits—and with this pleasant sense of superiority I could watch the discussion and often read most amusing opinions from those who would have been wiser to wait to publish opinions until they had tried the balls rather more fully. It is reported that the balls were submitted, on the American inventor's behalf, to several trades people at a very early date of their introduction; but the experts, probably of the professional class, to whom the British firms submitted the specimen balls for trial, pronounced against them, and the firms would not touch the invention.

The manner of reception illustrated by this story is typical. The Briton did not want to find the American ball a good one, so he did not find it a good one. Some one said that it had been bounced on the floor of the Stock Exchange and had gone on bounding about there, chucking one member after another under the chin, until it found its way to the fireplace, and from thence up the chimney and never was seen again. One quite expert authority said gravely that it was a good ball and would do all that was wanted of it, went very well off iron or wood, but would not putt off an aluminum putter. This is criticism that recalls the old days of chemistry or alchemy, when one substance used to be deemed to have a natural antipathy toward another. One expert, to whom I lent a ball to try, played with it for a round or two, then solemnly announced that it was useless as an invention for playing golf, not because it was an expensive ball—for that was the common, and rather natural, complaint—but because it was a bad ball. It was too jumpy, he said. It would not putt. The general, the natural, objection to the ball at first, was, as I have hinted, that it was too dear. This looked right on the face of it, and for most people that was enough. The ball cost twice as much as a first class "gutty." Naturally it looked expensive. The fact that it never was knocked out of shape and would last out three or four gutty balls only became obvious on fuller trial than yet had been given it. That was the kind of trial that required a little time, which also was necessary to establish the fact that the ball went very lightly off the club, subjecting its mechanism to far less strain and jar than the "gutty" ball, and thus reacting as an economy with the other principal instrument of the game. But what did not take any time to prove, but was obvious at once, was that if you lost a ball that cost half a crown it was a more expensive matter than the loss of a ball that cost a shilling, and also that if you were one of the class of players that hits the ball hard and often on top of the head with the iron, the American ball was a very doubtful item of economy, because a hit of this kind cleft a very serious wound in it. But it is only the bad and the violent kind of player that did this. For the rest the ball was distinctly economical.

Of course, when I make this claim for it I am not referring to the date when there was a "corner" in these balls, and prices up to a guinea apiece were asked and obtained for them. That was an abnormal condition in the relation of supply and demand that could not be expected to endure, and, of course, did not. With the ball at its reasonable price of twenty-four or five shillings a dozen, it was so superior to the "gutty" in ability to keep its spherical shape that the averagely extravagant player—the man who would use one "gutty" ball a round, let us say, as a fair average—would use an American ball at least three or four times as long; and even after that, the lack of paint was nearly all that was amiss with it. I shall not go so far as to say quite all, for even the best repainted ball is not as good as a new one in consequence of the little knobs being beaten rather flatter than when first they come out of the mold. So far as my own experience goes, no one has yet made a perfect success of remaking these balls. But on the whole, especially to the steady player, who hit his ball truly and not very hard, the new ball soon proved itself a distinct economy; so that objection to the ball gradually lost ground.

But it was slow work convincing the Britisher of the ball's excellence. He is not of a nature that quickly assimilates the new "notion," and there were those with vested interests in gutta-percha who did not counsel him in favor of the novelty, and they were counsels that carried weight. But in the end the qualities of the ball were too good to be denied, and the date at which the ball received the hall mark of approval, which it has never lost, was the date of the amateur championship in the spring of 1902. It was not so much that both winner and runner-up in a very remarkable final played with the ball, but that a great majority of the less successful players used it, that it was fully on its trial, and that it came out of the trial with very marked success. Since then it may be said that everybody, speaking in a general way, has played with the American ball. The supply has been equal to the demand. It is established.

So far, this is a little historical sketch. It may interest American readers to know in what way the new ball has, in my humble judgment, affected the game in Great Britain and the play of British golfers. The great feature of the ball, as compared with gutta-percha, is the ease with which it can be picked up from a hard, unfriendly cuppy lie, and the relatively greater distance that it can be driven with the iron clubs. These indifferent lies—not the bad lies, but the ordinary lies that one gets for the second stroke—have always been the point in which the second-class player has been distinctly inferior to the first-class. If one had to name the point in the game that was crucial, and made the difference in class, one would have said it was just this: that the first-class player could bang up his second shots from an indifferent lie as straight and as hard as his tee shots, but that the second-class player could not get the ball away from a lie of this character—really the general character of second shot lies—without cutting the ball. He could not get it to rise without this cut or slice. With the new ball, to take that ball as the type of all the rubber-filled kind of which I believe it to have been the pioneer, the second-class player, as he used to be, can play those second shots almost as well as the first-class. There are, therefore, a good many players that the ball has hoisted up a class, in this manner. There are other players that the ball has given a similar hoist in a different manner. Between first and second-class players there was not much difference in the length of the tee shots, nor, as between them, has the india-rubber filled ball affected this difference much. But as between second- and third-class players there was an appreciable difference in the length of the drive, and perhaps between them, this, rather than the way of dealing with the second stroke, was the crucial difference that distinguished the classes. For a gentle hitter, such as the third-class player was apt to be, the new ball came as a great advantage to him from the tee. It put him at once on terms with the second-class player, and so hoisted him again—though not quite in the same manner as the player who was originally second-class—into a class above his previous one.

So far it might seem as if I thought the effect of the new ball was altogether in the upward direction, but there is an exception to be taken. While preferring it for my own use to the "gutty," and thinking that on the whole I gain a slight advantage by its use, I am still quite certain that a little of what one gains through the green one loses in the putting and approaching. The balance is still in the new ball's favor, but its behavior in the shorter strokes reduces the inclination of the balance. The cause that makes it less easy for the short game than the "gutty" is the very cause that makes it superior in the long game; namely, its greater elasticity and liveliness. The truth is, that you do not want a lively ball for the approaching or putting; you do not want a ball that runs far off the pitch, nor one that is easily deflected by little roughnesses of the ground. And the new ball has these demerits. It is true that when the putting green is soft and the wind is not behind, you may drop the new ball quite as dead as a "gutty"; but if the green is hard, this is not the case. Its elasticity makes it bound and run more over a hard surface than the "gutty," and down a wind it is carried on with a lower trajectory at the end of its flight than the "gutty," and the natural consequence of this more acute angle of its fall, relatively to the ground, is that it goes forward more then a ball that falls more straightly.

The British golfer, according to my observation, has generally adopted the plan, probably in order to meet this difference, of approaching with a less lofted shot than he used to play with the "gutty" ball. It seems that the majority have found the best way of dealing with the novel element of difficulty introduced by the use of a ball that cannot be made to pitch as dead—in most conditions of ground—as a "gutty" is to attempt less loft and to calculate, with such exactness as he may, the run that the ball will make after pitching from a slightly lofted shot. I do not think that this is quite as attractive a stroke to watch as the more lofted shot, but there is reason to suppose that it requires even greater skill and delicacy. For one thing, one cannot fail to perceive that it is so, when one plays with the more elastic ball, after using the less elastic; and, in the second place, we in Great Britain have had striking evidence to that effect from the fact that those whom the use of the new ball seems to have benefited above their fellows are remarkably good billiard players. Mr. Charles Hutchings and Mr. S. H. Fry are instances of two men who are far and away above the average at billiards—and one could cite other instances to the same effect—and whose game has been very strikingly improved by the use of the india-rubber filled ball. It would seem as if their natural delicacy of touch enabled them to overcome to a greater degree than is given to those less gifted in this respect the difficulty of putting and approaching with the india-rubber filled ball. They have, therefore, less than most of us to set to the debit side of the ball as regards the short game, while they reap to the full all the advantages that are to be credited to it for the long game.

There is one respect, on the other hand, in which we should admit that the new ball gives a less exact test of skill than the old ball; namely, that a sclaffed, heeled, half topped, or toed shot goes relatively far better with a rubber-filled ball than with the "gutty," and in this regard the accurate striker hardly gets the value for an accurately struck shot that he used to have.

But, on the whole, striking the balance, the new ball seems to be the ball of the skilful and of the delicate player, the "gutty" the ball of the strong, hard smiter. In general terms, that is how we have to sum up the comparison, and beyond that we cannot go. It is, moreover, to nine men out of ten, a more pleasant ball to play with, making the game more amusing; which, after all, is a deal to say.

The question that is vexing golfing circles very badly just at present is whether the ball is not making most of our courses too short. The theory commonly held is that courses should be laid out in distances from tee to hole of a single shot or a multiple of a full shot. Other distances fail to give perfect play its true reward. That is the ideal. But while our courses continually get practically shorter, by reason of the increased hardness of surface, due to constant tramping over them, which has the effect of making the ball, of whatever kind, run farther than it used to, on top of that here comes this new ball, which, with most players and with most clubs, will go rather farther than the "gutty," and the distances are, in consequence, still further reduced from the ideal measure. There is force in this criticism; hardly so much force as to make one wish the india-rubber filled ball had never been invented, yet enough force to make it desirable that something should be done.

There has been vague talk of standardizing the ball, which means barring everything but the "gutty"; but people's wish to play with the ball that is most agreeable is too strong for such a step as this. Still

From an old print.

Golf a Century and a Quarter Ago.

Painted by L. F. Abbott, 1790, and dedicated by him "to the Society of Goffers at Blackheath."

Painted by Charles Lees, R.S.A.

" The Golfers "—from an old print.

A grand match played over St. Andrew's Links, December 20, 1850. Sir David Baird of Newbyth, Bart., and Sir Ralph Anstruther of Balcaskie, Bart., against Major Playfair and John Campbell, Esquire, of Saddell.

something is being done—something in the way of lengthening courses by putting back the tees, of making the courses more difficult by multiplying bunkers—and that, no doubt, is the way that things will adjust themselves, until the inevitable time shall come when some pernicious genius shall invent a ball that will go absurdly far, in which case restrictive legislation as to the implements of the game will become a necessity. In the meantime the result is rather to bring back the game to the condition in which it was in the time of feather balls; not because the feather balls were at all more elastic than the "gutty," but because courses were at that time much more narrow, and the sides of the courses were fringed with whins that made the punishment of crooked play quite dreadful. The result of the widening courses has been to put a premium on very hard hitting and far driving more or less irrespective of direction. It has made the game less one of skill than one of strength, speaking with relation to what it used to be. The new ball, by giving increased value to skill and less to strength, compared with the relative values of those gifts in playing with the "gutty," has done much to reëstablish the old proportions. We accept the American invention, as Britons will, of course, with grumbling, but with gratitude down in our hearts.

11

The Golf Clubs of Chicago

THE GOLF CLUBS
OF CHICAGO

ONWENTSIA—THE HOME HOLE.

BY ALEXIS J. COLMAN.

THE attractions of country club life have captured Chicago, and golf has been chief factor in the transaction. Just how much of open-air club life there would have been if golf had not come, it would be difficult to say; but this is true, that, whereas before golf came, there were one or two clubs devoted to outdoor recreation, with regularly established club-houses, now there are nearly twenty, and the number is still increasing.

Before golf came to Chicago the prosperous business man spent his summer in Wisconsin or Michigan, or in the East or West, or in Europe. If he had a summer home on the North Shore, in some one of the villages along Lake Michigan, he might spend the most part of it there, but even then he usually spent his few weeks' vacation away from both city and suburbs. For what was there here? Nothing except to be absolutely idle, and the business man found it hard to be that after his busy time in the office. He wanted something—he didn't know just what, but it wasn't to be idle. So he went away for a change of scene and air, to fish, perhaps to camp out. To be at leisure and at the same time do something enjoyable—that was his aim.

Now something has been found which will keep the business man busy in his idleness and at the same time keep him home. He has found that Chicago is as good a place to spend his summers as elsewhere, and the beauty of it all is that everything is so handy. He can sprinkle his vacation all through the summer and at very little cost, much less than would be the case in a trip away. It was golf that did it, and that is the reason golf has come to stay.

MRS. REGINALD DE KOVEN DRIVING AT ONWENTSIA.

Not tennis, nor any other game could have the vogue golf has had and is having. The game is in itself a good, a benefit to all who play. It is not a spectators' game, but a health-bringing, life-prolonging one, in

Photo by Stevens.
GEORGE R. THORNE,
PRES. MIDLOTHIAN CLUB.
TREAS. WESTERN G. A.

which anyone may participate; and in this fact lies its advantage.

Though the city was slow at first to take to golf, the idea was started aright and became firmly rooted. The city's location, with prairie lands on three sides, and its ample railroad facilities out to the suburbs, was favorable for the establishment of the game. Most of the suburbs served as abiding-places for Chicago business men. Most of the suburbs were surrounded by expanses of meadow-land and picturesque country. Naturally, then, Chicago business men located their clubs near their suburban homes. The scheme has also worked in the opposite way, as at Wheaton and Midlothian, where the tract has been picked out and members have built themselves houses so as to be near the links, after the manner of the Earl of Wemyss, in East Lothian.

MRS. H. C. CHATFIELD-TAYLOR AND MISS MARGARET DAY—"IT JUST DIDN'T."

Now the activities of the golfers have led them to form a Western association, and this month the annual amateur championship of the United States is to be decided on the links of the Onwentsia Club at Lake Forest, twenty-eight miles north of Chicago.

Quite the newest move in golf in Chicago has been the laying out of a public nine-hole links in Jackson Park, where the World's Columbian Exposition was held in 1893. Elaborate ceremonies marked the opening, the golfers who were instrumental in laying out the course presenting President Joseph Donnersberger, of the South Park Board, with a silver-mounted driver, and giving a similar trophy to Superintendent J. Frank Foster. Judge Murray F. Tuley, the local Nestor of golf, made the presentation speech, and the game has thus been officially recognized.

Members of the Quadrangle Club, composed of professors of the University of Chicago, and others, who were instrumental in having the course laid out, play on it considerably, and there are also several of the students who play. There is talk of organizing a university golf club, and it will probably be done. In time the West may see inter-collegiate golf contests between the teams of Chicago, Wisconsin and Michigan, as in the East.

Tradition has it that the first foursome ever played in Chicago, if not the first golf, was in Jackson Park in 1887, when four ardent Scots, who had brought clubs from the old country, played a foursome, using stakes instead of holes, and altogether enjoying themselves greatly, though at the expense of the scoffing of the natives.

The golf

Photo by Steffens.
H. C. CHATFIELD-TAYLOR,
PRES. ONWENTSIA CLUB AND
PRES. WESTERN G. A.

Photo by Dr. H. W. Bassett.

WESTWARD HO! GOLF CLUB HOUSE.

clubs about Chicago are sprinkled in nearly all quarters, though more lie to the north, along the line of the Milwaukee Division of the Chicago and Northwestern Railway, than in any other direction. Between Lake Forest and Chicago there are on this line six clubs whose chief object is golf. Other sports come in for a share, but a small one.

Lake Forest was long known as one of the prettiest suburbs of the city and as the home of Lake Forest University, before it won fame as the home of the Onwentsia Club. Its beauties lent themselves to the location of summer homes for city people, and it was but natural that in such a location there should be established a large country club like Onwentsia.

The evolution of this club is interesting as showing the great influence of golf in its formation. Senator Charles B. Farwell had built him a spacious summer home, "Fairlawn," a little way back from the bluff overlooking Lake Michigan. After a return from Europe in 1892, his son-in-law, Hobart C. Chatfield-Taylor, who had brought with him a set of golf clubs from Scotland, laid out a few holes on the bluff; and here, in this crude links, but nevertheless first real links about Chicago, because it was located beside the inland sea, Onwentsia had its foundation. Friends came and played, and were pleased.

The coterie of players grew, and more spacious grounds were sought. A large enough links on the bluff was out of the question, both on account of the fact that there is no clearing of sufficient size, and also because real estate there had long been pre-empted for summer homes, or was held at so high a price that purchase or lease was out of the question. So it was decided to move to the west side of town. A nine-hole course was laid out on the McCormick dairy farm in 1894, a very modest club-house constructed, and the "Lake Forest Golf Club" fairly started. The Chicago Golf Club, organized the previous summer at Belmont, about twenty-three miles west of the city, on the Chicago, Burlington and Quincy Railroad, and the Lake Forest Golf Club played team matches, and society woke to the realization that a true find in golf had been made.

OUILMETTE COUNTRY CLUB.

When the Chicago Golf Club moved to its admirable course at Wheaton, the Lake Forest Club, grown far beyond the capacity of the little links on the McCormick farm, crossed the Green Bay road to the west, and went a few hundred yards to the north, purchasing the farm and country homestead of Henry Ives Cobb, the architect.

Mr. Cobb had built a fine house, and was prepared to make the place his country home for aye, but the entreaties of the golf people were so importunate that he capitulated, and Onwentsia was the result.

Onwentsia's standard has always been high. When the Scotch professionals went over the links last fall in the professional tournament, they said the course afforded the best test of first-class golf they had played over in America.

Mr. Chatfield-Taylor has been president of the club from its inception, and to his efforts the place the club has attained is in most part due.

At first a nine-hole course was laid out, but later a large tract adjoining was secured, and an eighteen-hole course, 5,984 yards, arranged, former Champion H. J. Whigham making the final changes in location of hazards, greens and tees. The turf is excellent and the course affords opportunity for all kinds of golf. The great beauty of Onwentsia is that, although it is a strictly first-class, up-to-date course, there is no monotony about the play. There are opportunities for long and short shots, and bunkers to avoid or loft over; there is the "Skokie" to cross—a river which bisects the tract and which has to be crossed four times; there are other ditches, and there are trees, trees for shade and clumps of trees bounding the course to catch sliced and pulled balls. At one hole, the eighth, "Boomerang," there is a fine opportunity for a player to drive over the trees and land dead on the green, or he can play safe by going around. Most players prefer the latter way, though Champion Whigham regularly lofts the ball over.

As the fifth annual amateur championship is to be played at Onwentsia this month, the course will gain fame anew.

The distance out is 2,984 yards, bogey, 43; in, 3,000 yards, bogey, 42. Walter B. Smith, the Yale-Onwentsia man, holds the record for the course, 83, two under bogey.

Several members of the club have made the course under 90, and will doubtless put up a good game in the championship. Among those who are expected to qualify or do better are Harold Smith, younger brother of Walter, David R. Forgan, Slason Thompson and William Waller.

LAKE GENEVA COUNTRY CLUB.

Passing from Onwentsia south, the next links is that of the Exmoor Country Club, at Highland Park, twenty-five miles from the city. There had been a club, the Highland Park Club, before golf came, but it afforded no opportunity for outdoor recreation, so the Exmoor Country Club was born. The links is located somewhat similarly to that at Lake Forest, on the west slope of the ridge which runs parallel with the shore of Lake Michigan, and about a mile due west from it. The Skokie runs through the course as at Onwentsia, the stream which, a little farther toward the city,

Photo by R. Capes, Chicago.

WHEATON—A DRIVE FOR THE TENTH HOLE

Photo by Chas. Allgeier, Chicago.

MIDLOTHIAN—BACK FROM SECOND TEE.

SKOKIE COUNTRY CLUB.

at Glencoe, gives the name to the Skokie Country Club. A pretty club-house has been built, and the nine-hole course is well-drained, of good length with several "sporty" hazards.

The Skokie Club is at Glencoe, six miles nearer the city. Residents of Kenilworth and Winnetka, as well as those of Glencoe, belong to it. The course was rough at first, but has been improved. Mrs. Heaton Owsley, the sister of Mayor Carter H. Harrison, of Chicago, was in great measure responsible for the formation of the club, and the Mayor is himself a member. He is not a proficient golfer, but derives much enjoyment from the game.

At Wilmette is the Ouilmette Country Club, the founders preserving the old French spelling of the town. Here the organization is a social, family affair, organized for the purpose of having a good time. Croquet and tennis are popular with its members, and last year archery was revived with distinct success.

Leaving Wilmette, the next club is the Evanston Golf Club, to which belong many of the residents of Evanston. The club has this spring moved from its former location at North Evanston and located a mile to the south, and west of the temperance city which Frances Willard would have called "Heavenston." Although neither the members of this club nor those of Glen View are angels, they are sufficiently of that type for all practical earthly purposes. The new course will need considerable nursing to bring it up to shape. The unique feature of it is a railroad hazard, the double track "cut-off" of the Chicago and Northwestern Railway dividing the club's tract. As a test of lofting the club thinks this hazard cannot be excelled. A new club-house is being built.

The main club to which Evanstonians belong is the Glen View Golf and Polo Club, located on the North Branch, six miles west of Evanston. Here a club has been established which has won one of the first places in the galaxy of Chicago organizations. A forest innocent of an axe had to be cut out or tunneled through to lay out part of the course, and leveling, sodding, and all kinds of landscape work had to be done; but the results of this outlay of money and labor has been one of the most picturesque courses in the country. The club-house is on a knoll in the center of the grounds.

Back of the house is a reservoir of clear water, one of the hazards of the course. Sloping greens abound, and altogether the course is a beautiful one, a pleasure to play upon. There are several good golfers in the club, the champion being William Holabird, Jr., a youth of sixteen, who has twice won the championship cup. A close second is the captain, Phelps B. Hoyt, who is secretary of the Western Association.

EDGEWATER GOLF CLUB.

Photo by R. Capes, Chicago

GLENVIEW CLUB HOUSE.

Laurence Auchterlonie, one of the very best Scotch professionals who have come to this country, is teacher. Before coming to this country he was an amateur at St. Andrews, and always finished well up in the list. He won the gold medal given as first prize by the Royal and Ancient Golf Club, in 1897, the same trophy which Findlay Douglas took in 1896.

'Way to the northwest of the city, thirty-two miles as the crow flies, is the home of the Lake Zurich Golf Club. It is a beautiful spot, five miles north from Barrington, the nearest railway point, and in the heart of a farming community. The little lake is flanked on two sides by high wooded bluffs, and to the north, where the club is situated, stretch away broad prairie lands, wooded in parts and with small lakes and ponds bountifully sprinkled in.

Notwithstanding the small size of the club, there are many golf enthusiasts in it, and men anxious to win honor with mashie and driver. Some of them expect to enter at Onwentsia, though none is quite proficient enough to expect to win. It is not merely a summer club. All the past winter the men have been going out. The land is somewhat rough, and there are abundant opportunities for finding oneself in a cuppy-lie or losing balls in the numerous water hazards.

E. A. Mayo, Arch't.

THE NEW CLUB-HOUSE, EVANSTON.

Coming back to the city, the Edgewater Golf Club at North Edgewater, and just inside the northern city boundary, is naturally the next club. This also has a nine-hole links, plentifully supplied with bunkers and lying for a considerable part among tree-groves. Edgewater, originally a collection of sand-dunes, and avoided by the Chicago citizens seeking suburban homes, has been transformed during the past ten years into an attractive suburb of the highest class, filled with charming dwellings. In place of deep sandy roads there are paved streets, beautiful lawns and the best of everything. In fact, the surroundings of the golf club are too good, and it is expected that in a year or two the links will be converted into building lots. The club is admirably situated for business men who like to play in the late afternoon.

Besides the public course in Jackson Park and the Edgewater one, there are two others within the city limits: Washington Park and Bryn Mawr. At the former, the golf course is within the track, where the Chicago Polo Club used to play before its members decided that polo in the country would be better, and joined the Onwentsia Club, at Lake Forest.

To compensate for the level turf the bunkers are high, and there are ponds which afford good hazards. The course is 2,335 yards, and the record 33, made several times by Open Champion Herd and Alexander Smith, who are both at the club, Smith as teacher and Herd as clubmaker-in-chief. These men entered the open championship at Myopia last year and carried off first and second honors to the great pleasure of the club members. As Washington Park is but six miles from the City Hall, members find it very convenient for afternoon games.

Just south of Jackson Park is the Bryn Mawr Club. Though not primarily a golf club, many of its members are devoted and play at every opportunity. The course is nine holes and rather rough, but the members derive considerable pleasure there.

Just outside the city limits, to the northwest, is the Westward, Ho! Golf Club, composed chiefly of residents of Oak Park. The club last year was located upon a smaller tract, and decided to move to more spacious grounds. This spring an eighteen-hole course was laid out at Galewood, on the Chicago, Milwaukee and St. Paul Railroad. The backward weather delayed the work upon this, as upon the other Chicago courses, but new bunkers have been put in, and the grounds in time will be in first-class shape. The arrangement of the holes is somewhat different from the other full courses about Chicago, in that the ninth hole is farthest away from the club-house, instead of being near by, as in most courses.

One of the most proficient women players at the club is Miss J. Anna Carpenter, a seventeen-year-old girl who has demonstrated remarkable golfing abilities. Her step-father, A. Haddow Smith, is captain of the club. Miss Carpenter intends entering the women's championship at Philadelphia in September, and

EXMOOR COUNTRY CLUB.

if, as is rumored, Miss Hoyt intends withdrawing from golf play, the Western critics believe Miss "Johnnie" will prove a surprise to the Eastern women. The most famous women's golf match in Western golf annals was the twenty-hole contest which Miss Carpenter and Mrs. Chatfield-Taylor played at Onwentsia last fall in the women's tournament. Mrs. Taylor finally won, though it was a nip-and-tuck game throughout.

Other residents of Oak Park have organized the River Forest Golf Club, located near Oak Park, about nine miles due west of the city. This club is also convenient for men who wish to have an afternoon game after the day's work is over, for it is quickly reached by rail from the city. Oak Park and River Forest are both pretty suburbs of the city, and the two clubs number many of the best people.

Farther to the west on the same line, at Wheaton, twenty-four miles west of Chicago, lies the Chicago Golf Club, pioneer in golf organizations in the West. Originally established at Belmont, the club decided that it could do better, and sought a new location. A fine stretch of old meadow-land at West Hinsdale, four miles east of Belmont, tempted, but satisfactory arrangements could not be made for its control, and the club looked elsewhere, finally deciding upon Wheaton. A fine old farm, two hundred acres of rolling, well-turfed farming property was chosen, and here the club located. Transforming the old homestead into comfortable club quarters, with wide verandas on two sides, the beautiful course was made, which experts pronounce as on a par with the leading golf courses anywhere.

Charles B. Macdonald, who won the amateur championship at Newport in 1895, was one of the main factors in the establishment of the club and promoters of its welfare. Indeed, his position has been such as to win him the title of the "Laird o' Wheaton." The amateur championship of 1897 was held here, and Eastern golfers felt amply repaid for coming West and participating in it on such a fine course. Not content with its present excellence, the club members intend making several changes, as suggested by former champions Whigham and Macdonald. These will not be in the way of easy changes, either, but it is hardly expected the bogey, 86, will be changed. The length is 5,877 yards.

Pretty country homes, more ambitious than cottages, are being built about the grounds, and the number is increasing every year. This year an addition is being built on the northwest of the clubhouse, to be used as a ball-room and general gathering place for the members.

Photo by Chas. Allgeier, Chicago.

THE DINING-ROOM—MIDLOTHIAN.

Photo by J. W. Taylor.

WASHINGTON PARK CLUB.

Crossing country to the southeast for about seven miles, one finds himself at Belmont, cradle of Chicago golf and the Chicago Golf Club. After their abandonment by the club, the grounds were occupied by the Illinois Golf Club, an organization composed of men who did not care to incur the expense of the new club, and preferred to play the game in an inexpensive way and quietly at the old links. Then this club later gave up, and was amalgamated with Riverside in 1896, since which time, until this spring, the course has remained idle. But there were several golfers who did not like to see the old course go, and as it could be fixed up so as to be playable with little expense, a new club was organized.

Most of the members are novices, but the club numbers in its list at least three old-timers: Herbert J. Tweedie, who has been instrumental in laying out nearly every course in the vicinity of Chicago, and who was known as a first-rate player on his home links at Hoylake ; Richard Webster, who, while in Her Majesty's service in Ceylon in

Photo by R. Capes, Chicago.

ONWENTSIA—SEVENTH GREEN.

the early '70s, was secretary of the first Ceylon golf club in Colombo; and R. W. Chandler, one of the participants in the traditional foursome played in Chicago in 1887 in Jackson's Park.

Coming east to Hinsdale, where the club is located on the tract once figured upon by the Chicago Golf Club previous to its exodus from Belmont, a pretty nine-hole course, about 3,000 yards in extent, is found. The land is rolling, and readily adapts itself to golf. There are many good hazards, chief of them being "Hell," a startling name, to be sure, but an apt appellation for the bunker, a sand-pit sixty yards wide, and a sure trap for careless players going to the

Among the best players of the club are Raymond Driver and G. P. Bliss, who will probably enter at Onwentsia. The captain, Arthur P. Bowen, is vice-president of the Western Golf Association and one of its founders.

A giant in its infancy, the Midlothian Country Club has deservedly won the admiration and respect of the Chicago golf public. Just a year and a half old, Midlothian is well up in the forefront of country clubs in the West. The sole trouble with the club is that as the club itself is new, so the members are new at golf. But with the superb course and all the accompaniments of the game, there are bound to be players in time.

Photo by R. Capes, Chicago. GLENVIEW CLUB HOUSE—INTERIOR

eighth hole. This is the largest bunker on any Illinois course. A dainty little club-house is being built on a knoll.

Riverside, one of the older clubs, and one to which belong many good golfers, lies eleven miles from the city and seven east of the Hinsdale course. The course is only nine holes, but is interesting and picturesque. The Des Plaines River, a sluggish, old-fashioned stream, shallow all summer, and always except when spring rains sometimes make it overflow, bounds the course on the west. Trees fringe the links at several points, relieving the horizon of a course that is by no means otherwise monotonous.

The entrance to the grounds is through a grove, but otherwise there is not a tree on the course. This year the full eighteen holes are in use. The length of the course is 6,330 yards—3,132 yards out and 3,178 in. Various hazards are located upon the course, one of the best being the water-hazard at the first, a deep ravine, filled with water and dammed, to make a good, sporty hole. A feature is the club's practice golf-course, 2,672 yards, for beginners, and for women and children when the main course is crowded, on Saturdays and holidays. When a player has negotiated these nine in 72 strokes or under, he is

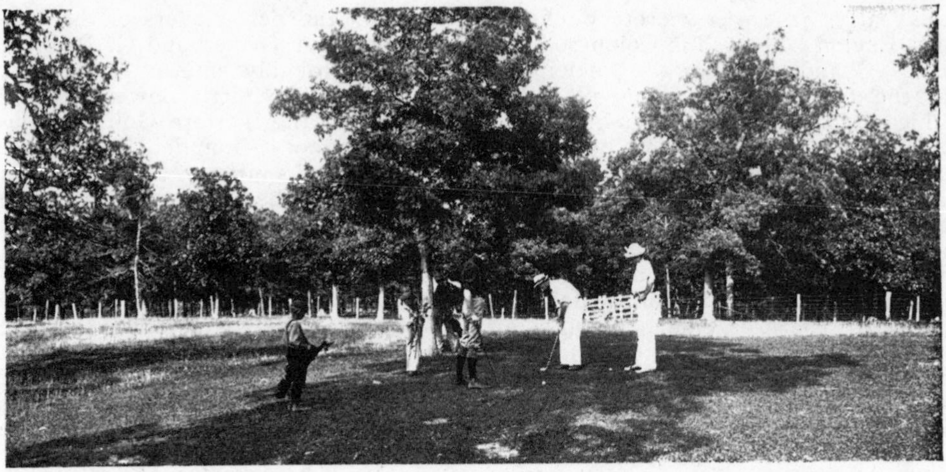

LAKE ZURICH—FIRST GREEN.

eligible to play on the main course. The investment at Midlothian is about $125,000.

George R. Thorne, the president of the club, and one of the prime movers for its organization, also treasurer of the Western Golf Association, has given a handsome trophy, to be contested for in annual club competition. "The Midlothian Cup" vies with the Havemeyer amateur championship trophy in beauty of design and value. Indeed, the designer of the championship cup was William Christmas Codman, and that of the Midlothian trophy, William Codman, his son. Both trophies are valued at $1,000, and in general design are similar. The Midlothian trophy model is that of a punch-bowl, surmounted by a figure in the attitude of putting.

Farther away from Chicago are two country clubs which derive their membership mainly from Chicago people—the clubs at Lake Geneva and Oconomowoc, both in Wisconsin. Lake Geneva is a beautiful summer resort. Surrounding the crystal expanse of water are the homes of many of Chicago's wealthiest people, who go up to spend the hot months. The Country Club is on the south shore of the lake, and golf is the main pastime. Though the club tract is but ninety acres, the president, George C. Walker, so contrived as to lay out a fine eighteen-hole course upon it, 5,658 yards in length.

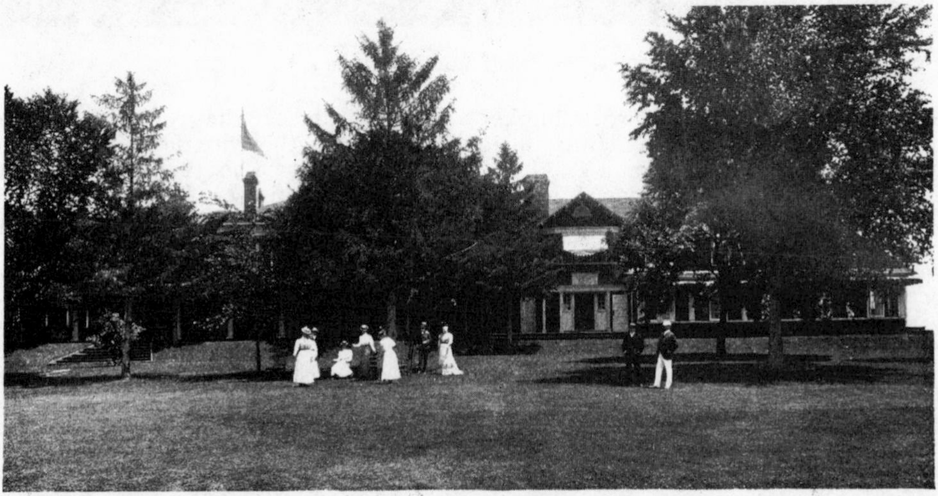

Photo by R. Capes, Chicago.

CLUB-HOUSE OF THE CHICAGO GOLF CLUB, WHEATON.

12

The Golfers' Open Championship

The Golfers' Open Championship 1899

Photos by T. C. Turner.

BY CHARLES TURNER.

TO the follower of golf, and to the lover of the game for its own sake, there is no gathering of the year that equals in interest that of the open tournament, when Greek meets Greek indeed, and the tug of war exhibits to the golfing disciple all that the best of the best can show.

It is a singular meeting, in the eyes of the followers of other forms of sport, forasmuch as, at it, amateur and professional are pitted against each other, without let or hindrance from the framers of cobweb laws, whose ingenuity and good but often mistaken intentions in other sports are defeated by equally clever framers of processes of evasion. In golf there has happily not arisen any occasion for a penal division of the two classes of players, and long may these conditions continue.

Of course, it follows from the very nature of things that, notwithstanding the permissibility of the amateur-professional contest, the entries of amateurs should be in the minority; for skillful though thousands of them are, they are aware that there is often more to be learned by an onlooker than by the contestant, and that it is the more profitable, as well as more pleasurable, occupation to follow from point to point and cross the field of operations of the two score professionals, whose very presence is a guarantee that they are the depositories of knowledge and exponents of practice which it is worth the while of the amateur to watch.

I was very much impressed with this at the first golf exhibition (it could scarcely be called a tournament), when in the fall of 1894 Willie Dunn and a corporal's guard, comprising nearly all the teachers then in the States, gathered at Grey Oaks by Yonkers, and gave as keen and as green "a gallery" as ever followed from tee to tee, the first public example of the prowess that comes from right principles rightly applied.

Since that really recent, but, in the history of American golf, almost forgotten date, the instructors of the game have risen from a corporal's guard to an army. Scotland and England have been ransacked for their best, and these have come. Annually the open championship has thereby become more useful as an itinerant exhibition of the possibilities of the game.

Newport saw the games of 'ninety-five, Shinnecock Hills those of 'ninety-six, Chicago welcomed the professional exponents of 'ninety-seven, and Myopia, Mass., was the chosen battle-ground of 'ninety-eight. It was fitting, therefore, that the South should share in the advantage of so useful an exhibit, and no more difficult, and therefore, desirable links could have been selected than the Country Club's, of Baltimore, Md. I say this advisedly, because in my opinion it is one of the most essential tests of skill in the players that the course over which they are called on to contest should be as different from their ordinary courses as possible, and as difficult to negotiate as can fairly be. Certainly the Baltimore course, to players mainly raised on the billiard-table, perfect courses of old Scotia, can claim to meet both the antecedent requirements. *Imprimis,* it has no sand. *Item*, it has every conceivable form that the scientifically perfect, orthodox course would not have. It has more humping hills than a herd of gigantic dromedaries; it has more varieties of hazards than were ever written down in the *index expurgatorius* of the veritable Colonel Bogey. It has hills of every variety of angle, from ninety in the shade upward and downward; ditches and car-tracks, fences and streams; woods of every conformation and in the most tantalizing and unexpected places, with avenues cut through, necessitating an accuracy that is fatal whenever the eye is out, or the wind is in.

For all which let me give much thanks, for three reasons: first, that it added many hundreds of difficult problems to be solved by the players for my edification, and that of hundreds more "chiels among them taking notes"; and, secondly, that it renders quite unnecessary any comparison between the individual scores made at the championship this year and all those which have gone before; and for a third and last reason, because it carried close home a lesson that instructors are prone to forget, namely, that the ability to execute strokes must be supplemented by the hardest kind of physical condition of wind and limb, and that to shine in an American open championship, even a professional must keep more out of the workshop than some have recently been inclined to do. Good clubs are good things, no doubt, and profitable too, to the maker, but the ability to wield them is the professional's *raison d'être*, and to maintain that is his first duty. More than one contestant to my knowledge had a punishment on his first day up and down the hills of the Baltimore course that he will not soon forget.

It was a great gathering in all respects. Great in numbers, for forty couples, bar one, started, one might almost say with the sun, for it was not much after seven, on the morning of Thursday, the 14th September, in as nearly ideal weather as can be imagined, on their first tour of the eighteen holes, which it was their task to complete twice before sunset, and yet again twice on the morrow. As the crow flies, this meant playing over five and a half miles each day; and, as the Bogey of the course was 156, putting the whole force of body and mind into certainly that number of strokes on each round, a formidable expenditure of muscle, nerve and brain power.

There were old friends and new faces gathered in from more States than formed the original Union, for there were representatives of fourteen States: Massachusetts, New York, Pennsylvania, Illinois, New Jersey, Ohio, Missouri, Maryland, Michigan, North Carolina, Rhode Island, Connecticut and New Hampshire; all had one or more representatives.

It was a notable gathering, too, and it speaks well for the healthy interest in the game, for its own sake, that every champion who has ever won the honor, was ready again to enter the lists, more, of course, for the mere pleasure of the game than for the possibility of new laurels. Willie Dunn, who won the premier honors in 1894, the patriarch of the champions in fact, played through the game, and put up a good game, too. His successor, who carried off the honors of 1895, at Newport, Horace J. Rawlins, placed to his credit 341; James Foules, the victor of Shinnecock Hills, in 1896, came within seven strokes of this; Joseph Lloyd, the victor at Chicago in 1897, was among the starters, and, of course, the Myopia champion of 1898, Fred Herd. But times and conditions were against him this year. Indeed, no man has won the title twice, nor is likely to, at least for some years. The importation of dark horses from beyond the seas, lusty and skillful, places that period, fortunately, a long way off.

And here let me say, lest I forget, in relation to that double trip round 36 holes, that I entirely disagree with the present system, which makes the whole 72 holes medal-play holes. I am of opinion that it would be for the interest of the sport if the first day's play were at medal play, and the second day's play (restricted to those who had reached a definite place in that portion of the contest) should be match play.

But conditions being as they are, we must take them as the basis of observation for this turn and purpose, and admit that they enabled the most perfect golf to be played. From start to finish the plane of play was higher than it has ever been, notwithstanding some apparent paradoxes.

For instance, the superficial observer may say "That cannot be ; for last year the champion covered the course in Bogey figures, whereas this year as the result of the four rounds the champion needed three more strokes than Bogey, for Bogey was 312, whilst the champion needed 315 strokes to carry him home." I might reply True ; but last year's Bogey for each round was 82, whereas this year's Bogey for eighteen holes was 78. Or one might still further confuse a superficial observer by a still more deadly blow, and say, Look you! last year the best score was 328, whereas this year the best score was 315, a saving of thirteen strokes. The controversial reply to this would be the exulting statement, perfectly true, too, "But last year's course of 36 holes was 11,940 yards long, whereas this year's was 9,756 yards only." And so on and so on, *ad nauseam*, as has literally been the case ever since the contest ended. The best test is that of ocular demonstration, and those who were there can testify to the truth of the quality of the play, and they only.

If it were desirable, as a parting shot at the scribes who write puzzles and juggle figures, I would say, show me any course presenting the infinite variety of conditions at Baltimore, where as many men have gathered for the first time, where Bogey has been placed as low, and where six times in one day Bogey has been gone one better, once equaled, and twice been approached within one shot! That is what happened at Baltimore, of which here is proof. Bogey was 78 ; Jack Park, of the Essex County Country Club, reduced it to 75 ; Willie Smith, the champion, lowered it twice out of four rounds to 77, as also did Ernest Way, of the Edgeworth Golf Club ; Peter Walker, of Onwentsia, and Willie Anderson, of Baltusrol ; whilst Lawrence Auchterlonie, of Glen View, was within one stroke of it, and

WATCHING THE RETURNS BEING POSTED.

THE 9TH GREEN.

H. M. Harriman, the amateur champion, and Alexander Campbell came within two strokes of the elusive colonel.

A better and more palpable test perhaps will be to compare the scores of the first few men of last year and of this. Last year the first five men were more divided than this year. This year, after the winner, came a bunch over which, as a huntsman would say of his pack of hounds "running so close you could cover them with a table-cloth"—in other words the second, third and fourth men were equal at 326; the fifth, 327; the sixth, 328; the seventh, 330, and the eighth, 331. Such a uniformity of result over so sporty a course as Baltimore, speaks volumes for the general high character of the performances.

Where the conditions of the course and weather are the same for every contestant, it is unessential to particularize. Yet a word may be added on one point which may throw light on a subject that lies immediately before all those in authority in matters golfing, and that is the condition of the greens. It is easy enough to lay out a course almost anywhere and at any period of the year. Time does not enter as a constituent element. The same hills and the same valleys will be there year in and year

WATCHING THE PLAYERS COME IN AT THE 18TH GREEN.

out, and no labor or thought can remove them. Nor do they form any obstacle to good play. It is comparatively easy to drive, especially to a professional, and to approach, too; but when the green is reached there is, at present, the pitfall of all good players, especially those who have learned on the older and more perfect greens of the older countries. It is against the greens of Baltimore, and against them only, that a discordant note could be heard the whole contest through, and although by comparison with other American links they were not bad, still as compared with the conditions to which most of the players had been accustomed, they were. Nobody but those who have played through the strain of such a conflict can appreciate the extent to which every irregularity and imperfection on the green is exaggerated. The mind involuntarily reverts to ideal conditions—the "what ought to be"—and all the ills of the game, and even the faults of the players in driving and approaching, are laid to the green.

Of course the judgment, as at Baltimore, may be biased to some extent; yet that more attention will have to be paid to the green is a self-evident problem, and the clubs that first appreciate this will produce the best results. Every player who leaves the ranks of the "sloggers" becomes a candidate for large, even, well-sodded, well-tended, well-drained greens; and he must have them, or his golfing life is made a torment to him. He is in the ranks of those humorously consigned to the punishment of the billiard player condemned to play

"With a twisted cue,
And a green untrue,
And elliptical billiard balls."

Photo by T. C. Turner.

WILLIE SMITH, MIDLOTHIAN CLUB, CHICAGO, OPEN CHAMPION.

Of golf it may be said, as of cricket, a game is never lost till it is won, and the open championship of 1899 is a case in point. On the first day the general voice and expectation were for Willie Anderson, yet the second day placed Willie Smith, of the Midlothian Club, Chicago, in the unprecedented position of eleven strokes below his nearest competitor, and crowned him victor with a record that will be long before it is beaten. The Baltimore course, with the greens set back, as they were in many instances especially for this contest, will be many a day before its eighteen holes will be covered in 77—77—79 and 82 in continuous play by the same player in two days.*

* Fuller details of the play will be found in our Review, at the end of the magazine.

13

Why Golf has Improved

WHY GOLF HAS IMPROVED

By HAROLD HILTON

I TRUST I will be forgiven the title of this article, as I feel assured that it will awaken in the breasts of many disciples of the old school of golfers certain feelings of resentment; for in the past, when improvement in the game has been discussed, those associated with the golf of the 'sixties and the 'seventies have shown almost more than a decided disinclination to believe that there has been an improvement since the days of Allan Robertson, young Tom Morris, and Davie Strath.

To what the improvement is indebted is the subject which I am about to discuss, and for the necessary scaffolding around which I am trying to build my beliefs, it must be taken for granted that the game has improved; that is why I ask to be forgiven my title.

Fig. 1. A Modern Set of Clubs.

Fig. 2. A Typical Set of Clubs Used Between 1880 and 1890.

With an ever increasing demand, it stands to reason that the wood as now supplied to the golfing trade cannot be so carefully selected as it was in the old days, when the supply was large and the demand comparatively small. I think nearly every clubmaker of even twenty to thirty years' experience will readily assent that the wood supplied nowadays is not of the same picked quality that it was in the days when they first joined the trade. I can remember myself when the majority of wooden club heads were made of apple, but as the demand increased apple became difficult to obtain and increasingly dearer, so substitutes had to be obtained. It may be that apple was not a better wood for the purpose than beach or dogwood, which are the standard materials at present. Personally, my experience leads me to the belief that the wooden club heads supplied in the present day are quite as efficacious as the old time apple heads. There are naturally more indifferent pieces to be met with, as the clubmaker cannot pick and choose as he was able to do in the days of old, but I may mention that I have now in my set two club heads which have been in continual use for over six years, and to prove that they were not specially picked wood, it is a fact that they were both bought from the stock in the clubmaker's shop.

But if we take it that there is not much difference in the driving powers of the wood, the same cannot be said of the alterations and modifications in shape, which have taken place during the past twelve years. It was about that long ago that the bulger was introduced, and I think its introduction is, in a certain measure, responsible for the extra length, combined with accuracy, attained by the leading players of the present day. It was some time before the bulger forced its way into the affections of the golfing public. By the older school of golfers it was looked upon with disfavor. They would have none of it, and one can appreciate the spirit of the ancients when I quote a passage culled from an article, which has as its author a worthy divine, who looks not with favoring eye upon the continuous innovations in connection with the game, and is far from loath to express his opinions. The article was written in 1890, on the occasion of a professional meeting at North Berwick, and after Sayers had received some sound advice as to how to play his home green, the author proceeds to say:

> Again it was most strange to see Simpson, who is, perhaps, on the whole, the best driver in the field, using that ugly club called the bulger. Fortunately, the other players used the old historical shape of head. The bulger is so small headed and unseemly to the eye that we of the old school would be afraid of missing with it.

Probably this was the opinion of many who had been accustomed to the long and narrow headed club. The bulger did not appear at all an elegant substitute, and, what is more, the fact of the face of the club being in front of the shaft, made the balance quite different.

I shall never forget my first attempt with a bulger. It was not my own club. It was the result of an experiment made by Mr. John Ball, Jr., on the advice of the late Henry Lamb, who is generally accorded the honor of being its inventor. The attempt was quite a disastrous failure, as neither could I strike a ball anywhere near the line I intended to, but, in addition, they seemed to travel no distance, and the only consolation I derived from the experiment was the fact that my old comrade in arms was even more hopeless with it than I. In consequence I dismissed the club as an impossibility. Great was my surprise, however, when some time after I met Mr. Ball driving with this self-same club, very far and very sure. I promptly came to the conclusion that my initial judgment must have been hasty, and I commenced the task of mastering the peculiarities of the bulger, with the result that I have never deserted it. It may be that the initial samples of the invention were carried almost to excess in the matter of the bulge; and, in consequence, the ball was apt to slip off the face, but time and experience have tempered this defect, and although many of the clubs used in the present day may be said to be almost straight in face, they are still, however, the children of this useful invention, in that the face is invariably in front of the shaft, and the head is cut down to workmanlike proportions. The old-fashioned club was certainly an elegant construction, but it was more elegant than effective. And it was almost impossible to strike with it in the same forceful manner that the leading players do nowadays with the newer implements.

To do full justice to the old club it was almost necessary to trust to the swing of the club. The *hitter* was all over the place, for, on account of the balance of the club, any extra pressure invariably resulted in the hands being in front of the head of the club and a horrible slice was the result.

Nowadays the leading player hits very hard; the head of the club shortened and more concentrated allows him to do so, and men like Braid habitually press with wonderful accuracy. Could they have done it with the old-fashioned club? I think not. Let any one try and see; then I think they will agree with me. I cannot help thinking that the alteration in the shape of wooden clubs has had more to do with the very apparent improvement in golf than anything else, and when one considers the time when the improvement began to make itself evident, about 1890 or 1891, it only confirms my opinion, as it was then that the bulger came into general use. Between the years 1880 and 1890 there was little difference in the winning scores in big competitions. They were somewhat on a par with those of the 'sixties and 'seventies, when the condition of the links was nothing like so good. But from 1890 the play of the game was improved by leaps and bounds; that unerring guide, statistics, proves it, and cannot be gainsaid. It may be that the links nowadays are kept in much better order, but, on the other hand, the material from which the implements are made is not superior; the present great demand precludes that; but I candidly think that more than a fair proportion of the improvement is due to the alteration in the shape of wooden clubs, which, in the hands of an expert, allows hard hitting with accuracy; which, in addition, allows balls to be played successfully out of lies that were impossible with the old-fashioned clubs.

Again, we find a similar state of affairs in connection with iron implements. I can remember the time when an iron made by Wilson, of St. Andrews, was considered a "pearl beyond price." Nowadays they may be said to represent "old iron." It has been a most rapid change, as Wilson irons were much esteemed only seven or eight years ago; but, as with the wooden clubs, it was generally found that a shorter head was more serviceable; not only did it drive farther, but it was an implement with which it was easier to play from indifferent or heavy lies, as when lying in such a position it is necessary to hit the ball, not swing at it; and the old-fashioned iron, long-headed and comparatively cumbersome, was a difficult weapon to wield in this fashion. So the iron club of the 'seventies and the 'eighties had to give way to the modern invention. The driving mashie superseded the cleek; and the lofting iron, with its broad, homely face, had to give way to the pitching mashie. They are old friends relegated to the portion of relics of the past, but, nevertheless, not forgotten. Certainly the cleek still survives, but its outward appearance is little in keeping with the weapon of old, as its head is short, and its face narrow. It is probably the outgrowth of the fact that in the craze for short-headed clubs the striking space became so limited that the balance of the club was destroyed, and the center of gravity was far too near the socket.

I commenced my golfing career with a wooden putter. It is not an extraordinary fact, as it is fast approaching thirty years since I first handled a golf club; in those days wood was the principal material for the instruments with which we were expected to put the ball into the hole. Then came the era of metal. It was slow but sure, very sure, as eventually, in the affections of golfers, it ousted the implement of wood; but it was a long time before iron putters became universally popular. I am one among many who are great believers in the efficacy of the wooden putter, but it is a weapon which not only requires great confidence, but in addition "touch," a combination which is vouchsafed to few; nothing could be more delightful than the manner in which the John Crow literally sweeps the ball into the hole with his "putter of wood." It is a delightful combination of touch and intellect, backed up by implicit confidence. But in my humble opinion Mr. Crow stands by himself as a manipulator of the old-fashioned wooden putter. How many are gifted with the same touch? And of the few so gifted, how many have the confidence to swing or sweep the club as Mr. Crow does. It is an art granted to few. But while the wooden putter cannot be said to be a relic of the past, it has had to give way to the putter of metal. There is, however, an innovation in putters which has done much to resuscitate the waning glories of the old wooden instrument. In shape, it is the implement used in the old days; but the material of the head is not a complication of wood and lead. It is solid aluminum, and, judging by the popularity it has attained, it has supplied the happy medium between the iron putter and the putter of wood. In reality, it is the latter in a new guise; but, on the other hand, in the matter of balance there is a slight kinship to the iron putter, as the balance is more forward on account of the fact that the club is all of one material. Personally, I am a great believer in this patent of Mr. Mills, as I think that while it can claim all the virtues of a wooden putter, it is not liable to many of the defects of the latter, as moisture has no effect on it whatever. But I hardly think there can be any material difference in the quality of the putting of the present day and that of the 'sixties and 'seventies. There is certainly more choice in the selection of weapons, but a really good wooden putter, in my opinion, cannot be beaten. It is said that the making of a wooden putter is now a lost art, and I can quite believe this to be true, as in the present days the demand for clubs is so great that the clubmaker has neither the inclination nor the time to waste precious hours over one single instrument.

Fig. 3. Wooden Clubs. Numbering from the Left, 1, 3, and 5 Are Modern; 2, 4, and 6 Were in Use from 1880 to 1890.

Fig. 4. Iron Clubs. 1, 3, and 5 Were Used from 1880 to 1890; 2, 4, and 6 Are Modern.

There is, however, one little item to which the improvement during the past ten or twelve years may, in a manner, be attributable, and that is that golfers nowadays are not bound down by the precepts and principles of their forefathers. They have found out that it is better to work out their own salvation and form their style according to the endowments of nature. I can remember the time when it was considered quite the correct thing to play every wooden club stroke what is termed "off the left leg," and that eminent judge, Mr. Hutchinson, advocated this procedure in "Badminton." But increased experience has taught us that the coat must be cut according to the cloth, and, in consequence, many of the old traditions are but memories of the past.

Now I am afraid I must commence to wander down the old trodden path for a short period. When did the decided improvement in play really commence? In my opinion, about 1893. It is certainly a little difficult to account for the fact that between 1880 and 1890 golf, as regards improvement, was in a comparative state of stagnation. But records prove that it is so; and from 1890 to 1900, feats which were considered almost beyond the bounds of possibility were accomplished with comparative ease. Was it due to the improvement in clubs? I give a decided affirmative to this query, as the gradual shortening of club heads allowed players to strike hard and, in addition, strike with accuracy. But at first the improvement was very gradual, as the sentiment and tradition of many years could not be rudely brushed aside. A score of eighty or under on any of the first-class courses was considered very great work, and players in competition instinctively played up to the standard. If they completed the first nine holes in a phenomenally low number, the home half was played in a safe and "pawky" manner; in fact, that was the spirit of the game—slow and sure. But at Prestwick, in 1893, there came a player named J. H. Taylor, who opened the eyes of our worthy Scottish friends. In his ignorance of precept and tradition he thought not of possibilities. "Excelsior" was his motto, and he played at the hole with putter, iron, and driver with the same determination and *sang-froid*. And the manner in which he placed his full iron and brassey shots was a revelation to all. Certainly he did not win that particular championship, but at the very first attempt he created a new medal record. Even if he did fail in the subsequent rounds, it must be remembered that this was his initial effort in the championship, and that possibly he was just a little overawed by his phenomenal success in the first round; in consequence, playing too much on the safe side, and not meeting with success, eventually lost confidence. That he was the best player in the world at that time I have never had the slightest doubt. He had unconsciously realized the possibilities of the game with the short headed clubs, and not being bound down by any traditions, had been able to work out his own salvation, a happy state of affairs, which culminated in his winning the championship later on.

But to the more workmanlike shape of the present club heads I attribute, in the main, the improvement in the game, an improvement which might not have been quite so marked had not the professionals had opportunity of meeting so often in serious combat, which has served to develop the latent talent of the leading players and provided that spirit of emulation which is the secret of the success of certain schools of amateur golf, like St. Andrews and Haylake, and others of the same class.

14

Women Who Play Golf Well—and Ungracefully

WOMEN WHO PLAY GOLF WELL—AND UNGRACEFULLY

By CAROLINE F. MANICE

Champion Metropolitan Association, 1902-3, 1903-4

PHOTOGRAPHS BY T. C. TURNER

Miss Frances Griscom Putting—a Good Stance.

"BUT how do I look when I'm playing?"

This is never a man's question, in the triumphant half hour after any game that he has won. He may wonder how he looked while he was playing; and he may hope that he didn't make such a spectacle as, privately, he thinks some fine player and good friend of his has made. But never, never will he ask any trusty soul, not even in the confidence of after dinner, what sort of figure he cut while he performed over tennis net, or on polo pony or in that fierce light that beats upon the links.

Whether a woman is more vain or more honest is not the point. That is debatable ground. But the quality of her playing is no longer debatable, and therefore her anxiety to look well on a golf course is no desire on her part to patch up bad playing by a picturesque pose. And to wish to look well on the course is the last thing to count as discredit. To look as well as one can is a part of one's payment for one's social keep, in golf as otherwhere. When a woman is dancing, dining or driving, she frankly wants to look well. Riding, half her pleasure is spoiled if she presents a sorry figure on her mount. Why in the world, then, should not a woman hope to look well while she is an observed figure out in the middle of a green course, playing her best golf?

"How do I look when I'm playing?" therefore should not only be an interest; it should be an issue. For no woman who skates well, dances well or walks well, need be ungraceful on the links; and yet very many women who can enter and cross a room like all the nine muses become, directly they tee off, far more like the three furies trying some of their most uncouth conclusions.

Naturally, whatever are the faults that make a woman ungraceful at golf, she is not by way of finding them out herself. She must be told. And yet, in golf as in hair-dressing and hats and tricks of manner, the little imperfections and unbecoming fashions are the thing that nobody likes to speak about. Consequently, a woman keeps on with trivial unconscious habits which are really ugly when a word would correct them. They are easily corrected in a child: "Don't swing your arms"; "Don't hold your head down"; "Don't raise your shoulders," amend many a little rising gaucherie and prevent and train and "whip into shape." In the same way, at golf, in which America is comparatively a child of fifteen, untutored ways should be individually corrected, and pretty, graceful women made

The Finish of a Brassey Shot.

to look their pretty, graceful best on the course. For there is many and many an expert golf player who is skilful and yet very awkward, a champion and yet graceless.

Graceful golf among women is made up chiefly of negative virtues. It involves a great religion of "Be careful not to do various things." And one of the first of these is "Be careful not to pose." For the woman who tries, by main strength, to remember to be graceful at every stroke is likely to defeat this end and the game as well. Graceful golf lies deeper than this. It must be striven for in the early practice, and must become a part of the actual way a woman plays, and not a remembered effort every time. For instance, the woman who stands for a full second with her club upraised, and who executes a little curve of shoulders or head, ending her stroke with ever so tiny a flourish, presents a far less attractive appearance than the player who is honestly awkward. Moreover, so soon as a woman is beset with a desire to be graceful at golf without having worked hard to insure grace, she is certain to try for a certain delicacy of stroke which nearly always results in topping.

"Be careful not to hurry," is a second negative injunction which sounds so alluringly simple, but whose disobedience is responsible for many an awkward play. The woman golfer is universally a believer in her own luck, if she can play well at all; so she rushes into her stroke without the one moment's consideration that is so necessary, as if she trusted to some kind spirit to lean out of the air and conduct her ball cup-ward. Sometimes the spirit does; but that hurried, pell-mell stroke is never "pretty." Before a stroke, she who hesitates—deliberately and not nervously—is, not lost, but graceful.

"Do not play with the wrong club simply because you have it in hand," is another warning that most ungraceful players do not heed. To take chances and make a shot with a brassey, for instance, simply because the caddy has given her the brassey and gone on, when a mashie or an iron either would have put the ball quite far enough, can result only in a strained, improperly calculated stroke which is anything but graceful.

Perhaps the most ungraceful woman player is she who is uncertain. The woman who plays golf the way most women cross a crowded street, may win her game just as safely as she usually gains the opposite curb, but she will make no less laughable a picture in the process. Nervousness not only disqualifies for a good stroke, but it is sure to produce a half-hearted stroke. To hesitate at a hazard is utterly to lose the freedom, and that buoyant, but leisurely, certainty which are essentially the qualities of the graceful player.

For of course the keynote of graceful, as of skilful golf, is complete freedom of motion. The acquirement of the long, free and proper swing—the orthodox swing which no temporarily brilliant trick of method can ever supersede—is the very first and indeed the constant aim of the player. And this, particularly if the player be self-instructed, may be so imperfectly acquired, that although her practice result in a sure, steady, record-breaking stroke, it results also in one quite without grace. This is the hardest detail of all to explain. Indeed, it is baffling to know why one woman will lift and swing her driver with such bewitching freedom and dexterity and ease and charm, while another, accomplishing quite as admirable results by her stroke, will yet look awkward and distressingly ill-at-ease. And the awkward woman, of course, never knows that she is awkward, though is she not observing most of the following details, the chances are that she at least has not freedom, and therefore no grace.

1. If she has not begun to play golf before she is thirty years old, it is probable that stiffness and lack of grace never can be remedied. It is virtually impossible for a woman to acquire and accustom herself to the free movements of golf, if she does not begin to play when she is young —the earlier in the teens the better.

2. If she is not able to poise lightly, firmly and naturally. To place the feet far apart usually means to increase stability of pose; and so it means in golf, but with this perfect balance must be also perfect lightness of pose, with the even turn of each foot from solid place on the ground to the tiptoe poise of the Mercury himself.

The distance at which the right foot is placed in advance of the left too is important in graceful playing. While this is supposed to depend upon the player's fancy, yet too far an advance of the right foot, or the reverse, hampers the stroke. The exact stance may only be determined by each individual, but it is not safe for the player to trust to her instinct alone. Only repeated experiments can determine the most advantageous position, and a difference of an inch may make a great difference in her appearance at the moment of the stroke. The distance of the advance of the right foot controls the weight of the body which it bears, and if the advance is too great there will be an awkward second after the stroke while the player is readjusting her weight.

At the Finish of a Tee Shot—Showing Great Force.

4. The grasp of the hands on the shaft is most important in graceful playing, and three inelegant strokes out of four, as likewise that proportion of inefficient strokes, come from the right hand too tightly grasping the handle of the club. The left hand should grasp tightly; the right hand should guide; and when both hands are nervously tightened the wrists are made taut and the entire movement is hampered and strained. The mere position of the hands also is no less important in a graceful play than in a skilful stroke. The thumbs should fall naturally, at their natural angle from the hands. If, on the other hand, the thumbs are too far around, or are straight down, freedom of movement is again prevented.

5. One of the most delicate adjustments of position is in bending the knee. The knees should be bent very little—just so that the knee-joint is not stiff. Most

women bend the knees too much for grace. This cannot but produce bad lines and an ugly pose. And the degree to which the arms should be bent is no less important. When the head of the club is behind the ball, the elbows are bent very little indeed—not in the least to the angle assumed by nearly all beginners. Arms that are too much curved are as ungainly in golf-playing as in ordinary carriage.

6. But the most important detail of all in the free and graceful stroke is the position of the head and waist. The correctness of this may always be determined by drawing an imaginary line from the crown of the head down the back to the hem of the skirt. Such a line should show a gradual curve, but absolutely no angle. And in an ungraceful player, the line usually shows two distinct angles—one above the shoulders and one at the waist. The involuntary thrusting out of the head and chin just before a stroke is purely the result of nervousness, and often of that inexcusable flight of the eye from the ball to the direction that it is about to take which results in so many bad plays. The chin down and the head drawn a little back give the position for the best play and the most graceful as well. The head that is tipped partly to one side or other is, after all, not the head of the graceful player.

But with the mention of the waist of the woman golf-player, the real cause of her grace or awkwardness is touched upon. There is no more subtle destroyer of grace on the course or off than a woman's management of her waist, and nowhere does its least movement show to such advantage or disadvantage as on the links. On the one hand that curious, unyielding waist of some women never can be trained to suppleness in golf-plays—the waist that turns only when the shoulders and thighs are turned. The possessor of such a waist can hardly accomplish great freedom in golf at any cost. She is, however, no more ungraceful than that other woman, no less frequently seen, whose back seems literally to have a joint, like an elbow, half-way down the spine. The best way for a woman to realize herself the possessor of this back is to notice her own position when she washes her hands. If, while standing over a hand basin of the average height, she bends only at the thighs, she will have small difficulty in taking position for, say, a drive; but if her back seems to bend higher up, and to describe a curve from shoulder to waist, a good bit of physical training is in store for her before her address will be good.

For a woman with this sort of back to play in corsets—not of course worn in the least tight—is an extreme advantage, in fact almost a necessity. But the woman whose waist is not supple would do well altogether to discard corsets at golf. For all other reasons, the debate as to whether they should be worn or not worn on the links is really unimportant, for in these days no woman who is sufficiently up-to-date and athletic to play golf, is far enough behind the times to lace.

If a woman will study carefully her own habitual degree of observation or neglect

Mrs. Charles F. Stout Playing out on a Bad Lie—a Mashie Shot.

of these six points to gain freedom, the ungraceful woman player will find herself immeasurably improved in her appearance on the course.

It is in the driving grip that so many women players present an ungraceful appearance. Often this is because care is not taken to let the end of the handle of the driver rest against the skirt, halfway between the waist and knee; otherwise the body will bend forward too far. Sometimes it is because the shaft of the driver rests on the palm of the hand, or on the fingers, instead of just at the base of the knuckles. Either of these incorrect grasps gives an uncertain, slippery look to the stroke. Also, if the hands are too closely held together, the appearance is bad, and though the closer they are held, in general, the longer the shot, still the extreme is bad.

A very ludicrous case of ungraceful appearance in making a drive is observable in women who insist that the best drive can be made only when the toes are turned in. This, in the short golf skirt, is very funny, and, as most experts agree, does not necessarily facilitate the drive. The careful turning out of the toes is just as absurd and ugly a position for a stroke in golf as in walking on the street.

Standing too great a distance from a ball that is to be teed, so that the player has really to reach for it, will always produce a cramped and unnatural position, and will result in a lifeless swing. The player who, when addressing the ball, has the toe of her club three inches behind the ball, is sure to give a cramped stroke. The other extreme of having the ball even with the neck of the club head does not give the freedom, either, that a medium position will permit.

In a desire to play gracefully, however, no less than in a desire to play expertly, it is a fatal error to try to imitate anybody else, either in position or in assuming one's distance from the ball. An imitative swing is almost always an awkward swing. And worse than this, the player who tries to place herself in exactly the same position for every stroke, and who worries and wonders about it instead of attending to her play, will be sure to be stiff, and will probably make a foozle.

Miss Rhona Adair at Top of Swing for Full Mashie.

Much of the ungraceful playing which one sees among women may safely be set down to improperly selected clubs. If a woman has been taught by a non-professional she is very likely to adopt for her own use the clubs that are his preference; and she may spend half her golf life using clubs with a limber shaft and a heavy head when the grace or "purchase" of her own stroke would be immeasurably improved by the wielding of a light head and a stiff shaft. She ought not to rest content with her instinct as a beginner in the choice of clubs; after she becomes a fairly experienced player she may change her clubs to decided advantage. But the woman who plays with a heavy club is not likely to realize that a long drive depends not on the weight of the club, but on its speed at its moment of contact with the ball, and that with a lighter club she can acquire greater speed for the down stroke and, usually, make a far prettier play.

To acquire grace no less than skill, the sure way is, given a knowledge of one's faults, simply constant, intelligent practice, if possible with a more expert and graceful player than oneself. One's errors in play are discernible by oneself, but one's faults of appearance one ought to be told.

And one need by no means confine one's preparation to actual ball practice. Armed with the various clubs, practice may be taken with a leaf or a bit of paper or any object to hold the eye, and freedom and grace and skill may be acquired by this very simple means. The mere swinging of a club on one's lawn will help. Above all, there are exercises which, if faithfully practised two or three times a day in one's room will greatly increase suppleness and grace in play. A most valuable exercise is to stand erect with arms extended, palms up, and simply rotate the arms slightly at the shoulder, keeping the hands and wrists in the same position. This will tend to make the shoulders supple. Standing with hands firmly on the hips and bending the body in all directions from the waist upward is extremely beneficial in correcting the stiffness of waist which is so unsightly in players. Especially if the player is not in the habit of taking regular gymnastic practice, it is essential to get the muscles under control. Any of the regular gymnastic exercises, with dumbbells or without, will not only develop and strengthen the muscles of the wrist and forearm and so improve the play, but will help the most awkward expert to become a graceful player.

Finish of Drive—Good Form above the Waist but Lacking in Firmness of Stance.

A golf course is the one place in the world where the clothes that a woman wears will not be responsible for her appearance. There have been women who, on muddy links on a cloudy day, have appeared in an old, badly hanging short skirt, with double-soled, hob-nailed shoes, and have played a game of such snap and vigor and unequaled grace, and have sent the ball far ahead with such beautiful swinging strokes that the name of the tailor who made the skirt was forgotten. And never so nattily dressed a player has over and over again made exhibitions of correct playing that were yet graceless and dead. Women on the links are superior to their costumes. But that is no reason for being careless, for all that, and it will be some time before American women golfers will forget the criticism of Miss Rhona Adair, the English and Irish champion, on her recent visit to America. While American women, she said, pay rather more attention to their clothes on fine days than do the women across the sea, in unpleasant weather she found that they do not care what they wear.

"In England," said Miss Adair, "dowdy and careless in dress as we are supposed to be, I have never seen women in such unbecoming and careless and rough golf costumes as I have seen here."

The matter of sleeves rolled up, or not; of hats on, or off, are alike unimportant. But the matter of shoes is very important, since in shoes that slip no woman can be a graceful player. For all weathers and

A Mannish Finish.

on all courses the consensus of opinion seems to be in favor of the heavy-soled shoes, with hobs. Whether they are low or high depends on the individual ankles to be supported or left free.

There is, however, no denying that the grace of a woman at golf is as indefinable a thing as is her charm. She can never acquire charm, though she may add to what she already has by her manner and her courtesy; and there are pessimists who declare that a woman simply plays golf gracefully, or she does not, and she can never very much change her way. But this is not reasonable. It stands to reason that a woman of thirty, just beginning to learn to dance and so using muscles not often used and not trained, will be a more graceful dancer if she tries to learn how to be graceful, than if she just dances to get over the floor!

"Graceful golf," said somebody, "bears the same relation to golf that culture does to education. You can start out in life with the determination to be educated; but you cannot say with equal determination: 'I intend to be cultured.' In the same way the golf-player, particularly a woman, may say: 'I will learn to play golf well'; but she cannot say, 'I will become a graceful golf-player,' with any assurance of her success. But she can at all events be more graceful if she tries, than if she never remembers it."

According to Miss Frances Griscom, most women are far too busy and too happy on the course to care how they look.

"I do not believe," said Miss Griscom, "when a woman gets in a game of yard golf, that she ever thinks twice about her appearance. The game simply takes her out of herself. If it does not, she is not a good player."

That is doubtless perfectly true—while the game is on. But afterward, when the day is won or lost, it is either new triumph or grateful consolation to hear ever so feminine a voice confiding:

"My dear, I dare say you play well. But I know that you *look* wonderful!"

When all is said, however, the vision of a healthy athletic woman in the midst of golf cannot be a very unpleasing one. But it is just because she is such a picture that she ought to be the prettiest picture she is able.

Finish of a Brassey Drive.

15

Miss Carrington's Professional

Photo by C. R. Pancoast.

"SHE IMITATED HIS STYLE IN EVERY STROKE."

MISS CARRINGTON'S PROFESSIONAL.

BY M. GERTRUDE CUNDILL.

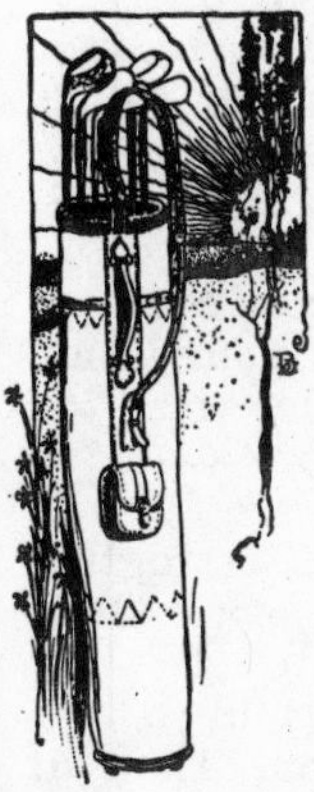

FOR the end of September the morning was wonderfully warm, and the links were deserted. Young Hilyard sat in the front of the Professional's workshop and polished a mashie, occasionally calling to Thompson, the instructor, in no gentle voice to hurry up. He had come early to practice, and had found a desired club not yet complete. Hence his impatience.

Though, in general, a young man who dressed well, this morning was the exception that proved the rule. His heavy boots were dusty and his coat and collar had been discarded. A corn-cob pipe and a faded college cap completed his costume.

The 10:30 train whizzed past, and Hilyard was idly speculating as to the chances of some men arriving, when the gate clicked, and a girl came along the pathway.

For a moment he felt inclined to retreat as he surveyed the neat figure in spotless piqué. He had not expected such a visitor and felt he was hardly fit to be seen by such a one, but, on second thoughts, what was the good? If she meant to play she would see him sooner or later. And he gave a finishing rub to a club.

By this time the young lady had cut across the grass, and was only a yard or two away from him.

"Good morning," she said briskly.

Hilyard glanced over his shoulder to see if the professional instructor was visible.

"I want you to give me a lesson this morning, please."

Evidently she was addressing himself, and he faced about.

It was an exceedingly pretty girl who confronted him and she carried a bag of the latest pattern, full of new clubs.

The young man rose and lifted his cap. This was non-committal. It might mean to allow her to pass, or it might be in respectful acquiescence to her desire.

"Miss Dawson," she went on, "told me you preferred giving lessons in the morning, and I should like to begin at once."

The die was cast. Hilyard reflected that Thompson was busy in the workshop on the favorite club. He himself was as competent as Thompson, and it was awkward to enlighten her now; besides, it would take Thompson off the much-desired club.

"Certainly—er—miss—one moment, please," he stammered. Then he dashed into the workshop.

"Here, Thompson, there's a lady outside who wants a lesson. You go on with my club; I will take her in hand, and she can pay you just the same."

"Yes, Mr. Hilyard, quite so, sir," assented Thompson, agreeably.

Coaching beginners was no sinecure.

"I am very anxious to get on well," said the girl as he emerged again, "and I want you to teach me all the correct positions for different shots. A few lessons, I think, put one in the right way, and one has nothing to unlearn afterward. Don't you think so?"

"Yes, miss, I do. The ladies here would be all the better off for some."

Then he summoned a caddie and led the way to "Tee No. 1." Thereupon his pupil drew from her pocket an enormous red and white paper "tee" and proffered it.

"Good heavens! where did you——" began Hilyard, but her astonished face stopped him, and he proceeded. "I don't advise your using such a high one, miss. It's better to make your own tee," and he took a little sand, and showed her how to place her ball.

She was as obstinate as most novices as to the way of holding her club, and Hilyard had to restrain himself as he explained why the thumb of the right hand must come round, not down the shaft, and her eye must be fixed on the ball, not its destination.

However, after hurting her thumb, and expending great vigor in beating the air, she came round to his way of thinking, and adopted his suggestions in other small particulars.

The first hole was not reached until the ball had traversed most of the surrounding country. By that time its form was barely recognizable, having been subjected to sudden "toppings" and severe poundings.

Amusing as the situation was, Hilyard wished he had met his pupil under more favorable auspices. It was quite impossible in his present rôle to be as nice as he well knew how to be. And this was somewhat of a privation.

He picked up the patent bag from its grasshopper-like position, gave it to the caddie, and prepared to follow the last erratic stroke. On the little silver plate the name "G. Carrington" met his eye. Why, the crack golfer who had lately come to reside near must be her father! And he wondered if it was permissible to ask her about it, but he decided that under the circumstances it was not.

"It is funny," said Miss Carrington, as he again showed her the position to drive from, "that Miss Dawson does not stand a bit like that to address her ball."

"Oh," said Hilyard, "no two people teach in the same style."

"Yes, but you taught her."

Hilyard was cornered.

"Well, you see one must let some people do as they can. It's no good following the teacher exactly if the style does not suit the pupil."

"Oh, I see. But Miss Dawson said she liked your style immensely. It was so simple——"

Never having, that he remembered, seen the lady in question, Hilyard had nothing to say, but he wished he had studied Thompson's attitudes more particularly.

And it struck him that the heat was becoming intense.

"Confound it all, I wish I'd introduced myself and offered to help her a bit. It is waste of time following such a pretty girl as mute as an oyster," he thought, as he trudged toward the second hole, having driven for her.

She used her iron through the green with great effect, and ran after r ball, in the pleasure of really hav sent it some distance.

"I am improving, am I not, Thompson? Miss Dawson was sure I would play well."

"That's a good lie," remarked her instructor, coming upon the ball at the same moment.

Miss Carrington's face was a study.

"Really, Thompson, I think you're forgetting——"

And Hilyard, for a moment puzzled, almost forgot his respectful mien, and only just checked his laughter as he explained that he was referring to the position of her ball and not to her remark.

"Now, miss, you can play a nice approach shot. I would take your iron."

She played. Then, as she tried for the hole under his instructions——

"You are a Londoner, aren't you, Thompson?" inquired Miss Carrington.

"Yes, I came from there originally," Hilyard ingenuously replied.

"I thought Miss Dawson said so."

"Oh, bother Miss Dawson," thought Hilyard. "I'll begin to think she is my fate."

"But I notice," she continued, "you have not at all a cockney accent. It is so ugly. Still, I suppose the Board Schools have helped to do away with that."

"Yes, miss, no doubt," Hilyard replied, demurely. He could hardly repress a chuckle, however. A good public school and Cambridge after, perhaps, had assisted him in placing "H" correctly. But he was perfectly grave as he turned his attention to her putting.

The third drive was not an unqualified success, although the pupil addressed her ball for nearly five minutes, swung around on one toe, dropped the left shoulder and went through several wonderful preparations which mystified Hilyard until reminded they were due to Miss Dawson.

A chat with Thompson and a little putting would have been a more profitable way of spending the morning.

Then he recollected what fun it would be when subsequently some fellow introduced him as one of the best players the club could boast. For Mr. Hilyard did not undervalue himself altogether. Of course, she would be angry at first; then she would see the amusing side of it, and it would put them on a very friendly footing.

He tried to persuade her to confine herself to what he called "the lazy man's course" and play back over the first few holes. But nothing would deter her from playing across the brook, and a good half hour was spent in trying to induce her balls to go over, not into, the water. After six new ones had valiantly taken a plunge, three only of which were recovered, Hilyard ventured his opinion.

"Your lesson will be over, miss, before we half finish the course, and you said you wanted to do the nine holes."

"Have you anybody else this morning?" she inquired.

"No, not until three o'clock."

"Oh, then, it is all right. I don't lunch till half-past one," and whack, went still another ball, while Hilyard groaned.

Finally she gave up, with tears in her eyes.

"I can't see what I do wrong," she said. "Oh, I detest this stupid game—and I haven't used my mashie or niblick or brassey yet!"

She threw down her club, and her instructor seized it and lifted the ball across.

"Now you can play a nice shot. Take your mashie, if you like; the grass is long. You play quite nicely through the green."

Miss Carrington brightened up.

"And I really don't put badly, do I?"

Hilyard thought ruefully of the six strokes it had required to put the ball in from a yard distant, but politeness is the rôle of the instructor, and a little ambiguity comes easily.

"Remarkably well for a beginner," he rejoined.

"But I must not be discouraged if I play worse to-morrow, must I?" she asked. "I know beginners generally do well, so I must not be too elated."

Worse to-morrow! Hilyard thought of the morose Thompson, and wondered if he would survive the round.

And then Miss Carrington declared herself tired, and, climbing onto the stone wall, sat down and fanned herself with her hat. Hilyard surveyed her lazily from his recumbent position on the grass, not quite sure whether he ought not to stand respectfully.

Evidently she was a young lady accustomed to being agreeable to her subordinates, for, after a moment's silence, she began:

"I suppose they don't require you here in winter, do they?"

Hilyard thought of the links in midwinter, and shivered. "No, miss ——" How that word always stuck.

"Well, then, when you are out of employment—do you make clubs?" Had she asked did he frequent them, it would have been more to the point.

"Not many. But there is the new curling club. I'm in hopes——" He paused before such an astounding prevarication.

"Oh, that they will make you caretaker. That will be nice."

She scanned the surrounding country, and her eyes fell upon the flock of ever-nibbling sheep, not far distant.

"I really think, do you know, it's rather cruel to have those sheep for—oh, obstacles, is it?"

"For what?" asked Hilyard, raising himself on one elbow and dropping the grass he was biting.

Miss Carrington reddened a little.

"Well, perhaps that is not the word I mean what they have to make play more difficult. Sometimes they are heaps of stones, I think, or sand-pits, or something——"

Hilyard saw daylight. "Oh, bunkers, you mean, or hazards of any kind. But what has that to do with sheep?"

"Well, aren't they 'hazards.' Every time I play they get in my way, and I thought they'd be more——"

But at the sight of the face before her, crimson in the effort to refrain from laughter, she stopped, and then laughed herself, as it was explained to her that their use was in keeping the grass short.

"I am very stupid," she ejaculated. "I'm always finding myself out in such stupid mistakes."

"There's a fine prospect of discovering another shortly," thought Hilyard, and nearly laughed again.

Play was resumed after a little by the undaunted lady.

"I wish you would play, too," she said, "for I should like to know how to score when I am playing with anybody."

So, helping himself to her driver, Hilyard drove in his best style, secretly pleased at a chance to distinguish himself. And the distance at which the ball dropped was a phenomenal one.

"How easily you play," said the girl behind him. "I have to take so much trouble, and my very best did not go so far."

And then she got mixed up with the scoring of the strokes. "I don't see what you mean. The like?—like what?"

"Oh, nothing. I mean it is your play. Now you'll have to play the odd. You are behind me still."

"I don't see anything odd. It is only natural I should be——"

She hit hard and badly.

"Play two more. Now I play one off two."

"Oh, dear, it's quite hopeless. No, I don't see a bit, and when I play with anybody I don't know what I'm doing. I never know whether I'm winning or losing. Can't you explain better?"

Hilyard was not, as a rule, "slow to anger," and what he would have blamed in a man he forgave in a pretty girl, though he marveled to himself, somewhat, at his painstaking explanation.

Some distant convent bell was ringing two o'clock, when he touched his cap and was about to retire to the workshop. "Half-past ten to-morrow morning, then, please," said Miss Carrington, smiling pleasantly. "I am very pleased with the way you teach. Shall I—pay you to-morrow or now?" "To-morrow, if you please. Good morning, miss."

Hilyard went in to have a "shower," in a very complex frame of mind. He felt rather guilty as regards his deception, and, furthermore, wondered if the amount of pleasure derived thereby counterbalanced the morning's work and a pump-like feeling in the top of his head. The sun was frequently too much for him.

"I WANT YOU TO GIVE ME A LESSON."

To-morrow morning would certainly find him quietly at home, and the proper Thompson in the field.

But by the time he was sitting at lunch in the cool dining-room, with an extra good salad before him, and a huge glass containing one of Hawkins' best concoctions and lots of cracked ice, his mood changed. Now and then a faint smile passed over his face. And as he raised his glass to his lips he bowed, as though drinking a health.

"To our next merry meeting, whatever capacity I am in," he said aloud. "And if the meetings continue I know in what capacity I'll hope to be," he added as an afterthought.

Of course, by to-morrow she might have found out her mistake. If so, his services, he thought ruefully, would be dispensed with. If not, the chance must not be lost of meeting her again.

Before he left the links, he ran into Thompson's. "Look here," he said, "I want you to keep out of the way to-morrow about half-past ten, in case I should be late. If that young lady should see you first, tell her you are only the assistant. It is just for to-morrow morning," and he made for his train. And Thompson, as he felt in his pocket something that had not been there before, hoped the day might come when he would be rich enough to do other people's work and pay for the privilege.

The next day dawned bright and clear, and Hilyard was up betimes and out to the links on his wheel. He had considered the advisability of an improvement in his costume. Surely even a Professional might indulge in a fresh colored shirt. He had discovered in the glass that a sweater, after all, was not conducive to beauty.

So when Miss Carrington came along the gallery from the ladies' room, she found him in the same position as the day before, looking a trifle more presentable. "Dear me," she thought, "he'd really look quite like a gentleman if he were only properly dressed."

Photo by T. C. Turner.

"THOMPSON WAS BUSY IN THE WORKSHOP."

Which somehow seems to disprove the old adage of "the coat not making the gentleman."

Fortunately, for the second time, there was no one about. At the second hole a foursome of ladies could be seen, but Hilyard had watched the start, and, as none of them was known to him, they were likely to cause him no inconvenience.

"I hope it doesn't matter, miss," he said, "but I can't give you any time after twelve. I am expecting a party (this sounded professional) then."

By lunch time there were sure to be lots of men and girls about, and he did not mean to have it made awkward for both of them. "Oh, twelve will do nicely," replied Miss Carrington. "I made myself too tired yesterday."

To give a beginner her due, Miss Carrington certainly did better. At all events, the difference was a marked one in Hilyard's eyes. With sincerest flattery she imitated his style in every stroke, and very gracefully, too.

Somehow the line between the lady of leisure and the Professional became less strictly drawn. Conversation seemed to come more naturally, though it was, perforce, confined to local topics.

As Hilyard holed out, when they were half-way round the links, he made some remark that fell a little strangely from the lips of a Thompson.

Miss Carrington looked up quickly. Then, as he replaced the flag:

"Have you never been anything better than"—she hesitated; "at least, have you always been in the position you are now?" she asked, rather shyly.

"Always," was the quick assent—"neither better nor worse."

Truthfully, his life had been singularly free from ups and downs.

"Oh!"—It was a disappointed "Oh"—"I thought, perhaps——" But she evidently decided to leave the thought unspoken, and she teed her ball quite expertly, and drove a fairly clean shot.

And Hilyard found it imperative to dally over the putting, and showed her many different tricks. Also, it must be confessed, the humble and inferior Thompson would have rendered his position an insecure one had he dared to look so often and so pleasantly upon a pupil, no matter what might be her charms

They played the last hole, which was before the door. Two of Hilyard's chums had just set off from tee No. 1, but they were too far off to recognize him.

No one was on the gallery, though voices and laughter drifted out from the club-room. Feeling such luck was more than he should have expected, Hilyard dismissed himself as speedily as possible, and made his way to the workshop. It was a realistic touch that would have been better omitted. As he sallied from the door with some new balls, Miss Carrington sped across the grass to meet him.

"You went without my paying you, Thompson," she said, breathlessly. She held a five-dollar bill, and Hilyard saw a loophole.

"I haven't any change," he began; then the gate opened suddenly.

Miss Carrington turned and bowed smilingly in response to a cheery greeting, and Hilyard felt a bang on the back.

"Hello, Hilyard, old man, haven't seen you for an age! So glad you and Miss Carrington have met. I have been trying to get hold of you to give you the pleasure," said "that ass Elmore."

Hilyard, speechless, waited for results, and in the perceptibly drawn-up figure and cold, expressionless face read his death-blow.

"We have not met," she said stiffly. "I was merely obliged to speak on a matter of business. You are lunching with father later, are you not, Mr. Elmore? I'll see you in a few moments," and she returned to the club-house.

Elmore looked after her retreating form and then at his friend's dejected face.

"What on earth have you been doing, Hilyard?" he asked. "I never saw Miss Carrington so furious."

"What have *you* done, you mean," said Hilyard, sulkily. Then he told his tale.

"Upon my word," exclaimed Elmore, as the recital ended, "for pure, unadulterated cheek! Really, Hil, I can't believe it. And to Grace Carrington of all people!

"I'll do my best for you," in answer to an appeal, "but it will make a poor showing I am afraid. You'd better lunch elsewhere if you wish to enjoy yourself," and he departed.

Hilyard's inward communings belong to the category of those things better left unsaid.

So the would-be Professional for several days felt far from happy in his mind. His susceptibilities had been worked upon in an incredibly short time. He was also unused to being denied anything that might add to his pleasure. Besides, it was not specially agreeable to keep continually coming upon his ex-pupil evidently doing excellent work with driver and cleek, and have to pass by, while the genuine Thompson studiously turned his head away to hide his smiles. And he concluded he was more sinned against than sinning.

Elmore's reports, too, were unfavorable.

"It's no use talking to her, Hil; she's ripping. She told me never to refer to the subject again. And she says, apart from any other annoyance, it has been very provoking to be obliged to unlearn all you taught her."

This was the most cruel thrust of all. Hilyard almost made up his mind not to think of her again.

Golf being the uppermost thought in everybody's mind that season, Hilyard was not surprised to receive an invitation to a "golf dinner" from the wife of the Golf Club president. Most of the guests were to be elderly, but a golf dinner without Hilyard would have have had as much point to it as a links devoid of holes.

Accordingly he put on his scarlet coat and set off, thankful that golf was not a drawing-room accomplishment, and therefore no exhibition of his talent would be expected after dinner.

He was late in arriving and everybody was ready to go into the dining-room. Mrs. Granton was talking to a girl by the deep window-seat, and Hilyard recognized Miss Carrington, with a slight tremor of excitement.

Mrs. Granton greeted him with a playful remonstrance as to his lack of eagerness to join them. She was a woman who always had a little joke or smart saying in readiness, and fired it off whether or not the occasion was suitable.

Hilyard forgot to smile, but muttered some excuse, and found himself bowing, with heightened color, to the young lady he was to take in. She was self-possession personified, for in youth it is never acquired in half measures.

So the procession wended its way to dinner, and Hilyard wondered vaguely how long the corridor really was. They seemed to traverse miles, and not a remark was volunteered by the possessor of the small gloved hand that barely rested on his arm.

Mrs. Granton had worked nobly to introduce an atmosphere of golf In the center of the table a miniature links was laid out in as detailed a fashion as space would permit. Even some tiny sheep grazed in one corner. The flowers and ribbons were of the club colors, scarlet and white. The dinner-cards were spirited little paintings of players in action; the *menus* fairly bristled with appropriate quotations—in fact, at a first glance they seemed to cater more to intellectual than bodily wants. The dinner-rolls were ball shaped, and the ices later were cunning imitations of the same. Everything of a golfing nature that could be made in confectionery was there.

Miss Carrington was having an animated discussion with her other neighbor, a gentleman of society. At least she looked animated and listened attentively, though the speaker was neither very able nor rapid.

Hilyard sat in silence, and resolved it was too late in life to learn to countenance being thus absolutely ignored.

He leaned forward.

"Miss Carrington," he began. She turned slightly.

"I'm sorry to bother you, but do you think it would be possible for us to address each other once during each course? I don't wish to make our hostess feel more uncomfortable than necessary. Couldn't you pretend we were utter strangers meeting for the first time?"

"I am afraid I am not very good at pretending anything, Mr.—Hilyard."

"Oh, I think everybody has some instincts of the actor; don't you?" He helped himself to some entrée, the chief merit of which lay in its wonderful resemblance to balls on tees. "I wonder," he continued easily, "why we were not asked to eat our food with small cleeks or mashies, after the chopstick method. It would have been the essence of realism."

Miss Carrington barely allowed herself to smile.

"I think this dinner is a most charming idea."

"Yes, so do I. Originality in any form is delightful, even if carried to excess. Though I fancy the 'Etiquette of Entertaining' or some such volume is responsible for most of this."

There was a pause for some minutes, and both the young people seemed engrossed in the course set before them.

Miss Carrington suddenly straightened as if steeling herself to something unpleasant. "I wonder, Mr. Hilyard—and I can't help telling you that I am a little surprised—that you seem to think any apology quite unnecessary."

Hilyard was a bit of a judge. He knew better than to play the abject penitent in this case. So he looked up slowly at the blue eyes fixed upon him, and said in a deliberate tone:

"Really, Miss Carrington, I assure you I depended on Elmore to express my regret more trustworthily than he evidently has done. But I don't mind admitting to you that I have been a little astonished that you — well, you know, a fellow is *not* highly complimented at being taken for the Professional, and you can't deny the originality of the idea was due to you. I merely assisted in carrying it out."

Miss Carrington broke her bread nervously. Their eyes met and they both laughed.

"But you could have easily explained my mistake."

"Then I couldn't have gone round with you!"

The blue eyes dropped. Hilyard noted afresh the length of the lashes.

"Wouldn't it have been more prudent to have gone without your cake and waited for another that would have lasted longer?"

"It takes a very big cake to satisfy me. But still, I have hopes"

The conversation then became general. With dessert came a lull, and Hilyard, noticing Miss Carrington and the talkative old gentleman seemed destitute of ideas, ventured again to turn the conversation to personalities by observing, in an apparently easy-going way: "By the bye, Miss Carrington, has Thompson shown you when to use a niblick yet? I remember——"

"Thompson has shown me everything," she somewhat tartly responded. "I know the use of every club, from a driving cleek to a bulger brassey. Oh," with enthusiasm, "*how well he plays!*"

"Indeed. Well, I hope he will get you thoroughly grounded before the new man comes. It will be a pity," with emphasis, "to be obliged to unlearn all he has taught you."

Miss Carrington tried to look unconscious of the hit.

"He is a remarkably nice man," she retorted, "and he does not expect to be taken any notice of."

"Seen better days, I expect," rejoined Hilyard; "and then, you know, the Board Schools," he added.

Miss Carrington's chair was pushed out from the table with rather too much vehemence. And she followed in the wake of the other ladies.

Hilyard, left alone with the men, was the life of the party. He told his own new jokes and laughed as heartily at the Captain's three-year-olds.

On returning to the drawing-room he devoted himself to the oldest lady in the room, apparently ignorant of the fact that the youngest one was being bored to distraction by the golfing anecdotes of her host.

Truly, he was a master of finesse.

As the party broke up he found himself side by side with somebody who would have looked demure enough if her eyes had not contradicted it, and a low voice said:

"Thompson is obliged to be in town to-morrow, Mr. Hilyard. So I shan't get a lesson unless——"

She received no encouragement.

"Perhaps you wouldn't mind showing me that three-quarter swing with the niblick you spoke of."

It is astonishing how easily a novice adopts the correct phrases.

"Shall I have to call you 'Miss' every second word, and carry all the clubs, and not speak until spoken to?"

"No; you can do anything you please."

"Then may I call for you at ten? I feel I am entitled to some little return for giving over to Thompson my most promising and only pupil. Don't you think so, too?"

Miss Carrington evidently did.

So, after that, Hilyard's friends found he was useless in a foursome, and, in fact, impossible to fix any engagement with, unless the party happened to include——But, after all, that is neither here nor there.

Suffice it to add that the two days golf Professional plays his new part quite as well as his first one—at least, if one can judge from the success with which the new venture, not an athletic one, is crowned.

16

Golfing in the Far West

THE PASADENA COUNTRY CLUB-HOUSE.

GOLFING IN THE FAR WEST.

BY THOMAS H. ARNOLD.

TIME was, and that not so very long ago, when the golfing world of the West was bounded by the Rocky Mountains; but away out in the "Golden State," where the sun smiles its last good night on this continent, the royal and ancient game has had a marvelous growth within the past two years, and more particularly during the last twelve months.

The term "far West" as it applies to golfing, embraces principally and primarily the State of California, for between Denver and the California State-line golf clubs are few and far between. In fact, there are none that are yet out of their "swaddling clothes." Denverites are grossly offended if alluded to as denizens of the "far West," so we must go beyond them for the application of the title.

And yet Denver must be included in the itinerary of a golfing circuit on the setting-sun side of this continent, as must also Colorado Springs and Salt Lake City, where golf clubs have recently been organized, and where a number of very enthusiastic players are to be found. Phœnix, Ariz., is also about to spring into the arena, and a professional has already been engaged to lay out a course there and to "start the ball rolling."

The golfing circuit of the "far West," however, now comprises that part of California lying between its eastern and western boundaries and between San Diego on the south and San Rafael—a few miles north of San Francisco—on the north. Within that area are to be found sixteen thriving golf and country clubs, and four courses attached to large resort hotels, which have been, and will again be, the scenes of many brilliant and exciting contests, during the winter season especially.

There is at present no complete organization of all the clubs mentioned, but the Southern California Golf Association, organized in August, 1899, with the Riverside Golf and Polo Club, Pasadena Country Club, Redlands Golf Club, Pachappa Golf Club, of Riverside, and the Los Angeles Country Clubs as members, is practically recognized, in so far as jurisdiction is concerned, throughout the entire territory; and all fixtures of any importance are arranged to suit the convenience of the S. C. G. A. Whether this is a matter of courtesy or necessity

THE OAKLAND GOLF CLUB-HOUSE.

is a question, but the fact remains that a majority of the best players of the State are identified with this organization, and without them no event would be particularly brilliant or exciting.

The officers of the S. C. G. A. are: C. E. Maude, Riverside, president; J. D. Miller, Pasadena, and A. S. Auchencloss, Redlands, vice-presidents; J. F. Sartori, Los Angeles, secretary; Ray Jones, Santa Monica, treasurer. The executive committee is composed of the above and R. D. Osborn of the Pachappa Golf Club and E. B. Tufts, of the Los Angeles Country Club.

For the sake of convenience, the touring golfer could, while doing the southern part of the circuit, make Los Angeles his headquarters, and from there, reach out in every direction. There are plenty of interesting sights and historical points round and about, and only a few hours, at most, are required to reach any of the courses in the southern part of the State. Coronado, opposite San Diego, and Santa Catalina Island, twenty-five miles out in the Pacific Ocean, are the farthest away, the former being four hours by the Southern California Railway, and the latter thirty minutes by rail to San Pedro, and two hours by boat from that point; Santa Monica and Redondo, eighteen miles away, are reached from Los Angeles by steam or electric lines; Riverside and Redlands are sixty miles to the east, in the beautiful San Bernardino Valley, on the "kite-shaped" track of the Santa Fé System, and the "inside track" of the Southern Pacific; while Pasadena is but nine miles away, and is reached by electric cars which run every fifteen minutes.

Thus, it will be seen, Los Angeles is the hub of this golfing arena. The Hotel Westminster, presided over by F. O. Johnson, himself an enthusiastic golfer, and a prominent member of the Los Angeles Country Club, and the Hotel Van Nuys are the leading hotels of Los Angeles, thoroughly equipped and up to date. Of course there are a number of other hostelries and private boarding places, all comfortable and accommodating to the purse of the tourist of modest means or the bank account of the millionaire.

Starting with the Los Angeles Country Club, I shall give an idea of the various points, in the order in which I visited them in September of last year, the route being given as a sort of directory that can be followed with the greatest economy of time and expense by golfing tourists.

Foremost among the clubs of the State stands the Los Angeles Country Club, which has but recently secured new property, removed and enlarged its club-house and established an 18-hole course—the second in the State. The grounds are located within two miles of the heart of the city, and are reached by electric cars or over beautiful drives.

This course is picturesque, extremely sporty, and offers excellent opportunity for the good player and severe punishment for the "duffer." The total length is 5,548 yards, the holes being so arranged that either a nine-hole or the full eighteen may be played over. The nine-hole course is made by playing the first six, and then 16, 17 and 18, which brings the finish in front of the club-house, the distance being 2,543 yards. The course differs from most of those of Southern California, in that it is rolling and is crossed at two points by huge ditches, which, with five artificial bunkers, form numerous and dangerous obstacles that can be avoided only by careful and steady play. The fifth hole, "Dinky," is a particular terror, being situated on a little neck of land—scarcely large enough for the regulation green—and encircled almost completely by a ragged ditch twelve feet wide and as many deep. "Vexation" would probaably have been a more appropriate name for this particular hole. The sixteenth green bears a striking resemblance to the fifth. It is evident the greens committee of the club laid out the course for genuine golfers, and in its calculations entered very thoroughly into the true spirit of the game.

The holding of the club represents an investment of about $36,000—the ground valued at $26,500 and the club-house at $9,500.

Santa Monica, eighteen miles from Los Angeles, is primarily a summer resort, but as they really have no winter in California, the resorts are kept open and the sports and pastimes continue the year round. The Hotel Arcadia, presided over by Frank A. Miller, is the leading caravansary, and is really a unique and interesting place. Its location on the ocean beach and its surroundings of beautiful grounds and handsome residences make it quite picturesque. Although the Arcadia has no golf course, there are two clubs with grounds at Santa Monica, to either of which guests of the hotel are welcome when presented by card. These clubs are the Santa Monica Golf and Polo Club and the North Shore Golf Club. The course of the former is about 2,500 yards in length, and the latter 2,455 yards. Both courses are flat and offer little opportunity for anything but mediocre playing. This flatness is the one

CLUB-HOUSE.—HOTEL DEL MONTE GOLF LINKS.

—and the only one—disagreeable feature in golf-playing on the southern coast, but the delightful atmosphere and the invigorating ocean breeze compensate for any other shortcomings.

Santa Catalina Island comes next in order, with its unique golf course and its host of other attractions. Not a moment can be wasted there, for when the clubs are in the bag other and very wonderful things are demanding the attention. Here is the one spot where the investigator can view as well what is in "Davy Jones' locker" as those things that are on land. Drifting about over Avalon Bay, in a boat with its bottom made of plate glass, the beholder gazes in mute wonder and admiration to the very bottom of the ocean, through a hundred feet of crystal water; every fish—and there are thousands and of as many colors as the rainbow—and every pebble and every piece of sea-weed as distinctly visible as though it were held in the palm of the hand. Gold fish, silver fish, electric fish, devilfish, rock-bass, and oh my! thousands that I cannot name, skim here and there among the submarine forests and grottoes, while the sea urchin, lobsters and sea cucumbers cling to every projection in perfect swarms. It is a sight that beggars description, a marvelous panorama never to be forgotten.

The golf course at Santa Catalina, as I have said, is unique. At one moment the player is in a smooth little valley and at the next on a plateau—called in that country "mesa"—perhaps, a hundred or so feet high, from which the players following look almost like so many ants crawling along, away below the beholder. The course lies from valley to hill-top, across tremendous ravines, back into the valley, up the steep once more, and then along a hill to where it starts from. It is verily uphill work playing golf at Santa Catalina, and few visitors go more than the nine holes before pausing for a long rest. The distance of the course is 1,926 yards, and those 1,926 yards are like the proverbial Jordan—a hard road to travel. Bogie of the course is thirty-six, and as yet the "Colonel" has never been downed.

The Santa Catalina Golf Club is an organization in itself, but the course and all its belongings are the property of the Banning Company, which owns the entire island—58,000 acres—and all of its means of approach. The company acts as guarantor for the golf club; that means that it pays the expenses in order to have the course as an attraction to visitors and tourists who travel on its boats and sojourn at its hotels—the Metropole and the Island Villa.

ON THE SEVENTH GREEN—DEL MONTE.

Besides golfing and the submarine view, there are wild goat hunting, fishing, sailing, rowing, bathing, and the most exciting mountain rides to be found on the coast. In fact, as I have said, there is something interesting for every moment.

The next point of the circuit is Coronado, which is 125 miles south of Los Angeles, and on a long peninsula extending out between the Pacific Ocean and San Diego Bay. This is the spot made famous by the great investment of the Sugar King, Claus Spreckels, in the Hotel del Coronado, one of the most noted resorts of California.

This is a "perfect wilderness" of hotel building, for it covers four and one-half

THE GOLF LINKS, SANTA CATALINA.

acres of ground, is four stories in height, and contains seven hundred rooms, besides offices, parlors, reception rooms, and corridors. The Coronado is the largest hotel in the State, and is almost a city within itself.

Golfing at Coronado is under the direction of the Coronado Golf Club, an organization of residents of the peninsula, but which extends the courtesies of its greens to guests of the hotel on payment of very modest fees. The course is nine holes, extending in a circle, along the shores of San Diego Bay almost its entire distance ; it is flat, and the soil is of such a sandy nature that it constitutes a continuous hazard from the first tee to the ninth green. This ninth green, by

THE OAKLAND GOLF CLUB.

the way, is the only turf green of the course; there were nine turf putting greens once upon a time, but eight of them have gone the way of all grass in Southern California—burned up for want of rain.

In California turf greens are a luxury that very few clubs can afford to indulge in. It does not rain enough to keep even an imitation of life in the grass, and it would cost a small fortune to irrigate the green properly. And so it is that we find all of the putting greens there made of hard-packed earth sprinkled over with a fine layer of white sand. The course of the Oakland Golf Club and that at Del Monte are the only exceptions to this rule. About the most lucid description of the earth greens that can be given is that they look like huge grindstones sunk into the earth. Golf playing on sand-greens is a vastly different matter from playing on turf. Sand-greens are decidedly easier for putting, because the surface, being perfectly smooth, offers little resistance, and the ball rolls with a precision equal to what it would be on a billiard table.

Accurate approaches are next to impossible where there are sand-greens, for if the ball lands short of the green it lies dead, and if it strikes on the green it shoots across and off the other side. This makes the game partake of a very undesirable element of luck.

But to return for a moment to Coronado. The golf club, with its pretty little club-house and goodly membership, is quite a feature of the place. General tournaments are held two or three times during the year (their season for playing being, as it is at all other California points, 365 days), with local tournaments each month and medal play and special contests every week. This keeps up a continual and never-flagging interest in the game. In the breathing spells there are excellent fishing, boating, tennis, bathing, hunting, and, in fact, all sorts of recreation to demand the attention of the sojourner.

Doubling back from Coronado and passing through Los Angeles, the route lies over either the "kite-shaped track" or the "inside track," along the beautiful San Bernardino Valley to Riverside and Redlands, which are verily in the heart of the fruit-producing section. It is a magnificent stretch of fertile country, long and narrow, hemmed in on both sides by great mountains, carpeted with exquisite flowers even in December and January, and with miles upon miles of orange trees, upon which the luscious fruit hangs like golden globes and ruddy moons.

At Riverside there are three golfing organizations—the Riverside Golf and Polo Club, the Pachappa Golf Club, and the Rubidoux Golf Club. It is not a wonder that there are so many clubs here, for, although the city of Riverside claims but 8,000 people, its corporate limits cover fifty-six square miles, and it is necessary for residents of each portion of the town to have their own amusements. It is a wealthy community, and the citizens can, as a class, well indulge in every desirable amusement. The golf courses are not vastly different from others I have described, only that they are devoid of that flatness which characterizes those nearer to the ocean. From the Glenwood Tavern, the leading hotel, presided over by Mr. Frank A. Miller, whom I have already introduced as the genial proprietor of the Hotel Arcadia, at Santa Monica, all points of interest are easily accessible.

Seventeen miles from Riverside is Redlands, another pretty and picturesque little city of the San Bernardino Valley. Here is located the beautiful Casa Loma Hotel, with Mr. Joseph H. Bohon presiding over its destiny—a clever, congenial, whole-souled host. Catching the spirit of the times, Mr. Bohon has just completed a very attractive course, 2,425 yards in length, and with nine holes. The course is flat, but is furnished with enough earth bunkers and road hazards to make accurate playing a necessity.

Four miles to the east, but still within the incorporation, is the green of the Redlands Golf Club. The course is not easy of access, and the lay of the ground, along the foot-hills, is quite undesirable for golfing. Besides this, the course is badly laid out, and is sadly in need of remodeling.

One of the principal attractions of Redlands is "Smiley Heights," famous the world over for its beautiful drives, magnificent panoramic view, and world of exquisite flowers and palms. It is a private holding of the Brothers Smiley, but the hundreds of acres of lovely park are ever open to the public.

Pasadena, that beautiful resort of the

San Gabriel Valley, nestling at the foot of old Mount Lowe, and where is situated the famous Hotel Green, completes the circuit of Southern California. Here the golfing fever has struck with full force. From 500 to 600 guests at the Hotel Green, from 200 to 300 at the Hotel Pintareska, all the members of the Pasadena Country Club, and about half of the inhabitants of the city play golf all winter, and many of them keep it up all summer.

Three courses are available here, those of the Pasadena Country Club and the Hotel Green being nine holes each, and that of the Pintareska six holes. Were it not for its out-of-the-way location—which demands a private conveyance to reach the grounds—it might well be said that the Pasadena Country Club possesses the most pleasing green in Southern California. It is on a high point of ground, from which a magnificent view of the entire valley may be had, and it is a sight that cannot but be greatly enjoyed. The golf course is well laid out and very sporty, and is kept in excellent condition. The one point for adverse criticism lies in the fact that, through ignorance or carelessness, the greens committee allowed wire netting to be placed for bunkers. These things disfigure even a mediocre course, and are an abomination to true golfers. Where the idea of using them first originated I am at a loss to know, and why it is clung to is still more a mystery.

The course of the Hotel Green is situated a mile from the Caravansary, on the electric car line that connects Pasadena and Altadena, and is the best hotel course in the State. It consists of nine holes, the distance being something over 2,700 yards, and bogey 37. The ground is rolling, with a small ravine and an old railroad right-of-way to offer natural obstacles, while a number of great oaks, standing in excellent positions, form hazards that if disregarded in the least will prove very disastrous. Two earth bunkers, one on the fourth and the other on the eighth course, complete the list of obstacles. On the northeast corner of the grounds a pretty little club-house has recently been erected, with reception rooms, lunch room, lockers, etc., and a large veranda on three sides. There is nothing lacking in the golf grounds, and it is thoroughly in keeping with the Hotel Green, which, by the way, is one of the most magnificently constructed and equipped and most perfectly operated resort hotel of this continent. It is the property of Col. G. G. Green, of "Green's August Flower" fame, and is under the management of Mr. J. H. Holmes.

The Hotel Pintareska's course is of six holes only, and was designed simply for the use of the guests of the hotel, last season. I understood it to be the intention to extend it to nine holes during this winter.

There are many interesting points about Pasadena, not the least of which are the ascent of Mt. Lowe by the incline cable road, a visit to the ostrich farm, and miles upon miles of beautiful drives and cycle journeys. The most delightful season at which to see "the queen city of the San Gabriel Valley" at its best is during the early months of the year, for then the flowers are all in their most prolific and beautiful bloom, the fruit is ripe, and the hotels are crowded with guests.

Leaving Pasadena the objective point is San Francisco, which is reached from Los Angeles, on the magnificent "owl train" of the Southern Pacific, in 14 hours. It is hardly possible here to go into anything like detail as to the many attractions of "The Sunset Metropolis." Chinatown, Golden Gate, Sutro Park, Cliff House, the Seal Rocks, and many other points of interest will demand much attention from the tourist.

Including that of the San Francisco Golf Club, five golfing courses are easy of access from that city, any of which is worth a visit. They are: Hotel Del Monte, at Monterey, about 70 miles south of San Francisco; Burlingame, just a few miles south, on the road to Del Monte; Oakland, across San Francisco Bay, and San Rafael, about 30 miles northward. Either of these can be visited in a day if time is pressing, but more time than that should certainly be spent at Del Monte, if possible, for it is certainly the garden spot of the earth.

No matter what one may have heard or read of Del Monte, he is not prepared for the beauty and grandeur that are there encountered. It simply beggars description. Imagine, if you can, 162 acres of exquisite exotics, magnificent roses, giant palms, symmetrical hedges, huge oaks, covered with graceful, clinging ivy, tremendous cacti, and hundreds of the most delicate flowering and foliaged plants, the beds cut into the most pleasing and fantastic shapes by white walks that look like silver snakes creeping away under overhanging foliage; and you may have a faint idea of a tithe of the beauty of the grounds of Del Monte.

Then there is the "seventeen-mile drive," an ever-changing stretch of picturesque and romantic scenery; the lake, for sailing and rowing, ocean and plunge bathing, hunting, tennis courts, and a very attractive golf course. This last is situated just north of the hotel grounds proper. It is nine holes, the distance being 2,900 yards. The land is hilly and quite sporty, and, taken all in all, is of good character. On this course some of the most interesting tournaments held in the State have taken place. The most recent of these was held in August, when the Southern California representatives carried off the honors in handsome style, the championship of the State being won at that time by C. E. Maude, of Riverside, with Ed Tufts, of Los Angeles, a close second.

The international tennis tournament was also held at Del Monte in September. Both events were largely attended by people from all over the country.

There is no fixed time for tournaments or other fixtures at Del Monte; they are arranged at various periods during the entire year, the idea being to so place them as not to interfere with other important events elsewhere, and to provide suitable attractions for the guests of the place. Del Monte is a holding of the Pacific Improvement Company, one of the wealthiest corporations of the Western coast. It is under the management of Mr. W. A. Junker, and the hotel and its conduct are thoroughly in keeping with the magnificent surroundings.

Returning from Del Monte a stop can be made at Burlingame, where an excellent nine-hole course is owned by the Burlingame Golf Club. This is an organization made up principally of wealthy residents of San Francisco; in this respect it is on an equality with the San Rafael Club. Theirs also is a nine-hole course. Play on these greens is entirely of a local nature, and as it does not differ materially from what is met continually in the East, it does not demand special explanation.

SANTA CATALINA GOLF CLUB-HOUSE.

The course of the San Francisco Golf Club is a decided novelty, in that it is by far and away the poorest course in the State. It is a matter of great surprise that, with all the wealth of San

Painted for OUTING by Jas. L. Weston.

OVER THE HILLS AND FAR AWAY.

Francisco and the many enthusiastic golfers to be found there, the only green in the city should be such a poor affair. The course is badly laid out, the approaches unkempt and rough, the putting greens are as corrugated as the face of a washboard, and there are cracks in them in which a golf ball will almost drop out of sight; the teeing grounds are dilapidated and uneven, and, altogether, the course would seem to be a golfer's nightmare. But the club-house is a very pretentious affair, handsomely built and prettily furnished. It is a great pity that more effort is not devoted to the green and less to the club-house.

In preparing to leave California the farewell visit is made to the best course in the State—that of the Oakland Golf Club. This organization, although comparatively young, has a membership of 225, and employs two high-class professionals. The club-house is small, but very tasty and attractive in arrangement, while the course is eighteen holes, and over ground that is beautifully adapted to the true spirit of the royal and ancient game. Here the putting greens are all of an excellent quality of turf, and the fair greens are in splendid condition at all times. There are no mountains and tremendous ravines to strike terror to the golfer's heart, but gently sloping hills, even little valleys, just enough obstacles and uncertainties to put the best players on their metal. There is, too, a progressive, energetic spirit ever prevalent that keeps up an interesting series of fixtures during the entire year, but the principal events lie between November 1st and June 1st, as a rule.

Oakland ends the tour of what is properly known as the "Far West," and the homeward journey—for those who sojourn east of Denver—should include, as before stated, Salt Lake City, Colorado Springs and Denver, the latter especially having a good club and very attractive course.

There is one unsatisfactory feature about golfers of the "Far West," as a class, and that is, a very large majority of them play *at* the game, rather than play it. They have learned it unaided, and have followed out the lines they imagine should be followed. They are much in the same position as a person who tries to master a foreign language without a tutor—they learn to speak it after a time, but with the wrong accent. Up to November 1st, there were but five professionals in that territory—Tetley, at San Rafael; Melville, at Del Monte; Grindley, at Los Angeles; Robinson, at Riverside, and Stephenson, at San Francisco. Since November 1st, Alex. Smith, of Washington Park, Chicago, has gone to Coronado; Willie Anderson, of Baltusrol, has taken up quarters at Oakland, and William Watson, of the Minikahda Club, Minneapolis, has established himself as instructor on the Hotel Green course, at Pasadena. These are all high-class professional golfers, and will do a vast deal of good for golfing in the Far West.

CORONADO GOLF CLUB.

17

The Common Sense of Golf

THE COMMON SENSE OF GOLF

by H. J. Whigham

Illustrated with Photographs

OUT of a possible seventy-five millions (allowing for infants and infirm octogenarians), there are less than a million people in this country who play golf. At least seventy-four millions are willfully depriving themselves of one of the most certain methods of attaining health and happiness. If you were assured that without imbibing any new-fangled religion and regardless of all the new dietists and doctors who fill the human body full of parasites for the sake of destroying other parasites, you could not only add twenty years to the normal span of life, but secure in the present at least one good day out of seven by the simple process of swinging a golf club, would you not rush to the nearest golf links and begin to take lessons from the local professional?

There really is no question about the results any more than there is doubt about the pleasures of the game. Every other form of outdoor sport loses its votaries sooner or later. Baseball, football, riding, polo, even lawn tennis abandon us or we abandon them as our wind gets shorter and our bones more brittle. But once a golfer, you are wedded to the game for life. Nearly all the men who ever played golf and gave it up are those to whom athletic exercise in any shape is abhorrent. A few—perhaps even more than a few—have attempted to learn the game and have renounced it in disgust either because they could not see any fun in it or because they were such hopeless duffers that any sort of proficiency seemed out of the question.

These might well have been saved if they had only gone about it the right way. It is to these and to the many millions who have never even attempted to play that a few words of advice may be offered. If they will follow the advice given we guarantee health, sleep, immunity from nervous prostration and business worries, good temper, mental control, and lastly long life barring accidents from taxicabs or air ships. If those long-lived people who discovered for Professor Metchnikoff the virtues of the lactic acid had been nurtured on a golf links they would never have required germ tabloids to keep them alive.

It is easy enough to become a golfer if you happen to have been born in Scotland or even on Long Island; but how about the inhabitant of Keokuk or Kankakee, who has an equal right to liberty and happiness? When you come to think of it the wonder is not that so few people play golf, but that so many got along quite happily with such a bad imitation of the game. Most of our inland courses are so bad that to the uninitiated observer the game must appear a very futile kind of sport. In many cases the lies are abominable, the putting greens so coarse that no finesse in the short game is possible and in nearly all it is heavy odds that you cannot get round the links in summer without losing several balls.

I played over a course last year not a hundred miles from New York, where my adversary took out a dozen new "dimples" and lost every one of them before he got to the eighteenth hole. He was always in long grass or bushes. He never played from a good lie except on the teeing ground, because he invariably lost his ball before he reached the putting green. It is true he was rather a bad player, but the majority of men are indifferent golfers. The extraordinary thing is that they do not give up the game altogether. Golf, according to the President, is the poor man's

Photo by Brown Brothers, N. Y.

FRED HERRESHOFF PLAYING AN IRON ON THE FAIR GREEN.

game. So it ought to be. But a poor man cannot afford to spend nine dollars on "dimples" for one day's play.

And even when you find your ball on these courses there is too much hammering away from one bad lie to another for the poor players. You will never become a good player by hacking at your ball in long grass with a heavy iron. That is just the stroke which a novice should practice least; for it gets him into all sorts of bad habits. Indeed the beginner should avoid playing with an iron club altogether if possible.

The individual, however, does not make the links. He has to be content with what he can find in his immediate neighborhood. But let him at all events, when he has a chance, visit a good course and watch some good performer at work. The common jest about golf on the English stage used always to have reference to a feature of the game which should be absent from all good courses. "Chasing a pill round a cow pasture," was one definition. "You tee your ball and hit it into the next field; if you find it the same day you win the game." That was another jibe. All of which goes to prove that when golf first became popular in England the inland courses were just as bad as they are in this country, if not worse. On a real seaside course it is almost impossible to lose a ball except in the whins which used to abound at St. Andrews, but are fast disappearing.

If you are in New York, then, go out to Garden City and see Walter Travis of Fred Herreshoff hitting the ball. If you are in Boston visit Myopia. Out West they will show you at the Chicago Golf Club what can be done with an inland course. No real golfer on a real golf course digs interminably at his ball half out of sight. If he plays more than two shots in a bunker the hole is lost anyhow and he picks up his ball and goes on to the next. You wouldn't think much of the game of billiards if you saw it played on a Brussels carpet, would you? Well, golf on most of our

Photo by Brown Brothers, N. Y.

THE "FINISH" OF WALTER TRAVIS'S SWING WITH THE WOODEN CLUB

inland courses is just as poor an imitation of the real thing.

The next task is to learn how to hit the ball. There is only one way to do that. You must watch a good player and imitate what he does. Most beginners make the mistake—a serious one—of taking lessons from professionals who watch their pupils play and try to correct them. The pupil would get twice as much good out of the lesson if he would watch the professional play and think as little as possible about himself. The human being is naturally imitative. If you sit and watch a good tennis match between first-class players you will unconsciously finish your stroke better the next time you take up a racket. With golf this is particularly true because nothing is so important as the rhythmical timing of the stroke which distinguishes a good player from a bad one.

My advice is of course addressed mainly to grown-up beginners. A boy needs little or no advice. He is purely an imitator, and being young and supple he very soon learns to swing easily and smoothly. The grown-up novice is self-conscious, self-concentrated, and will insist on trying to reason things out; and he is apt to be terribly obstinate. He learns by adopting several bad tricks to hit the ball a good distance occasionally; and nothing will induce him to alter these tricks which he imagines are adapted to his peculiar style of anatomy. He asks you to correct him if you think he is wrong, but he will not accept the only correction of any value, which is to forget all he ever knew, give up thinking about himself, and do nothing but watch you, the instructor, hitting the ball.

The instructor should have common sense too. The beginner should never attempt what is called a full swing. For that reason the best example for him is Walter Travis. The ignorant often comment upon the Travis "form" and think it is eccentric just because he plays with what is usually called a half swing. In reality Travis has the best possible golfing style for anyone who does not begin as a boy; and boys, too, would do well to watch him play. He gets all his effect by perfect timing and by a straight follow through so that the weight of the body is thrown into the stroke just as the head of the club hits the ball. The same accuracy may be acquired in time with what is called a full swing, but it is much more difficult for the adult beginner to adopt this and he is almost sure to swing too far back, which is the worst fault of all.

A Good Way to Begin

Begin then with a half swing, keeping the hands well away from the body and never let them go higher than the shoulder, except in the follow through after the ball has been hit. And be sure to swing slowly. Watch the good players and see how slowly and easily they swing back. At first sight you may think that they go back rather quickly, but that is only because the whole action is smooth and without apparent effort. But imitate them exactly as they stand in front of you and you will find that the backward motion is much slower than at first you imagine it to be. The backward swing should be just twice as slow as the forward movement to the ball. It isn't a bad plan to count "one—two" going back and "one" coming forward. By thus counting you compel yourself to go slowly.

Half the battle of golf consists in taking it easy. Irritation over a bad shot, anxiety about a bunker in front of you, and especially the effort to drive against a strong wind, may tempt you to hurry your swing. If you give in to the impulse, the result is almost sure to be bad, and the habit of pressing grows upon you.

The details of the grip and stance you must get also by constantly watching good players. The grip is an absurdly simple matter, yet most beginners hold their clubs in a manner which effectually prevents them swinging properly. There is one thing you must not do, and that is to hold the left hand under the club. The first two joints of the fingers *must* be invisible. With the right hand the grip is optional. Walter Travis favors the old St. Andrews grip, with the right hand well under the shaft. There is no doubt that this method makes for straightness and especially prevents pulling, though it may curtail the distance just a trifle in the longer shots. Look at the way Fred Herreshoff holds his hands. His right hand is well under the club; you can see both the first two joints of the fingers. But the shaft is not so well home in the palm of the right hand as it is in the case of Walter Travis. You cannot do better than imitate this grip. There are other refinements which may come later.

A great number of good players hold the right hand over the first finger and thumb of the left for the shorter approaches and in putting. And there is the Vardon grip, which has ruined many a young golfer, and there are several other variations. The beginner will do well to employ the ordinary straightforward method and he should remember to keep his hands as close together as possible.

It is a truism of the golf books that the follow through is more important than the upward swing. Look at the pictures of Fred Herreshoff and Walter Travis and you will see how the whole body seems to move on the spine as an axis, and at the end of the swing the right shoulder is brought forward until the body of the player from the waist upward is facing the hole squarely. The beginner may argue that it cannot matter much what the body does after the ball has left the face of the club, and in a certain sense he argues well. No action of the arms or body can affect the flight of the ball once it has been struck. But the easiest way to strike the ball correctly is to think of the follow through.

It is by concentrating your efforts on letting the arms follow the flight of the ball that you succeed in swinging straight at the ball and in timing your stroke correctly. Cause and effect are here inextricably mixed. In order to follow through correctly you must come straight at the ball, and in order to

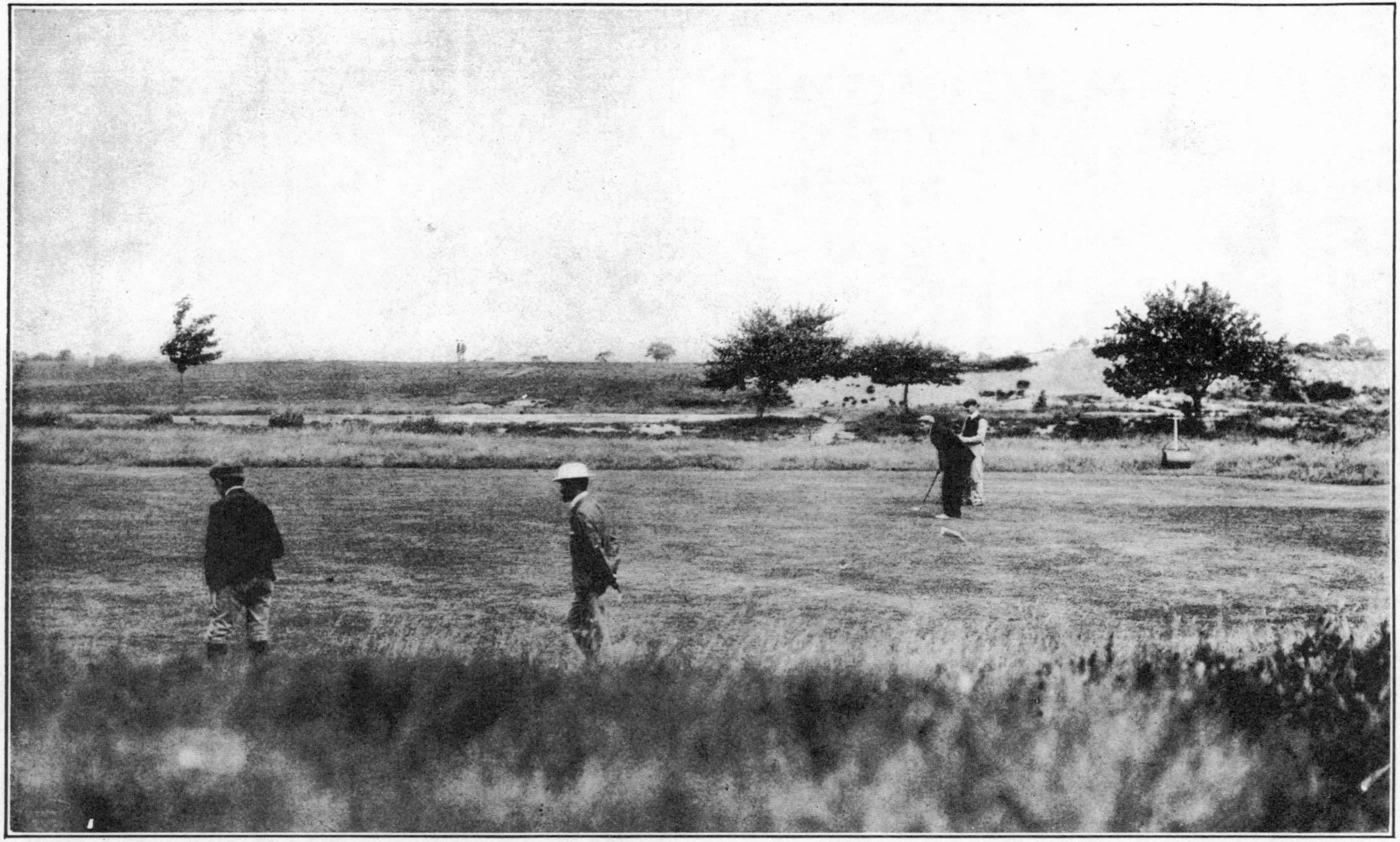

Photo by Edwin Levick, N. Y.

GOING THE ROUND AT GARDEN CITY.

come straight at the ball you must think about following through correctly. And here again an ounce of example is worth a hundredweight of instruction.

Remember to get your hands well away from the body in going back; you will find it impossible to swing straight if you don't, and instead of following through straight after the ball the hands will be drawn around to the left. Look at the picture of Findlay Douglas swinging and you will notice at once how the hands are kept away from the shoulders at the top of the swing. Douglas has the perfect style which it is so difficult to acquire after one is of age. Even in the photograph you can see the nimble foot action, the perfect timing by which quite unconsciously the center of gravity moves from the right leg in the upward swing to the left in the downward attack. You can see, too, how easily the hips turn on the axis of the spine. There is hardly a muscle of the body that is not brought into play. What would not some of our millionaires give for a style like that!

Notice, too, how Findlay Douglas finishes the approach shot; hands, club, eyes are all pointing toward the hole. The attitude is perfect all but the eyes. The beginner would do well to try and keep his eyes fixed on the spot from which the ball was hit. There is no fault more prevalent than the fault of lifting the head too soon, and so it is well for the novice to err in the other direction and keep the eyes glued to the ground until the ball has stopped rolling. I am sure that one secret of the remarkable success of Walter Travis is his determination to keep his eye on the ball.

Nearly all players when they are photographed at the finish of the stroke have their eyes directed toward the flight of the ball. You will observe that Travis even at the end of a full swing keeps his head as far as possible turned toward the spot from which he has just struck the ball. Notice the marked difference in this respect between Travis and Herreshoff.

The common faults of the golfer may

Photo by Brown Brothers, N.Y.

FINDLAY DOUGLAS FINISHING AN APPROACH SHOT WITH THE IRON.

Photo by Edwin Levick, N. Y.

A TEST OF A GOLFER'S SKILL—AND TEMPER.

be named in the following order of importance. Swinging too quickly; taking the eye off the ball; holding the left hand under the club; keeping the hands too near the body; and standing too near the ball. The easiest, indeed the only satisfactory way of curing all these faults is to go out and watch some one like Findlay Douglas or Walter Travis or Fred Herreshoff play. If you cannot find any expert of the first class, go for the best available; and if you have to fall back on professional advice make your teacher play the ball himself and imitate his stroke.

This, of course, is rudimentary advice and certainly not original. The youngest caddie at St. Andrews has learned to request his master to keep his eye on the ball and not to press. The trouble is that no amount of book teaching will make you follow this advice. You have to assimilate it by practice. There are a few other points about the game which I should like to dwell upon, and which are applicable to older players as well as beginners.

The game of golf is in a fair way of becoming unplayable in America on account of the amazing and unconscionable slowness of American players. The prevalent idea that the American is a born hustler is sadly belied on the golf links. It may be that just because he has learned to travel in express subway trains the American has forgotten how to walk. On the golf links he walks terribly slowly.

But that is not the only reason why he takes such a long time to get round the course. Because Walter Travis takes a practice swing before most of his shots the beginner appears to think that he cannot become a good golfer unless he does the same thing. So he takes a preliminary swing and then he waggles his club needlessly over the ball, or he crouches over it with glaring eye as if by sheer hypnotic power he would compel it to fly. The result is that it is almost impossible to get around any crowded links in less than two hours and a half. There are many days in the autumn when you cannot play two

Photo by Brown Brothers, N. Y.

HOW THE "OLD MAN" FINISHES HIS IRON SHOTS.

rounds at Garden City at all unless you start about daybreak.

Something ought to be done to stop this creeping paralysis which is coming over the game. Most of the delay is quite avoidable. No good player was ever a slow player. Some are faster than others, but I have never seen a good golfer who could not easily get round Garden City (which is a very long course) in two hours with a clear green. If the dawdlers only knew it, they would play a far better game if they would give up dawdling.

I know one player at Garden City who habitually takes nearly two hours and a half to play the course even when there is no one in front of him. Once he went out to play in a four-ball match with some faster players and as there was not a great deal of daylight remaining it was made a condition that the fast players should not wait for him. The slow player hurried along putted boldly at the hole without studying the line too long; walked up to the tee and drove off without any preliminary swing and did not stop to discuss the cost of living between shots. The result was that the four players completed the round in two hours. When the slow man came to think it over on the club veranda he discovered that he had actually putted out at every hole and had finished the round in 78, a score which he had never equaled before and which almost anyone may be proud of at Garden City.

If the average American player would only realize how much easier it is to play well when he is swinging along at a good rate, he would surely gird up his loins and walk a little faster. I shall never forget seeing Mr. Harold Hilton win his first open championship at Muirfield a good many years ago. He actually did his last round in 71 with the old gutty ball, thereby cutting the record by several strokes, and he walked so fast and played so fast that he kept the large gallery trotting nearly all the time.

Photo by Brown Brothers, N. Y.

HERRESHOFF'S STYLE IS A GOOD MODEL FOR THE YOUNGER GOLFER.

Perhaps the slowest match on record was a famous game for a big purse between two professionals, Andrew Kirkcaldy and Willie Park. When these two met at Prestwick they took three hours to cover the course in the morning. Andrew not only studied all his putts from both ends but even his longest iron shots called for the most minute examination of the ground. I forget who won, but it was a miserable exhibition of golf. The scores were about 85 and 86. Robert Maxwell, the present amateur champion, has scored a 66 at Prestwick and he probably got around the course on that occasion in an hour and three quarters or less. There is a limit even to speed, but as a general rule it holds true that the more time you take the worse you play.

There are one or two other reasons for the congestion of the courses in this country. One is the prevalence of long grass and bushes already referred to. I believe that if some one would make a course with nothing but smooth turf and sand bunkers upon it he would soon have all the golfers of the country at his feet; no one would play anywhere else. Nothing spoils the game so much as the losing of balls, which not only ruins the temper of the players who lose them, but of everyone else on the course who is kept waiting.

Then there is the much-vexed question of the four-ball match. The four-ball match is a pleasant pastime, but it has many bad sides to it. Four good players can get around the course about as quickly as two bad players, but the majority of players are bad, and when they take to playing four-ball matches they occupy the links for the best part of the day in accomplishing one round. It is not sufficient to say that a single can always pass a four-ball match. It can; but the mere delay of passing tends to hold back the entire field, and in their anxiety to get through the players of the single generally miss a few shots and so their game is spoiled for two or three holes.

Four-ball matches should only be played when the green is rather empty, or after all the rest of the field has started. Morally speaking, they are bad for the young player. They put a premium upon a careless and slashing style, and they are apt to make a great deal of the play perfunctory. What is the good of my doing a hole in a par four if my partner has already secured an abnormal three?

In its social aspects the old-fashioned foursome is just as amusing, it is a far finer test of skill and mental control, and it has the advantage of taking no more time than a single. In Scotland, where a man goes to St. Andrews or North Berwick for two or three weeks at a time and plays nearly every day except Sundays, the pleasantest way is to play a single in the morning and a foursome in the afternoon; indeed you soon find that more than this is bad for your game. But golf in this country is hardly ever indulged in to that extent. If a man gets his Saturday afternoon and Sunday rounds he is lucky and he wants to do all the hitting he can. He is out for exercise rather than golf, and he cannot afford to waste his time in playing a foursome. He plays a four-ball match in preference to a single because he not only gets in plenty of exercise that way, but can play about five matches at once with bets on each.

Why Travis Likes the "Four-Baller"

The great advocate of the "four-baller" is Walter Travis, although he gets more play than most people in this country. It is easy, however, to understand his point of view. Generally speaking, he is playing with a weak partner against two strong players; Travis cannot depend much on his partner and has to play every shot just as carefully as if he were playing a single. The responsibility and the fun and the glory are all his.

But how about the partner? He cannot expect to help his side more than once or twice in the round; if he does he gets roundly abused by his opponents; most of his shots realy do not matter at all. If he were playing a foursome everyone of his shots would be just as important as his partner's. On the whole the "four-baller" is to be discouraged especially for young players; as a test of golf it does not compare with the single or the foursome since it is quite possible for two poor players with luck to beat two much better players.

After having said all this, I must now confess that personally I almost invariably play four-ball matches in preference to anything else, but that is because I belong to the "commuter" class. If I could play golf for a week at a time I should hardly ever play anything but singles and foursomes.

Another pernicious habit is the counting of strokes. Time was when no one ever had a handicap and cups were unknown. An annual medal round was sufficient for all the pot-hunting proclivities which even the best golfers sometimes hold concealed. In those days if you asked how such and such a one played, the answer was not "his metropolitan handicap is six," but "Laidlay can give him a third," or "he beat Horace Hutchinson with a half." Sometimes it is a dangerous question to ask of a Scotch caddie, as for example:

"How does Captain Stewart play?"

"Captain Stewart? He canna' play a damn."

"How much shall I give him?"

"You? You canna' give him onneything."

There is one person you cannot deceive in this world and that is your caddie. He knows all your shortcomings, both of skill and character, and he is not slow to let you find them out. No golfer is a hero to his own caddie. The Scotch caddie had, and still has, the most supreme contempt for the golfer who goes around the links with score card and pencil. Old Crawford's saying is immortal.

" D'ye see that fellow?" he said in a loud tone of voice, indicating an Englishman who was laboriously adding up his score on a neighboring putting green; "D'ye ken the best club in his set?"—then with great contempt, "It's his pencil."

There is reason for this attitude, for

the real game of golf is the play by holes and not by score. It is in the play by holes that all the elements which make the game so human come in. A man may go around in eighty by himself, but when he comes across a player who is just a class better than himself and has to try to defeat him in match play he is more likely to take ninety. To the young player the score card is particularly injurious because he is apt to try all sorts of tricks in order to get there somehow and so he loses all freedom of style. It is better to miss the shot a hundred times in the right way than to play it successfully in the wrong.

Photo by Brown Brothers, N. Y.

WHERE IT TAKES NERVE TO PLAY A BRASSIE.

To most of us medal play is nothing more nor less than a beastly nuisance, but we should not despise it altogether. In the first place, it is excellent discipline for the finished player; it teaches above all control of the nerves, for it is absolutely impossible to do a good score if you get either anxious or irritable. In the second place, it is a capital test of steadiness and temper, and for that reason the American system of deciding the amateur championship, including as it does both medal play and match play, is distinctly better than the English system which excludes medal play.

But, after all, the most important thing for golfers of all ages and handicaps is not that they should play golf well, but that they should play it cheerfully. One often wonders why some people choose to play a game at all which apparently gives them about two hours of complete misery. The habit of being irritable at golf grows upon a man without his knowing it, until at length he is a burden to his partner, opponent, caddie, and most of all to himself. If he is not careful he will carry this irritability into everyday life and become a burden to his family as well.

For golf is like a patent medicine; it either kills or cures. If you realize at the beginning that to be a good golfer you must, before all things, control your temper, you will find after a while that it is just as easy to be cheerful as not and a great deal more pleasant. And the result of this schooling of the temper is that you are a better and more lovable person in all relations of life. But if you once begin getting angry and morose at golf, you will rapidly become worse and worse until there is no playing with you or living with you. So be warned in time. When you top a drive into a bunker or miss a short putt at a critical point of the match, remember that you are playing a game for amusement, even if you are desperately keen to win, which you have every right to be. Tell yourself that your only chance of winning lies in forgetting past errors.

About Good Losers

When you have any bit of hard luck, don't keep talking about it for several holes afterwards. In the first place your opponent, though he may condole with you for form's sake, really does not think that you had such bad luck; if he were honest with you, he would tell you that he thinks you played the shot badly. The more you talk about such things the more he thinks that you are getting old and cranky and really rather a nuisance to play with. In the second place, talking about your bad luck only makes you dwell on your sorrows and tends to spoil your play. It is not true that you consistently get worse lies than other people. When a man tells you that he always holds bad cards at bridge you never think of believing him; you take him to mean that he always plays them badly.

Perhaps the best way of curing yourself of the tendency to become irritable and morose when you are playing badly is to pull yourself up and think how objectionable and ridiculous other people look when they are in the same state. Nothing in the world is so unlovely as a bad temper; real loss of temper is deplorable.

It has often been said about bridge and other games that the only thing worse than a bad loser is a cheerful winner. Surely this is true of golf. The man who gloats is singularly detestable. Remember here again that you are playing a game and you want your opponent to have as good a time as possible, even though he is losing. Nothing indeed is more necessary than courtesy to your opponent. If you find that it annoys him to get too near to him when he is playing, or to walk ahead of him, or to make remarks to him just as he is going to attempt a difficult putt, remember that to do any of these things is just as unfair as it would be to tee your ball in a bunker when he is not looking. The best advice to all golfers is to play the game for the fun of the thing; take your defeats cheerfully and your victories with modesty.

Finally to make the game enjoyable and at the same time to improve the skill of players, your courses should be well laid out and properly bunkered. I lay stress on this point because the science of bunkering is so woefully misunderstood in this country. I do not at all insist on penalties. There must always be luck about the game; that is one of its charms. On the contrary, I object very strongly to the penalty of having to hunt for your ball in long grass every time you go off the course. But I do hold that the bunkers and penalties should be so arranged as to make the player try the fine shots. A course is hardly worth playing on which has not several really big carries off the tee and also for the second shot.

Why do all golfers like the Alps at Prestwick and the Sahara at Sandwich? Surely on account of the great carries. Secondly, the putting greens should vary in size and contour and the bunkers close to the hole should be deep, although you may easily go too far in this matter of depth. Of course, mud holes are bad. All bunkers should be filled with clean sand and then you will find it is not at all difficult to get out of them. But unless your greens are well bunkered you lose half the fun of the game. Jerome Travers found in Scotland that men like Hilton and Maxwell could play shots which he had never thought of.

Our players in this country do not learn to play golf in the best sense of the word because they never have to put back-spin or side-spin on the ball to hold it on the green; and they rarely have to play for a slice or a pull.

It is all nonsense to argue that the majority of players being poor performers ought not to be punished by having to play over difficult courses. All the bad players in England flock to St. Andrews and Prestwick and Sandwich. And Americans do just the same thing. It is a noteworthy fact that most Americans praise Prestwick more than any other course abroad, and Prestwick is noted for the size of its bunkers. Bad players have a way of objecting to new bunkers before they are put in; but they very rarely object to them once they are made.

It is only those who do not play golf as a game, but take it as a medicine, that really object to bunkers being properly placed, and we cannot make our courses to suit the physically and mentally weak. There was a lot of talk about driving away the poor players when the new bunkers were put in at Garden City; some bad players became quite fierce about it. I have yet to hear of a single player who has left Garden City now that the bunkers are there. In other words, no one has suffered and a large number get more pleasure out of the game.

No one really knows anything about golf until he has played over a course at least as good as Garden City. And so we get back to the original point of this article: if you want to become a golfer—and you are very foolish if you do not—go and play on the best courses available and watch the best players.

18
Acquiring Form in Golf

ACQUIRING FORM IN GOLF.

SOME ADVICE TO BEGINNERS.

By Harold H. Hilton,

Amateur Champion of Great Britain.

WHEN invited to subscribe a short article by the proprietors of this magazine, I was particularly requested to make my remarks practical, so as to be as useful as possible to

No. 1. No. 2.
Grip of Fingers at Top of Swing.

the average golfer. This I have attempted to do, and I can only sincerely trust that they will bear the fruit of my intention in that they will prove at least of some slight service to golfers in America.

In the majority of the athletic pastimes which are in any way kindred to golf, the ball is "hit." It may be that there are certain ways of hitting it, which may be classed the scientific and the unscientific, but they all differ from golf in that they do not require any necessarily concerted action of all the parts of the player's anatomy, at least in as great a degree as golf does.

In cricket, for instance, a player may strike the ball with great power and precision, in a firm or fast-footed attitude, with little of the motive power coming from the lower limbs, but in golf it is the unison of all the parts, the feet, the legs, the hips, the shoulders, and even the head, backed up by what would aptly be deemed the keys of the situation, the wrists and hands, which result in what is rightly termed, in golfing parlance, a "swing."

A swing it undoubtedly is. A rhythmical motion of all parts of the body, working in unison together, which enables an apparently weakly stripling who has been gifted with the power of applying all his forces at the right moment, to outdistance a matured man of herculean build, who trusts but in the force with which nature has endowed him.

To commence with the most important factor toward the desired consummation. A player must learn to slide the club in the palm and fingers of the right hand, on the upward swing, before he can successfully attain a correct golfing swing. It does not matter how he holds the club handle in the preliminary address to the ball; he may hold it well under, like Mr. Ball and Mr. Tait, or with the fingers interlocked, like Vardon and Taylor; it matters not, provided that he has mastered the science of sliding the club until it is resting lightly between the thumb and forefinger at the very top of the swing.

This is the great secret of a golfing swing, one which a boy, when learning, picks up instinctively. It is a species of natural golfing touch, more than difficult to acquire when a golfer takes up the game in later years. Practice it; it is worth practicing.

The accompanying illustrations, numbered 1, 2, and 3, will, on close observation, give a certain idea as to grip of the fingers at the top of the swing. It will be seen that in each instance the grip of the club is almost entirely controlled by the fingers. In No. 3 it almost looks as if the grip were too insecure to put on the requisite pressure on the downward journey, but the grip may be as light as light can be, provided the player still retains command over the club.

Golf is not a simple game, and requires an abnormal amount of practice to arrive at anything like perfection. I do not mean the practice which arises from playing round after round. This is naturally merely mechanical. I mean the practice which admits of experiments being attempted, for all clubs vary, one from the other, and have to be carefully tested, like children, and the player, when he can find time for a short period of solitary practice, should always favor the wayward and willful child—the club with which he is the least at home, the club with the peculiarities of which he is the least acquainted.

It is easily to be understood that the natural inclination of all golfers, be they good, bad, or indifferent, is to favor the club which gives them the most satisfaction. It may be a driver, a brassey, or an iron. It is indeed pleasant to take out such a club and play half a dozen balls with almost unerring accuracy, to see them soar away in the distance, or drop, one after another, in the vicinity of the spot to which you intended them to go; but beyond that feeling of satisfaction and pleasure it profits you nothing. You knew previously that you were a master, or a comparative master, of that particular weapon, and the pleasant time spent has probably only had the object of indorsing that knowledge.

That is not the way to improve your game, and surely the ambition of all players is to improve their game. Better

No. 4.
At the Moment of Impact.

No. 6.
Right Elbow Close to Body.

leave your favorite club at home and take out some obstinate wretch of an instrument over which you have little or no control.

Every golfer has some weakness in his game. It may be only a comparative one —that is, comparative with the rest of his game—but the weakness is invariably there. A golfer should always try and conquer that weakness, and it cannot be overcome except by assiduous practice—practice in solitude, with but the club and the balls for companions. I am speaking from personal experience, as for many years there was one stroke in the game which baffled me, a stroke which I never approached to play except in fear and trembling; but I eventually overcame it—overcame it simply by assiduous practice—and I can only advise all golfers to follow the same mode of procedure. It is not a pleasant task whilst on hand, but it may save the necessity of a great deal of heartburning in the future.

No. 3.—Grip of Fingers at Top of Swing.

Keep your hands low and the elbows, particularly the right one, well into the body, as in that position it allows the club to make a longer sweep, and the power is consequently greater. What is more, I can hardly call to mind a single player who has any claim to be considered in the front rank, with the probable exception of Mr. Hutchinson, who does not follow this principle, whilst, in addition, Messrs. Charles Hutchings and Sidney Fry, who, of all the players who commenced the game comparatively late in life, may be said to be pre-eminent, are both great disciples of this cult. Taylor, the present open champion, is a remarkable example of the efficacy of this method, as his elbows appear almost glued to his body, both on the upward and downward swing, and even in the follow through.

A besetting sin of nearly all golfers is to what may be termed "underclub themselves"; that is, to take a club with which they cannot possibly reach the distance they require. Even in the very first rank of golfers this fault is very marked, and one has only to stand and watch the approaches to any individual hole in an open championship meeting to note how repeatedly approaches are short of the hole where there is no hazard to carry immediately in front of the green. A friend of mine amused himself at St. Andrews by standing at a certain hole and noting the percentage of approaches which were short of the pin, and he found that only twenty per cent. made their way past the hole. The remaining eighty per cent. were short in a greater or lesser degree.

Of course, it may be that a certain percentage of those which were short had not been hit quite truly, but even that is only an argument in favor of playing to be past the hole. It is just as well to be ten yards past the hole as ten yards short; and, as you cannot rely upon striking every ball truly in the center of the club, it is better to allow a little for this fact, even if you do go a little past the hole.

The hazards on the majority of courses are less numerous past the green than short of it. This feature of playing firmly past the hole has always struck me as one of the great merits of the game of both Vardon and Taylor, particularly the former, who seldom underclubs himself. Follow his example and you will not rue it.

If there is a doubt as to reaching the hole with an iron, take a cleek, or its equivalent. If there is a doubt as to reaching with a cleek, always take a wooden club.

When playing short approaches, keep the body comparatively still, not absolutely so, as there must always be a slight swing of the body in which the feet are a party, or else the freedom of the arms would be restricted, but do most of the work with the arms and wrists. They are quite capable of accomplishing the task in hand, and they are more easily managed than the remainder of one's anatomy.

No. 5.—The Finish of the Swing.

One often witnesses a first-class player pitch a ball up to the hole with an abnormal amount of spin upon it, the ball, on landing on the surface of the green, appearing as if a piece of string was attached to it, so quickly does it pull up; and there is an impression that, by some occult means, the player has imparted a mysterious screw on it, an impression which, from my own experience, I think is an erroneous one. It certainly is possible to impart an extra spin on the ball, but I have found that very few players attempt it, as it is a dangerous stroke, necessitating a dropping of the shoulders just at the moment of impact, and a ball struck truly off the face of a highly lofted club will always have sufficient spin upon it for ordinary circumstances. My advice is, when playing short approaches, try your utmost to strike the ball truly and leave the rest to nature. It is a principle which I have always followed and never regretted.

To beginners I have one word of advice. Put yourself under some competent man straightaway. You may spend a round or two getting through the initiatory stages of learning to hit the ball on the face of the club. Then arrives the time for the tutor. It is easier to form good golfing habits in early golfing youth, and difficult, very difficult indeed, to eradicate bad habits when once acquired. What is more, the powers of imitation are great in the golfing race.

In the majority of cases the imitation is quite unconscious, but it is probably more marked in connection with the Royal and Ancient game than in any other class of pastime. One has only to watch the younger generation on any of the first-class links in England and Scotland to note the similarity, in a more or less marked degree, to some giant of renown. It may be that the similarity is only remarkable in the address to the ball; it may be that it is only noticeable in the freedom or length of the swing, or some peculiar action of the body; the Jersey school of golfers, of whom Harry Vardon is the great master, being a noticeable example.

All of the players who hail from that little island are blessed with a peculiar heave of the shoulders. Just at the top of the swing it is most marked in the case of Tom Vardon, the younger brother of the champion, who rises on his toes at the top of the swing, almost jumping from the ground; but, as I said before, all the Jersey boys have this peculiar heave in a more or less marked degree, and it cannot be anything but the natural power of imitation, probably to be found in a more marked degree in the would-be golfer of younger years, but nevertheless always apparent in some form or another in the player who has taken to the game in maturer years. Do not, therefore, fail to put yourself in the hands of a good man, one who has followed the game from childhood preferred. Even if he does not succeed in imparting to you any principles of lasting value, your bump of imitativeness will have a good model to work upon, and imitation is half the battle.

One word before concluding regarding the illustrations which accompany this article. Nos. 1, 2, and 3 show the player at the top of the swing, from different positions, whilst No. 4 was taken just at the moment of impact; in fact, the ball has just left the club face. Following the series through, it will be noticed that even the head can claim some of the credit of the motive power, as it is taken back on the downward swing, and comes through with the hands and the body, and eventually finishes in the direction in which the ball has taken, as will be seen in No. 5.

19

West Beats East on the Links

CHARLES EVANS, JR., EDGEWATER, IS WESTERN CHAMPION, BUT HE LOST TO EGAN IN THE NATIONAL SEMI-FINALS.

WEST BEATS EAST ON THE LINKS

THE distinguishing features of the fifteenth national amateur golf tournament on the course of the Chicago Golf Club at Wheaton, Illinois, this fall was the elimination of the Eastern representatives. All four of the semi-finallists were Westerners, and only two Easterners, W. J. Travis and T. M. Sherman, lasted into the second match round; Travis alone of the Eastern contingent survived into the third. There he met his downfall at the hands of Gardner, the winner in the finals.

The field was smaller than in many years, only one hundred out of the one hundred and twenty-one entrants starting on the qualifying round. Jerome D. Travers, the champion of the last two years did not appear.

In the semi-finals H. Chandler Egan, twice a national champion, had trouble in disposing of Charles Evans, Jr., present Western champion. The match went the full thirty-six holes, Egan winning by one up. In the other semi-finals, Mason E. Phelps, the Midlothian representative, stuck to Gardner for the full round, although the latter finally came out two up. Phelps was handicapped by a badly blistered hand and could not take the lead from his opponent at any time, although he was always close on his heels.

In the finals Egan made his appearance at this stage of a national tournament for the third time. On the two other occasions he came through successfully, but "the third time's the charm," and the Yale youngster was too strong for the older man, winning by four up and two to play. At no stage of the final round was Egan in the lead, although he had the match squared two or three times.

Gardner, whose home club is Hinsdale, is a new figure in national golf, but if he keeps to his present form and rate of progress he should be a hard man to play against for a number of years to come. His age, nineteen, is greatly in his favor, and steady playing combined with reasonable study of the game should keep him in the front rank for a long time. It would be refreshing to see a youthful golfer of promise for once run true to expectations.

MASON E. PHELPS, MIDLOTHIAN, WHO LOST TO GARDNER IN THE SEMI-FINALS.

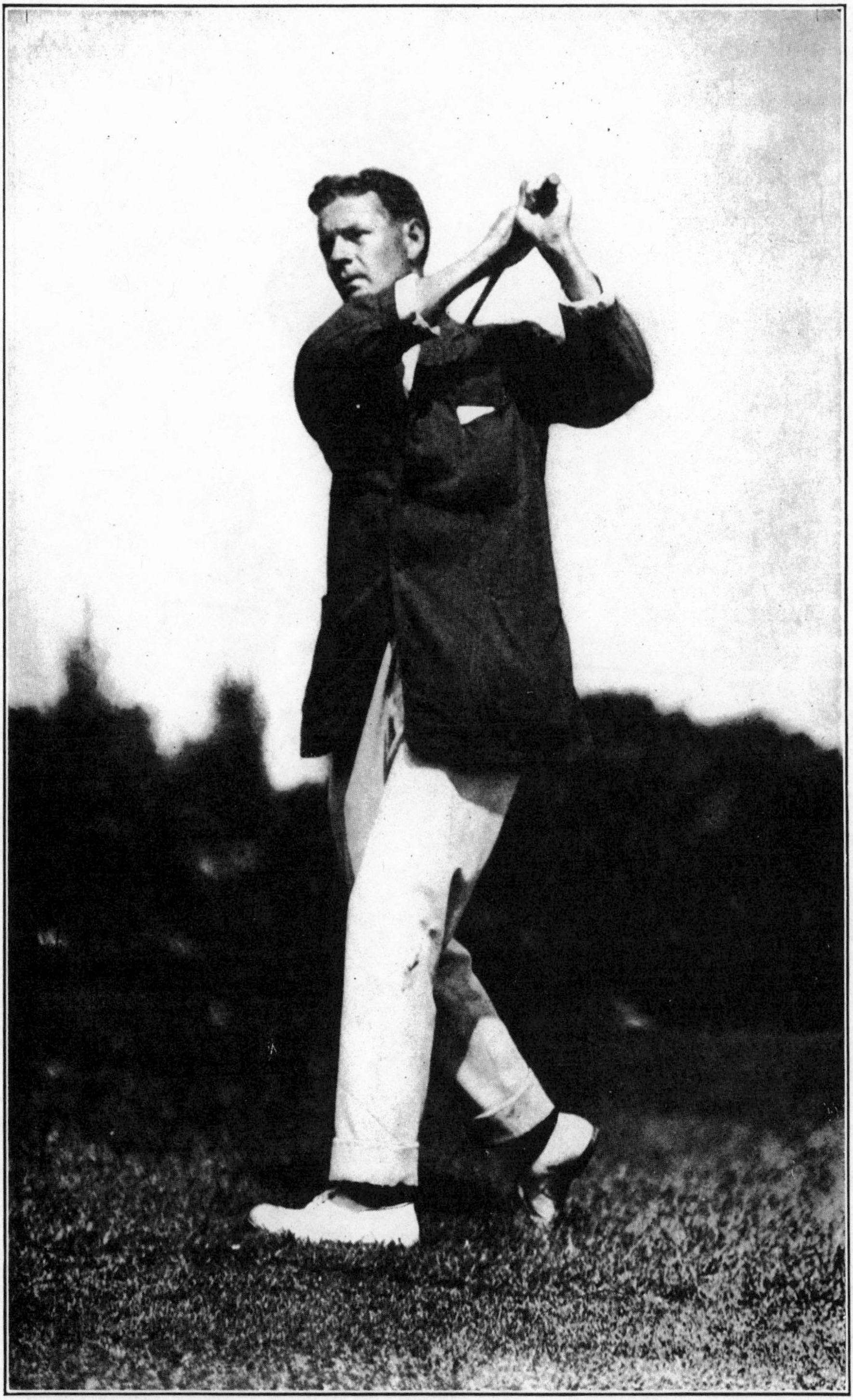

H. CHANDLER EGAN, THREE TIMES A CONTESTANT IN NATIONAL GOLF FINALS, BUT THIS TIME A LOSER.

ROBERT A. GARDNER, THE NINETEEN-YEAR-OLD GOLFER, WHO WON THIS YEAR'S NATIONAL CHAMPIONSHIP.

20

Some Golf Pictures by A. B. Frost

SOME GOLF PICTURES

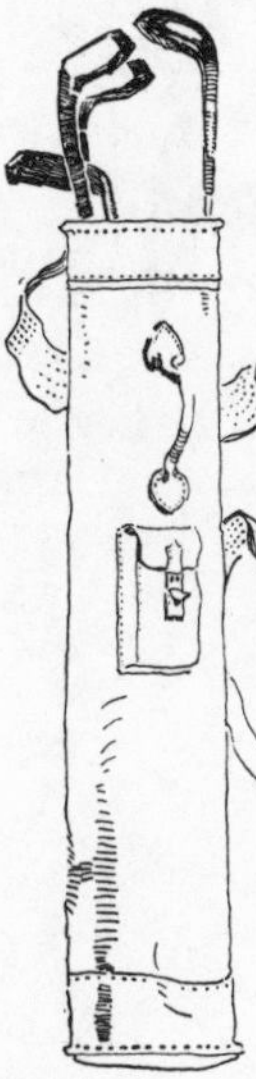

BY A B FROST

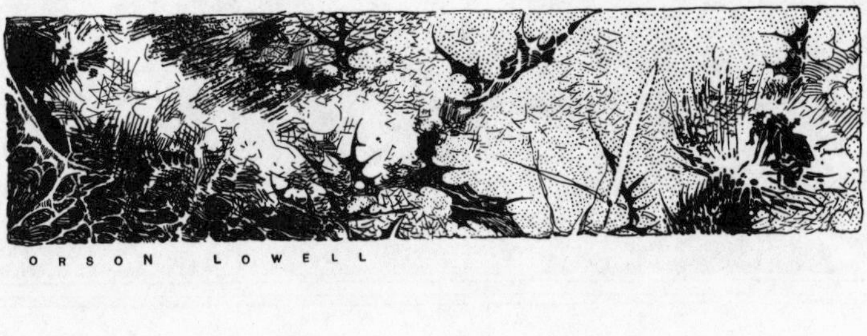

Dormy Two.

“Fore!!”

In a Bunker.

Just Missed It.

Stymie.

A Foursome.

21

Tommy's Master-Stroke

TOMMY'S MASTER-STROKE

By RALPH HENRY BARBOUR

TOMMY was feeling sore. Dickie had beaten him badly that afternoon and Tommy didn't like being beaten at golf, especially by Dickie. Tommy—Tommy Winslow, you know—is quite a dab at golf; he won from Travis once at Garden City; the Duke says Travis wasn't feeling well that day, but Tommy denies it. Dickie isn't much at the game; I downed him once myself, and I'm considered about as rotten as they make 'em. That's what made Tommy rather hot; that and the way Dickie rubbed it in. Tommy's the best-natured chap in the world, but Dickie Boswell was certainly beastly exasperating that night.

We were sitting around in the Duke's room drinking mint juleps. We were all in our pajamas, for it was an awfully warm night; when it *is* hot at Island Lake, it's—worse than that! We'd all four of us been up there three days, staying at the Medford Arms, the big, long hotel on the hill back of the links; you know the joint I mean, the one with the big veranda all around it and red chimneys sticking up here and there through the roof. The boy had just brought up fresh drinks, and we were smoking the last of my Egyptians.

"You see, Tommy, it was that long drive to the tenth hole that queered you, my boy." Dickie took a straw out of his glass and swept it through the air.

"Here, quit sprinkling me with juice!" growled the Duke. He isn't really a duke, you know. That's just a nickname; his real name's Hastings.

"I made the tenth in two and you took four," continued Dickie. "If it hadn't been for that you might have done better, Tommy. It was my master-stroke that beat you."

"Master-stroke be blowed," sputtered Tommy. "It was a bally fluke, that's what it was!"

"That's envy speaking," replied Dickie, wagging his head sadly, "that's not you, Tommy."

"Bally fluke, I said!" reiterated Tommy, sitting up suddenly and spilling his julep on the pillow. "Why, you were the worst surprised man in the country when you found you'd hit the ball! It was the first clean swipe you'd made; you'd been topping and slicing all the afternoon! Master-stroke—!" Tommy gulped—"master-stroke thunder!"

"Then how did I happen to beat you?" asked Dickie sweetly.

"Fool luck!" cried Tommy. "You had fool luck all the way; no one can win against luck! But I'll play you to-morrow for any money you like and give you a handicap; that's what I'll do!"

"Cut it out, you two," groaned the Duke, nibbling his orange peel and looking disgusted. "Neither of you really knows a golf ball from a hen's egg."

"I'll take you," Dickie cried, "but I don't want your old handicap. I'll play you for fifty a side going out and fifty more coming back! And what's the good of waiting until to-morrow? I'll play you right now, Tommy!"

"Ah, that's a sporting proposition for you," said the Duke, looking interested. "Annie, see if Bill the moon's up."

I slid off the bed and went to the window.

"No, darker than Egypt; you couldn't see a ball ten feet away."

"Hard luck," said the Duke, going back to his julep. "I suppose, though, we might get lanterns," he added grinning.

"Poppycock!" said Dickie. He was silent a minute, but the light of battle still shone in his eyes.

"Just wait until to-morrow," threatened Tommy, "and I'll give you a chance to make all the master-strokes you want!"

"I'll tell you what I'll do with you, little Tommy," cried Dickie explosively, "I'll play you from here to the office for fifty dollars a side, loser to pay for damages!"

Tommy stared; then he put his glass on the floor and dropped his cigarette into it.

"Done!" he said. The Duke applauded loudly.

"But isn't it a bit late?" I ventured.

"Late nothing," said Dickie, "it's only half-past eleven. What if it is late?"

"The halls are dark, aren't they?"

"Well, we'll light 'em up then."

"Now, hold on," said the Duke, "let's understand this proposition. I'll act as referee. You're to play from here to the office; the one holing out in the least number of strokes wins the match and takes the money; is that it?"

"Yes," chimed Tommy and Dickie.

"All right. And if you lose a ball you may drop another, eh? And the loser's to put up for breakage. Where are you going to hole out?"

We all thought intensely; at least, I did. Finally I said:

"The ink-well on the office desk!"

"Good eye!" said the Duke. "Only we'll have to put it on the floor. Aniseseed, you be caddy."

My name is Annismead; but nobody ever calls me that; it's generally Annie, sometimes Anise-seed; that's the trouble with having a name that sounds like something else. I got the clubs and the Duke armed himself with a rule book.

"This match is going to be played right," he said.

Dickie put a bath gown on and so did I; but Tommy and the Duke said it was too warm. So Tommy got into a red golf jacket with green sleeves, and the Duke went in his pajamas. We went out into the hall and Tommy teed. Our rooms were on the third floor. The corridors were about twelve feet broad, but there were more than twenty trunks between us and the first corner, and that made it difficult. Tommy got away with a long, low drive that put the ball pretty near the full length of the hall and beyond the turn. Dickie followed and went high, rolling behind a big trunk.

"You'll need a lofter to get out of there," chuckled the Duke. But Dickie swore a little and got back onto the carpet in three. The carpet, by the way, was green, and the Duke said that helped out the illusion. On the next stroke Dickie banged the ball against the door of Number 68 and it flew behind another trunk.

"Well, aren't you coming?" jeered Tommy, who was sticking his head out around the corner.

Dickie swore some more and pushed his ball out into the open, the Duke pretending not to see. Then he banged away at it again and got a good lie just where the hallway turned toward the stairs. Tommy had to make a short approach here, and the score was 2 to 5. From the corner to the stairway was about twenty yards and Dickie called for a wooden putter. He had fine luck and landed right at the head of the stairs. Tommy got his ball about half way, when it rolled up onto a door sill. It took him three to get it away again. Of course, he banged the door a good deal, and pretty soon it opened and a man's head popped out.

"What in thunder's the row?" he asked calmly.

But Tommy was swinging for his next stroke and so we merely told him to shut up. He came out into the hall then and looked on. Tommy's ball rolled against the banisters.

"A good lie, Tommy, my boy," said the Duke. I took up the two bags and started after.

"Say, what's up?" asked the man we had disturbed. I told him; match for fifty a side to the office ink-well.

"Good stuff," said he; and went in and put on a bath robe. When he returned he brought cigarettes and we all lighted up, all except Tommy; he said he never smoked while playing; it was bad for the wind. We were making a good deal of a rumpus, I fancy, about this time; anyhow, doors began to open and people put their heads out and asked silly questions. One old lady wanted to know if it was fire. We told her no, it was golf, and she seemed quite satisfied and went back to bed. But a chap down the hall yelled up to ask if we thought that was a links, and the Duke said:

"Sure, Bill; don't you see the green?" He pointed to the carpet and we all laughed; and the man swore a lot and threatened to have us put out of the house. We could hear the bell ringing down in the lower hall and pretty soon a bellboy came crawling up stairs. The Duke caught him half way up.

"Nothing doing, Bill," he said. "Go back to sleep and tell me about it in the morning when I have money with me."

The boy said "Yes, sir," and went back.

A young chap whose room was at the head of the stairway looked on for awhile and then crawled into a box coat and joined us. It was Dickie's play and he dropped his ball neatly down onto the first landing. Tommy followed and did better yet, for his ball went to that landing and then rolled half way down to the next. But Dickie was after him and reached the next floor below in one. The score was 8 all. The chap in the bath robe and the one in the box coat made a wager of ten dollars a side, the bath robe taking Tommy and the box coat Dickie.

Tommy had a lot of trouble finishing the flight and reaching the second floor; when he got a good lie close to the banisters at the head of the next flight the score was 8 to 11 in favor of Dickie, and Tommy was swearing like a trooper.

"I'll raise the stakes another fifty," said Dickie, grinning.

"Take you," said Tommy, like a little man.

"Can't be done," the Duke said. "But you can make a side bet." So they did; and the ink-well meant a hundred to the one who made it in the best score. The excitement was getting intense. Doors were opening and closing all over the shop and bells were ringing and folks were asking what in something was up. We told them the truth, but, generally, they didn't believe it and had to come and see for themselves. So pretty soon we had about a dozen spectators, all making suggestions and laying wagers. Dickie was a prime favorite now and the best odds were ten dollars to six; I took some of that myself, getting the Tommy end without trouble. You see, I knew that Tommy was better at putting than Dickie and knew besides that he was feeling sore about the "master-stroke" and was resolved to win out. About that time the man in the bath robe began backing Tommy for all he could get. He laid about fifty dollars and then took Tommy aside and whispered to him. No one noticed it except me, I fancy, for the rest of the bunch was watching Dickie. The bellboy crawled upstairs again and said he was going to rooms 28, 36, 42, 61, and a lot more. We sent him back for ice water; told him the occupants of the rooms were thirsty, and promised him a dollar if he'd take twenty minutes to get it. He was a sensible kid and did it.

Dickie slammed his ball hard with the idea of hitting the wall at the turn and rolling. But it didn't work and he got no farther than the first landing. Downstairs some one was thumping the office gong to beat the symphony orchestra and a stout, baldheaded man on the floor above was dancing up and down and talking a blue streak. We told him to go back to bed and be good, but he wouldn't; wanted to know how in smoke he could sleep with a lot of damphools raising Ned around the place. The Duke told him that he didn't know what the answer was and offered to lay him two to one in fivers that there wasn't any. The baldheaded chap was a sport all through and took the Duke for twenty. That calmed him down and he sat at the top of the stairs and tried to think what the answer was.

The score was 9 to 11 now, and Tommy's play. His gutty was right alongside the railing. He took an iron putter and gave the ball a little tap that sent it between the spindles and down the well; we heard it hit the floor below and bounce around. Everybody stared; everybody except the bath robe chap; he grinned: so did every one else after a moment; everybody except Dickie.

"You can drop another ball there, you know," he said to Tommy. Tommy shook his head.

"No, thanks," he replied sweetly.

"But you have to!"

"Not a bit of it, Dickie; it's your play."

"What—what——?" Dickie stuttered.

"It's all right," answered Tommy; "that's my master-stroke."

"But you can't do that!" shouted Dickie. "I'll leave it to the Duke! He can't do that, can he, Duke?"

The Duke opened his rule book and stood under the light, pretending to search the pages. Everybody was laughing except Dickie, and Tommy, and the Duke. Dickie was frothing at the mouth; Tommy was merely grinning pleasantly; the Duke was frowning while he turned the leaves. Finally he said:

"There appears to be no rule bearing on the point in dispute. It is very thoughtless of the committee, but it can't be helped. As there is nothing forbidding the play, I presume it to be allowable, and so decide."

We all howled, and Dickie ranted and went on terribly. But we shut him up and the play went on. Dickie was mad clean through, and as a result he slammed around for five minutes. Of course, he followed Tommy's example and dropped his ball down the well, but he had a lot of trouble getting it through between the spindles, and when he did the score was in Tommy's favor, 12 to 13. The Dickie chaps tried to hedge, but there was nothing much doing. We all trooped down the last flight and met a sleepy-looking man in his shirt sleeves who said he was the night clerk and what was the trouble?

We explained the matter to him at some length, as he was a very dense sort of chap; and even when he got it through his head he tried to make objections; said we were disturbing the whole house and a lot of poppycock like that. But the Duke called him "dear Bill," and smoothed him down, and we went on. The two balls were lying side by side between the stairs and the elevator. No one knew which was which, but, as the Duke pointed out, it didn't matter. From there to the desk was about sixty feet. We got the ink-well down and placed it half way between the desk and the other side of the lobby and built up around it with the register and a lot of cards, blotters, and note paper. The night clerk turned in and helped and proved to be a very accommodating sort. When we had finished we had a very decent hole.

Tommy got to work with a putter and rolled his ball to within ten feet. Dickie managed a better lie, a foot or so nearer, and where he had a nice ascent to the ink-well by way of the blotting papers. Then we all made a big circle around the two and watched. The night clerk wanted to pour the ink out of the well first; said it might get on the floor. But we reminded him of the blotting papers and refused to have the green disturbed.

The score was 13 to 14 in favor of Tommy. Every one smoked hard. The annunciator began to buzz again, so the night clerk went over and did something to it. Dickie was vilely nervous and on the first put went two feet wide, and swore.

"Better make it in two and be sure of holing," some one suggested. But Dickie thought he couldn't spare two and tried again from a distance of about four feet. The ball started up the ascent all right but was stopped by the edge of the register, about six inches from the ink-well.

"Sixteen," said the Duke.

Dickie straddled the book and blotters and things and shortened his grip. "Remarkable stance, eh?" murmured the chap in the box coat. Then the ball rolled and the ink spurted out.

"Seventeen," said the Duke; and every one clapped loudly.

Dickie fished the gutty out of the ink-well with a toothpick and stood aside, watching Tommy anxiously. Tommy had four to tie and three to win; and it looked like hard work to most of us; but they didn't all know Tommy's putting. Tommy went to work very carefully, picking a piece of lint out of the path and finding the line by means of a dark spot in one of the oak boards. Then he tapped the ball gently and it rolled straight for the hole. Every one held his breath. When the ball reached the foot of the little hill it was going so slowly that it didn't seem as though it could get half way toward the top. But it did; it went over the strewn cards and made the writing paper, going slower and slower, seeming always on the point of stopping but not doing it. Straight for the ink-well it rolled and right on the very edge came to a pause. Tommy went toward it to drop it in when, presto, over it went of itself!

Then every one clapped and shouted and shook hands with Tommy. Dickie was feeling pretty well cut up, but there's nothing mean about him, so up he marched with the rest of them. Tommy shook hands and clapped him on the shoulder.

"It was that master-stroke of mine beat you, Dickie," he said grinning.

"The match goes to Mr. Winslow," announced the Duke, "the score, 14 to 17." Then we all cheered some more, and the chap in the bath gown went over and talked to the night clerk. At first the latter shook his head; but in the end he led the way down the corridor.

"Gentlemen," said the bath robe chap, "we are going to have liquid refreshments in honor of the victor in the most unique golf match of history. After you, gentlemen!"

So we all trooped into the bar and turned on the lights and sat around in pajamas and dressing gowns and blankets and drank Tommy's health. And just when the bath robe chap, who had won about ninety dollars, had finished a speech of congratulation the door was quietly opened and in walked the old codger with a bald head.

"Hello, Bill," said the Duke, "you're just in time."

"Thank you, with all the pleasure in the world," said the other. "And I'll thank you, too, for that twenty, sir."

"Which twenty is that?" asked the Duke, who had forgotten the wager.

"Why, sir, you bet me twenty to ten that there was no answer to the question."

"What question, Bill?"

"The question, sir, as nearly as I recall it was this: 'How in blazes can I sleep while a lot of damned idiots are raising Ned in the corridors?'"

"Ah, to be sure," replied the Duke. "I recollect. And there is an answer?"

"Yes, sir, and I have found it."

"And what is it?"

"The answer, sir," replied the old chap soberly, "is, Take a narcotic!"

"The money is yours, Bill," answered the Duke, laughing. "Now have a drink."

The old chap joined us, and the night clerk opened some more bottles. When the glasses were refilled the Duke got up.

"Gentlemen, to the Master-Stroke!"

We drank standing.

22

Miss Griscom's Game of Golf

MISS GRISCOM'S GAME OF GOLF

BY ARTHUR POTTOW

WITH PHOTOGRAPHS BY T. C. TURNER

IT seems to be generally conceded that the standard of play amongst the women golfers has advanced, and that it requires great skill now to win the championship. One evidence of this is the two successive defeats of Miss Beatrix Hoyt—three times champion of America—in 1899 and 1900.

Miss Hoyt has not retrograded in the slightest degree. She shows the same admirable form that enabled her admirers for many years to claim, with good reason, that she was in a class by herself. It simply means that the others have advanced, until now there are so many woman golfers in the

MISS GRISCOM.

APPROACH SHOT.

TOP OF SWING.

front rank that it is becoming increasingly difficult to pick out in advance the winner of the great national event. Miss Genevieve Hecker, Mrs. Caleb F. Fox, Miss Eunice Terry, and at least half a dozen others are good enough to win the championship, and so equally are many of the players matched that it seems as if the luck of the game only determines the result.

Very few experts selected Miss Frances Griscom, of the Merion Cricket Club, Philadelphia, for the honor of being woman champion for 1900. This was not because of lack of faith in her merits as a golfer, for to have doubted this would have bee flying in the face of facts. In ever one of the five tournaments played for th Cox trophy, Miss Griscom has qualified, Mis Hoyt being the only other golfer who ca make the same claim. In 1895, the first yea Miss Griscom played in a championship con test, she tied at 102 in the qualifying roun for the second medal with Mrs. Willian Shippen, of Morris County. In 1897 and 189 she reached the semi-finals, and in 1899 sh was put out in the first match-play round b her neighbor, Miss Elsie Cassatt. This is long and consistent record which certain ly entitles her to friendly consideratio at the hands of the critics. But the

IRON-SHOT—FINISH OF SWING.

new she had been in Europe for nearly three nonths, during which time she had not even een a golf-course, and they were afraid that his rest had spoiled her chances of success.

As a matter of fact, it had, no doubt, maerially helped her, because she was saved rom falling a victim to the disease of being ver-golfed, which killed off so many candiates at Shinnecock for national honors, and articularly Miss Genevieve Hecker, who tood on an equality as a popular favorite vith Miss Beatrix Hoyt.

Knowing the game thoroughly, all that was ecessary for Miss Griscom to do was to obain a few days' preliminary practice over the hampionship course, and this was quite

FINISH OF SWING.

BRASSEY SHOT—FINISH OF SWING.

enough to fit her for the week's trying ordeal. She never played steadier or better golf in her life than she did in the preliminary round, and it was probably nothing but her unfamiliarity with the course which caused her to finish two strokes more than Miss Hoyt, who was on her native heath.

The Shinnecock course is an extremely difficult one for a golfer who has been accustomed to play on an inland course, every stroke having to be played absolutely clean, but Miss Griscom soon showed that she had mastered this difficulty. It was apparent, too, that she had lengthened her game, which was always somewhat a weak spot with her,

FINISH OF DRIVE.

without falling off in her short game, which was always her strong point. At Shinnecock, too, she simply excelled in putting, and perhaps it was to her steadiness in this respect that she owed her success. In one game only was she at all weak in her putting, and that was in the match with Miss Terry, which enabled the latter to halve the game on the home green. Her iron play was splendid, and time and again her approach shots excited the admiration of the gallery, as she laid her ball dead on the green.

It seems a pity that with all this excellence she should be unable to acquire a different style of driving from the tee. She has a tremendous swing, and at the finish of her drive it is no uncommon thing to see her pull her self completely off her feet. Under these cir cumstances it would be reasonable to expec that she would slice or pull her ball badly but somehow this seldom happened, the gen eral direction of her tee shots being for th most part sufficiently accurate.

No attempt at a follow through is appar ent in her driving, and therefore her succes from the tee must have been due to luck to very great extent. This may at any time de sert her, and therefore it is advisable for he to make every effort to modify and perfec her style. The failure of Miss Ruth Under hill, last year's champion, should be an ob

PUTTING.

ject-lesson to her in this respect. She was put out in the first round at Shinnecock, due to weakness in her long game, the result of as bad a style as it is possible to conceive.

For a full swing Miss Margaret Curtis, of the Essex County Club, Manchester, and for a three-quarter swing Miss Hoyt, furnish excellent examples for imitation. The former was the surprise of the tournament, by reason of fine, free style, and terrific long game; and full as was her swing, she was steady as a rock at the finish, following through in good style, and using her wrists to obtain extra driving power. It seems a pity that she cannot use her irons better, but she is very young, and a year's practice at the short game should make her a formidable candidate at next year's contest.

For general all-round excellence Miss Hoyt still reigns supreme, for she is strong at all points of the game. She uses a short swing only, yet few can outdrive her, and in her iron play and on the green she is in the same class as Miss Griscom. Of course, as the latter won the championship, she must be accepted as the premier golfer of the year, but if the two should meet, it is probable that the superiority of Miss Hoyt at the long game would bring victory to her.

MISS UNDERHILL AT FINISH OF SWING.

MISS UNDERHILL AT FINISH OF SHOT.

Miss Caroline Livingstone, of the Westbrook, drove about as long a ball as Miss Margaret Curtis, but was unsteady like her, and so neither of them gained to any appreciable extent by their driver and brassey work. Mrs. Caleb F. Fox is as good a golfer as there is in this country. Notwithstanding Miss Livingstone's terrific driving, Mrs. Fox put her out by 5 up and 3 to play, and was only beaten by Miss Hoyt by 1 up after a desperate fight. Miss Hecker was undoubtedly not playing the game that made her the winner at the Women's Metropolitan Tournament at Morris County earlier in the summer, showing unusual signs of weakness in her short game, and so she fell a victim in the second round to Miss Eunice Terry, who played consistently throughout the week, and in good style, as she always does.

Miss Hoyt won by 2 up and 1 to play in 1896, 5 up and 4 to play in 1897, and 5 up and 3 to play in 1898, while Miss Underhill beat Mrs. Fox in 1899 by 2 up and 1 to play. This year Miss Griscom won by 6 up and 4 to play.

23

Canadian Golf

BY JOHN P ROCHE.

W. W. WATSON,
President and Captain of the Royal Montreal Golf Club.

THE delineation of preposterous little Dutchmen on preposterous Dutch pottery, wielding hugely disproportionate clubs, may, in the very long ago, have given rise to the idea that the royal and ancient game of golf is of Hollandish origin, but the generally accepted idea is that golf is as Scotch as curling; and there is never a loyal Scot, and Canada is full of them, but will lay claim to a first mortgage on these two finest pastimes the ingenuity of man ever invented.

But that is not the question for discussion here. Golf in Canada is the subject. It is no wise strange, seeing how deeply tinctured with Scotch, who are still actuated and moved to a greater or less extent by the traditions of the British Isles, Canada is, that golf should have found an early home there; and it is a fact of which latter-day golfers are justly proud that the Royal Montreal Golf Club was twice as old as the patriarch of clubs in the United States, St. Andrew's, of Yonkers, is now, when the first course in the States was laid out.

As far as reliable information is available, golf was played in Montreal between thirty and forty years ago by a few enthusiasts who happily brought with them to the new world the healthy ideas of sport imbibed in the land of their fathers. In those days there was a common called Logan's Farm, that would have delighted the heart of any golfer. Logan's Farm has been transformed into the picturesque Logan's Park, but there are still with us a few gentlemen who speak with feeling of those good old days in the sixties. If Mr. W. M. Ramsay or Mr. R. R. Grind-

OLD ROYAL MONTREAL GOLF CLUB.

lay could be prevailed upon to write his reminiscences, they would supply the golfing world with some very interesting reading matter anent them.

The golfer is gregarious, and golf naturally led to organized clubs, the first of which, the Royal Montreal Golf Club, will celebrate its twenty-fifth anniversary on the 4th of November next, a glorious fourth. In an old book of rules belonging to the club, the following entry fills the first page :

"A meeting convened to arrange the preliminaries of a golf club, for playing the royal and ancient game of golf on Mount Royal Park, was held on the fourth day of November, 1873, when it was resolved that the club be called 'The Montreal Golf Club.' The officers for the year were appointed: Alex. Dennistoun, president; W. M. Ramsay, vice-president; D. D. Sidey, treasurer; Jos. Collins, secretary. The rules of St. Andrew's Club (Scotland) were adopted. According to the club minute-book there were also present at this initial meeting Hon. M. Aylmer, J. G. Sidey, H. McDougall, and T. Holland."

The gentleman, however, who is recognized as the father of golf in Canada, that is, who fostered and encouraged the game, and was the means of starting the Royal Montreal Golf Club, was the Mr. Alexander Dennistoun who was elected the club's first president. He recently died in Edinburgh, but for many years was a resident of Canada. Mr. Dennistoun had played in his early days over the famous links of St. Andrew's and Musselburgh, and was a member of several other leading clubs in Scotland and England. He was not only an enthusiastic player, but an excellent exponent of all the intricacies of the game. Among other early players were such men as Hon. Geo. Drummond, J. K. Oswald, F. Braidwood, Eric Maim, Jno. Taylor, Homer Taylor, Rev Dr. Campbell, Rev. Canon Ellegood C. C. Foster, and R. M. Esdaile. Among the younger generation may be mentioned Mr. W. Wallace Watson, the present captain ; Rev. Dr. Barclay, F. Stancliffe, W. J. S. Gordon, J. R. Meeker, K. R. Macpherson, J. Hutton Balfour, G. W. MacDougall, J. L. Morris, Q. C., A. H. Harris, W. A. Fleming, Alex. Macpherson, Rev. W. W. McCuaig, A. A. Wilson, Rev. Mr. Dobson, Jno. Dunlop, Fayette Brown, Dr. Macdonald, Dr. Andrew Macphail, and A. Piddington.

ROSEDALE GOLF CLUB HOUSE

Until the autumn of 1896 the club played over that part of Mount Royal Park known as Fletcher's Field. Owing to the increase in the number of people visiting the park and consequent danger to them from flying golf-balls, it was then decided to acquire the property now occupied by the club at Dixie. This step necessitated, for proprietary reasons, the conversion of the club into a company. This marked a new phase in the club's career. The new grounds, which are laid out as a nine-hole course, are rapidly getting into shape ; indeed, they were sufficiently improved last season to admit of the Royal Canadian Golf Association meeting, including the contest for the amateur championship of Canada, taking place there in September last.

The disused links over Fletcher's Field were eagerly snapped up by the Metropolitan Golf Club, a young but enthusiastic organization.

In 1892 the Montreal Ladies' Golf Club was formed, with nearly a hundred members, among the founders and first officers being Mrs. George H. Drummond, President; Mrs. H. Vincent Meredith, Secretary; Mrs. W. W. Watson, Mrs. Halton, Misses P. Young, A. Lamb, and A. Peterson. Since this club was formed the membership has largely increased, and the ladies are even more enthusiastic than the gentlemen.

The next year after the formal launching of the Montreal club the Quebec club was founded, and it was two years later (1876) these two pioneer organizations met. This is the first golf-club match on record in America, and according to Mr. Morris "it was played in May or June, 1876, Quebec winning with twelve holes to their credit." A second match seems to have been played in the following September, of which we have a record of the teams. As it is the first recorded golfing event of the continent, it is worthy of a republication to a wider circle than its first issue reached:

Quebec		*vs.*	*Montreal.*	
Mr. Scott	0	vs.	Dr. Argyle Robertson (Edinburgh)	4
Mr. Thomas Scott	0	vs.	Mr. Dennistoun	13
Mr. McNaughton	4	vs.	Mr. D. D. Sidey	0
Mr. A. Nicoll	3	vs.	Mr. J. G. Sidey	0
Mr. C. F. Smith	0	vs.	Mr. J. K. Oswald	2
	7			19

Montreal thus won by 12 holes. The draw was played off in Montreal, the home team winning by 13 holes, and so the Royal Montreal Golf Club won its first club victory.

Individual and match play was then of course, as it is indeed now, the backbone of the pastime; and some few years ago Mr. John L. Morris wrote a very interesting sketch, from which the following extract is made as illustrating what was considered good play in those early days: "A match was played on November 26th, 1876, between Messrs. Taylor and J. K. Oswald. The play was about the best ever seen on the Montreal links. Mr. Taylor made the 18 holes in 115, Mr. Oswald 105 strokes."

It may surprise some of our readers, whose ideas of Canada and its climate may have been gathered from the perusal of "Our Lady of the Snows," to note the date of this match, November 26th. It will, perhaps, surprise them more to learn that, the next year, play was continued until New Year's Day.

But to turn from the lesser-chronicled individual play to club play, annual matches between the Montreal and Quebec clubs have, ever since 1877, been fixtures eagerly looked forward to.

Several valuable prizes are competed for every year, among them being the Drummond Silver Cup, the Sidney Medal, and the Burnett Cup. The Dennistoun Scratch Medal is a much-coveted trophy. Last year it was won by Mr. T. R. Henderson, the acknowledged champion of the Province of Quebec, and the year previous was captured by Mr. Wallace Watson, one of the keenest golfers in the country.

Quebec's golf links form part of the historic battle-ground, the Plains of Abraham. Scarlet coats are still numerous there, where Wolfe and Montcalm led, but the contest now is a bloodless one. As has before been pointed out, the Quebec Club was founded in 1874, but there is no doubt in the minds of old curlers that the game was played many years previously by a relative of old Tom Morris, one Mr. Hunter, who with several companions negotiated the somewhat difficult links on the Plains. One great advantage of the Quebec links is the unparalleled beauty and grandeur of the scenery, and their historic interest is enhanced by the fact that some of the hazards are formed by the ruins of Montcalm's fortifications. There are fifteen holes, the first three being played twice to complete the eighteen. The grounds are of a markedly sporting character, and all golfers are welcome in the ancient capital of the Dominion, come they from the West, the East, or yet the South.

In 1892 a Ladies' Golf Club was formed in affiliation with the Quebec Golf Club. Special prizes are played for over a nine-hole course, in May, June and September; all three competitions were won last year by Miss Sewell.

When Montreal and Quebec golf clubs

have been considered, the other Canadian clubs seem by comparison to be growths of yesterday, with, perhaps, the exception of Niagara, which was founded in 1882.

The Niagara links, which are splendidly situated on the government reservation, within a short distance from the dépot, consist of eighteen holes. The ground is broken and sandy, and the course a very sporty one. The International Trophy is the leading club prize competed for annually. It was won last year by Mr. G. T. Brown, of the London Golf Club.

In point of antiquity Kingston comes next. This club first came into existence in 1886. It has a course of thirteen holes and a club-house near the Military College. Associated with it is a ladies' branch, the combined membership being about one hundred. The principal club prize is the Hewat Trophy, which is held by Mr. C. F. Smith. The course runs along the line of the Grand Trunk Railway.

From 1886 to 1891 there were no additions to the number of golf clubs in Canada. Then the Ottawa Club was organized, the Hon. E. Dewdney being elected president. Play was begun in the fields near Rideau rifle-ranges and on Sandy Hill. A club-house was erected on a lot of land given by Mr. Magee, and in a very short time the club numbered seventy members. The succeeding presidents were Major-General Herbert, 1892, Lieut.-Colonel Irwin, 1893,-4,-5,-6; A. Z. Palmer, 1897, and A. Simpson, 1898. This last gentleman had served as secretary since the formation of the club. In 1894 the present Governor-General, Lord Aberdeen, replaced Lord Stanley as patron.

The first tournament for the amateur championship of Canada was held on the Ottawa links in June, 1895. His Excellency had given a magnificent silver challenge cup. The championship was won by Mr. T. A. Harley. Shortly after the commencement of the season of 1896 it was found necessary to abandon the club-house and links hitherto used, and links were obtained on the Chelsea Road, and the old Bingham homestead was occupied as a club-house. A course of twelve holes was laid out, crossing the Chelsea Road and the railway twice in the round, and the course remains practically the same as used at present. This year Mr A. Simpson succeeded Mr. A. Z. Palmer as president, and the secretaryship vacated by the former was taken by Lieut.-Colonel Irwin. The club now has a membership of sixty-five gentlemen and forty-eight ladies, of whom the majority are playing members. The club-house has been refitted and furnished, and very many improvements have been made in the links and putting-greens. Handicaps are held every Saturday afternoon, and the ladies have been accorded the use of the links every morning except Saturday, and on Monday, Tuesday, Thursday, and Friday afternoons.

The Rosedale Golf Club was the pioneer in Toronto, having been organized in 1893. It is now most active and progressive, having almost three hundred members, of whom nearly half are ladies. The course is a magnificent one, within easy distance of the city, and the hazards comprise everything from bushes to ravines. The club holds several valuable trophies, and three monthly handicaps for medals are held.

A boom was reached in 1894, when five new clubs were organized, namely, London, Toronto, Winnipeg, Hamilton and Stony Mountain. Lieut.-Colonel Bedson was the gentleman who founded the club at the last place, laying out a links consisting of nine holes, covering about three miles of country, the nature of which gives many opportunities. Later on four more holes were added; bowlders, ploughed land, and badger-holes made some pretty pronounced hazards. This was the introduction of the royal game into Manitoba; and in the same year Mr. John Balsillie and Mr. Oswald took the initiative in Winnipeg, and a club was immediately formed, which at present has a membership of nearly one hundred and a nine-hole course.

Toronto was the next city to take up the game. The Toronto Golf Club was incorporated in 1894, and now hasupward of one hundred and fifty on the roll. The course is eighteen holes, over which the amateur record is seventy-five. The professional record, held by the green-keeper, Arthur Smith, is seventy-two. Several valuable trophies are held by this club.

The London Golf Club was organized in 1894, but only laid out last year. It has been remarkably active ever since. It now has about fifty members; and adjoining the London Golf Club is the Ladies' Golf Club, which has seventy-five players on the roll.

In October, 1894, a golf club was organized at Hamilton by Senator D. McInnis, Messrs. A. G. Ramsay, Geo. Hope, A. D. Stewart, H. D. Braithwaite, P. Banker and M. Pattison. In 1897 the club was incorporated, and now is in a very flourishing condition, having over a hundred members and a mile and three-quarters course.

The year 1895 saw the completion of the trans-continental circuit by the establishment of a club at Victoria, B. C., while Cobourg, Ont., St. Andrew's, N. B., and Kincardine were added to the list.

The Victoria, B. C., Club is the possessor of an excellent course—nearly three miles from the city, but the distance is more than compensated for by the beauty of the surroundings. There are one hundred members, including lady players, and the course is a full eighteen-hole one.

In Cobourg, a nine-hole course was laid out this spring, and already the greens are in excellent condition. The club has nearly one hundred members, and a club-house will soon be erected.

The Murray Bay Golf Club, beautifully situated at a charming summer resort on the St. Lawrence, is, to all intents and purposes, a summer club, play being only indulged in during the warm months. The course covers a distance of about three miles. There are usually a large number of lady members.

At St. Andrew's, N. B., the Algonquin Club has its headquarters. The links are on the shore of Passamaquoddy Bay. The course is a full eighteen holes. This is another distinctly summer resort club.

The Kincardine Club is not possessed of a large membership, but it has plenty of enthusiasm. A nine-hole course is laid out over pasture-land.

ROYAL MONTREAL GOLF CLUB.

The year 1896 saw Oshawa, Lennoxville, Sherbrooke and Halifax come into the fold. The membership of the Oshawa Club is not large, but there are a very well-appointed club-house and a nine-hole course. A ladies' club adjoins the gentlemen's.

Lennoxville and Sherbrooke both have a large number of golfers, and in the case of the latter, a ladies' club is attached.

There is every prospect of an excellent year for the Halifax Golf Club. The Studley grounds have again been

ON DIXIE LINKS.

secured. The links are not the best in the world, but they will be considerably improved this year. The course is one of nine holes.

Fredericton and St. John were the only additions to the ranks of golf clubs in Canada last year. The former has a very attractive nine-hole course. In St. John the golfers are blessed with a splendid course almost in the city. As far as surface of ground is concerned, it is much too short, but it will be improved.

The latest golf club to be added to the list, is Brockville, where a new club was organized in the middle of April last.

Such is a brief outline of the history of golfing in Canada; but a word is necessary about the Royal Canadian Golf Association, which was founded in 1896.

The associate clubs of the Royal Canadian Golf Association are: Royal Montreal G. C., Quebec G. C., Toronto G. C., Kingston G. C., Ottawa G. C., Rosedale G. C. (Toronto), Winnipeg G. C., London G. C., Hamilton G. C.,

TORONTO GOLF CLUB HOUSE.

J. S. GORDON.

Niagara G. C., Toronto County and Hunt Club, Cobourg G. C.

The allied clubs are: Lennoxville, Oshawa and Murray Bay.

In 1896 the amateur championship of Canada was won by Mr. Stewart Gillespie, Quebec Golf Club, and in 1897 by Mr. W. A. H. Kerr, Toronto Golf Club.

As to the interprovincial matches, according to a resolution passed last year,

MR. HENDERSON.

"The maximum number of players in the match between the Provinces of Quebec and Ontario shall be twenty players from each Province, and in order to constitute a match at least ten players from each Province must compete. Either Province failing to produce ten players shall be considered in default, and the Inter-Provincial Cup shall be awarded to the team complying, as to number of players, with the above conditions."

The following table shows the result of the interprovincial matches since the beginning:

1882	Won by Quebec at Montreal by 18 holes.
1883	Won by Ontario at Niagara by 30 holes.
1884	Won by Ontario at Montreal by 5 holes.
1885-'86	No matches.
1887	Won by Quebec at Montreal by 40 holes.
1888 '91	No matches.
1892	Won by Quebec at Montreal by 51 holes.
1893	Won by Ontario at Ottawa by 30 holes.
1894	Won by Quebec at Montreal by 37 holes.
1895	Won by Ontario at Toronto by 47 holes.
1896	Won by Quebec at Quebec by 20 holes.
1897	Won by Ontario at Montreal by 6 holes.

GORDON MC DOUGALL.

Mr. Stewart Gordon, secretary of the Royal Canadian Golf Association, lately received a letter from Mr. Kerr, secretary of the United States Golf Association, stating that the United States Executive Committee had formally accepted the invitation of the Royal Canadian Association to play a match in Toronto on or about October 1st; and, of course, this event is looked forward to with great interest by all golfers in this country. There is every prospect also of some of the local clubs of the States accepting the invitations which have been sent to them from localities in Canada, so that we may see not only international but inter-city and inter-club matches in the coming season.

24
The Strokes of Golf

THE STROKES OF GOLF.

PUTTING.

By Walter J. Travis, Metropolitan Champion.

IT is a matter of common knowledge that I have perhaps experimented with more kinds of putters than any other player in this country, and should therefore be expected to have at least learned what not to do.

I have tried wooden putters, gun-metal putters, straight-faced putters, cylindrical putters, mallet-headed putters, putting cleeks, cleeks, left-handed putting cleeks—in short, the whole family of every conceivable kind of weapon that human ingenuity has evolved for the purpose. I have tried them all in every imaginable position—off the left leg, standing square, off the right leg, facing the hole; have had them equipped with long and short shafts with straight faces, with varying degrees of loft and, antithetically, with the face turned in—and, at times, have putted extraordinarily well with each and every member of the tribe. I have tried putting with cut, with a follow through, with a chip, with a tap; with the hands taken well away from the ball before striking it, and the reverse; with light grip, with firm grip, with the left hand only, and again the right gripping firmly—all with varying degrees of success.

The sum of it all is, that my experience shows conclusively that the really good putter is largely born, not made, and is inherently endowed with a good eye and a tactile delicacy of grip which are denied the ordinary run of mortals. At the same time, less favored players may, by the adoption of methods which have stood the test of actual experience, materially improve their game.

There is no royal road to the hole. Some men play well in the most awkward and contorted positions—positions which seem to invite a lack of success. Their success, however, proves that by whatever means the result is brought about, one thing is clear—the face of the club must have met the ball squarely at the crucial moment of sending it on its errand—which is the essence of good putting. That's about all there is in it: to strike the ball truly in the center and with the necessary strength. There is no mystery about it. If the ball is struck exactly at the central point in line with the hole, by the middle of the club, with the face of it at right angles to the line to the hole, and kept so for an inch or so after the moment of impact, it is bound to go straight.

This double-barreled problem, however, of striking the ball truly and with the requisite strength is not by any means so easy as it would appear. While wrestling with the question of true striking, the equally important matter of force to be applied intrudes itself, and it is extremely difficult to consistently succeed in getting both factors to work harmoniously. More often it happens that when the line is right the force applied is either too weak or too strong—generally the former—and when the force is right the line is wrong.

This matter of strength is infinitely harder to regulate and control than that of striking truly; and little can be said which would aid this weakness other than that the player, having measured the distance with his eye, should invariably endeavor to allow the muscles to act upon the information so conveyed. After the eye has told the muscles what they are to do, leave the matter entirely to them. Too much employment of the eye is ruinous to good putting. The first estimate is usually the correct one. Prolonged studying of the distance or the character of the turf induces conflicting opinions as to the necessary strength, and this halting, undecided state of mind is fatal. There is no definiteness of purpose; the player is see-sawed between the prospects of being away over the hole or equally short, and with such vacillating mental forces at work the stroke is usually a failure.

Putting is largely mental, and on this account becomes so difficult. The novice who has not back of him recollections of scores of missed putts a couple of feet or so from the hole is more apt to bring off a putt of this distance, especially on a keen green, than the other fellow. He is not troubled with any thought of being a yard or more away on a miss, and in blissful ignorance confidently bangs away and holes.

Confidence is a prerequisite to good putting. Some players naturally possess this quality in a greater degree than others—and accordingly are better putters. This heaven-sent gift may, however, be cultivated and developed to some extent—primarily by at all times allowing the hands to be strictly governed by the first impression produced by the eye in the calculation of the necessary force to be exerted, and secondarily by practice, preferably by playing against an opponent, which is far more valuable than solitary practice.

No. 1.—Ball Nearer Left Foot.

No. 2.—Ball Midway Between Feet.

No. 3.—Ball Nearer Right Foot.

From Instantaneous Photographs.

We all know how easy it is to knock your ball in with the back of the putter three or four feet away when the hole is won or lost—when it doesn't make a particle of difference if the ball doesn't go in. It is pretty much the same when putting alone. The metal attitude is different. It is so easy to run a putt down in one when you have two for the hole, and equally easy to take two when you have one for a half to win. "Why is it, papa," asked the little girl, "that when you have two for the hole you always go out in one, and when you have one for the hole you always take two?" Confidence on one hand, and lack of it on the other. Therefore, too much solitary practice is not conducive to good putting when under the strain of a tight match.

There are putters and putters. If a man putts poorly it isn't so much the fault of the club as of the putter—"the man behind the gun." A naturally good putter will putt fairly well with any old weapon. At the same time, I am of the opinion that the best all-round results can be secured by a putting cleek, with a pretty short shaft. The slight loft on the face enables the player to strike the ball more firmly—and firmness and decision are here invaluable. The face, being somewhat laid back, imparts a back spin to the ball, which is very helpful on a keen green. This is due to the fact that the ball is struck below the center, and the spin asserts itself in a large degree after the more dominant propelling power of the stroke exhausts itself. The result is that the ball does not travel so far as it would off the regular straight-faced putter. In the latter case the point of impact is just a shade above the center, and a rotary spin is given the ball in the direction of the hole. It will thus be apparent that with the straight-faced club the measure of force applied to cover a given distance is less than that employed with a putting cleek, and greater delicacy is required. The fear that one may overrun the hole on a keen green often leads to a weak, flabby sort of stroke, lacking both direction and strength. Weak strokes of this kind are not so common with a putting cleek, where you are obliged to hit the ball a bit harder.

Allusion has been made to a short shaft. It seems to me that a short shaft possesses several points of merit. The principal one is that the stroke must necessarily describe a truer circle because a smaller one, thereby increasing the chances of the ball being struck truly. Take, by way of illustration, a hoop of large diameter and place it in front of you, letting the part touching the ground represent the head of the club, and the center the hands. Now do the same thing with a much smaller hoop, and observe the difference. With the latter it will be found that in reference to the line from the ball to the hole the segment of the circle in the same plane is much greater. In other words, the club-head is moving longer over the line to the hole with the short-shafted putter, and there is less likelihood of the ball being diverted from that line than when the longer-shafted club is used.

It is, of course, possible, by standing very erect, to get the longer club to move along in much the same circle as the smaller one, but apart from the fact that this will bring the heel of the club over and run the toe into the ground, there is not the same command over it. In short, there is greater margin for error the farther the hands are removed from the head of the club.

There is another point also in favor of getting down to the ball—you are not so liable to take your eye off at the critical moment of striking. This is a fruitful cause of many a miss. It is rather a good plan to go to the other extreme and keep your eye for a second on the place where the ball was, after striking it. Looking up a fraction of a second too soon induces a tendency to pull the hands around to the left somewhat. This is usually attended by a slight circular curl described by the ball in the last few inches of its roll, to the left of the hole.

Reference has been made to the three leading positions assumed. The first illustration shows the ball close to the left foot; the second about midway between the feet, and the third with the ball nearer to the right foot. There is no particular advantage in any one of these styles. All are affected by good putters—and poor ones, too. It is, of course, a matter of personal choice. Simply because A putts well off the left foot is no good reason why B—who putts equally well off the right foot—should seek to change his style.

As a matter of fact, very many really good putters humor themselves and affect one or other of the alternative positions when they find themselves doing poor work—frequently with good results. It is proper to state that the effect on the ball is not the same in each case. In playing off the left leg a shade of loft is put on the ball by reason of the face of the club being slightly laid back, while playing off the right foot causes the club to present a more perpendicular face and makes the ball hug the ground more closely.

A word or two respecting the grip. Generally speaking, the club should be held pretty firmly with the fingers of both hands—firmly, not tightly. A very tight grip robs the fingers of the guiding sense of the necessary strength. If anything, the grip of the right hand should slightly predominate. A firm grasp seems to give a truer run to the ball, which is not so liable to be deflected from its proper course by any irregularities of the surface of the ground. A loose grip is more apt to cause the ball to run in a wabbly, indecisive sort of way, and is less effective except you be playing on a very true and consistent green.

Addressing.

Top of Swing.

Finish of Swing.

DRIVING.

By Charles B. Macdonald.

GOLFERS who have recently taken part in or heard discussions on the correct form of driving, know that there is the widest divergence of opinion as to the most desirable style—that is, the one giving the best results. Whereas there are only two or three recognized correct methods in putting and approaching, there seem to be almost as many different styles in driving as there are individuals.

For years the form of the veteran Allan Robertson and of young Tom Morris stood as a model for those seeking to attain perfection in the game; but in these days, golfers are hopelessly at sea when they attempt to instruct the beginner in driving. They are lost in explaining the various grips, stances and swings. The very grip which has always been considered orthodox, and concerning which two varying opinions have never before been ventured, is not used by either Vardon or Taylor, the two most remarkable players of the present day. The overlapping of the fingers was, I believe, never attempted before Taylor and Mr. Laidlay adopted that style.

Instantaneous photography has enabled us to study more in detail the reason for long and straight driving. In the old days the driving was more of the character of *sure* and *as far as possible.* To-day it is *far* and *as sure as possible.* While 20 years ago 180 yards was considered the average length of drive for professional champions, to-day 200 yards is nearer the usual distance. This can be attributed neither to the clubs nor to the balls. In my opinion, it is due to the scientific manner in which every muscle of the body is made to utilize weight and momentum at the moment of striking the ball. The man who drives the straightest and longest ball is the one who accomplishes to the greatest perfection the follow through, and the timing of the stroke. Timing of the stroke is a phrase which has become known to the golfing world only in late years, and really refers to the instant you throw your wrists forward on the change of your center of gravity at the moment of the club-head's contact with the ball. That is the beginning of the follow through. To do this as perfectly as Vardon does, one gets anywhere from 20 to 30 yards' longer ball.

Many golfers claim that Vardon violates all the laws of golf. As a matter of fact, he violates none, so far as I have been able to discover. His follow through is the most perfect I have ever seen. Any one who may pick up a photograph of his position after the follow through, will see that the position of his body shows an absolutely straight line along his face, right shoulder, left hip, left knee and ankle. This is rarely true of any other of the leading golf players.

The Finish in the accompanying photograph is not correct, for the body is not forward with the leg—that is, in a straight line. The end of the swing is far more important than the beginning. The address and the backward swing are simply poising one's self for the purpose of striking the ball correctly. There are two or three positions in which one can stand to the ball, none of which is essential in getting a long ball. Some get a longer ball in playing off the right foot than off the left, and *vice versa*. A heavy man will play off the left foot because it comes easier for him to follow through and he is less liable to slice, while a youthful man, who is supple, will probably get better results playing off the right leg, as he can follow through more easily. There are as many intermediate positions as there are intermediate weights, but the stance is not a very important matter.

As for the backward swing, the best results are usually found in a man turning well up on his right toe, giving him greater freedom of action when it comes to timing his stroke for the follow through. In this respect the accompanying photograph is also incorrect, as the subject plays from the side of his foot, as does also Mr. Harriman.

It is not necessary for a player who has a three-quarter swing, such as Mr. Harriman, to turn so much on his toe, for he does not need to describe the same arc as one taking a full swing.

Pure strength never accomplishes long driving. In men who drive the longest balls, you will usually find the muscles of the back, forearm and wrist well developed, while the development of the upper arm is not pronounced. The wrists play the most important part at the moment of timing of the stroke, which is, in a very large measure, the secret of very long driving.

The questions most frequently asked are: What is a long drive? What is the longest drive?

One hundred and eighty to two hundred yards is a long drive. Conditions, of course, direction and velocity of wind, and slope of ground, go toward creating distance in the drive. Mr. F. G. Tait's record drive of 351 yards was made over frosty, hard ground. The conditions under which this drive was made remind me of a well-authenticated story of a drive made on the Ardsley-on-the-Hudson course.

At a 300-yard hole at Ardsley, where the course slopes from tee to putting green, an enthusiastic golfer was playing one windy day over ground covered with sleet. The ball was on a snow tee. The player made a labored and terrific swipe at the ball, narrowly missing it. The wind from behind, together with the current of air created by his exertion in trying to hit the ball, caused it to roll off the tee, and the wind blew it over the slippery, icy surface, until it finally reached the putting green and rested near the hole.

When asked the longest drive, I like to tell the foregoing story.

25

Golfers in Action

Painted for OUTING by A. W. Van Deusen. See "Golfers in Action."

"A TICKLISH MOMENT."

OUTING.

VOL. XXX. AUGUST, 1897 NO. 5.

Golfers in Action

By Price Collier.

1. C. B. MACDONALD, ADDRESSING THE BALL.

MANY golfers nowadays, as they read of this man's and that man's prowess on the links, wish that they might see these players actually swinging a club. OUTING has collected here a number of instantaneous photographs of some of the better-known golf-players, to enable its readers to see just how these men look when they are actually playing. In short, when we hear of the brilliant play of one or another of the prominent players, we would like to see what is called their *style*.

There has been a great deal of non-

2. C. B. MACDONALD, FOLLOWING THROUGH.

3. C. B. MACDONALD, AT TOP OF SWING.

sense written about style: whether it is style in writing; style in running or walking; style in rowing, or fencing, or boxing; or style at golf. Architecture, and painting, and landscape-gardening, and literature, are said to have their styles. At one period it is this style, at another period it is that, and so on. This

4. H. T. WHIGHAM, ADDRESSING THE BALL.

means that during a certain number of years men working at painting, or writing, or building, are apt to adopt the same model, and to give their work a similar air. So men are said to have the same or similar styles at cricket, or tennis, or golf. The nonsense that is written about all this, consists in not analyzing what *style* is! A man's *style* in anything that he does, is his individual method of doing what he undertakes, with the greatest comfort to himself, combined with the greatest effectiveness possible. It follows, therefore, that there is no one superlatively good style, whether in writing, or painting, or golf. The nonsense written and talked about

5. H. T. WHIGHAM, AT TOP OF THE STROKE.

style, consists then in taking it for granted that there is one way, and one way only, to do things, thus leaving out of account altogether the most important factor of all, namely, individual idiosyncrasies. A short, fat man cannot row, or spar, or play golf, as a tall, thin man can; and if he tries to do so (fooled by all this clamor about style), he leaves out of account the first of the two factors which go to make up style, namely, that he must do what he has to do, *with greatest comfort to himself*. One man achieves the greatest effectiveness by one use of arms, legs and trunk, while another man achieves it by quite another use of his limbs

But this does not mean at all that there is no such thing as a bad style, or a good style; it means only that there is no one model of style, and it means, too, that where a man plays with greatest comfort to himself, combined with greatest effectiveness, he plays in good style; while a man who copies some other man's good style, and does not play comfortably, or with the greatest effectiveness possible, plays in bad style.

When a student of such matters says of one man, that he has a good style, and of another that he has a bad style, he does not mean that the man does, or does not, swing like Fernie, or play his

7. H. T. WHIGHAM, FOLLOWING THROUGH.

6. H. T. WHIGHAM, COMING THROUGH.

iron like Mr. John Ball, Jr.; he means that the man is not using his own peculiar physical abilities in the most comfortable, combined with the most effective way.

For example, here is a player whose swing in driving is short and not smooth, and with a tendency not to sweep away the ball, but to chop down upon it, or behind it. We do not say he has a bad style, because he has not the long, smooth, sweeping swing of Mr. Whigham (4, 5, 6, 7), or Taylor (p. 422), or Sayres (p. 422); we say he has a bad style, because he has the thumb of his right hand down along the shaft, and not around it; hence, when his club goes back, that thumb stops it, and swerves it, and makes the player both uncomfortable and inefficient. Here are several illustrations of Mr. Tyng at play (18). His club goes back, hardly further than the baseball bat he was wont

7*a*. H. P. TOLER.

SAYERS, DRIVING.

to wield so effectively. But he hits the ball, hits it hard, and sends it straight and far. This would be a very bad style to imitate, but it is a very good style for Mr. Tyng, as the late tournaments at Lakewood and Meadowbrook can testify. He shortens his swing because thus he is more sure of hitting the ball, and he makes up for the shortness of his swing, by the power he puts into the club with that right arm of an old baseball pitcher. No better illustration of how hard a good player can hit the ball would be easy to find, than our illustration of Taylor (p. 422), kindly sent to the writer by Mr. Hutchinson. The gritted teeth, and the tension of the body, show what power this player has put into his shot. He makes up for a defect by a good quality. But if some other man attempts to imitate the defect, without having this particular good quality to compensate for it, he is bound to fail; and the critic sees at once that the trouble lies in the simple fact, that what is Mr. Tyng's meat is his imitator's poison.

VARDON, OPEN CHAMPION, '96.

Carlyle and Dr. Johnson had some very important things to say to the world, and because the former said his say in eruptive and Teutonic phrases, and the latter with sesquipedalian sententiousness, made no matter; but when their microcephalous imitators come along with nothing in particular to say, the imitation of the mere manner of those literary giants is highly ridiculous. The style of the two former is good; the style of the latter is abominable.

W. Hilton (p. 423), who has just won the open championship with an almost unprecedented steadiness of scoring, doing the seventy-eight holes in 314, swings along the course with a lighted cigarette in his mouth, hardly stopping at each stroke to address his ball. But Mr. Hilton has worked his way to the condition of an almost perfect golfing machine, and he makes his shots without delay, and without hesitation. On

TAYLOR, OPEN CHAMPION, '95.

the other hand, another player, probably quite as good, namely, Mr. Horace Hutchinson, waggles, and waggles, as he addresses his ball, before each shot. Yet Mr. Hutchinson is the man who can drive ball after ball off his watch-face, without the least danger of resultant visits to his watchmaker as a consequence.

In these, and in all other examples, there are these two factors to be considered always: first the physical, and then the moral make-up of the player; and the comfort and the efficiency of his play are dependent not on one, or the other of these two factors, but on both. From a misunderstanding of this arises all the ignorant discussion of style, of which we hear so much. Here is a man who swings smoothly, and who apparently plays his shots correctly, but who never gets very far up the lists in the golfing world. "He has a good style," men say, and yet he accomplishes very little. The truth is, that he has not a good style at all. He is merely mechanically doing what the professional has taught him to do, but he gets no power into his shots, and he lacks confidence and concentration. He is trying to write like Carlyle, or Dr. Johnson, without having anything to say; or he is like one of those high-stepping cobs, which can go all day on a tin plate.

H. H. HILTON, ENGLISH OPEN CHAMPION, 1897.

The fascination about this game of golf, which makes it the game of all games to those who have studied it, lies in the fact that it is something more than a machine-made affair; it requires higher powers than that, and no man who lacks these can ever hope to excel at it, no matter how mechanically correctly he plays. That is the reason, also, why men who break every known rule laid down by the experts, still play good golf.

Mr. Thorpe (13), last year's runner-up in our amateur championship, has already pardoned me in advance for what I am about to say touching his style. But he is too good an example not to use for the benefit of his less proficient fellow-golfers. In the instantaneous photographs of his play here, you will notice that there is no whip-like motion of his driver as he swings (14, 15), as in the case of the photograph of Mr. Whigham driving (5 and 6), or in that of Sayres driving (p. 422). On the contrary, the motion is slow and perhaps a little stiff; but notice how his eye is glued to the place where the ball was, even after it is gone; notice how firmly and steadily he keeps his feet (16). Here is a man who plays with his head. He atones for his deficiencies by giving the utmost attention to steadiness of stance, firmness of grip, and that point—by far the most important of all—keeping his eye on the ball.

Even Mr. Thorpe is the first to admit that his is not a good style, *quâ* style, but as he is doing what he has to do with greatest comfort to himself, combined with very considerable efficiency, it may be said to be a good style for him. Indeed, herein lies the beauty of the game. An older and naturally stiffer man finds that it is impossible to get the long, whippy, lightning-like swing of his younger opponent, and he compensates himself for that by slower, surer, more careful play. Each man has certain characteristics that another

8. A. H. FENN.

man has not; and what we mean when we say that a man is *doing what he has to do with the greatest comfort to himself* is, that he is making use of the peculiar powers he possesses, to compensate himself for other powers that his opponents may have, that he has not.

For example, some men are well-known non-stayers. That is to say, if you hang on to them long enough they become impatient and fretful; they try to play better than they can play, with the result that they become erratic, and lose holes that they ought to halve or win, and in the end lose a match, not to the better play, but to the cooler head and steadier nerves of their opponent.

All men have their off days as they are called, when head, hand, and eye are not in good working order. But there is a certain class of players who are seldom badly beaten—you may discover who they are by watching the scores now so generally reported in the newspapers. No matter who the opponent may be, they travel along at a good even pace, and except on an occasional day of golfing doldrums, they are seldom more than two or three down, as the case may be. This is as it should be. For, an average game of forty-five or forty-six for a nine-hole course, or of ninety to ninety-five for an eighteen-hole course, is not easy to beat, even by a first-rate man, if the average player will only keep his head. There are always a certain number of short holes which the average man is pretty certain of in 4, and which the first-rate man will not do in 3 very often—there are very few holes, however short they may be, you will notice, that are done very often in 3. Then there are the fairly long holes of from 380 to 450 yards that our average man can do in 5 or 6, if he will only play his own game, and not permit himself to be carried away by emulation of his smarter rival; and at the end of eighteen holes he will find that he has halved a good many, and perhaps won, here a hole, and there a hole, and the first-rate man must have made very few mistakes, if he is to be many holes up on the round.

Too many men will not remember this sage advice in a match. They lose a hole or two; then they try to win a hole, instead of letting their opponent lose a hole, which is, after all, the only safe way to win one. You cannot beat a man by playing a better game than you can play; you can win only by playing your own game and permitting him to beat himself; if you try to beat him, you almost invariably play worse than usual. Take for example a hole that you occasionally do in 4, but more often in 5. Your opponent plays a longer ball than you do, and after the drive it is your shot. There is a running stream between you and the green. You may carry it and you may not; your opponent, lying nearer, is pretty sure to carry it. If you were playing a medal round you would lay up in 2, be safely on the green in 3, perhaps have a put for it in 4, but be sure of it in 5. Your opponent has a long shot to get over in 2, must approach in 3; and as this approach shot

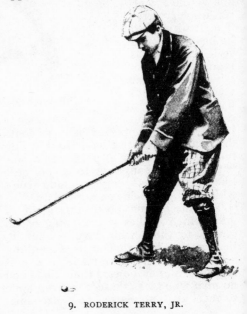

9. RODERICK TERRY, JR.

is of all others most difficult, he is probably not dead in 3, and must play 4, with a chance of missing. How much better then for you to make sure of a 5, than to play a long 2 and get into the stream; and yet where a man is two or three down, how seldom is he willing to play this so much safer game.

It is at such crises as this illustrates, that the wise man redeems his lesser physical prowess by his judgment. That very judgment which prevents his taking unusual risks, and which keeps him playing inside his game all through the round, is just as much a part and parcel of his style as the way he uses his arms, and legs, and feet. To revert to what was said at the beginning and to repeat: a good style is where a man plays the game in the greatest comfort to himself, combined with greatest efficiency.

This is one—and the most important—reason why there are so few good teachers. Most men who teach, want you to play as *they do*, instead of, as *you can*, two widely different things as a rule. It is the reason also why some men find it so difficult to learn, because in studying somebody else's game, they omit the far more important point, namely the study of themselves. It is thirdly, and lastly, the reason why it is possible to say that one man has a bad style, and

11. JOHN REID, PRESIDENT ST. ANDREW'S CLUB.

10. JASPER LYNCH.

another man a good style. For it is easy to see now that a bad style is where a man is doing uncomfortably what he might do just as well comfortably, or doing inefficiently, though comfortably, what he might just as well be doing both efficiently and *comfortably*. For example it is just as comfortable, after a little practice, to play with the right thumb *around* the shaft of the club, as *down* it. It is just as comfortable to turn the body a little, and swing the club around at about the height of the shoulders, as to hold the body, and swing the club around at the level of the right ear—with a frequent consequence of chopping down on the ball. It is just as comfortable to come back, as the club strikes the ball, with a slight knuckle in of the right knee, which allows the club to follow through and on after the ball, as not. Not to do these things is bad style, for the simple reason that not to do them is to lessen one's efficiency. It is most efficient, on the other hand, to have a long full swing; but for elderly men, rheumatic men, gouty men, this is so uncomfortable as to be most uncertain of execution in their case, hence for them it is a bad style. They gain nothing in efficiency, and lose much in comfort. For such men, too, it is almost impossible to get that pivotal motion on the hips, which brings the club around with a switch as though it came from a bow-string; see the illustration of Sayres (p. 422); and because that Scotch professional can do it with perfect accuracy, is no reason why they should even try. It is good style for him, but bad style for them.

There are photographs here of the six men, Messrs. Whigham (4), Macdonald (1), Fenn (8), Toler (20), Tyng (18), and Thorpe (14), who may be fairly considered the six leading amateur players in this country; and only one of them, apparently, has that lithe, free, whippy swing, that old-world golfers deem to be the perfection of style. But mark you, it is considered the perfection of style, not because some golfing Paderewski wears his hair long, or grips his club thus or so, or stands with his right foot a little behind, or a little in front of his left; not on account of any such finical reason as this, but because, after some two hundred years of study, golfers have found that it is the most efficient way of getting the ball away, straight and far.

Your average Britisher, whatever other faults he may have—and some of our sugar-coated Senators can name you a good many—does not go in for frills, at either his work or his play, unless the said frills prove useful to the end to be attained. The stance, the grip, the swing, that together make up, what they call a good style, are only such an adjustment of the physical machinery as they have found effective, most effective, for this particular game. Now, a good style for you or for me must needs be, not a copy of this style as produced by some professional who has played for twenty years and more, but a modification of these perfections which will best adapt them to our imperfections. If you are of a quick, volatile (some people call it irritable) disposition, cultivate a slow swing and use a stiff club. If you are of a lethargic temperament, tinctured with gout and perforce slow of execution, you may permit yourself a somewhat whippier shaft. In a word, if you are irritable, then play with a phlegmatic club and a stolid swing; if you are phlegmatic, then indulge in a little irritation in the shaft of your driver, and just an imperceptible display of temper in your swing. At all events remember that you cannot be efficient for any length of time if you are uncomfortable, and also that you will be uncommonly uncomfortable if you are continually inefficient.

Study the attitudes of some of these players, and if possible keep your eyes upon some good player on your own links and study his methods. See how near you can come to doing the same thing. You will discover that certain of their ways are physically impossible to you; you are too stiff, or too old; or you have played some other game so much, that you cannot rid yourself of its tricks. Then with what powers you have, and by some method of your own, see how near you can come, if not to their style, at least to their performance. If you can learn to drive the ball off every tee, straight, and a distance of from 165 to 180 yards, then stick to your own method, and to the winds with style! If men tell you that you have a bad style, follow the advice of the late Master of Balliol, Dr. Jowett: "Make up your mind, do what you set out to do, and let 'em howl!" which, by the way, is very good advice in other matters almost as serious as golf.

But, as a matter of fact, you will not have a bad style if you are efficient and comfortable. The very essence of grace is that it should give the appearance of ease; *ars est celare artem.* What you do comfortably, you are doing, so far as in you lies, gracefully. It is when you become a contortionist, in the attempt to do something like somebody else, that you are awkward. Of course, some men are doomed to awkwardness; just as others are doomed to early baldness, or thin shanks, or inappropriately placed rotundity; it is congenital with them. But for the average man to be comfortable is to be, so far as he can be, graceful. A dog or an elephant on its hind-legs is doing uncomfortably on two, what it can do better on four legs. Though most of us get about on two, and call it good style to do so, we are bound to admit that an elephant is more graceful, goes in better style, in short, on four. And be it said, some of us are veritable elephants at golf, and we might as well give up the tricks of the superior bipeds at the game, and go meekly on all fours, in our own lumbering fashion.

But the faults of our better class of

American players are, in most cases, not faults of imitation, but faults of bumptiousness. They assume that they can play the game just as well as anybody else, and play it their own way. No swing, thumbs down the shaft, the eye off the ball—a common fault of some of our best men — an unsteady stance, and so on, make no difference to them ; and they go on playing a game of their own manufacture, which is only passable because there are only a few first-rate players here to beat them. It has been hinted that perhaps Mr. Hutchinson, Mr. Balfour-Melville, Mr. Boothby, and Mr. McFie, and perhaps some other British players may run over here in the early autumn ; and nothing could be better for us than to have these gentlemen as our guests and to learn by observation, and probably by a series of good, sound lickings, just wherein and to what extent we are deficient in the finer points of the game.

To the neophite there seems to be comparatively little difference between the man who does eighteen holes in 95, and the man who does eighteen holes in 89 ; or between the 89 man, and the man who does eighteen holes in 83 ; and still less difference between the 83 man and he who does eighteen holes in 79. But as a matter of fact, there is the difference between style and no style ; the difference between a duffer and a past-master of the art of golf, in just the saving of those few strokes. Practically any man, sound in wind and limb, of average strength and fair eyesight, can learn to go round in 95, which is 5 for each hole, and 5 strokes to spare for mistakes. This same man if persistent and painstaking, can get down to 89 ; but when it comes to cutting six more strokes off the round to do an 83, then something more is required than mere painstaking and patience. A man must acquire some kind of a style to do that. He must play comfortably, with a certain confidence in just what he can do, and with the ability to do it not here and there occasionally, but every time. He is no longer a problem to the handicappers when he reaches this stage ; he knows, and others know, just what can be expected ; he has settled down into a style of his own. So far as doing eighteen holes in 79 is concerned, or even in 80 or 81, we have practically no men here, who like Ball, Tait, Hilton, Laidlay, Hutchinson, and a score more in Great Britain, can count upon, not infrequently, touching the 80 mark. Whatever be President Eliot's opinion to the contrary, when a player at golf can get round inside of 80, he is a great artist at a great game. He compares favorably in physique, temper, and moral fibre with the best cross-country riders, the best shots, the best bats, the best sparrers, and very favorably indeed, with contemporary Harvard oarsmen.

Once when Mr. Herbert Spencer's London club was being renovated, during the summer months, he with others accepted during those weeks the hospitality of a neighboring club. Mr. Spencer's only exercise is playing billiards, of which he is very fond. One afternoon he strolled into the billiard-room of this neighboring club, and promptly challenged a man he found lounging there, to a game of billiards. They banked for the first shot. Mr. Spencer won, and led off. When his opponent came to play, he put the chalk in his pocket, and went at it in professional fashion, running out the game before he missed. Mr. Spencer walked to where his coat was hanging, and as he passed the stranger he said to him : "Sir, I have always considered the game of billiards an innocent amusement, and a game well adapted to the recreation of a student. But sir, when a man plays as you play, it bespeaks a wasted youth. Good afternoon, sir!" Though to play golf like Mr. Hilton does not bespeak a wasted youth, for Scotch moors are healthier than smoky billiard-rooms, it certainly does imply that a first-rate man has put a lot of hard work into the game. No game is worth a Continental Congress that does not demand the exercise of much the same qualities to win at it as are required to win at the more serious professional and business problems of life. No man wins at golf who only brings to the game what President Eliot unwittingly opines to be necessary, namely: the senile lethargy and clouded vision of advanced age. On the contrary, golf is unique in having had, and in still having, among its foremost devotees men who have won victories in more extended fields. The amateur champion of Great Britain is a student ; the amateur champion of the United States is a professor, and the open champion, or as

12. W. B. SMITH, PRESIDENT, TUXEDO CLUB.

Mr. Chuck Connors would phrase it, "the champ of champs," is an educated gentleman.

No other game has this peculiarity. The professional, at rowing; at fencing, or sword-play of any kind; at riding; tennis, indoors and out; at sparring, football, baseball, running, bicycle riding, shooting, is superior to the amateur. At golf he never has been and is not now. There have been all through the history of the game, as there are now, amateurs who are the equals, if not the superiors, of the best professionals. This indicates, what the real lovers of the game contend for it, that it requires, as does no other game, a combination of qualities, found most often in the gentleman. Any "rough" can be trained into fighting shape for most of our games, and make a passable showing at them; but many years might be spent in the training, before a potential "Babe" Anson, or a potential Sullivan, or Fitzsimmons, could be brought to the point where he could play eighteen holes of golf in 79, and many more years still, before he could play 72 holes in 314. The most typical golf professional, and by all odds the best-known professional of to-day, is known far and wide—by his play, you will say—not at all, but because he is a natural gentleman, because he is a kindly, sweet-tempered, pure-minded and charitable old Scotchman who goes to church and says his prayers, refuses to play even golf on Sunday, and never took advantage of anybody wittingly in his life. To put him in a group with "Babe" Anson, and "Jim" Corbett, and illustrious professionals at other sports, would be like setting off a dignified old lion with jackals. Indeed he would look askance even at the methods of some of our amateurs, I opine. Golf is a game requiring just as much, that a man be of a certain character, as that he be of a certain physical prowess. It is a game that knows no underhand methods, and which even makes very slight provision to prevent them. The rules, people are saying now-a-days, are complicated, are insufficient, and so on. Yes, 'tis true. They are, and they always will be insufficient, and inefficient, if professional methods creep in. If you are playing to take every advantage; if you are playing to win, no matter how—and I may be pardoned (or not, it matters little) for saying that there is a deal of that kind of play at all our amateur games; if you are playing the way Kelly—"King" they called him, which shows the popular estimate of good sport—used to play baseball, then the rules are quite insufficient to keep you from taking advantages or to prevent

13. J. G. THORPE, ADDRESSING THE BALL.

14. J. G. THORPE, TOP OF SWING.

your opponent from so doing. But suppose you set out to play golf, in the way gentlemen ought to play every game, with the intention of accepting, and taking no advantage of your opponent, think you, that you would have any difficulty with the rules ? Certainly not! There used to be a certain chivalry among gentlemen in such matters—there is still, I think, here and there—which dictated that if your opponent broke his sword in two, you should do the same by your weapon, before continuing the fight. They say that competition in business, in the professions, in life, is too severe nowadays for that kind of Don Quixotism (Donkeyotism some might call it derisively), and that this fierce competition has found its way into sport. If this is so, more's the pity. It is vulgar, it is of the very essence of the cad and the bully, it is the *canaille oblige* of the ignoble ; it has spoiled our football, ruined our baseball, except for the "tough" ; almost put an end to horse-racing, and sent some of our best men to race abroad, and made sparring (one of the very best of all exercises) more like chicken-fighting than like sport. Fancy, in a club of gentlemen, a knot of men listening to the story of one of their number who recites with glee how he took advantage of a professional jockey, against whom he happened to be riding, by bumping him at an opportune moment, unseen by stewards or judges.

This is just as low and vulgar as cheating at cards, or any other form of stabbing a man in the back ; just as bad as kicking your ball out of a bad lie at golf, stabbing a man in the throat with your elbow at football, or spiking a man with your spikes at baseball. Some men seem to have the idea that there is such a thing as *splendide mendax*, that a man can be an heroic cheat, a glorious liar, a tricky sportsman, and that their first duty is to win. Nothing could be, nothing is, worse for sport than such an estimate of it.

Some of us have fondly imagined that the place of sport in life was to compensate in some measure for the paucity of virile adventure, brought about by civilization. The wild beasts and wild waters have been tamed ; the explorer has smoothed out the roads everywhere ; machinery has made the use of the muscles less necessary, and steam and the telegraph have taken the place of endurance, wind and nerve. Sport is an artificial form of adventure and excitement adapted to keep alive the virile qualities of mankind, and in-

15. J. G. THORPE, AFTER THE SWING.

16. J. G. THORPE, ADDRESSING THE BALL FOR IRON SHOT.

tended to make him strong, self-reliant, temperate and courageous. But the moment the element of cheating and trickery enters in, the whole excuse for being, of sport, is gone. Sport then merely becomes a matter of prize-money, gate receipts and sly methods,

17. J. G. THORPE, SHORT APPROACH (AFTER).

and debauches the moral tone of everybody who takes a hand in it.

It may seem that we have wandered from our subject, which was "style" at golf. But we have not. One of the elements to be considered in analyzing "style," is temperament; and character is temperament brought into training. The man who is to play golf well must consider his own temperament, and use its advantages, offset its disadvantages, and make for himself in some sort a golfing character. A character not like that of some other man; a character not pared down and pruned and shaped to suit the fashion of the hour; not changing and shifting, to fall in with what

18. J. A. TYNG, AT TOP OF SWING.

other men do, or say, but something of his own; something that he can take care of, and which can take care of him in any emergency. Style is then what Buffon claims it is—the man!

In watching other men play, or in looking over these illustrations, what a man is, will be found to be the predominant factor in the game he plays, or *vice versa*. As you study his game, you will discover the man. And of no other game, perhaps, is this so true as of golf. For no other game requires such a variety of physical and moral adjustments to the vicissitudes of the game as does this. You may use all your power, and then you must hit as softly and neatly as at billiards; and of the variety of lies, accidents, hazards and opponents there is no end, and to each of these the player must adapt himself as occasion requires. No other game, unless it be cricket; no other sport, unless it be hunting big game, is so complete a measure of the whole man, as is this game, when played under proper auspices. And of this game, as of cricket and big-game hunting, with very few exceptions, it may be truly said that it is played better by men than by boys. In a word, it requires not only the energy and lithesomeness of youth, but the steadiness, the resource, and the reserve power, not of age, but of maturity.

20. H. P. TOLER, ADDRESSING THE BALL.

19. J. A. TYNG, IN POSITION FOR IRON SHOT.

Youth may play all around you at tennis, or baseball, and do his hundred yards, or half-mile, or the hurdles, at a pace that leaves you far behind; but until you are sixty you ought, with care, and by securing for him a little more time at the office, and for yourself a little more time on the links, to be able to put up a game at golf that the youngster will find hard to beat. And for us, old fellows, surely that is a feature of the game by no means to be despised. For there are none too many sports that father and son—and we have known one instance of grandfather also—may participate in on fairly even terms. All our sports and games will be less childish when our older men are drawn into them. Golf is doing this as nothing has ever done it before in this country; and the more we can tempt our mature men to take an interest in the sports and pastimes of their juniors, the better it will be for all concerned.

21. H. P. TOLER, FULL IRON SHOT.

26

What Golf Means to a Big City

WHAT GOLF MEANS TO A BIG CITY

By ARTHUR RUHL

PHOTOGRAPHS BY T. C. TURNER

ONE of the cartoons which Du Maurier drew for *Punch* years ago represented a very esthetic young man seated at a table in a restaurant gazing at a tumbler of water in which were a couple of lilies. The glass was the only thing on the table, and the young man regarded it with a certain air of ecstasy, as was evident from his liquid eye and the intenseness with which his nether limbs twined one about the other. Opposite the young man, with his fingers resting deferentially on the edge of the table, bent the honest, round-faced British waiter.

"Can't I get you something more, sir?" he asked. The young man had merely requested a glass of water and dropped his lilies into it.

"Thank you, this is quite sufficient," the young man replied, devouring the lilies with his eyes; "soon I will have done."

Although the purpose of the cartoon was to satirize the cult of esthetes, just then beginning to appear, it was doubtless suggested by the anecdote, since become almost classic, of the prophet of the new order, who, as I recall it, being late at a dinner party of which he was a guest, seized a bouquet of violets from a vase on the table, pressed them to his face, and with great apparent satisfaction sighed: "A-a-ah! I have dined!" The mental attitude therein implied is one which, in these days of athleticism, is rather distinctly deprecated. If one poses now, it is on the other side of the fence. One is rather embarrassed than otherwise to disclose the fact that he possesses sensibilities. The development of the more virile and Spartan virtues is generally reckoned to be the essence of the sports of the out-of-doors.

It is with a somewhat whimsical interest, therefore, that I recall a certain spring day on a golf course tucked away in the hills to the north of town. It was one of those days when the spring seems to come all at once, when the stir of growing things and the warmth and richness overpower and conquer us. All the things of winter seem suddenly old and dusty and frayed about the edges. We shuffle off our winter ideas and our hearthstone point of view as serpents shed their skins. Before we can quite adjust ourselves to the new world we drink to intoxication of the air and the colors and the sunshine. The greenness of the fresh grass, the smell of the earth—mere lights and colors and odors become for the moment overwhelmingly vital.

The St. Andrews course, than which none in the neighborhood of New York is prettier, was that day covered with violets. The fair green in the lower levels near the brook was purple with them. The air above them, hemmed in by the hills around, seemed to have an almost tangible velvetiness. One strode softly and played with a sort of exaggerated leisure and dignity as if afraid of breaking the charm. As a pair met in the greens they greeted each other with deference and conversed in lowered voices as though they were in church. The moving figures, specking the green here and there in the distance, seemed less actual persons with whom one had come up in the train an hour or so before than parts of a painted picture or the fabric of a dream. Now and again a man would stop and raise his head and look all about him as though he wished to *feel* the day and the spring even more. And yet those playing were almost as far as possible removed from the type of person who would plunge his face into a bunch of violets and murmur, "I have dined!" They were lawyers and bankers and brokers and busy men generally, who, twenty-four hours before, had been hard at it in downtown New York, at downtown New York's cruel pace—fighting hard-headed battles in the realm of stock tickers and roaring exchanges and skyscrapers and trucks and trolley-cars.

It is this esthetic value of golf, its appeal to the sensibilities, the rest and stimulus

The Natural Hazard to the Twelfth Green, on the Deal Course.

From the Eighteenth Green of the Deal Course One Looks Across to the Lake.

which it gives to the fagged-out and the world-weary which makes it more, probably, than any other sport to those who live in town. It is a game which we take up at any age and which we can play comfortably without any previous training or preparation. Almost any one may ride, but park riding is at best a somewhat artificial sport —an urban rather than a country recreation. Rowing is too violent an exercise for any but the young or very fit, and, as done in this country, one who goes in for it is likely to be lonesome. Walking without any object but exercise is a bore, and to all but the insatiable muscle-maker gymnasium exercise is likely to be more so. Tennis and squash, although they answer the requirements of exercise, have little of that restful appeal to the sensibilities which one finds in the more leisurely, open, and freer sports. To a man nervously tired, as most tired city men are, the mere keying-up one's self to the strenuous pitch of violent exercise has somewhat the same grating effect that harsh sounds have to ears already wearied with noise. In short, from the point of view of pleasure, of practicability, and of results there is no sport which seems to be more adapted to the needs of the city man than golf. While it is putting air in his lungs and blood in his veins, it is smoothing out his puckered brain and attuning it to the eternal harmonies. The sum of the effect of a perfect day on a good course is similar to that of a cross-country run, a visit to an art gallery, and a symphony concert rolled into one.

No city in the country, probably, is surrounded by so many courses of the better sort as New York. New Jersey, Long Island, and the beautiful country to the north of Manhattan are dotted with them—Garden City, Baltusrol, St. Andrews, Ardsley, Knollwood, Essex County, Englewood, Montclair, Dyker Meadow—there is no end to them.

Then, too, there is Van Courtlandt—the house of the Philistine. Perhaps you do not care for the public links, but lots of other folks do. To a good many hundreds of them, a day up and down the wooded valley in which the course is laid means the one brushing away of the mental and physical cobwebs that have gathered during the week's grind in town. We do not venture to hazard an estimate of the number of golfers that play at Van Courtlandt. It depends a good deal on the number of times you are hit. If you are hit, say three times, in making the circuit of the eighteen holes, and also lose half a dozen balls, the course is disgustingly overcrowded. If you don't lose any balls, beat the man you've picked up as a partner while waiting in line at the first tee, and manage in a polite and accidental way to send a low hard drive into the back of the player ahead of you some time during the day, you will find the course not half bad.

The sight which we may see on any holiday in fair weather, from April to December, is calculated to cheer the heart of any lover of the out-of-doors. The railway station is close by the first tee, and the locker-building which a paternal municipality has provided is only a stone's throw away, and as the trains pull in from town every half hour or so the whole place is alive with golfers—husbands and wives and young men and maidens—hurrying to get into their playing clothes and to a good place in the line. On a bright morning there will be waiting in line at the first tee, while the breezy young bloods from Harlem smack out their 200-yard drives and the embarrassed middle-aged ladies blush and top and foozle—some thirty or forty players. Each one must get his little ticket from the greens keeper, so that he may not cut in where he does not belong, and when he has made the circuit of the first six holes and is ready to start on the straight course up the valley, he must exchange it for another little ticket which says to the attendant at the seventh tee: "I have played the hill." This is the only reminder of the city's hard and fast lines and its routine. Few courses have a prettier setting than Van Courtlandt and none are so easy to reach, and as the game grows older there is less and less of the roughshod play of a few years ago, and more of the dignity and considerateness which are so much a part of the game. And it is good to stand on the hilltop at the sixth tee and view the quiet valley dotted from end to end with moving figures, and to remember that were it not for such a sport a good part of those, who bare-headed and with sleeves rolled up are drinking in the sunshine, would be mooning over colored supplements in boarding-house bedrooms or squatting half asleep on the front steps watching their play-day go by.

Those whose daylight time is pretty much their own have found in golf a new and val-

Golf Is Largely Responsible for the Athletic Girl.

uable occupation. I have in mind one man whose work does not begin until the ordinary dinner time nor end until two or three o'clock in the morning. By noon he is up and about with the best of the day ahead of him. "But *what*," asks your lily-livered office slave, "can a *man* find to do in the daytime unless he's downtown and at work?" Loaf about the house boring himself and worrying his wife? Not a bit of it! The moment his breakfast—your luncheon—is down he is off for the country. If the day is fair and the house things are running smoothly Mrs. Blank goes with him. And the result is that our much-to-be-pitied friend gets better acquainted with his wife and

An Interesting Crowd of Spectators Always Follows a Championship Match.

The Deal Golf Club's Attractive Home, Where the Metropolitan Championship is Held This Year.

keeps more lively and fit than the most of us do in spite of his unearthly hours. It is supposed by many that one cannot keep in shape and yet turn night into day One has only to see the actors and newspaper men and such unconventional birds on some of the courses near town of a likely afternoon to know how far from the facts this impression may be.

The Deal Beach course is, naturally, more in the public eye at the present moment than any of the other courses in the neighborhood of New York. The Metropolitan Championship, which went to Deal this year, is generally regarded as next in importance to the two national events, the Amateur and the Open Championship. To those who live and play near New York the Metropolitan has, of course, a local and personal interest which is not felt so warmly for the two greater meets. Every golfer who has got beyond the duffer class has a friend or a clubmember entered for the Metropolitan, and then there are such players as Mr. Travis and Mr. Douglas whose names are known all over the country. The winner of the Metropolitan is pretty sure to be the likliest candidate for the Amateur event, and the significance of the winning of the first championship is indicated by the fact that since 1899 the victor in the Metropolitan has been a national champion.

This is the fifth of these Metropolitan events. The first, which was held in 1899 on the Garden City course, was won by Mr. Harriman, who in the same season won the Amateur Championship from Mr. Douglas, at Onwentsia. In 1900, the event was contested on the Nassau County Club course and won by Mr. Travis, who followed Mr. Harriman's example of the year before and won the national amateur championship a few weeks later. On the Apawanis course, at Rye, the next year, Mr. Charles H. Seeley beat Mr. Travis, but could get no better than second place in the national event. The fourth Metropolitan Championship was won last year by Mr. Travis at Tuxedo.

The Deal Beach course was laid out in 1898, but it was not until 1900 that it became known as a course of the first class by the best-ball play between R. B. Wilson and Willie Norton, the American professionals, and the English professional J. H. Taylor. The course was then very tolerable, but in the three years since it has improved with age as all properly cared-for courses do, and the polishing off which it received in preparation for the present championship put it, as a playing course, in rank with any in the neighborhood of New York. The Deal course is laid over pleasantly undulating surface and on turf which is firm and close and remarkably free from stones. There is more play at Deal, probably, during the summer than at any of the other Metropolitan courses, except the public links at Van Courtlandt, and yet even during the dog days of July and August and September, the turf remains in good condition. There are two courses at Deal, the regular one of eighteen holes and the nine-hole course reserved for women, both covering in all about 200 acres. The playing length of the regular course was 6,255 yards before the special preparations for the championship began, and since then it has been increased to something like 6,400 yards by setting back the trees. To players who have mastered the long game. as compared with those who have to depend more on the finesse of approach shots, the long course is an advantage. One may imagine Mr. Travis, for instance, with his startling drive of 382 yards last winter up his sleeve, viewing all such increases in the playing distance with complete equanimity.

Deal is a course of comfortable sportiness, and, judging from the scores made on it up to this year, of tolerable difficulty. The amateur record for the eighteen holes is seventy-nine, and is held jointly by Mr. Travis, Mr. George Brokaw, and Mr. Archibald Graham. Bogey is eighty-two. That the score had not been brought lower up to this season than a seventy-nine was attributed by some observers to the peculiarities of the Deal greens. They are smooth but not level, having been allowed to follow to a certain extent the natural conformation of the turf, and to players used to playing only on greens as level as a ball-room floor they doubtless presented some embarrassments. As for the various holes in the course, the seventh, of 550 yards, is the longest: the twelfth, of 475 yards, is perhaps the most difficult, its green being fortified by a most uncomfortable ditch. The thirteenth hole is, in a way. the sportiest. It involves merely an approach shot of 100 yards, but this must be lifted over a deep pit of soft earth, and the ball that is n't sent over by the first stroke must be lofted up an almost perpendicular bank some fifteen

Bunkers in Line of Play for the Ninth and Tenth Greens, at Deal.

feet or so in height. As for the general aspect of the course, it is one free from trees and other obstructions, and agreeable alike to both players and gallery.

It is a pleasant thing to watch a championship match, strolling along on fresh green turf, in the air and sunshine, at the polite distance of the gallery. It isn't so

The Twelfth Green, at Deal, Comes Close Down to the Lake.

bad just to read the story of the play in the press dispatches, sitting in a comfortable chair in a country-club veranda a thousand miles or so away. Every one who is interested in the game is interested in such an event as the Metropolitan and in the other greater and lesser contests of the year. But the really big and important thing, and the thing which should have the most potent interest for every sportsman, is the fact that all these "set-pieces," so to speak, are but the frills and furbelows of all that honest, every-day, just-for-fun golfing which is going on all the time, in all sorts of weather, and in all sorts of places, wherever in the land can be found an available bit of open comfortable country.

Hundreds of thousands of persons go to see football games and rowing races, but it is only the few who may be one of an eleven or a crew. There is scarcely another game in which the big public contests are not more important in the ordinary man's eye than the every-day playing of the duffer. In golf, things are ordered differently, and although Jones and Robinson may buzz like anything on their way down to their offices in the "L" in the morning of So-and-so's chances and Such-a-one's form they are much more vitally concerned over those eighteen holes which they are going to play next Saturday afternoon for the Jones-Robinson championship, or, perhaps, as a desperate stake for as many balls as the winner is "up," or a dinner at the club-house. The golf bag is almost as typical an ornament of the suburban train and the ferry-boat as the parcels of the commuter.

It is a cheering and healthy sign when busy men in the fragmentary pauses of their business are of a mind to gossip about the tremendous drives that they made the last day they were out, and to apostrophize the good time they are going to have on the next fine afternoon. It is a fine thing when multitudes go in for a sport, not because the crowd goes, not because it is swagger, but only because it 's healthy and it 's fun. And that is just what golf means to those who live or work in town.

There Is Never Failing Interest in the Crowd Roped Back From the Last Hole.

27

Through the "Green" with the Iron Clubs

OUTING.

VOL. XXXIV. JUNE, 1899. No. 3.

THROUGH THE "GREEN" WITH THE IRON CLUBS.

BY FINDLAY S. DOUGLAS, AMATEUR CHAMPION OF THE U. S. A.

THERE is a tendency in beginners at golf to consider the end of good golf is accomplished when they are able to drive from the tee with a certain amount of confidence, skill and success. Of course, so soon as the days of tuition are passed the novitiate begins to discover that it is not all golf to drive. It dawns upon him that the drive, in fact, is but the beginning of his troubles, and that, valuable as is the capacity to drive from the tee in such a manner, and with such certainty of direction, force and pitch, as to get into the best possible position for the succeeding strokes, the real problems of golf come when one is confronted with the question, "What club shall I use through the green?" a problem as various in its component elements as greens are numerous, and recurring with well-nigh every stroke under differing conditions. It is this variety which is the very spice of golf. 'Tis these never-ending, ever-changing conditions, indeed, which give golf its virility and surround its open fields with a fascination akin to that which is awakened in the student by the inexhaustible diversities of chess. Were it not for this mental gymnastics, if I may be permitted to use the simile, golf would be a mere exercise, but with it as its very essence, it claims the rank of a splendid outdoor science.

DOUGLAS ADDRESSING THE BALL, CLEEK SHOT.

Time deals hard with the golf player of to-day. Fifty years ago a golfer's set contained, at the very most, two iron clubs, a driving iron and a niblick. Where to-day we use a cleek, they of the past obtained like results by means of a spoon, long, middle or short, as the distance required. They played, if I may so call it, a clean game. There were fewer pieces of loose turf

DOUGLAS, PLAYING OUT A SAND BUNKER.
THE START AND FINISH OF THE SHOT

lying on the course and consequently less bad lies were to be found. Leather balls were used, and a "bad top" with an iron rendered them unplayable. They were expensive, too.

The increase in the number of iron clubs carried began with the introduction of the gutta percha ball. To-day, the average golfer carries six irons in his bag, viz., driving cleek, driving iron, mid-iron, mashie, putting cleek and niblick. The wooden clubs are generally limited to a driver, brassie, and, perhaps, a middle spoon.

To be able to play well with the iron clubs is a most important factor in the game. While stance, swing and grip are practically the same for all wooden clubs, it is not so with the iron. The swing with the wooden driver or brassie is always a full one. The stance, in relation to the ball, ought never to vary, except in exceptional cases, such as when the ball is hanging, or where the player is standing below or above the ball; whereas, with the iron clubs, the stance and length of swing are constantly changing, according to the lie of the ball and the distance from the hole. It is truly said that the difference between the first and second class players is that the former approach the hole better; that is, they are more adept in the use of the iron clubs.

Accuracy is the most important thing, no matter whether the distance to the hole be 50 or 150 yards. To obtain this accuracy at varying distances requires years of practice; not so much practice in playing a full round as in going out to vacant parts on the links and there mastering the particular clubs, playing shots at all distances and marking the carry and run after the balls fall.

One good way to improve your iron play is to play over different courses. If your experience is limited to one particular club links, you will most assuredly be entirely at sea when the time must come that you play over a strange course. While the driving and brassie play required will be similar to what you have been accustomed to on your home course, your approaching, for the most part, will be guesswork, and a bunker guarding the green, which you imagine 120 yards distant, may be 150' or only 100 yards from you. Beginners, especially, will find that distances on a strange golf course are very deceptive.

AT THE TOP OF THE SWING, CLEEK SHOT.

While we would not advise the beginner to carry the list of iron clubs before mentioned, it is absolutely necessary that he should carry the cleek, iron, and mashie before he will be able to get around the course in an at all respectable score. It is absolutely necessary that he master those three clubs. This can be done in the course of a few months' earnest practice.

Select a medium driving cleek, with a fairly stiff handle, driving the ball in the same manner as though using the driver. The position of the feet, in relation to the ball, are the same; if anything, the grasp is a little tighter with both hands. The swing and "follow through" are exactly the same as with the driver.

It will repay one well to practice with the cleek, so that one will have every confidence in using it. It is the favorite club of many of our best players. No matter how the ball is lying, if it is not quite unplayable, and distance is required, the cleek will be found to be the club to be used. There are very few courses where there is not a short hole about the distance of a cleek shot.

The man who can play his cleek well has a distinct advantage, especially so on a windy day. The wind does not seem to affect the ball and its flight so much when struck with an iron club as it does when it is driven with a wooden one.

It would be almost true to say that the cleek ought never to be used except for a full shot, were it not that there is a stroke known as the three-quarter cleek, which is recognized to be the most difficult shot to play with success.

To play this stroke is never absolutely necessary if one carries a driving iron, and this is the safest thing to do. The driving iron is used exactly as the driving cleek, and the distance of the full driving iron and the three-quarter cleek are the same.

The driving iron is a most useful club in long grass and when the ball is hanging, or lying in sand.

One of the strokes with the cleek which I have not mentioned is what is known as the "wrist stroke." This stroke is very much used at "old St. Andrew's" in approaching the hole.

"THE NIBLICK WILL STAND ROUGH USAGE." * (*p. 226.*)

There it can be used with impunity, as very few of the holes are guarded by bunkers in the direct line of play. However, it is a stroke which is not necessary, as the holes on most courses are guarded by some hazard over which it is necessary to pitch the ball.

For all ordinary approaching, the mid-iron will be found most suitable. It can be used with full swing, half-swing, or wrist. Care should be taken when selecting this club that it is not too heavy. If too heavy it will be found that in taking a full swing you feel as though you were being swung off your feet; it should balance well, and the shaft should be stiff.

The position of the feet for a full iron is the same as for the cleek. The shaft of the iron being a little shorter necessitates your standing nearer the ball and bending slightly more over it. Both hands are held tight, and here I would remark that care should be taken to see that the grip is fairly thick. If the handle should be thin, it will be found that the club head, on coming in contact with the ground, is apt to slip from the grasp, in which case there will be a lack of distance.

The most useful shot to practice with the mid iron, however, is the "half-iron."

*Reproduced from "How to Get Out of Trouble in Golf," in OUTING, August, 1898.

By applying different force, the ball can be made to travel from 100 to 150 yards with a "half-iron." Here the position of the player, in relation to the ball, changes. The right foot is advanced nearer the ball and more in a direct line with it. The club handle is grasped shorter and the body is kept stiff. The weight of the body rests almost entirely on the right foot. In the backward swing the club head travels closer to the ground and in a direct line from the ball. The right arm is bent and the elbow is kept close to the body. The left arm is kept almost straight, bending the least bit at the elbow. In coming down on the ball the left arm and shoulder do most of the work; the force they exert is in the nature of a pull During the stroke the weight of the body is transferred from the right to the left foot. As will be seen from the illustration, the club and arms follow through in the line of flight. This half-shot with the mid-iron is of great service when approaching against a head wind.

"THE NIBLICK IS USEFUL IN A SAND BUNKER." * *(p. 225.)*

The wrist stroke with the mid-iron, when properly executed, is very deadly; especially so is this the case when the turf between the player and the hole runs true. In fact, it is much easier and much surer to play a "long putt" with the mid-iron than to run it with the putter.

If the players in this country would throw away the club which is known as a "lofter" and would use the mid-iron more in their approaching, their game would improve thereby. The "lofter" is a delusion; it is not a sure club to play with at all; you either get too much under the ball with it, when you will be short, or you don't get down to it, in which case your ball will run twice as far as you intended it. It is absolutely no use, excepting, perhaps, when your ball lies buried in a heap of stones and you run the risk of breaking a club. The mashie, which is coming to be a very popular club for approaching within the last few years, is, however, used too frequently. This club was only intended to be used in approaching a hole which was up close behind a hazard. In this case, the ball had to be pitched a certain distance, and yet not run off upon falling, as it would do if played with an "iron."

Nowadays, people seem to think that

ADDRESSING FOR THE "HALF-IRON" SHOT.

the mashie is the proper club to approach with, no matter what the conditions of the ground are. There is perhaps nothing whatever in the shape of a hazard between them and the hole, and yet because it is, as they think, the proper thing to use the mashie, they prefer to run the risk when they would be more effective and much safer had they used the mid-iron. There is no doubt that an approach with a mashie is much prettier than an approach with a mid-iron, but it ought not to be "which is the prettier stroke" but "which will get you nearer the hole."

The different varieties of strokes with the mashie are very hard to master, and even when mastered require constant practice to keep. If it were not that it is a club which is necessary at some stage of the game, I would also say, "Throw it away."

In playing the mashie, a full swing should never be attempted. A swing with a half-shot will be found to carry just as far, and you will be much more accurate in direction. For the ordinary half-mashie, the stance is the same as in the case of the half-iron. The knees are bent a little more, and the body is nearer and more over the ball. In "following through," the club and arms follow the ball; the feet are kept perfectly stationary. In playing this stroke with the mashie, the ball will be found to run considerable after falling; and if one wants to increase that length of roll (and this is sometimes necessary where the ground is in bad condition and where the safest turf to pitch on may be further from the hole than the ordinary stroke of the mashie would make the ball go), then we take up a position in front of the ball, as on figure, page 225. The right foot is in a direct line with the ball and the weight of the body rests entirely on the right foot.

And now we come to a stroke with the mashie or iron in which the best player can never hope to attain perfection. It is what is known as the "cut stroke." The object is to get the ball to carry a certain distance and drop dead. The usual method to attain this result is to impart a "spin" to the ball by drawing the club across the line of flight. The hands in the upward part of the swing move out from the body, and coming down they are drawn sharp-

THE FINISH OF THE "HALF-IRON" SHOT.

ly in again. Aim should be taken to the left of the hole, as the spin will cause the ball to break to the right. This stroke is comparatively easy when we have a good "lie." Alas! however, good "lies" are the exception rather than the rule. Unless one is absolutely accurate it is impossible to put cut on a ball when turf is taken in playing the stroke, and it is just as impossible to get a ball away from an indifferent "lie" without taking some turf. One way by which a fairly uniform result will be obtained, no matter whether the "lie" be good, bad or indifferent, is to play the stroke off the left leg, taking a little turf. The left foot is in a line with and near to the ball. The right foot is drawn back. The weight of the body rests on the left. The right hand grips loosely, and the right thumb (as in the case of all wrist shots) should rest down the shaft, not across it as in the case of a full swing. During the swing the right elbow is kept close to the body. In this case the hands and club do not follow after the ball to the same degree as in the ordinary wrist stroke, but are brought up sharply through holding the elbows close. In playing with the mashie it is well to remember that if you want the ball to run after it pitches, stand in front of it, and *vice versa*.

THE WRIST MASHIE—BODY WELL IN FRONT OF THE BALL.

THE FINISH OF THE WRIST MASHIE—BODY WELL IN FRONT OF THE BALL.

One stroke in playing with the irons through the green that I have not mentioned is the "jerk" stroke. When the ball is lying in a cup it is obvious that it cannot be swept away as though it were "teed." It has to be "jerked" out. When properly played, there is very little distance lost. Swing in the ordinary way, but aim to hit into the ground between the ball and the turf. The "jerk" will be felt after the ball is on its way.

By taking a little turf in playing the iron clubs, better direction is insured. One is not so apt to pull or slice. Do not, however, take too much; just skin the ground. See that the caddie replaces all divots. This is a part of his work and helps the preservation of the course.

While not absolutely necessary, the niblick is a most useful club to carry. It is especially so on courses where there are heavy sand bunkers. It should be heavy, with a strong and stiff shaft. In playing out of sand, swing, or rather lift, the niblick back almost as you would a hammer. Aim not to strike the ball, but the sand back of it. Think nothing about following through, but hit hard into the sand. The force of the impact coming almost immediately under the ball will cause the latter to rise quickly and will enable the player to clear the opposing bank of the bunker. There will not be much distance to this stroke, but distance is not to be thought of when the ball is lying up close behind the face of a bunker. Get the ball out, and if possible play it so that it will be in an advantageous position for the next stroke. It is foolish to attempt to use an iron in a bunker for the sake of a few more yards gained in distance. If it is your last chance for a "half" that you must reach the green from the sand, then go ahead. In the majority of cases, all you want is to extricate yourself in one stroke, and the niblick will be found to be the safer club. The niblick will stand any amount of rough usage, and for this reason is well adapted for playing from very bad "lies," such as cart-ruts, roots of trees, and stones, where there is a danger of destroying the head of a favorite club.

To sum up: Iron clubs should balance nicely. The shafts should be stiff, the driving cleek alone having a little spring to it. Make up your mind what distance the hole is and what club you will use, before you begin to address the ball. Whenever the distance and nature of the ground will permit, approach with your mid-iron. Play half-shots with stiff arms and strike the ball firmly. Take a little turf, and, above all things, keep your eye on the ball. Remember that, in wrist shots, when you stand behind the ball it will fall dead; if you want it to run, stand in front of it.

PLAYING A WRIST MASHIE—THE BODY WELL BEHIND THE BALL.
THE START AND FINISH OF THE SHOT.

28

Golf in Gotham

OUTING.

VOL. XXXIV. AUGUST, 1899. No. 5.

Photos by T. C. Turner.

THE THIRTEENTH GREEN, CRESCENT CLUB, OVERLOOKING THE NARROWS.

GOLF IN GOTHAM.

BY CHARLES TURNER.

THERE are pleasant aspects of life even in the busiest city in the Western Hemisphere. It is certainly one of them to stand amidst the bustling throng of the lower Broadway, the great artery which carries the impetuosity of the concentrated impulse of the most earnest business people in the world, and to know that within a cannon-shot in any direction, up or down, north or south, and eastward of the living stream, there are golf links holding out the fair hand of peace, contentment, rest, and good health. That in fact within the radius of the city limits, and thereby of course excluding those over in Jersey, there are eighteen golf clubs, each the center of an enthusiastic crowd drawn from the very vortex of this tumult and this striving.

But this is to put golf in Gotham in the straitest of strait-jackets, because, just outside the limits prescribed by necessity in this article, are the principal points of pilgrimage, those real Meccas of the enthusiastic golfer, St. Andrew's at Mount Hope, Ardsley Casino by the Hudson, Garden City in Long Island, and Tuxedo, to say nothing of the great Jersey centers where so many thousands of New Yorkers take their leisure, the Oranges (a pleasant basketful), Morris County, and the bevy of clubs that dot the Palisades.

Even this enumeration falls short of the real extent of Gotham's golfing necessities, for every summer her ardent sons and daughters lay under contribution the string of pearls which lie along the seacoast from Sandy Hook to Barnegat Bay, and on Long Island from St. Lawrence and Rye to the far-off Shinnecock Hills, to say nothing of their tithe which may be reckoned in the Adirondacks, and indeed in every resort where Columbia gathers her beauty and her chivalry.

In fact, golf has become the game of

THE EIGHTH GREEN, RICHMOND COUNTY COUNTRY CLUB, S. I.

the people, using the term in the broadest sense; and, paradoxical as it may at first seem, nowhere is it so much so as in the great metropolis. If I were asked for proof of this assertion I should not have to rely upon the premises I have already laid down or on the variety, extent, and popular support so freely extended to the eighteen clubs within the city's limits, which are maintained by its supporters; I should but have to point out that beyond all these, and outside the provision they so lavishly make, there are two thousand players who are mostly unattached to any club, and who are content if once in a week they can hie them to the two hundred acres of public links at Van Cortlandt Park.

The finger of scorn is often pointed, and often recklessly, at Gotham and its greed, and at the sins of omission and commission of its municipal govern-

THE TENTH GREEN, HARBOR HILLS, S. I.

ment. Let me as a golfer and inhabitant of much-maligned New York, raise this one little candle in honor of the powers that be, who were the first, and for a long time were the only ones, in the United States, to provide for the general public a public links. It may take more than ten righteous men, in these latter days, to save a city, but Gotham is not without hope in more respects than this provision, singular as it was. That its influence has been more than local is attested by the fact that Boston followed suit, and even now the pick and roller are at work in Jackson Park for the benefit of the rank and file of the royal and ancient game in Chicago.

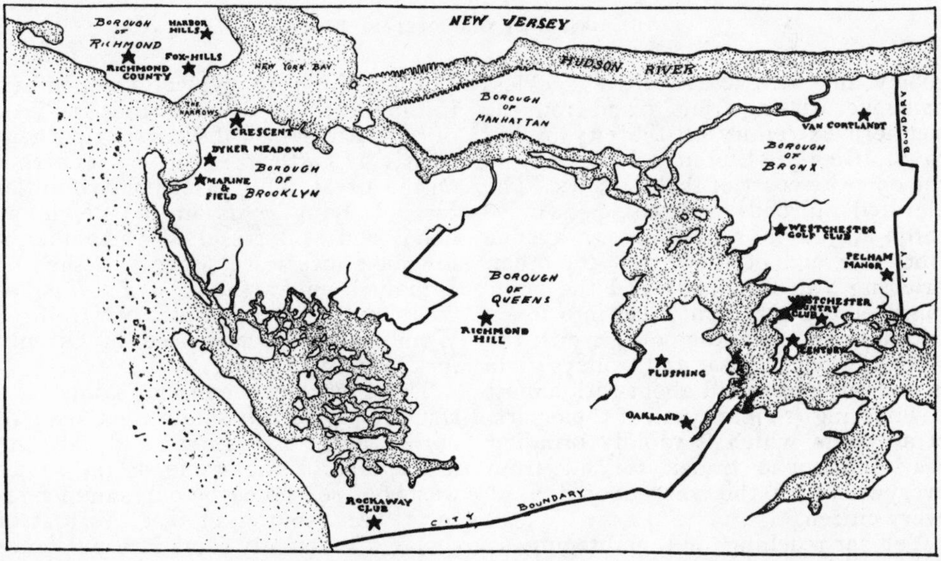

If nature had planned so that golf should, in the great metropolis, have opportunities commensurate with the great demands it would create, and that it should arrive at a time coincident with the possibilities of reaching the city's outermost borders, she could not, in either respect, have planned more wisely.

No city in the continent, indeed it may with truth be said, no metropolitan city in the world, has the peerless position of New York. Miles on miles of water front girdle its teeming millions. On one side wide wildernesses of sandblown dunes, cast up and ground and threshed by the mighty Atlantic's winter storms, are left soft yet solid for summer's recreations. On two others, for yet greater distances, the gentler waters of the Sound lave the feet of "boweries," to use a good old Knickerbocker and appropriate phrase, which sink, verdure-clad and tree-embowered, down to its margins. Its tide-swept, breezy harbor's coast-lines, a compromise between the Atlantic and the lake-like Sound, present in the undulations of the Narrows and the terraced heights of Staten Island, a series of sites for golf unequaled for position, salubrity, and beauty; whilst the uplands that rise and fall from the moment Manhattan isle's northern boundary is left, until the furthest city limit is reached, present a combination of pastures, orchard, country road and lane, barren rocks and trickling streams, lake and forest, the like of which may be equaled but cannot be excelled.

What nature prepared with the patient diligence of untold centuries, the remarkable achievements of science, in these latter days, have made accessible in a degree never before equaled. We may lack some facilities in city locomotion, and at certain definite times, when in a few minutes all the world is desirous of converging at the narrowest end of the wedge, there is undoubtedly an undesirable congestion; but taken large and by, as the golfer disciplined to larger views will gladly do, there is little that is left undone. Boats swift,

THE FIRST TEE, VAN CORTLANDT PARK.

roomy and safe weave their trackless and never-ceasing trails to and from the southern extremity of the city proper to St. George, Staten Island, and to the opposite coast of the Narrows. The elevated railroads with ceaseless pulse throb through nearly every avenue from one end of the city to the other, bringing Van Cortlandt and the outer range of the northern parks into touch within the limit of the hour; whilst the serpentine electric car and trolleys glide in and out and round about with almost bewildering frequency all of them parts of a system which is rapidly bringing easy and cheap transit to and from everywhere to the very door-step of every citizen.

Yet far-reaching and embracing as the results are, it has all come about as a law of nature. Well do I remember, in the fall of 1890, yet lacking one year of ten since passed, discoursing, perhaps effusively, with the editor of OUTING on the great and glorious opportunities for golf lying *perdu* in the neighborhood; and still freshly I remember, a few days afterward, feeling abashed as I mailed under the *nom de plume* of "Albion," the limited plea of "Golf for Women," which appeared in OUTING for December, 1890.

There was not then to my knowledge a single player this side of the Canadian border, and I had in my mind only the utilization for the game of the sandy wastes of seashores by our summer resorts. As a matter of fact, the first of such clubs actually came into existence the next year at Shinnecock, among the

THE ROCKAWAY HUNT CLUB, CEDARHURST.

summer cottagers of Southampton on the coast of Long Island. The spread of the game since that grain of literary mustard-seed was planted is public property, and only indirectly part of the subject now under discussion, "Golf in Gotham."

The first physical, visible indication of golf in Gotham came in 1892-3, when the curious might have detected a few, a very few, of the faithful, once or twice a week, wending their way, with mysterious receptacles of sticks with iron ends, which might easily have been mistaken for improvised umbrella-stands, to the improvised links adjacent to the Cricket Club of Livingstone, S. I.

That golf should find a welcome among the kindred spirits who have for so long a period wielded the willow in cricket on Staten Island, is a matter of no surprise. The whole history of the Staten Island Cricket Club has been one of catholicity and welcome to all kindred sports either on sea or land. Rowing and yachting even, far removed as they may seem, from the parent motive, cricket, have been auxiliaries; whilst a baseball diamond is blazoned on the face of the fairest cricket-field that New York possesses, and the westernmost section of the same fair green has been for many years monopolized by the lady lawn-tennis players amongst its members. Indeed, time was when in the full blast of the popularity of lawn-tennis they might have fairly been taken as its most characteristic exponents.

Golf, therefore, had a natural ally in the good fellows who have so long held aloft the gospel of fresh air and outdoor sports in the metropolis. Indeed, there may even be an historic claim to its position as the premier welcomer of the game in the metropolis, for there is a tradition, with more than the usual basis on fact, that far away in the antebellum days of 1863, one Mr. Betts, a member, brought over from Scotland a set of clubs and displayed their uses to his brother members. Good Mr. Betts, I rejoice to record your loyalty to the ancient and honorable game. Like many another disciple, your propaganda was born before the times were ripe. Would that those venerable clubs could now be put on exhibition as a standing memento, to whom it may concern, of what has been lost to two generations!

THE NINTH GREEN AND CLUB-HOUSE, DYKER MEADOW, BROOKLYN.

Desultory and tentative golf existed on a course over the country east of the club-house and at the back of Sailors' Snug Harbor for quite a time before the first regular course of nine holes was formally laid out in 1896 with a playing length of 2,287 yards. The new links at

Fox Hills may produce, and probably will, players of greater skill than did the old familiar and well-beloved first course; but it should not be forgotten that the zeal and skill of the primitive round produced, as early as 1894, two competitors in the first national championship ever played in the States, at Gray Oaks, St. Andrew's, by Yonkers, and the names of G. E. Armstrong and S. S. Robinson stand on this the first bede-roll of honor of the game.

The new eighteen-hole course at Fox Hills differs in nearly every respect from the original lowland course of the club, and from all other courses in the metropolis. Indeed, it is so barren as to suggest the bleak moors of Yorkshire or lowland Scotland rather than the city of New York. Treeless, or nearly so, windswept and bare, it yet affords to the golfer looking for ideal conditions the very best course, not only within the metropolis, but for many a league around. It is scarcely yet in condition for play, and is, except to its selectors, very nearly unknown, but, ere many years, the name of Fox Hills will, I opine, have become a household word amongst the golfers of the United States.

Harbor Hills, the second of the Staten Island Golf Club in point of time, has the distinction of being the first established to play golf and nothing else. It is the real simon pure of the sport. Its location, high on the backbone of the island, isolated its district, to a certain extent, from easy participation in the play of its more lowland neighbors and forced the enthusiasm to find the lines of least resistance at home. Its origin was of the most primitive and hardy sort, but, crude and circumscribed as was its first grounds and difficult to negotiate, they did but whet the appetite of the ten good golfers and true who, in 1895, organized the club. By the next year its original six-hole course had become nine, of the very respectable length of 1,933 yards; its membership had increased by leaps and bounds; its little club-house had become the center of the social life of quite a community, and its team, including the redoubtable Dr. Burdett O'Connor, has attained a notoriety that may be found victoriously recorded in the annals of the past and present years.

THE CLUB-HOUSE, HARBOR HILLS.

At the present time, the club's membership of 300 is full to overflowing; its course is a full one, too, of 18 holes, extending over 4,331 yards, and the prowess of its members has been proven in many a golfing fray.

The situation of its links is very commanding, and when it is stated, as the fact is, that it embraces in one view the whole upper bay, with Brooklyn Bridge hanging in lace-like fantasy across the vista, enough has been said to indicate the possibilities and beauties of Harbor Hills' site.

Light lingers long on the crest of Staten Island, and this is no small factor in the time which can be devoted to

THE FIRST GREEN, WESTCHESTER COUNTRY CLUB.

the acquisition of the requisite skill for success.

Women form an important element in the ranks of the Harbor Hills players, and their influence is represented amongst the officers by an associate captain, Miss A. K. Robinson.

The last in point of time, yet perhaps the first in point of golfing importance of the three Staten Island organizations, is the Richmond County Country Club, whose members, from their eerie on the crags of Dongan Hills, overlook the whole lower bay, and, except for the spit of Sandy Hook, receive the untainted breezes of three thousand miles of salt water. Surely a links in this respect, although to be more conventional it should have been on the rich undercliff, rather than on the cliff tops. But what is lost in conventionality is gained in picturesqueness and in health-giving qualities. So salubrious indeed was the situation that eight years before the advent of golf the club was the center of social and equestrian life, and the baying of the club's hounds woke the echoes of many a hunter's morn.

When in the fullness of time golf claimed its recognition, what better home could it have fallen heir to than the old Alexander mansion and estate,

THE MARINE AND FIELD CLUB. THE MAIN HOUSE.

THE RICHMOND HILL CLUB-HOUSE (BROOKLYN).

and no better sponsors could it have had than Captain James Park and his colleagues, John R. Chadwick, Albert E. Patterson, W. W. Lowry and Edward Beckett, under whose guidance in 1896 the nine-hole course was first laid out. Since the days of the game's apprenticeship it has been found necessary to complete the course to eighteen holes varying from 144 yards to 469 in length and presenting as great a variety of problems as of length. The amateur record of eighty is an indication of the nature of the course on Dongan Hills.

The third hole is of so unusual a character as to deserve special mention, the ball having to be driven in little over a hundred yards down into a green in a valley some two hundred feet below.

Whilst none of the 325 members of the club have obtained the highest honors of the game, yet it has many prominent players, and the club's team is known and feared round a wide circuit where victory has lit on their banners. There is seldom a week when the players of the Richmond County Country Club are not giving or taking blows on their own or on neighboring links, setting a commendable example of pluck and neighborly feeling, prominent among whom are the veterans James A. Park, G. E. Armstrong, J. R. Chadwick, C. P. Stout, A. E. Patterson and C. A. Fry.

The trinity of clubs upon the Staten Island side of "the Narrows" is matched by a similar trinity upon the opposite or Brooklyn side, "Dyker Meadow," "The Crescent" and "The Marine and Field." Of those, the first in order of establishment, and the only one of three exclusively devoted to golf, is "The Dyker Meadow Club," established in 1895 on links that come down to the sea at Gravesend Bay. The accessibility of these links, for they can be reached from any part of the two cities, via Brooklyn Bridge and Fort Hamilton electric street cars in a very short time at any hour of the day or night, would alone have insured their popularity, but when to that availability is added the fact that, although but a nine-hole course of 3,003 yards, the links are, from a pure golfer's point of view, one of the best in the United States, it is not surprising to find that its membership of 250 is backed by a portentous waiting list.

Nature has done more than man for the deserved popularity of the Dyker Meadow course. The turf is old and close, and of that variety that only comes from generations of freedom from the plow and the presence of close nibbling, and when this is stretched over a series of natural undulations gradually approaching the sea, and in addition it receives the most careful and skillful attention for the purpose to which it is now put, good results must follow, with so good a team as are made by Daniel Chauncey, Alfred Norris, Duncan Edwards, W. B. and W. H. Crittenden, J. H. Merritt, W. K. Fowler and J. C. Burns, Norman S. Dike and others close on their heels.

From the club-house and ninth green, looking to the south, nearly all the greens can be seen in one view, backed by the dancing waters of Gravesend Bay, where the white wings of the Atlantic Yacht Club flit by and the lighthouse on Sea Gate lifts its portentous finger like an exclamation point!

"The Crescent Golf Club" owes its magnificent home on Bay Ridge, the east cliff of the Narrows, to the parent club, the Crescent Athletic Club, whose colors and crescent, like the scimitar of the conquering Moors, has for many a year mown swaths of conquest on turf and field. It was not until the fall of 1896 that a sufficient number of the general members of the club had developed golfing tendencies to need a separate organization and a separate course. The Crescent is the nearest club to the core of the city, from whose center the advancing locusts of the dire speculative builder swoop like the plague and devour every green thing. Even now its links are gridironed with actual or designed roads, and its possession cribbed, cabined and confined by obstacles and inconveniences. However, the Crescents are nothing if not plucky, and, after delays and annoyances which are trying to the temper of even the mildest golfer, they are surely more than compensated by the magnificence, nay the splendor, spread before the piazzas of the fort-like club, as the sun bathes the cloudscape beyond the misty Ramapos and swathes the heights of Staten Island and the bays, from the Statue of Liberty to the Navesink Highlands, in a glory of color impossible to describe, and to be seen in such perfection in but few favored spots. Happy Crescents! You can sacrifice much for such a privilege!

The Marine and Field Club, of Brooklyn, the last of the three ocean-facing clubs, is our old friend, whose little colony, devoted to "all lawful land and water sports," has lived a happy and prosperous life on the waterfront of Bath Beach in Gravesend Bay since 1885. What answer could a club with a charter so catholic as that say to golf? For surely here was "a lawful land sport," and so to the broad piazzas of "the Main House," where ladies most do congregate, to "the Cottage," sacred to bachelors, and to "the Tower Hall," came golf with the summer colonists of 1896. It was welcomed warmly, but modestly, for the Marine and Field is conservative, and had assigned to it a small five-hole course. But golf, like Cleopatra's appetite, doth grow by what it feeds on, and so in 1897 it devoured additional property for a 1,900 yard nine-hole course, and in 1898 had extended 2,400 yards up and down and to and from and this way and that, over rolling ridges and natural hazards, where stone walls are not, and trees, when present, are disciplined. The taste must be epicurean to the border of the troublesome that cannot find ideality, rest and health in the conditions which surround golf at the Marine and Field Club.

THE CLUB-HOUSE, OAKLAND.

Its club and team play is as wide and varied as its hospitality and its more prominent players include Frank N. Doubleday, Arthur P. Clapp, J. Temple Gwatheney, H. N. Curtis, L. Daniels, E. H. Kinney and Percy S. Mallett.

Before taking a flight to the city's northern coast lines, there is one other southern course, at Cedarhurst, L. I., which must be disposed of.

The club, of which the links at Cedarhurst is one of the outcomes, is one of almost patriarchal age, and certainly formed originally to foster the most patriarchal of pastimes, the sport of kings—the horse. It was little foreseen in 1878, when the Virginian pack of foxhounds found a welcome and subsequently a home at the headquarters of the Rockaway Hunting Club at Cedarhurst, that within twenty years the encroachments of time and the builder would make golf a welcome auxiliary, and the fields and fences that once on a time were the delight of the intrepid horseman and the terror of the "duffer" should become an equal source of joy and tribulation to the wielder of the mashie and the niblick. Polo still flourishes with more than its pristine glory where the hound was once supreme, and golf, a kindred sport of kindred spirits, has come to help along the love of robust outdoor life upon which Cedarhurst was builded those many years ago.

The course now in construction in lieu of the older nine-holes, will be an eighteen-hole one; the soil is sandy and the turf very good. When it is stated that it was laid out by that Napoleon of link designers, Thomas Bendelow, it may be assumed that every advantage has been taken of the opportunities offered. Good golf, and not eccentricity or startling results, is the guiding principle of Bendelow's work, and it is not out of place here to acknowledge the obligations the game in the metropolis is under to his ability. Of the eighteen courses we are considering, he laid out nine and has influenced several others.

When we turn from the extreme south to the extreme north, and stand on the northern shores of the Sound instead of upon the fiercer Atlantic, we shall find the same sporting equestrianism to have been the precursor and foster father of the class from whom golf naturally had its early recruits. It was the horse over the stone walls of Westchester that was the chief diversion of the Country Club at Westchester, and on the polo fields he holds still an unrivaled supremacy, but the click of the golfer over so fit and picturesque a country as that of Westchester could not long tarry.

The Country Club of Westchester has a grievance against the public recognition, to its own exclusion, of Shinnecock as the workshop which has turned out the greatest woman player America has yet seen, the incomparable and unconquered Champion Beatrix Hoyt, whereas, in fact, Westchester is her home links. There is enough honor for both to share, and my modest claim is only that a links within the city limits should not be ousted entirely from its share of this golfing glory.

Like all the early links, the beginnings here were tentative. Hole was added to hole in 1895, until seven covered a playing distance of 1,400 yards, and each year since has seen it grow and grow, until its nine holes cover one of the longest courses in the country, 3,017 yards.

The nearest neighbor to the Country Club of Westchester is a new organization, "The Century Club." It is well supported, it has an excellent club-house, and excellent links running down to the Sound; but that is not its peculiarity. Its distinction amongst the clubs of the metropolis is that it is the one club of Hebrews devoted to *outdoor sport*. The Jews in all nations and times have produced, and never more so than to-day, more than their share of leaders in art, in drama, in music, in literature and in law; in fact, in all those walks of life in which intellectual acumen and close application to books, and to the study of mankind, is the main force; but they have hitherto, as a people, shown little aptitude for, or application to, the sports of the field and of sustained interest in outdoor recreation. The members of the Century Club have somewhat broken away from tradition and recognize the value of the adage that though "all work and no play" does not always make a dull boy, at any rate the more settled conditions resulting from their civic and religious freedom in America demand, as a corrective, more attention to the corporal upbuilding which comes from systematic outdoor exercise and relaxation.

The third Westchester Club is really, if I may use the expression, "a son of the

THE EIGHTH GREEN, OAKLAND (WITH GIRL CADDIES).

soil," in the sense that it is the natural result of the congregation in that favored district of the homes of so large a proportion of people of means and leisure. Its club-house is not at its links, the one being at 167th street and Westchester avenue, the other, at present, on the east bank of the Bronx. It is a nine-hole course, plentifully besprinkled with Westchester's specialty, "stone walls," than which no more exasperating hazard could be designed. The turf is natural and good, and the links well cared for. There is a rumor current, which indicates the ambition stirring in this new organization, that an eighteen-hole course is already the subject of negotiation in a not far removed district.

The fourth and last of the Westchester group is the Pelham Country Club, a nine-hole course laid out in the spring of 1898, whereon the pupils of a well-known near-by school for young ladies have the happy privilege of becoming early initiated into the health-giving pastime, wherein so many of them in after years will find so welcome a refuge and diversion.

And now we must hark back again to Long Island, on the opposite side, however, to that on which we last were, and pick up on the Sound side "The Flushing Golf Club," the pride of the golfers of that old and aristocratic settlement, onto which modern progress has grafted a new colony altogether in harmony socially with the ancient régime. The course is a nine-hole, laid out by Bendelow, over a country which, without giving anything remarkable, has, in the language

THE FIFTH TEE, FLUSHING. TRAVIS DRIVING.

of one of its members, produced "a very nice" course. That is exactly its best description — very nice. Everything about is just that, and thereby it is exactly suitable to the discriminating taste of a very nice neighborhood. Its distinguishing characteristics appeared to me to be the youthfulness of the majority of its players—a commendable trait.

From Flushing it is but five miles, to the east, to the club that has produced by far the most prominent men playing on the metropolitan links, the Oakland Club at Bayside, the home club of, amongst others, Walter J. Travis. The Oakland is in more than the usual sense his home club, because it was upon its links he taught himself the game, and to the diversity of its holes he attributes the great success which has followed his apprenticeship to himself. He did not begin practice until the fall of 1896, but so persistent and successful were his efforts, that by the opening of the season of 1898 he had achieved a position in the highest ranks, and in that year he won eight prizes, five of which were gold medals for lowest scores at medal play. Among his winnings were the gold medals of Seabright and Lakewood, the Archbold cup, at Knollwood, and the first cups at Dyker Meadow and Oakland. The total of his medal cups was 400, an average of 80. In the amateur championship he beat T. L. Blair, of Morris County; I. H. Thorp, of Cambridge, and Foxhall P. Keene (Oakland), and was only defeated in the semi-finals by the Champion Douglas.

A GOOD PLACE FOR A NIBLICK, WESTCHESTER GOLF CLUB.

Already this summer Travis has started another victorious campaign by winning the open championship of Lakewood over H. M. Forest (Philadelphia), H. M. Harriman (Meadowbrook), and C. Watson, Jr. (Westbrook), following that by winning the open championship of the Marine and Field Club, over Cornelius B. Van Brunt and H. S. Bowns, and his home championship cup over Watson, by nearly faultless golf.

Next to Travis the best player in the club is that veritable Admirable Crichton, Foxhall P. Keene, who is at home and in the highest flight alike at polo and at the traps and in golf.

Another player of whom much is expected, and who began this season by beating Douglas, is Herbert M. Harriman. Last year he won three prizes. Herbert L. Riker, who also hails from Oakland, won last year the Consolation cups at Oakland and Norwood.

In passing, let me not forget to note an experiment which has been made at Oakland and been found very successful, and that is the employment of girls for caddies. Not to the exclusion of

THE RICHMOND COUNTY COUNTRY CLUB-HOUSE, DONGAN HILLS, S. I.

THE WESTCHESTER COUNTRY CLUB-HOUSE.

Photos by T. C. Turner.

THE CRESCENT CLUB-HOUSE, ON THE CLIFFS OF THE NARROWS.

THE NEW CLUB-HOUSE, FOX HILLS, S. I.

boys, but in coöperation, and, from all I have heard, the attention and eyesight of these ministering maidens of the links are superior to that of their male competitors. When one comes to think of it, why should they not be preferable company for our sisters and our cousins and our aunts?

And yet again, to dispose of the Long Island clubs within the metropolitan metes and bounds, there is the Richmond Hill Country Club, perched on the backbone of the island, on the borders of the seven miles of forest that have so providentially been saved by the municipality from the ravenous maw of the speculating builder, and held in trust for the people as a park. High up on dry and timbered heights which catch the wafting winds from the ocean on either side, Richmond Hill occupies a most desirable site, and its nine holes, of a total length of 2,176 yards, pass up hill and down dale amidst the wooded outposts of the near-by forest and present natural hazards that render its negotiation in more than a usual degree difficult for the stranger within its gates.

Finally, in a class by itself, for the reasons already detailed in the opening of this article, stands the public links at Van Cortlandt Park, situate, as all such links should be, immediately adjacent to a railroad station through which two

THE MAKING OF A GOLF COURSE. FOX HILLS, STATEN ISLAND, IN TRANSITION.

lines run, one in connection with the network of the Manhattan Elevated system at One Hundred and Fifty-fifth street and the other direct to the Grand Central Depot at Forty-second street.

The first tournament, open only to those who were not members of clubs in the United States Golf Association, was held over the nine-hole course November 28, 1896.

The years from 1896 to 1899 were years of anxiety, for, whilst numbers increased, discipline and order decreased. It remained for a wiser policy (thanks largely, if not solely, to Commissioner August Moebus) to be inaugurated, and a green-keeper of the wide experience and distinct firmness of Thomas Bendelow, to be left in almost autocratic charge, to bring chaos to order in this year of grace.

The course has been extended to eighteen holes, and so much are the powers that be encouraged that they are now laying out a still further public course in Sunset Park, Brooklyn. More power to the good cause!

The original nine holes at Van Cortlandt form a vision of delight to the eye, and, though capable of being made more satisfactory to the golfer, they could scarcely be more artistic. A long, flat valley, all grass, with wooded hills coming down on one side close, and on the other a lily-covered lake and parklike uplands, inclose a moving panorama of color-dotted players, who, in variety of costume, give to the pasture an effect not to be equaled for brilliancy and life on any links in the world. A Saturday afternoon on the old nine-hole course is one of the sights no citizen, much less a golfer, should miss.

And now, in conclusion, lest it be thought that the students of the metropolitan university, Columbia, were behind their contemporaries in golfing sport, let it be noted that that institution has a flourishing golf club and enjoys the best of opportunities for exercising it, but, from the peculiar geographical conformation of the Manhattan isle, not within the city limits. The university, as all the world knows, crowns the Riverside heights, and it is easier for its golfing members to cross the Hudson by the Fort Lee Ferry and take the cars to Englewood, over in New Jersey, than it is to reach any other links in the metropolitan area. So that they are in the metropolis, but, as golfers, not of it, and hence, by the necessities of the limitations of this article, are not legitimately to be reckoned with in an article on golf in Gotham.

29

Form in Golf

•

Vardon and His Ideas

FORM IN GOLF.

By Harry Vardon.

I HAVE never before written, or had published, any matter regarding my ideas of playing golf; and I will commence by contradicting the statement so universally made by people when speaking or writing about me, that I " infringe every known rule laid down in the books and play a game which is peculiar to myself." The only peculiarity about the way I play is in the manner in which I hold my clubs, and this I will endeavor to explain, with the aid of the accompanying illustrations from life.

I grasp the club about two inches from the top, and I always play with very short clubs, my driver being only forty inches long, measured from the top of the shaft to the heel of the head; my brassey is the same length, my idea being that I have better control over a short club than over a longer one.

I place my left thumb along the center of the shaft and completely cover it with the palm of the right hand, the little finger of my right hand overlapping the knuckle of the first finger of my left hand, the end of the little finger being half way between the knuckle and the second joint of the first finger of the left hand.

I neither hold my club in the palms of my hands nor in the fingers; the shaft lies across my right hand and rests between the palm and the fingers of the left hand, and I grasp the club equally tightly with both hands. I use the word tightly because I mean tight, and do not mean to convey the idea that I merely hold the club firmly.

My idea in holding the club as I do, is that I, to all intents and purposes, make the two hands into one and consequently only have to consider the swing of one arm instead of two.

I adopted this grip after trying all kinds of methods of holding clubs, some seven years ago; and not until then did I feel the perfect confidence in myself which is absolutely indispensable to a proper control over the ball and the consequent control over direction.

I ought to add that I put my right thumb on the left-hand side of the centre of the shaft when driving, and straight down the centre of the shaft for all kinds of iron shots. I never allow my club to move in my hand after addressing the ball until I have completed my stroke.

I carry the club for a full swing back behind my shoulders, almost parallel with the ground, my two hands a little above the top of the shoulder, about on a level with my jaw, and the point of the elbow almost squared a very little above the level of my hands, probably an inch, or possibly two.

I come down much straighter than men who carry their clubs further back

VARDON ADDRESSING.

and I stand very much more upright; my club thus describes a truer arc from the top of the swing to the end of the follow through than if I described a wider circle.

A great deal has been said in the papers about my method of approaching. It is perfectly true that I always run a ball in preference to pitching it, if the nature of the ground permits; as it is very much easier to simply have to calculate the amount of strength to put behind a ball to roll it a certain distance than to have to gauge the strength required to pitch a given distance and allow for the roll after, especially as it is very frequently impossible to tell whether you are going to pitch on an exceptionally soft spot or vice versa.

I consider putting, next to the mashie approach, the most important stroke in golf. I always carry two different kinds

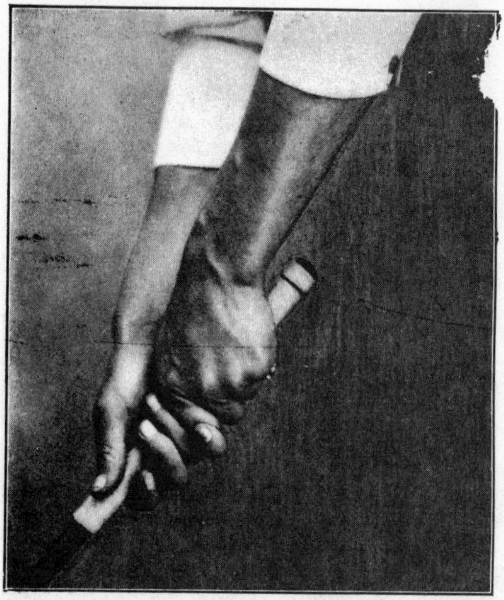

VARDON'S GRASP.

of putters and I have several different stances, and if I find I am off with one putter I try the other and keep altering my stance until I feel perfectly comfortable; for without this feeling you can not have confidence, and without confidence good and accurate putting is an impossibility.

The expression "a wrist shot" is to me an absurdity; there is no such thing as a wrist stroke alone. In all my so-called wrist shots I make the arms and the wrists act together, but I do not turn my wrists back. My left arm is almost straight, and my right elbow is close to my side and my right forearm is held stiff. It amuses me very much to hear people remark when I place an approach shot close to the hole, "Goodness gracious, what a cut he did put on the ball! He must have drawn his club clean across the ball to make it stop so dead." Now as a matter of fact, I do not put any cut on the ball with my club; but instead of striking the ground about half an inch behind the ball and pitching it straight up, I strike the ball itself almost on the side, a little above the center, and drive it into the ground, from which it ricochets. The ground puts the cut on which stops the ball, and not the club.

I believe I am the only man who makes this stroke, and it is another of the instances in which I am supposed to infringe the rules of golf as laid down in the books.

Newspaper critics always say that it my second shot which wins me the ıampionship. This I believe myself to ɜ perfectly true, and I will endeavor to describe how it is that I make it. The most important point, which results in long accurate playing, is the keeping perfect time between the raising of the club, after addressing the ball, to the top of the swing, and the raising of the left heel over the left toe as it pivots around. These two motions should take place simultaneously; and the downward swing and the return of the left foot to the exact position it was in when the upward swing commenced should also be simultaneous. At the precise moment when the left heel reaches the ground and the club head strikes the ball, the

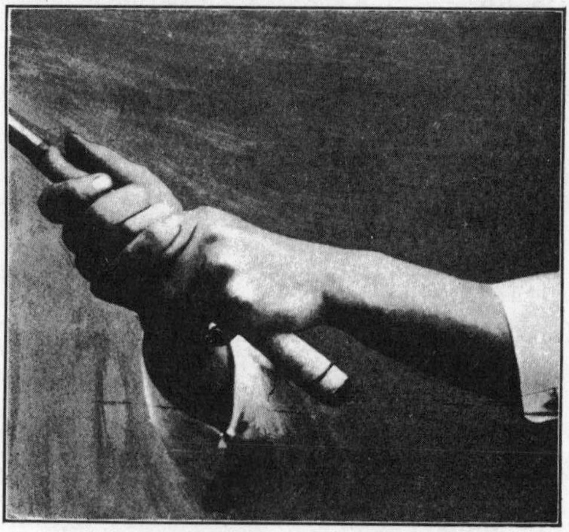

VARDON'S GRASP.

raising of the right heel over the right toe commences; and it rises in the same proportion as the club rises in the follow through, until both reach their limit, which limit is the very point of your right toe. The minute that point is reached the swing is completed, and unless you allow your arms to follow through until your toe reaches that point, you check your swing and lose distance.

In regard to my method of training, or rather, to my lack of training, I have what seems to me to be common-sense reasons for acting as I do. I am naturally a healthy man, with a good appetite, and I live about the same all the year round; I always drink whenever I feel like it, but never to excess, and I am an inveterate smoker. This mode of living, combined with an outdoor life, keeps me in perfect health, and I consider that my normal condition is the one in which I am the most likely to play my best; my nerves are not irritated either by extra abstinence or by any sudden excesses, and I feel no more excitement when entering for a big match than I do when playing a mixed foursome, which, after all said and done, I consider the most pleasant way of enjoying a game of golf.

VARDON AND HIS IDEAS.

By Charles S. Cox.

IN writing about Harry Vardon and his style of playing golf, a most important point in my opinion is the man's temperament.

He is naturally very quiet and unassuming in his manner and gives you the idea of being phlegmatic and not much given either to study or thought; but underneath his outward appearance of "don't care much about anything" lie a very shrewd head and a bundle of nerves, which supply him with an inexhaustible fund of vitality, directly he is interested in anything.

The shrewd, common-sense style of analysis which he brings to bear upon subjects about which he knows absolutely nothing, invariably leads him in the right direction, and he seems to get to the very bottom of whatever he attempts to do or to talk about. If he had not been a golf player he would probably have been a great man in any other line of business requiring a good eye, perfect control over the nerves, and the faculty of accomplishing anything by the power of deduction.

He is supposed to infringe every known rule laid down by the best writers on golf, such as Horace Hutchinson, Simpson, and Park. As a matter of fact, I do not think he does anything of the kind: he simply supplies the missing links to the chain which they attempt to make when describing their ideas of what constitutes a perfect style when playing.

They give an idea of a swing, which no doubt is mathematically correct, but as there are no two men made alike, their ideal swing is one which very few men can adapt to their varied styles of physique.

I have heard it frequently stated by men who have seen Vardon play since he came over here, that he drives with a three-quarter swing. Now, with a three-quarter swing, the elbow of the right arm is down, and the hands are below the level of the arm-pit, or about on a level with it, and the club is pointing up; while for a full swing the elbow is square on a level with the face, and the hands are about on the same level as the elbow. The general idea of a full swing is, that it is the length of the arc described by the club, which constitutes a full swing. This is not correct. It must depend on the height to which you raise your arms. Whether, when at the top of the swing, you allow your club head to drop until it points to the ground behind you, or whether you keep it about parallel with the ground, as Vardon does, is perfectly immaterial as far as the fullness of the swing is concerned.

The men who describe an arc, which is commonly called a full swing, are the men who hold their clubs loose in the palm of their hands and allow it to drop out of the palm into the hollow of the thumb when at the top of the swing. This is an impossibility when the club is held as Vardon holds it, perfectly tight with both hands; in such case you cannot get your club below the level of a line which is parallel with the ground.

When first Vardon became a professional he always used to grip his club with his thumbs around the shaft, and sometimes he could drive a few holes and keep direction, but he says himself that he never had any confidence in himself; as after letting his club turn in his hand, at the top of the swing, he never felt sure when he grasped it tight again in the downward swing, just before getting to the ball, that the face of the club was at right angles to the line of direction in which he intended the ball to go.

Vardon gets distance by the tremendous rapidity with which he makes the club travel through the air in the last few feet before the lead reaches the ball, and this he does with his wrists only, which are exceptionally strong. He regularly snaps them, the same as a man does when he plays racquets, and it is this snap of the wrists which enables him to get the tremendous brassey shots for which he is famous.

He has the most sound common-sense ideas of what constitutes a perfect follow through I ever heard; and he has described them so perfectly in his own article that it is not necessary to say anything about them except to add that Taylor himself says that Vardon is the only professional in England or Scotland who has "a perfect follow through."

Mr. Hérbert Leeds, who is a shrewd critic about any sport which he goes in for, remarked at Aiken that at first he thought Vardon seemed to jump at his ball, when playing for distance, but that after observing him more closely he came to the conclusion that it was simply the way in which his arms and his feet kept perfect time with one another. This is exactly what Vardon himself says. I have seen him play with Smith, the open champion, Findlay, Low, Nicholls, Jones and Machrell; and by comparison with the wide swings they all take around the shoulders, Vardon immediately strikes you as taking a very much more up and down one. This, of course, to a certain extent is due to the very short clubs he uses, which compel him to take a more up and down swing or else crouch very low, which he does not do.

He has the most perfect judgment in regard to distance, and seems to be able to place a ball just about where he thinks it ought to go.

What really counts in his matches is his steadiness. I don't mean that he never foozles a shot, but his foozles probably don't average one per cent. Put him on any 18-hole course in the world, and the probabilities are that his score will not vary more than four either way, however long he plays.

I asked several men at Hoylake just recently how they graded the professionals on the other side, and the unanimous reply was that Vardon was one, two, three, four, five, six, then came Herd, Taylor, etc. Willie Park told me that there was only one Vardon, and that he himself could see no one who was likely to beat Vardon for some time to come.

30
A "Pocket" Golf Course

A "POCKET" GOLF COURSE

BY VAN TASSEL SUTPHEN

THEORETICALLY, the golf course is an indispensable adjunct to the country estate, as much so as are the tennis lawn and the squash court. In point of fact, private links exist in little more than name. Seven or eight years ago, when the madness was at its height, many so-called courses were laid out over private grounds, and while a few of them were well planned and properly installed, the great majority afforded but a mediocre arena for the practice of the royal and ancient game. Nor is it difficult to assign the reason why. Even premising that the requisite acreage is available, golf and landscape gardening do not meet on common ground. Putting greens, adorned by pretty red and white flags, are all very well, but bunkers are distinctly out of place on a gentleman's lawn and shrubbery, and flower-beds and trees are particularly poor golfing hazards. The view-points of the head gardener and the greenkeeper must remain irreconcilable, and the ordinary compromise simply results in the mediocrity already alluded to; golf in a stage setting is an absurdity.

But even if we dismiss the puerilities of lawn-golf there are other difficulties in the way. How about the up-keep? On a large estate it may be practicable to set aside sufficient acreage for a nine hole course that shall be properly laid out and adequately bunkered. To keep it in really playable condition is another thing. Of course to the multi-millionaire this is merely a matter of money, but if expense be an object, then the question becomes a serious one, for it is no light thing to keep the fairway and putting greens of a nine hole course in the pink of order. It must be remembered that there is a minimum of play on the average private course, and every golfer is aware of the extraordinarily beneficent influence of the human foot. As a rule, the more play the better for the course, and there is never any waiting at the tee on private links.

The obvious remedy would seem to be the substitution of quality for quantity. If the golf budget be insufficient for the proper maintenance of a nine hole course let the number of holes be reduced. Six good holes are better than nine poor ones, or we may even content ourselves with a triangle and play around it six times to complete the orthodox match. The objection here is as obvious as the remedy—monotony is fatal and a round of this artless character quickly degenerates into a sporting treadmill.

A difficult problem, then, yet an alluring one to the contemplative golfer, and my solution is admittedly untested, but on paper it would seem to be feasible, and I submit it in the hope that some enthusiastic confrère may think it worth the trouble of working out in actual practice.

References to the map of our imaginary "pocket" course at once reveals its cardinal principle—condensation. It is unnecessary to argue the point that such a course would be unplayable under ordinary club conditions. Cross play is manifestly impracticable on a crowded green, but on a private course we have only to allow for the solitary couple, and that gives us our opportunity.

Considering the diagram in detail, it will be observed that the playing area lies roughly in the form of a triangle. Its width should be about 400 yards at the base, and this may be reduced to 100 yards at the apex. The total length may be placed at 550 yards. A comparatively restricted space, and yet it contains nine complete and markedly individual holes whose playing distance aggregates 2,900 yards—a very respectable showing when compared with the cramped measurements of the average private course and not a few club links.

Although there are nine separate holes there are only four greens, and this means at once a saving of fifty per cent. in the up-keep. In a modified sense this economy also applies to the fair green, as will be apparent at a glance. Virtually, the whole of the fairway is in constant use and may be cared for *en bloc*.

In considering how to make the best possible use of the purposely limited area at our disposal, we will eliminate all question of local topography and deal with the problem under the simplest and withal the severest conditions. In other words, we will assume that we have nothing but a cleared and level pasture at our disposal. To transform it into a golf course will entail a certain initial expenditure depending upon the more or less elaborate nature of the bunkering, and may be modified at pleasure. The pond and brook at the back of the 5–9 hole are not essential, as their office may be assumed by a shallow sand hazard.

In the planning of the course the prime object has been to conform to correct golfing standards as regards the length of the holes and the disposal of the hazards; and secondly, to introduce the utmost element of variety. It is in this last essential that most nine hole courses are weak, and so indeed are many links of the full size. Variety is the spice of golf, since the latter is assuredly an epitome of life.

Examining the four putting greens, it

will be noticed that the 5–9 and the 1–8 are situated on the natural lie of the land and that they are plotted to be 20 yards in diameter. Thirty yards in diameter would be a preferable measurement, and of course their shape may be square instead of round.

The 2–4 green is also 20 yards in diameter, but it is placed at the bottom of an artificially excavated "punch bowl" with a circular sand hazard on its upper rim. The material taken out, together with that removed from the various pot-bunkers, has been utilized to elevate the 3–6–7 green and also to form the turf banks that back up the latter. This green is the largest of the four and measures about 80 by 60 yards. It will be noticed that it contains three separate holes, but, if preferred, only one actual "tin" may be used. On the map, a sand pit is plotted before the green, extending about half way around it. The earth from this excavation may be used to still further build up the green above the general lie of the land. The putting surface, being artificial, should be approximately level, while that of the other greens should preserve the natural undulations. We may now examine the separate holes and the play in detail.

No. 1 (350 yards). Theoretically, a "first" hole should be of fair length and of moderate difficulty. A drive and a brassey should place the player on the green, and the regulation two putts make up the bogey of 4. There is a half-moon sand trap behind the green to punish an over approach.

No. 2 (200 yards). This seems like a long distance for a one shot hole, but since the green lies at the bottom of a "punch bowl," a carry of 165 yards will clear the circular sand hazard and the roll of the ground will do the rest. There is a patch of woodland on the left, but the fair green is wide enough for all practical purposes. Failure to carry the hazard means, of course, an extra stroke, and only the far and sure driver can hope to equal the bogey of 3.

No. 3 (300 yards). The direct road to the green lies over a pot-bunker 150 yards from the tee, and the trap is 15 yards in length. We may play to either side, but preferably to the right. In front of the green is a sand pit bunker which is 20 yards at its widest, the near cliff being perpendicular and the depth ranging from six feet in the middle to zero at the extreme ends. A drive and an iron should place us on the green, and we may approach with confidence as the high banks at the back will stop a running ball. Bogey is 4.

No. 4 (350 yards). The play runs back over virtually the same golfing territory, and it is therefore necessary to obtain as much variety as possible. We therefore notice that the tee is elevated while the green is the "circus ring" or "punch bowl" that was used a short time before for No. 2. This serves to differentiate the play, but we want length as well and the distance in a straight line is only a trifle over 300 yards. We therefore provide that the player's ball must pass the line flag B (see map) *on the left* before it is in position for the hole. In other words, the ball can be only played for the green when it lies in the triangle marked by the line flags A, B and C. It requires a good drive of about 180 yards to accomplish this; anything shorter or wilder will necessitate an extra shot to place the ball in position for the approach. This is a new principle in golf, although it has its counterpart in the "elbow" holes occasionally encountered on ordinary courses. In the latter case, however, the obstruction to the straight course is a material one (generally a piece of woods), while here the restriction is purely arbitrary. But the principle is a perfectly simple and practicable one, and its exercise adds much to the interest of the hole. Two perfect shots will put the ball on the green calling for a bogey of 4.

No. 5 (470 yards). This is the long hole. There are sand traps to catch a pulled or sliced ball, and the third shot must be a lofted approach over the bunker that guards the green. A pond behind the green imposes an appropriate penalty for an over-approach. Bogey is 5.

No. 6 (360 yards). The first one hundred and forty yards of the way lies over a wide and shallow sand hazard. A bastion-like bunker waits for the topped brassey and the approach is a gentle run-up. With ordinary play, the bogey of 5 is not difficult.

No. 7 (290 yards). The actual distance is only approximated, as the "law of the links" provides that the ball must lie behind the bastion bunker before the return journey to the green can be begun. A moderate carry of 140 yards will accomplish this, and the player will then have a brassey or a cleek shot back to the green, depending on his position. Of course, if the ball fails to clear the bunker, or does not lie behind the line indicated by the flags D and E, it will be necessary to play a short shot for position. The principle is a modification of that employed in No. 4. With no mistakes, the hole should be played in the bogey of 4. The high banks back of the green provide against an over-play, but a pulled ball will find the sand pit hazard at the left of the green.

No. 8 (125 yards). This is only a mid-iron shot, but it must be accurately lofted if the ball is to clear the half-moon bunker and stay on the green. Of course, a bad top finds the depths of the sand pit. Bogey is 3.

No. 9 (425 yards). Again we have recourse to the "out-and-back" principle of No. 7 in order to secure both length and variety of play. The law provides that the ball must lie *behind* the water hazard before it can be played for the green. Two

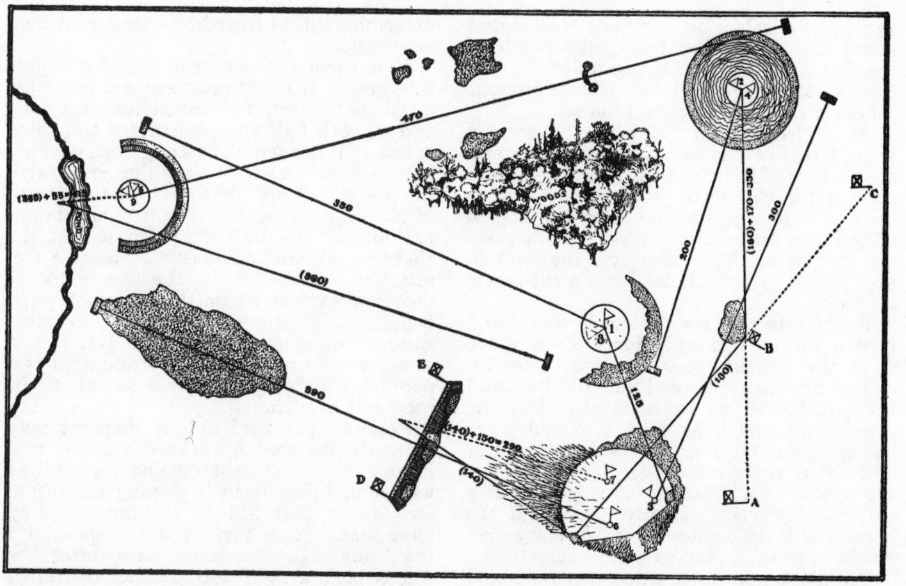

really good shots, that aggregate about 360 yards, will accomplish this result and the normal bogey is consequently 5.

Summing up, we find that the total length is exactly 2,900 yards, or 5,800 yards for the double round. In the play, there will probably be brassey shots on the first, fourth, fifth, sixth and ninth holes, or ten for the double round. This is rather a high average for, as a rule, the ordinary course is weak in affording opportunities for full shots with wood through the green. But brassey play is a most important factor in differentiating a first and a second class course, and it would be perfectly possible to lay out a nine hole course approximately 2,900 yards with not a full second shot in the whole round of play. Average your holes at 320 yards apiece and there you are.

Another element that must be carefully considered in the lay-out of a "classical" course is the construction of the greens. Many links have all their greens artificially leveled, and this, of course, is opposed to all the traditions of the game. But for the sake of variety in putting, we may allow a certain proportion of the greens to be leveled up while the rest are on the natural lie of the land. In our "pocket" course, the third, sixth and seventh holes are on the level, and the others follow the natural undulations of the soil.

Again, greens may be elevated, depressed or situated on the general level of the fair green. Referring to the map, it will be seen that the 3–6–7 green is slightly elevated while No. 2–4 lies in a marked depression, and No. 1–8 and No. 5–9 conform to the level of the fairway. This again adds to the variety of play and consequently to its interest.

A third consideration concerns the protection of the greens. On some courses we are eternally running our ball up to entirely unprotected greens, while on others we are constantly confronted with the lofted approach. Moreover, we do not want *all* our hazards either in front of the green or behind it. On our "pocket" course, the first, sixth and seventh holes call for a running up approach, while a loft is necessary at the third, fourth, fifth and ninth. (Note that the second and eighth holes are theoretically one-shot greens only to be reached by a stroke representing the full value of the respective clubs used.) The proportion is in favor of the lofted shot, but the balance should properly incline in that direction as tending to eliminate luck and flukes.

As to the disposition of the green hazards, the third and eighth greens are guarded by bunkers, placed in front. No. 1 has a trap behind and No. 7 is (partially) protected by a bunker on the left. Nos. 2–4 and 5–9 are entirely surrounded by hazards. Nos. 3, 6 and 7 are built up at the back to stop an ordinary overplay, but a ball pitched beyond the bank finds itself in the rough. The bunker in front of the third green belongs to the pit class, while the back hazard at No. 5–9 is water. As much variety as possible has been the object in view.

In the general bunkering of the course the cross-bunker is used only on the sixth and seventh holes. But it has been made of sufficient length (90 yards) to prevent sneaking off to either end. As it is in play both ways there is a trench on either side and the cop proper may be from three to five feet in height. Pot-bunkers are indicated on the third and fifth and sixth holes, and others could be introduced, if thought desirable, on the first, second and ninth fairways. The triangular patch of woodland or long grass, bounded by the first, second and fifth holes, has its obvious function in punishing wild shots.

As to hazards in front of the tees, a topped ball at the fourth, fifth, sixth and eighth holes finds itself in difficulty—quite enough for this variety of hazard. Out-of-bounds is supposed to skirt the course of the fifth and sixth holes—in both cases on the right. The tees for the fourth, seventh and eighth holes have a moderate elevation.

Bogey totals 37 for the single round and it is a rather stiff one, for a short drive from the second, fourth, sixth, seventh, eighth or ninth tee will inevitably entail the penalty of an extra stroke, and the second shots on holes Nos. 4, 6 and 9 are by no means kindergarten golf. The first and eighth holes are easy; Nos. 3, 6 and 7 are moderately difficult; Nos. 2, 4 and 5 call for first-class, steady play, and the home hole is the hardest of all. Average play would indicate a card of 42 or thereabouts.

On the map, sand traps are indicated by dotted areas, and built up cops by parallel lines. The wavy, concentric figure at green 2–4 represents a depression. Return lines of play (seventh and ninth holes) are marked by hyphen dashes.

Our "pocket" course should accommodate three separate matches without crowding or danger, provided that the second and third couples should not start until the preceding match shall have holed out on the *second* green. This is necessary to avoid meeting face to face on the 3–4 and 6–7 holes.

The practical construction of our course is a question that is difficult to discuss on paper. But a few hints may be of service.

To begin with the general characteristics of the land, the heavy clays and the thin, stony soils are both of them ill-adapted to golf. The rich meadow loams look well to the eye, but the herbage is apt to be too soft and rank to give the best results, particularly if the proportion of clover be large. The ball does not sit up properly on clover and has to be scooped away or even dug out. The ideal country for golf is the sandy subsoil covered by a close growth of thin but rather stiff turf from which the ball may be nicely picked up with the wooden clubs. The famous seashore courses of Great Britain are all of this true golfing character, but in this country it is difficult to find even an approximation to the ideal, with the exception of a few especially favored localities—for example, Garden City on Long Island. Speaking generally, we must make the best of conditions as they are, for it is impossible to change the vital characteristics of our whole playing area. Obviously, we will clear it of stones, trees, bushes and all coarse growth. If there are rabbits already in possession they must be exterminated, as their holes are a continual annoyance.

It is upon the construction of our putting greens that we must expend our most intelligent effort, for unless they are true and smooth half the pleasure of the game is lost. What we want are greens covered with a close sward of very fine grass with the roots thickly matted. The presence of clover on a putting green is an abomination, for the ball drags on it and the slightest amount of moisture makes a tremendous difference in the run; one is nearly always short on the approach putt. Equally objectionable is the so-called summer or crab grass. This latter is a weed of the creeping variety and as it is a perennial the only remedy is to cut it out, root and branch.

Possibly the turf at our disposal may approximate the thin-leaved variety, and in that case constant cutting and rolling will soon bring it into playing condition. Or, failing that gift of fortune, we may have some good turf at our disposal for resodding. In the latter case, after the sod is laid, a light top-dressing of soil or road scrapings should be applied to fill up the cracks, and then a sowing of grass seed. After the first heavy rain, the surface should be pounded with a maul to remove minor inequalities, and frequent waterings and rollings will be necessary before the resodded green is really playable.

If it be impossible to build up a green on the old turf and good sod is not available, we must then begin at the beginning. No one has given more thought and study to this subject than Mr. Travis, and I take the following paragraph from "Practical Golf":

"Plough up the surface to the depth of a foot or so and remove all loose material. Then proceed to fill in a layer of sand a few inches in depth and cover it with loam about an inch or so thick; on top of this put a thin crust of well-rotted manure, and then another layer of loam of two or three inches. At this stage apply a dressing of bone dust with a touch of slaked lime. Cover this with a suggestion of sand and top off with loam, the surface being raked and finely pulverized. Sow liberally with a mixture of recleaned Red Top, Rhode Island Bent, Crested Dog's Tail and Kentucky Blue Grass, and level off and roll with a very light roller."

As a rule, the chemical fertilizer should be avoided and the potash mixtures are particularly provocative of clover. Pulverized sheep manure is about the best enrichment for average soils and it contains no weed seeds. The free use of sand will work wonders on heavy soil, and as a general thing putting greens err on the side of being too rich. Remember that it is not the over-luxuriant growth of a lawn that is wanted.

The best cop-bunkers are those whose embankments are of sand, rather than the ordinary turfed-over mounds, since the latter often permit the rubber-cored ball to run through them. The ditches should never be less than six feet wide, comparatively shallow and filled with several inches of fine sand *that will not pack*. The same considerations apply to the construction of pot-bunkers or traps; their whole value lies in their capacity to stop a ball, and this they will not do if the sand packs. The proper quality of sand may have to be imported, but it is worth the trouble and expense.

The tees on our model course are all on the level of the land, as they should be, and only require to be made approximately level and their limits designated by iron marking pins. These should be changed as the ground shows signs of wear.

The special problems in the construction of our "pocket" links include a depressed "punch-bowl" green and an elevated one (Nos. 3, 6 and 7) backed by sodded banks. This, of course, necessitates regular grading operations with road scrapers and carts and entails a considerable expense. The amateur golf architect must decide for himself whether the increased interest and variety of play thus secured are worth the money it will cost. As already noted, the earth from the deep pit in front of the 3–6–7 green may be used to build up the level of the green proper, and also for the flanking walls at the back.

It would be an interesting experiment if some enthusiastic amateur should undertake the construction of a model miniature course as herewith indicated (or on analogous lines), and the writer will be glad to lend his assistance in the practical working out of any particular problem that may present itself.

31

My Golf

MY GOLF.

BY CHARLES BATTELL LOOMIS,
Author of "The Four-masted Cat-boat," etc.

WITH PICTURES BY FANNY Y. CORY.

I AM naturally very nervous. All my friends say that I lack repose, that I am too strenuous. "Take up golf, old man," said one. "It is what you need. It will keep you out in the open, it will teach you the value of deliberation, and it will cure your nervousness, and give you a repose of manner that you can get in no other way."

I am spending the summer in the country, and although there is no course near us, the country-side is full of natural advantages for the pursuit of the game, and I determined to take it up.

I did not care to go to the expense of a whole outfit, as I might not like the game after I had learned it, but the next time I went down to New York I bought a driver, thinking to practise repose with it.

I bought a particularly stout one that cost me five dollars, as I figured that if I put a little more into the purchase price I 'd gain in the end. But now I 'm sorry that I did not buy a very cheap one, because then, when I had tripped up the old gentleman in the Fourth Avenue car on my way to the Grand Central, it would have broken the club, and that would have ended my golf. But the stick was stout, and the old gentleman fell and broke his leg instead, and also dropped a bottle of wine that he was taking home, having just received it from a returning sea-captain.

He told me that he did not mind the break in his leg, because he had broken it before in the same place, and he knew just how long it would take to mend it, and he needed a rest from business cares, anyway, which he never would have taken if he had not been forced to it in some such way; but he was all broken up over the spilt wine, as it was a very rare vintage, and he never expected to receive any more.

I apologized all I could and offered to put him up at any hospital he might select, but he would n't hear of it, and as the wine was priceless, there was nothing left for me to do except to feel miserable and show it plainly, which I did.

He was an old golfer himself, and after I had helped him out of the car (and lost my train by so doing) he showed me the proper way to hold my stick so that I should n't trip up anybody else. The pleasantest part of my golf experience was while we were waiting for an ambulance—for I had telephoned for one at my own expense. We sat on the curbstone, and he would n't hear of my accompanying him; said he believed in the rigor of the game, like Sarah Battle, and he ought to have seen that I was a beginner and kept out of the way of my club.

He was so entertaining that I was really sorry when the ambulance came and he rolled off toward his home.

As for me, I had missed the last train for the day, so there was nothing to do but to put up overnight at a hotel, and that with dinner and breakfast cost me four dollars more. So far, the game had come to nine dollars, and I had yet to make my first inning.

I will hastily pass over the broken car window on the way up in the train next morning. I might have pushed an umbrella or a cane through it, and I contend that it was not because it was a golf-stick, but because I lacked repose, that I did break the glass. Of course I had to settle with the conductor, but I think that three dollars was too much to charge me for the glass. The car was ventilated after I had opened the window in this artificial way, and thousands rose up and called me blessed in different parts of the car, for, needless to say, the car was warm and the other windows were too tightly wedged to open, even with superhuman efforts. I should like to recommend to the Consolidated Company a judicious use of golf-sticks on their windows; then there would not be so much smothered profanity

"HE WAS AN OLD GOLFER HIMSELF."

on the part of men, and overstrained muscles on the part of women who foolishly attempt the impossible.

I hold that the London way is preferable to ours. There you know that the bus windows cannot be opened, that they were manufactured shut; but in this country you know that a car window may be opened in a perfectly normal way under proper conditions. The fact that the conditions never are proper, coupled with the knowledge that the windows were meant to open, is what makes travel in summer in America so absolutely unendurable.

"I LET DRIVE."

But I digress.

I was unable to do any golfing after I had reached my abiding-place in the country, as I found in the mail an order for a Christmas story, and as it was July the affair cried haste and kept me busy all day. But next morning I awoke early, aware that the golf fever had seized me, and I was up before any one else in the house, as every one else knew, for my lack of repose caused me to express my exuberance of spirits in merry roundelays—that is, they were merry to me, but disastrous to the dozers.

My youngest son soon joined me, and was delighted at my request that he act as my caddy. He prepared my tee—I had had coffee in bed: I never take exercise with stomach empty.

I adjusted the ball, gazed earnestly at the object I desired to approximate, swung my club in the air, made several false starts in the most approved fashion, and then I let drive.

My next-door neighbor, a wealthy gentleman from New York, was awakened by the crash of glass, and came running down-stairs in his pajamas. I tried to cultivate repose as I reflected that I had disturbed his, and while cultivating it I went over to see just what damage I had inflicted. I had put quite a curve on the ball, for it was fifty feet to the left of its intended destination.

I walked over and gazed at the ten-dollar opening I had made in his plate-glass window. My son was overjoyed both at the crash and at the jagged opening. That is youth. *I* felt no joy.

My neighbor was not gazing at the opening I had effected, but at a little faience vase which had tried in its ineffectual way to stop the rapid progress of the ball.

Even as the old gentleman of two days before had overlooked the damage to his leg, but had grieved at the spilt wine, so my friend could have overlooked the broken glass, but the vase was an heirloom and virtually priceless.

Here let me stop long enough to ask why it is that people will load up their summer houses with priceless treasures. I never yet bought anything that was priceless; in fact, I always insist on having the price plainly marked. And when people give me priceless things I do not put them in my summer house. I go even further than that. The place where I spend my winters I regard

"MY SON SAW HIM DROP."

simply as a house of detention until I can return to my summer place, só I never load it up with priceless treasures; therefore at no season of the year could such an accident have befallen me as I had caused to fall upon my neighbor.

He would not hear of my buying him another vase,—he is a little deaf,—and I was glad he would not, nor did I raise my voice. My golfing had cost me enough already, and when I buy faience I want it for myself.

But he was somewhat sarcastic at my expense, and that I did not like. I like sarcasm to be prepaid, although I like to do the shipping myself. He said that I was not cut out for an athlete, and that at my time of life if I did want to take up games of skill I 'd better go out to the Bad Lands, that could n't be damaged, or to the Desert of Sahara. Altogether he made me feel very sorry that I had not bought a putter instead of a driver. Putting is wholly innocuous and innocent. Those who made a name for themselves in the late sixties at croquet, as I did, should be able to putt with ease, while driving of all kinds is and always has been dangerous and difficult.

Still, there is too much of the sportsman in my make-up to allow me to submit tamely to setbacks. It was now breakfast-time, and I had had a little ten-dollar practice,—for of course I insisted on paying for the pane I had caused to be broken,—and, like Dewey at Manila, I felt that breakfast was necessary; but afterward I would go on with the fight and master driving.

The morning mail brought me an order for a hundred-dollar story that an editor wanted written while he waited in his office; that is to say, he wanted it within twenty-four hours.

I generally pay immediate heed to such orders, because I think that editors who take the trouble to order things in this world, where so much is forced upon the unwilling, ought to be encouraged; but the golfing fever was on me, and after breakfast, instead of going into my workroom, I secured my son once more and sallied forth to try a little more driving.

This time I went farther from the haunts of men, and took up my station in a very wild field full of shrubs and weeds, and, as I supposed, containing nothing valuable—certainly no vases or rare wines.

I have heard people say that they found it hard to hit the ball squarely; that they generally dug up earth, or chipped slices of gutta-percha from the cross-hatched sphere, or fanned the circumambient air. But my troubles were of a different nature. I hit the ball every time I strove to, and the first time I hit it in that field I seemed to conceal it in a lusty whortleberry-bush some fifty feet distant.

My son and I consumed nearly the whole of a pleasant morning looking for that ball. We visited every bush and shrub that was big enough to harbor a ball, but we could not find it, and at last, after several hours' search, I reluctantly gave up and sent my boy home after another one. While he was gone I threw myself down upon the grass to rest, and I found the ball, or, to speak more accurately, my hip found it. And it was n't ten feet from the place where I had stood when driving. I can account for this in only one way. When people lose their way in the great woods they circle round and round, and at last bring up where they started from. I dare say that lost balls do the same, and that this one was on its way back when I found it.

While yet my son was gone, I placed the new-found ball on a little tee of my own making, and with a strength born of long waiting I whirled my club through the soft July air and smote the ball.

"LOOKING FOR THAT BALL."

Will somebody tell me why farmers in New England should raise Angora goats, and if so, why they select wild and scrubby pastures to raise them? I am told that it is a profitable industry, and that in a few years, instead of the cattle upon a thousand hills, it will be the thousand Angoras on a single hill, so prolific and so useful are they. But they are inimical to golf, and hard as their heads are, they are not so hard as a ball driven by a strong man with a five-dollar club.

There were little kids in that field not worth more than twenty-five dollars apiece, and they went scot-free after my terrible drive. They bleated and leaped and cropped the rank herbage, all unaware of the fact that the father of the herd, imported from Turkey, had been laid low by a golf-ball. My son saw him drop, and my son found the ball on the ground in front of him.

I did not know that he was highly valuable, but small boys have a way of picking up information, and my son told me that Mr. Hermance, a gentleman farmer and a neighbor of mine, who had just gone into the industry, had paid one thousand dollars for this miserable animal that was now worth no more than its wool and its hide and its carcass would bring. It did not interest me to recall, as I did immediately, that I had read in an afternoon paper that Angora leather made the best golf-bags in the market. I did not care to buy a golf-bag just then.

I decide quickly. I took the next train for New York and proceeded to get insured for one thousand dollars in favor of Mr. Hermance. Then I registered an oath to play no outdoor games more dangerous than puss-in-the-corner.

Then I returned to my summer home to write the story that the editor was waiting for so patiently, and nothing better coming into my head, I wrote up my experiences at golf under the foregoing title. While they were not written by an expert golfer, they should hold much of interest to the average beginner, and if the reading of them shall save to the world a few pieces of faience, a few rare vintages, a few legs, and a few Angora rams and other cattle, I shall not have written in vain.

32

Amateur Golf Championships

AMATEUR GOLF CHAMPIONSHIPS

BY H. L. FITZPATRICK.

THE Golfing Amateur Championships are over, and there are some very thankful golfers in the land, especially amongst those of the selected band who won their way to the coveted honor of the contest; for although golf is, and rightly, claimed as the game that calls the least upon the reserve forces of the physique, yet there is no championship based upon exertion that calls upon the contestants for so prolonged an exhibition of skill and endurance.

Think of it, ye happy mortals whose contest begins and ends in a ten-second sprint, and ye the fewer and often condoled-with athletes whose mile-long course is covered under five minutes, that the successful golf champion begins his competition at almost break of day on Monday, and continues it over a course several miles long every forenoon and afternoon until the next Saturday's sunset.

Who shall gainsay, then, that the golf champion is entitled to his honor, or shall not see a good and sufficient ground for the great company of interested spectators, or, still better it would be to say, of lay participants, who will merrily plod and keenly follow the players through their prolonged, but never uninteresting, week of striving.

The standard of the championship has been set high, as high, indeed, as in the home of golf; and in that fact alone is one of the most striking exemplifications of the width and depth of our practice and playing of the "royal and ancient game." That within ten years of the acorn being planted the oak should be able to stand the stress of such an effort, speaks more than volumes. And as for the quality of the playing itself, may we not safely continue the parable and ask, if this be the green twig, what may we not look for in the seasoned tree?

Four years seems but a trifle scarce worth consideration in the lifetime of a game, and such a lapse in the long years to come will be of lesser moment; but the first years, the advent and infant years, of the championship games, seem worthy of a place in that one repository of passing events that will pass the sports of the day down to posterity, OUTING.

Having been present at the whole of the championship contests, I make no excuse to fellow golfers for gathering together the main facts relating to them ere they pass into oblivion, or become the happy hunting ground of speculative and often untrustworthy antiquarians.

The United States golf contests which have culminated in the amateur championship began only in 1894, and then were really the outcome of a zealous disagreement. The golfing pulse was just changing from the calm to the quick, and both the Newport Golf Club and the St.

Andrew's Golf Club determined to hold championship tournaments. And so, in the last week of August, when the social season was at its height at Newport, some thirty golfers met at medal play, over a short but well-planned course. None of our home-bred players were in the finals, for the winner, by a stroke, was William Lawrence, who had learned the game at Pau, and the second contestant, C. B. Macdonald, learned his golf while a student at St. Andrew's University, Scotland's famed Mecca for golfers.

The tournament at St. Andrew's, which followed, and was played on the nine-hole course on the Sawmill River road, was a more pretentious one, being at match play, and the winner of the gold and diamond badge was to be proclaimed the "Amateur Champion of the United States." A circular embodying the conditions, signed by John Reid, H. O. Talmadge, W. E. Hodgman and J. C. Ten Eyck, had been sent to every golf club that could be discovered, and the field that met on October 11th, 12th and 13th was a thoroughly representative one. Places in the semi-finals were claimed by L. B. Stoddart, St. Andrew's; C. B. Macdonald, Chicago Golf Club; Archibald Rogers, Shinnecock Hills, and William Lawrence, Newport Golf Club. Here Macdonald atoned for the defeat at Newport by beating Lawrence by 2 up and 1 to play. On the sixth hole Lawrence ran down in 2 with a long cleek shot, one of the earliest instances of the marvelous in golf on record here. Stoddart, who had learned to play as a boy in England, beat Rogers, who at that time, was more devoted to yachting than to golf, by 5 up and 4 to play. In the finals, played on soggy links, Stoddart won from Macdonald by 1 up. All the rounds were at eighteen holes.

FINDLAY S. DOUGLAS, CHAMPION 1898.

In view of the conflict, it could not be said that the amateur championship had been satisfactorily settled.

The disagreement regarding the respective value and importance of our two championship meetings made it evident that there was need of some permanent body to guide the affairs of the game. The result was the creation of the United States Golf Association at a meeting in New York on Dec. 24, '94.

The five clubs represented at the first meeting were the nucleus of a society now containing nearly two hundred clubs as associate and allied members. To its first President, the late Theodore A. Havemeyer, we owe the present perpetual championship vase, which is but one of his many deeds to foster the cause of golf in America. In formulating the championship conditions the system adopted was substantially the same as in Great Britain, the one a meeting open to amateurs only, and the other an open tournament, in which professionals and amateurs might meet on equal terms. The amateur championship is open only to members of clubs in the United States Golf Association, a restriction framed as an inducement to all clubs in the United States to become members of the national organization.

The first amateur championship under the new order of things was held at Newport in October, 1895, the late date having been chosen to avoid a conflict with international yacht races.

Thirty-two players left the first tee in this meeting on the first day, the field

PUTTING AT THE FIRST GREEN.

including doctors, lawyers, clergymen, and men of business prominence, but the college player had not yet developed into championship form. He was already in existence, but the late date of the meeting, even if he had desired to put the question to the test, compelled an attendance at his lectures. A fine crop of club champions had mustered together for this competition, but the finals narrowed down to a match between Macdonald and Charles E. Sands, a lawn tennis player of repute, but who had been at golf for only some three months. Good luck brought him to the finals, much to his surprise.

It was the first instance in the United States of madcap youth overleaping the set plans and prognostications of the golfing sages and elderly athletes. Sands had foozled his drive from the first tee in every match of the week, and he did the same in starting out with Macdonald, but in this case the match ended right there, although the exact score for the thirty-six holes showed that the Chicagoan won by 12 up and 11 to play. His brother, W. H. Sands, was regarded as a likely winner, but he was put out in the second round by Dr. Charles Claxton, Philadelphia Cricket Club, who had picked up a knowledge of golf while attending Trinity College, Dublin. Claxton was then on his game and lasted until he met Macdonald in the semi-finals.

Undoubtedly the best match of the meeting was between Winthrop Rutherford, who had been playing abroad in the preceding summer, and L. B. Stoddart, champion of 1894. Stoddart had the match dormie, but Rutherford ran down a long put and took the home hole in 4, making a tie. Rutherford, although he made a barefaced foozle of his second shot, made the green of the extra hole in 3, Stoddart playing a mashie somewhat short on the link, the

FOLLOWING THE PLAYERS OVER THE RAILROAD TRACK.

ball hitting the bank of the terraced green and running into a bad lie, so that Rutherford won in 5 strokes to 6. Macdonald put him out by 5 up and 3 to play, in the succeeding round.

Visitors to Newport found the new club-house a magnificent structure, but the links were as full of reminiscences as a modern comic opera, for at that period cop bunkers and terraced putting-greens were the rule on every links.

After disposing of Sands, Macdonald played out the last round with James Foulis, the Chicago Club's professional, in an endeavor to lower the amateur record of 1887. By strokes his score was 88, 87—175. Sands needed 101 for the first eighteen and 48 for the next nine holes. That Macdonald was on his game was revealed by a comparison with the scores made the next day by the professionals in the open championship, when H. T.

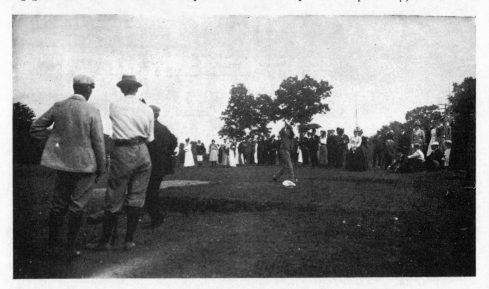

ON THE SIXTH TEE.

SILENT PARTNERS IN THE GAME.

Rawlins won with an 89 and 86, while W. F. Davis made the best round, an 84.

It was at this amateur competition that Richard Peters, of Newport, put into practice an attempt to put with a billiard cue, to the great grief of the more orthodox exponents of golf.

Macdonald's reign as champion lasted until July, 1896, when the amateurs met on the sand dunes at Southampton. At last they had an eighteen-hole course to play over, although the Shinnecock Hills Golf Club links then measured but 4,423 yards in playing distances, and

THE PRIVILEGED.

would now be termed a short course. A qualifying round at thirty-six holes medal play, the first sixteen to keep on at match play, was the system introduced for the first time. Four tied for the sixteenth place out of eighty starters, and, as L. B. Stoddart withdrew from the play-off, which L. P. Bayard, Jr., Princeton, won, only five who had started in 1895—Macdonald, W. H. Sands, A. L. Livermore, E. C. Rushmore and H. G. Trevor—gained a place among the elect. Of the others, two were college boys, and two, H. J. Whigham and A. M. Coats, graduates of Scotch links, the rest being self-taught and self-reliant golfers, who made up in zeal for any deficiencies in style. H. J. Whigham with his wooden putter was the sensation of the meeting. Few of our players had ever seen a wooden putter, and, indeed, to run up an approach instead of pitching up, was considered, until then, to be rather "bad form;" in brief, it was often croquet, not golf. Whigham won the gold medal with 163 in the qualifying round; then, defeating in turn Bayard, H. R. Sweny, Coats and J. G. Thorp, he held his title clear to championship honors. Formerly a baseball and lawn tennis player, Thorp played a brainy, "get-there" sort of a game, that enabled him to beat Macdonald, who was ill, however, W. H. Sands, and H. P. Toler, and gain the semi-finals. Thorp has since changed his style, and now is orthodox to Badminton in swing and short approaches.

C. B. MACDONALD, EX-CHAMPION.

As at Newport, the life at the Shinnecock Hills Golf Club ended each day with the posting up of the scores, and there was a constant round of dances and dinners at the country houses during the week.

In this respect there was a decided change at Wheaton last year when the amateur championship was played on the fine eighteen-hole course of the Chicago Golf Club. Possessing a large and well-arranged country club, the Wheaton organization was the host of a score of dinner parties each evening, and, as dances in large tents followed, the club-house was a gay scene by night as well as by day. At midnight a special train conveyed the guests to Chicago, the golfers seeking a brief sleep in the club-house or at the near-by country houses. The week on the social side was a whirl of gayety. On the links, after the preliminary skirmish of the qualifying round, it was learned that Macdonald had won the gold medal for the best score with 174, and of the sixteen to qualify, the veterans of the previous year were Macdonald, H. J. Whigham, A. H. Fenn, J. A. Tyng, A. M. Coats, H. R. Sweny and J. R. Chadwick. Two college boys had a place, W. R. Betts and John Reid, Jr., both of Yale, and the most prominent of the others were Findlay S. Douglas, formerly a player at St. Andrew's, in Scotland, but now a resident here, and W. Girdwood Stewart, a well-known golfer at Troon and other links abroad, who was on this side on a visit. The element who had not qualified the year before were Deveraux Emmet, Herbert M. Harriman, James A. Stillman, of the East, and D. R. Forgan, a Scotchman, and G. S. Willetts, both entered from Chicago. Douglas, who had brought a grand reputation as a golfer with him from old St. Andrew's, was regarded as a likely winner, but he failed to equal the expectations of his friends, for, when the progress of the game brought Douglas and Whigham together in the semi-finals, the champion had little trouble in winning, by 6 up and 5 to play. In the thirty-six-hole finals, Whigham won with equal facility from Betts, who, catching Macdonald off his game, had beaten the ex-champion in the semi-finals. Yale, as the recent championship again brought out, is a stumbling block in Macdonald's golfing path.

So much for the past and its statistics. They reveal that to the time of this year's championship the United States had not produced one player equal to Whigham or Douglas in class, although some were capable of great performances in an erratic way when on their game. The query that clubmen asked each other as the date for the Morris County tournament drew near was whether time had produced the man fit to cope with the golfers trained abroad.

Only two of the players in the championship of 1895 were among the qualified at Morris County; and, more sad still, two more failed to qualify, finishing in the unplaced division with H. J. Whigham, but, unlike the ex-champion, they could not put forward a Cuban war record or a tale of vile malarias to account for the downfall. The two survivors were C. B. Macdonald and W. H. Sands, representatives of the best types of the exotic and the homebred golfer. Macdonald, aside from his zeal in the affairs of the U. S. G. A., has done an incalculable amount of good among our players by his advocacy and practical illustrations of good style in the game, while Sands has been one of the most diligent pupils of the links developed here. Both play better golf now than at any earlier period in their careers, but the others are moving faster, which is the only reason why the two do not figure more prominently as winners today. Of the fate of the two veterans in the present contest it is to be recorded that Sands was put out in the first round by F. H. Bohlen, the noted Philadelphia cricketer, who chanced to play one of his dashing games; but Macdonald lasted to the semi-finals, when he was beaten by his young fellow-townsman, W. B. Smith, a Yale senior, by the close score of 2 up and 1 to play. While the brilliant play of the younger golfer may not be questioned, nor his pluck impugned, Macdonald was undoubtedly somewhat over-golfed. Smith, it is true, had a close match with L. P. Bayard, Jr., the ex-Princetonian, in the second round, but he had had easy matches with J. H. Choate, Jr., in the first round, and with G. D. Fowle, in the third; while Macdonald had defeated in turn such clinking good golfers as G. G. Hubbard, Newport; John Reid, Jr., Yale, and A. M. Coats, Newport. He showed at Wheaton last year that a week of continuous golf unhinged him, when, by succumbing to W. Rosseter Betts, he opened the finals to a Yale man, a precedent that his unlucky star made him follow this year.

The "luck of the draw," however, was, in a general way, more fair than usual, yet the goddess who guides the destinies of the golfers may not be accused of favoritism in the case of Walter J. Travis, of the Oakland Club, who certainly had his week's work cut out for him. He had to defeat, in turn, to win the right to play, Findlay S. Douglas in the semi-finals, J. I. Blair, Jr., Princeton; J. G. Thorp, Cambridge, and Foxhall P. Keene, Oakland. It was a succession of well-earned victories, and the meeting with Keene brought out about the best match between homebred players witnessed on the links. It was a contest that brought out to the quick the real spirit of golf, earnestly fought out, but in a manly, generous way, that would have won the hearty plaudits of the most captious stickler for Scotch traditions and customs.

This, then, brought to the semi-finals Douglas, Macdonald, Smith and Travis, representatives of four distinct schools of golf: Douglas, only two years ago Captain of the St. Andrew's University team, and embodying the modern and aggressive in the game; Macdonald, who was at St. Andrew's nearly two decades before; Smith, a college boy who has a natural aptitude for the game and the energy of youth, with Travis, who learned the game when somewhat past thirty, and who owes his prominence to a diligent study of golfing methods and style in the library and on the links. Smith, to the honor of the homebreds, plucked a victory from Macdonald, but neither Travis nor he was a match for Douglas, who had simply to wait to win. Including the medal-play round, Douglas ran down the ball into 191 holes during the week, and was as fresh as the proverbial daisy at the end. The meeting made it clear that a succession of thirty-six-hole match-play rounds is a true test of golfing skill, far more so than eighteen-hole matches, in which the young and less experienced player may, by a lucky streak, either win or halve with a superior man. Undoubtedly the longer game is the more perfect test of "form," but the elimination of the unexpected does not enhance a championship meeting as a spectacle, except to those within the cult.

At the Shinnecock Hills Golf Club, on the day of Whigham's first triumph, President Havemeyer prophesied that within three years a native-born golfer would win the amateur championship from the foreign players. Two of the years have passed, and, while young blood has twice been second, the Scots are still supreme. With the increase in golf links of the best class, time should bear out the truth of the prophecy; but the consummation is more apt to be a decade than twelve months away, that is, with men entered of the class of Douglas and Whigham, not to speak of the possible advent of H. H. Hilton or F. G. Tait, or others in their ranks from the other side. In a recent letter, in mentioning the two amateurs named, W, Girdwood Stewart, who was a visitor here in 1897, states: " The leading men here now are really so good that further improvement seems impossible. They drive further, approach more accurately and put better than of old." It is evident that the golfing pilgrims Scotland is still to send us will be no less skilful than those who have preceded them, a condition that our ambitious golfers must face. It is not sufficient to learn to golf well enough to win cups at club competitions; for the ambitious wight must labor unceasingly to acquire style and force, if the grand climax is to be attained.

Uniformity in style is not an essential —the short swing of Hoylake is as effective as the heel-tapping swing of old St. Andrew's—but it must be a golfing style, not one that suggests either baseball, cricket, racquets or tennis. There are men on our links who play well in the most heedless of self-taught styles, like Arthur H. Fenn, who is still the best player the United States has yet brought out, although no longer eligible to amateur competitions, but his strokes are made with an ease and steadiness that is in itself graceful. To most men who take up the game when over thirty, when muscles and joints are set, like Fenn, Travis, Thorp, Keene, Tyng or Toler, execution must be cultivated at the expense of the graces. The one great desideratum is that the club-head shall move with the ball at the impact—even in jerk strokes—and shall follow after it as far as possible. Those who fairly meet and follow through in each stroke, even though the method may suggest a gymnastic feat, may attain a considerable degree of proficiency; but, and this is the one great lesson of the Morris County championship, they must succumb in the competitive phase of the game to the youths, whose supple muscles have made possible a style orthodox in every detail. How many of our older set who qualified this year will be among the elect in 1899? Yet, and this is the great glory of golf, when their day of competitive prominence will pass, they will be the better for the knowledge of the most healthy and rational of games. They may tramp the links, over greens bordered by forests and with great mountains in the distance, or through park-like lawns, or where sea and river bound the view, and gain a pleasure that never cloys nor punishes. There is no senility in golf.

Good-fellowship, in the best sense of the word, was in the air at the meeting. There was so little of that spirit of rivalry that borders on contention—the recklessness of the jockey or the ill-humor of overzealous baseball or football adherents—that the odd lapse or two gained a fictitious prominence. The handshake at the end of each match was from the heart, and not the perfunctory finger-touching of pugilists entering the ring—or else there was no handshake! An incident or two revealed that even our scratch players have sometimes only a very elementary idea of the golf rules. It will be recalled that in the match between Douglas and A. H. Smith, of the Huntingdon Valley Club, the latter laid a half-stimie, and objected when Douglas, in the prescribed manner, lightly brushed the line of his put with his hand. Douglas merely stated his right to do so, and then ran the ball down by a most accurate put. It was a case where hair-line accuracy was required, and with a player of less experience the objection might have superinduced a miss. Thoughtlessness, in another instance, worked to the disadvantage of the individual. A local rule, created because on two holes the woodland approaches too closely the line of play, permits a player to drop another ball without penalty save the loss of distance should he send one into the obstruction. Keene, in the match with Travis, drove into the woods from the tenth tee, and, in taking advantage of the rule, he inadvertently teed up instead of dropping the second ball. After the play Travis asked for the hole on account of the infraction of the rule, and, as it was a proposition that did not admit of demurrer, Keene conceded the point. The two instances, while they reveal that the rules should be conned as diligently as a mariner learns to box the compass, are hardly in the same category, for Smith displayed an ignorance of his golfing A B C, while Keene, in the stress of conflict, ignored a local rule that has almost no parallel in match play.

Local rules are often a fungous growth of excessive legislation, an evil our countrymen are said to be prone to, and the competitions at many links would be more inviting to the golfing pilgrims if they were rigorously cut away. There is one rule enforced on many links that seems to have a degree of right on its side, which is, that when a straight, true drive of 210 to 220 yards is trapped by a bunker, the player shall lift and drop clear of the hazard without paying any penalty.

H. J. WHIGHAM, EX-CHAMPION.

The local reason for this rule is usually that, in the early days, when the course was laid out it was impossible for anyone in the club to carry such a bunker except on the second play, and when the ratio of skill has so advanced that to drive into it is not unusual, a decree is framed to free the long stroke from a penalty. It is implied that circumstances forbid the placing back of the tee. The third hole of the championship course, 234 yards, has a cop bunker just at the putting green, which is generally made by a drive and a "wee pitch." Smith, in the finals with Douglas, drove into this bunker, taking two to get out, but rolling close to the cup, so that he ran down in four. As it happened, he won the hole, but if the quite generally established local rule was in force at Morris County, Smith would not have been penalized, and might have made a three. Some half-dozen players drove into this bunker during the week, all of whom felt that they had been unduly punished. W. H. Sands, of the Country Club of Westchester, made the green on the drive, the ball bounding over the cop. There are two sides to every question, and, in the opinion of C. B. Macdonald, it is right that a drive into this bunker should be punished, for the true golfer should play short, either by sparing the wooden club or by using a cleek, and reach the green on his second stroke. The play, in his judgment, should be modified by the place and nature of the hazards, and the smashing, headstrong driver deserves no more consideration than he who foozles, pulls or slices. Under this argument there would be little need for local rules on any links, and the tendency is to abolish them. There were very few at Morris County, and there will probably be still less when, in its appointed cycle time, it again brings the amateur championship to Morristown.

There was something unique in the position of the Morris County Club to the championship. When the club, through its representatives, asked for the amateur championship at the annual meeting of the United States Golf Association in February, it was frankly stated that the course was not then what it should be as a fair test of golf, and the promise was made that if the boon was granted the links would be altered until every expert would be satisfied. The promise was nobly kept, for, after consulting with professionals and amateurs, the best links now in the United States was evolved from the former short course. The playing was 5,960 yards. Best of all, the Greens Committee intends to keep on improving the already excellent course.

33

On the Links

ON THE LINKS.

BY GEORGE HIBBARD.

WITH PICTURES BY C. J. TAYLOR.

IT was a trying moment. In the clear sunlight the links lay trim and clipped before me. At varying intervals the little red flags dotted the course, while here and there the vermilion coats of the players shone brilliantly against the emerald grass. The scene was a pleasant and peaceful one, but I did not enjoy it. My heart sank, and my hands grew cold while my head grew hot, for Emily—only in the last few days had I dared to think of her as Emily—stood looking on.

My visit to the Harrisses had at first been delightful. If Emily at times appeared indifferent, at other times she was gracious, and I was not hopeless. Then suddenly the blow had fallen.

But, in order to be understood, I must explain the state of mind of the Harrisse family. I saw, a short time ago, a book, "The Manias of the Middle Ages." I am sure that no medieval persons were ever more thoroughly "possessed" than the members of this very modern household. They were all golf enthusiasts, or fairly golf mad. Harrisse *père* never thought of anything else, and Emily of but few other things. I had tried to appear interested, and they had been politely indulgent. Then the fateful moment came. One evening, on entering the drawing-room dressed for dinner, I saw that Mr. Harrisse held a letter in his hand. I could not help noticing a singularly beaming smile on his jolly old face, and with some astonishment I detected a new light of interest gleaming in Emily's eyes.

"My dear boy," he cried, hastening forward in his impetuous way, and grasping me by the hand, "why have you been so modest? To have one of the best golfers in the country here in the house, and not to know it! We can't forgive you."

In an instant I saw what had happened. Some person, knowing that I was staying in the house, had mistaken me, Launcelot Schaw, whose reputation as a minor poet, I will confess, extends beyond my own country, for my cousin "Sam" Schaw, whose collection of cups, won at everything from tennis to polo, is almost as great as my collection of first editions. The same thing had occurred before. I should have been equal to the occasion, but I was not. I saw Emily's admiring glances. These were something I had never hitherto encountered, and, in my delight, I yielded to temptation. Not actively. I did not assert anything; still, I did not deny anything. In a moment I wished earnestly that I had; but then it was too late. Almost at once I began to discover the difficulties and dangers into which I had plunged myself. Dinner was a torture. With an air of profound deference, I was asked questions by my host, and even by Emily, that I could not answer, and that, indeed, I could not in the least understand. It was delightful, but distressing. After-dinner was for me something like a session of the Inquisition. I do not know how I passed through it; but the worst was yet to come.

"There 's one thing you must do," whispered Emily's father, pushing his chair toward mine; "you must beat Stewart Elyot for us."

Beat Stewart Elyot! Beat a man who did nothing but talk golf, who did not attempt to make any concealment of his victories, and who was clearly my rival with Emily!

"I tell you," said her father, "ever since he has been staying at the Blakeleys' his boasting has been insufferable, and you must take him down a bit. You must do it for me."

What could I do? I was asked by Emily's father to "take down" my own rival, and to do it for him. No human being could have had the strength of mind or character to own up then and there. Better go on and be found out, since I had already committed myself, gaining at least a few days in which something might happen.

But nothing had happened, and there I stood. A caddie was beside me with my bag, holding a number of knobbly sticks, that reminded me, with my disturbed imagination, of the bunch of instruments from which

"'HUSH!' EXCLAIMED MR. HARRISSE."

my dentist made selections before he said, "A little wider, please." Emily's father was there, intently absorbed; Emily's friend Miss Allyn was there, coldly critical; Emily herself was there, charming in her loose golf cloak, and looking maddeningly enigmatical. Stewart Elyot, my opponent, was there, and, to my surprise, visibly anxious. I knew what they expected me to do. I had seen many do it. With one of those sticks I was to knock that miserable little pebble of a ball some altogether absurd distance. What if I had only the night before written the lines beginning,

> In ambient loveliness my goddess queen,

a poem I think not unworthy of Emily, and certainly one that will take its place among the sonnets of the early twentieth century!

"Watch the stance," I heard her father whisper.

The hour had come, if not the man. But I must act or stand confessed the impostor—the unwilling one, to be sure, but still the impostor—that I really was. I did not know what the "stance" was. I did not care. I seized a club.

"Hush!" exclaimed Mr. Harrisse as Miss Allyn giggled in the way that always annoyed me.

A solemn silence fell on the party. A silence seemed to fall on the universe. There was a certain haziness before my eyes. The ball was there, for I had seen the caddie put it on a little heap of sand. I grasped the club despairingly. I also shut my eyes firmly. I drew back the stick, and seemed to swing it through illimitable space. Suddenly I heard a dull click. I opened my eyes.

"Where is it?" I demanded wildly, scanning the heaven.

"There," said Emily.

Looking down, I beheld the glittering little thing peacefully reposing on the grass, and as the sun shone on its brilliant surface, it would seem, almost winking at me in derision.

"I 'll venture you don't 'top' it often like that," said her father, consolingly.

"Very strange," I stammered.

I glanced at Elyot. The anxious expression that I had noticed on his face lifted a little. He came forward, placed his ball, and with an airy swing sent it rolling—at most fifty feet. I felt perceptibly encouraged. If a great performer like Elyot did no better, I might for the moment escape. I caught a surprised whisper as I advanced to take another stroke. I hit the ball this time. I actually hit the miserable little object, taking, to be sure, a good deal of ground with the stroke, but still sending it, with a rise, on and on down the side of the hill.

"That 's better," said her father, critically.

I had thought it something wonderful, and was distinctly disappointed. However, I remained silent. The walk was short to the place where my ball had fallen, and I tramped on, with Emily by my side. I could seldom manage to speak to her alone, and I blessed the occasion which gave me the chance.

"There is no other game in the world that would give me such an opportunity—such a blessed opportunity as this," I said tenderly.

"Oh," she exclaimed, "can you play and talk? So few great players can."

I found I was in the wrong, but I braved it out.

"Of course, under ordinary circumstances; but to speak to you—alone—I can do it so seldom."

She was silent, but did not seem displeased.

"Look!" she exclaimed suddenly. "Mr. Elyot is going to play."

I glanced in the direction of my opponent and my rival. I watched him as he drew back his club, watched him with growing anxiety, and saw him miss his ball altogether. I could not understand it at all. Was he so "rattled" because Emily was there?

There was a queer light in Emily's eyes that I did not comprehend. Elyot tried again. This time he did not miss. It was my turn. Once, twice, thrice, then I hit the ball squarely, and away it spun. The mocking glance in Emily's eyes increased. I was decidedly troubled by it.

"You must see," I said with what I considered great presence of mind, "that there is an influence that makes accurate play for me difficult, and golf is a game requiring perfect poise."

"Have you a headache, or is it the day?" she asked in her direct way.

"It is you," I replied bluntly.

"Then I will remove the influence," she said haughtily, and joined the others.

I had made a fool of myself when I had thought to do so well. Viciously I hit the ball, and, to my amazement, it rose grace-

"I HEARD A HUMMING SOUND; IT SEEMED WITHIN A FEW INCHES OF MY EAR."

fully. It fell, rolling hardly six inches from where it struck the ground, and rested within a foot of the flag.

"Bravo!" cried her father. "A splendid approach!"

And I would have given worlds not to have made that shot exactly at the moment Emily left me, after I had said what I had. I thought I saw in her face an expression of displeasure, also of surprise. In the next I

"I FELT IT STRIKE THE SOD, AND BELIEVED THAT ALL WAS LOST."

"holed out"; no one could have helped it. I had won. I did not understand how it could have happened.

At the next tee I started first. I say "started," for that was all. I may have gone ten feet. I doubt it. This time Elyot missed altogether. I was puzzled. So was Emily's father.

"Gentlemen, gentlemen," he exclaimed reproachfully, "you 're both woefully off your game."

It really hurt his kind old heart to see such golf. I don't wonder.

This time Emily walked with Elyot, and I plodded on, cursing my blundering stupidity. Before, my desperation had enabled me to make a good shot; now the result was quite the opposite. I swung over the ball, I hit behind the ball, I went on both sides of the ball. My score on the putting green was something awful—fourteen, I think. And Emily and her father were looking on. However, Elyot, although he won easily, was eleven. I was certainly perplexed.

At the next hole Elyot led off, or, as I heard them express it, he had the "honor." He did well. His ball rose with a sudden up slant and shot off into the air. Her father applauded; so did Emily. Again I missed altogether. Miss Allyn giggled. I liked her less than ever. Clenching my teeth, I hit wildly, and missed again. It was getting serious. They must see the truth.

"Curious game—golf—*very*," commented her father. "There are days when *I* am almost as far off myself."

They would not find me out. There seemed some malevolent destiny in it, some diabolical play of Fate, to make me suffer to the uttermost for my deception.

At last I got away; not very far, in truth, but it was something. I glanced at Elyot. He did not seem to be having very much better luck. What was the matter with the fellow? Suddenly I found Emily again with me. She was distinctly smiling.

"Oh," she exclaimed, as I looked at her, "I am *so* amused!"

"It 's serious enough for me," I said gloomily, and I have no doubt that my looks proved the sincerity of my words. "But you misunderstood me," I hurried on, "about the influence. You inspire me. I can do better. I want you by my side—always."

I had never ventured to say so much, and I was terrified by my own boldness.

"There!" she cried as I again missed the ball, "is that my inspiration? You pay me a poor compliment to play so badly. You must do better, or I will go."

What could I do? The ball was so painfully small, and the space about it where the club's head might go so absurdly great. I felt that I must concentrate. There were times when I had been mildly facetious about golf. I wished that I had not. I did not feel that way now.

"Stay, stay!" I besought wildly. But by some accident the next shot was a fairly good one, and as we talked I advanced little by little. At last I found myself on the green.

Elyot was a stroke or two "more," as they put it, but after going past the tin-lined orifice several times, and once or twice over it, I was even with him. At last, when in despair, I went in. He missed, and I won.

We had played two more holes. Suddenly I found Emily again by my side.

"I have concluded to forgive you," she said sweetly.

"For what?" I gasped.

"I don't know exactly, but for something."

"You are so good!" I murmured.

"Besides, I want you to beat."

"You do!" I exclaimed ecstatically.

"I like Mr. Elyot so much, but if he beats *you*," she said seriously, "he would be made so vain that it would not be good for him."

The more I considered this sentence the more I was puzzled as to whether I should be pleased with it or not. There was certainly one for me in this accented "you," but were n't there two for Elyot? Emily was often maddening.

"See!" she exclaimed, "Mr. Elyot has lost his ball!"

I expected she would go to look for it, as all were doing, but Emily was unexpected. She sat down on the grass near me. I sat down too. There was no reason why I should look for Elyot's ball; moreover, I had quite forgotten about him and it and almost everything else. With Emily's last glance all prudence fled.

"I have so few chances to speak to you," I murmured, "and I am going away."

"Not at once," she said quickly.

"In a day or two," I said, sighing hopelessly.

"I know."

There was something in her tone that encouraged me.

"Emily," I said tremulously.

As I spoke the name a perfect panic seized me. I was appalled at my own daring; it seemed as if something must happen, but nothing did. Emily remained motionless, with her head averted.

"You know I never want to go away from you—that I want to be always with you—that I only live in the hope of winning your love—that—"

"Fore!" cried Stewart Elyot, and I jumped perceptibly.

I heard a humming sound; it seemed within a few inches of my ear. The next moment they were all down on us, and her father announced that it was my play.

I was too dazed to understand as I staggered to my feet. I had spoken,—not in the poetic words in which I had fancied myself speaking, but still I had spoken,—and I was appalled by my temerity.

I appeared only to regain consciousness at the "quarry." I had seen it before, and viewed it merely as an ordinary excavation of some size, with water covering its rocky floor, and luxuriant vines trailing along its steep sides. Now it seemed endless in width, bottomless in depth. I was thankful Elyot had to go first. I was more thankful that his ball, when hit, rolled gently across the intervening grass, over the edge, and into the stagnant water below.

I stepped forward. As I did so, I passed Emily.

"He is two up," she whispered.

The fact that Emily had listened to me encouraged me. I felt that I could do anything. What I did was to drive the ball into the water with a sounding splash. I saw Emily clasp her hands. Elyot's second attempt was no better than the first, but no more was mine. Elyot's third was even worse. I had given up all hope as I stood again over a new ball. I was astonished, therefore, as I opened my eyes, to hear a burst of applause.

"Neatly placed!" said her father.

Emily's eyes sparkled, and I tried to look as if I were not surprised.

"I might be starting on," I said airily.

As I spoke, Elyot cast a glance at me that, for utter downright loathing, I never saw equaled. I moved away. As I did I heard the rattle of Elyot's fourth ball as it rolled down the stony bank.

I have had my rare moments, when the "Athenæum's" praise—but never mind that; when the third edition—but let that pass; still, I had never experienced such a period of perfect bliss as was mine when I stood on the opposite shore while Elyot sent ball after ball into that water. I had often derided my cousin Sam when he had described to me the delight of feeling an opponent's arm slip over one's own in a neat parry in boxing, the pleasure of taking a stiff jump in the lead of the field, the joy of gaining a well-contested yard at foot-ball, or a long drive between the flags at polo; but at that moment I felt that I had been wrong. The bays of the poet are good, but there are more exhilarating conquests.

At the eleventh hole a long stretch of over four hundred yards lay before us. Both Elyot and I drove miserably and wildly, he to the left, I to the right. I expected Emily to go with him. She did not. She came with me. I could feel my heart beat. I did not care about the game, for I was with her. But her first words troubled me.

"You *must* win," she said decidedly.

"But my mind—my heart is so full of so much else," I replied gloomily.

"Of course," she replied as we strolled along. "I have been thinking of what you said just now—and of course you did n't mean it—"

"But I did," I interrupted quickly; "and you know it," I added impatiently.

She seemed a bit taken aback by my tone, and went on more meekly.

"Why, if you did, I must think it all over again—in a different way," she murmured.

"But don't you know?" I continued, emboldened by my success.

She looked at me for one short instant, as I thought, appealingly.

"I know that this is no time for me to speak," I continued desperately, "but there are so few times when I can."

"But if I—give you other times?"

What I felt was beyond utterance.

"You see, I did n't understand," she said slowly; "I did n't know what you thought—or," she concluded slowly, "what I did."

"And you do now?" I cried.

"Y-e-s," she answered.

I started with joy, and then it occurred to me that what she thought might easily be unfavorable to me. I was assuming too much. Instantly I was cast into the deepest gloom.

"But you must play *now*," she urged.

"How can I," I exclaimed, "with this awful suspense—if it is suspense," I concluded mournfully.

"Don't you know what I think?" she said again, glancing at me.

"No," I cried.

"But—but I can't tell you now," she continued, looking about.

"When, then?" I demanded.

"I had made up my mind to tell you—before you went," she continued.

"Then you knew what I was going to say!" I exclaimed joyfully and stupidly.

"How could I?" she replied, rather disconcerted, but haughtily. "Still," she went on, "if you will not let him beat you—"

"Yes," I said breathlessly.

"—I 'll tell you—" she paused, "twenty-four hours sooner."

"Won't you—without?" I begged.

"That 's my condition," she said, and quickly left me.

I looked, and found that, while I had been pounding the ball along, Elyot had already reached the green. I gathered myself together. One stroke hit the sod; the next, though, brought my ball beside his.

"What 's against me?" I demanded.

"Ten," said her father, reproachfully.

I was nine, but in a distant corner of the green. I putted.

"Dead!" he cried delightedly.

I did not understand, but I felt it were better so. Elyot was within six inches of the hole. His next shot would put him in it. With deliberate care he bent over, for he was afraid of hitting too hard. Miss Allyn again giggled, and this time I did not mind. His putter just stirred the ball. I went in. Elyot was again only one up.

Elyot won the twelfth hole. The thirteenth we halved. I saw that my state was desperate. Twenty-four hours—how could I?—twenty-four hours, when it lay with me to shorten the time!

"Two up and five to play," muttered her father.

Elyot, of course, had the honor, and marched proudly to the tee. After he had placed his ball, I saw him glance rather anxiously before him. The hazard in front was a peculiar one in this: the end of a narrow pond came half across the course, thus leaving any player a choice whether to drive over its hundred yards of water and its sandy shore, or go round the bend, where there was open land with smooth grass. I saw Elyot hesitate, then gently drive his ball off the tee in the safer direction. My blood boiled. In my heart I said it was a most unsportsmanlike thing to do. I had hoped that he would attempt the pool and go in. It was my turn. I felt that in boldness was my only hope. Anyway, I had noticed Mr. Harrisse's disapproving look as he had seen Elyot's action, and it was better to fail grandly, since fail I must. I made up my mind to try to drive directly across.

"Take the cleek, sir, take the cleek," my caddie whispered. I had feed him well before we started.

I took what the boy gave me, and hit. Again, as I opened my eyes, there was applause. I had gone over. I had gained a stroke, at least, on Elyot. All might not be lost. I was on the green.

"Your mashie," suggested my caddie.

I took the proffered club, and brought it down with all my strength. I felt it strike the sod, and believed that all was lost; but no: almost straight up the ball rose, and going higher and higher in the air, fell finally, beyond the hole, to be sure, but still within putting distance of it.

"'YOU 'RE STYMIE!' CRIED HER FATHER."

Passing Elyot angrily pounding his ball, I waited at the hole until he came up. Then I went in on the fourth stroke. It was a glorious moment.

I was excited, I will confess. Never, even when I wrote "Roland at Roncesvalles," had I felt so thoroughly stirred by the white heat of intense emotion. I had the honor. I understood what that meant now. The cleek had saved me before, so I took it again, although I saw Mr. Harrisse's astonishment. I clung to it as my only hope. I hit, and hit well; at least, the ball rose and then rolled. In the semi-unconsciousness of many mingled emotions I walked forward.

"Fore!" cried Elyot, and I dodged.

His ball, I saw with consternation, had gone farther than mine; but I might gain on the next stroke. I did. He missed his ball altogether. I swung the club once, and once more I hit. Elyot was away behind. I was almost on the green. Suddenly I heard a buzzing in the air, a whir, and something passed me. It was Elyot's ball; he was beside me.

"That 's something like," commented her father.

I was too dazed for utterance, for the strain was telling on me. As I putted, a dozen holes danced before me. It was not golf; it was roulette. But I went in. I expect Fortune to take it out of me some day for that outrageous piece of luck; but I went in.

The hole was mine. We were even.

Even! Even! It seemed incredible to me, when I considered with whom I was playing. But I had to play. Golf, it seemed to me, was a constant repetition, with infinite variation. In this case the variation was not great. I abandoned my cleek, and my drive was as bad as ever. But, again, so was Elyot's, and there was no advantage for either of us. As I walked forward, I felt, rather than saw, that Emily was beside me.

"Don't you *want* to know sooner?" she whispered.

"*Don't* I want to know!" I exclaimed almost angrily. "What would n't I give to know—the best!"

"Then play!" she commanded, and left me.

I groaned inwardly. I may have groaned outwardly, for my caddie looked at me curiously; but it was only for a moment. He was evidently accustomed to all possible expressions of human emotion on the links. But I felt perceptibly better. If it should be that she really—

"Fore!" cried Elyot, and again his ball whizzed past—hurrah! only to bury itself against the post of a fence far out of the course. I watched him with delight as he dug at it, beat at it, pounded at it. At length it rolled out. He had counted seven strokes. Made careless with delight, I hit jauntily, lodging under the very same fence. I had thought what a fool he was to get excited. As I look back at it, I must have become quite frantic. In a sort of automatic frenzy I used my club. At last I, too, was free, and together we played for the green. Why go into detail? We halved the hole.

Still even, and still my honor. I felt as if I were staggering up for the last round. But the end was near. I had made a brave struggle. As I looked back it seemed almost pathetic to me that all my efforts should at last go for nothing. I found myself pitying myself in anticipation.

"An exciting game," said her father, rubbing his hands, "although I must say, gentlemen, it might have been better played."

Again the honor was mine. The stream that we had crossed in coming out again lay before me. It was at a distance nicely calculated to catch all balls not well driven. I could not drive at all. I was safe so far, for I fell short of the hazard by fifty yards. I saw that Elyot was preparing to follow my example. His idea, evidently, was not to hit hard, but he did what he had not done before. He hit cleanly and truly, and the small force accurately applied was enough to land him squarely in the ditch, for it was little more.

"Hard luck, old fellow, for a fairly good stroke!" I cried.

He glowered thunderously at me and passed on. A stroke more took me to the edge, another over. He tried three strokes, paused, and wiped his brow; then tried two more. My heart bounded. I am sure my eyes lighted up. But he was across, and we were pounding in for the green. I got in a rut. I got in a thistle. When we reached the verge of the green we were even.

"You 're farther off," said Mr. Harrisse.

I obediently took the club my caddie gave me, and, stooping, played. Elyot's ball was within a foot of the hole, and our strokes were even. I saw I was lost, but I played. My ball stopped directly between Elyot's and the hole.

"You 're stymie!" cried her father. It sounded like a deadly insult, but I knew that he could not mean it.

Still, I did not know what this was, and for a moment I thought all was over. But it was all right.

Elyot had to play round me. Mr. Harrisse said something about lofting a stymie, but it was after Elyot had played. This stroke left him as far from the hole as he was before, but one more. He played again and missed—missed by half an inch, but missed. He had played too hard, and his ball was still farther off than mine. I could see his hand tremble. He played. Again he missed! At the next putt I went in. The hole was mine.

I was dazed, but I played. Playing had become a second nature to me, and I believe that I could have played in my sleep. Indeed, there was something of a somnambulistic character in my action. At least, it seemed almost as if I awoke when I heard Emily speaking.

"I am *so* glad!" she said.

"Why?" I asked stupidly.

"Why," she replied impatiently, "you 're dormy now, and he can't beat you."

She seemed to describe my condition, but I understood that she was speaking of the game.

"Why?" I gasped.

"Because you are one up, and there is only one hole to play."

"Oh!" I exclaimed, with a glance of intelligence. "But I have n't beat him yet—and I suppose I can't know."

"I—I," she murmured, "only said that you must not let him *beat you.*"

"Oh!" I cried, this time rapturously. "And I may—you say he can't beat me. Then tell me. I have waited so long. Tell me. You are not unwilling to have me love you."

"What a way to ask me!" she said impatiently.

"How should I ask?" I demanded anxiously.

"So that I could answer you properly," she said gently. "You should say, 'Do you love me?'"

"Do you?" I cried.

"Yes," she whispered.

It was exasperating. I could not take her in my arms then and there out on the broad expanse of the sunny links. I had dreamed of quite another scene when I learned my fortune. But I did not care. I had her. She was mine at last for good and all. I wanted to say something intense, poetic.

"This is a beast of a game," was all that I managed to answer.

She smiled.

"Do you think so?"

"No, no," I exclaimed hurriedly; "I 'll always think of it with gratitude, with rapture. It has made me the happiest man in the world. But, thank Heaven! there 's only one more hole, and we can walk to the house."

"Yes," she said shyly; "and now beat."

"I can't," I replied hopelessly. "I only wonder that I have done so well."

"*Do* you?" she said, with the same curious smile I had noticed at first.

"Yes," I replied, "against such a great player as Elyot." I could afford to be generous now.

"Why," she said, "did n't you know?" Then she laughed outright. "He never had a club in his hand before to-day. I found it out, and I have been so amused. He was only boasting, and that is why I wanted him beaten."

I was astonished. And I had been pluming myself on coming off so well against a "crack." Suddenly my conscience smote me.

"Do you know," I said contritely, "I think perhaps I ought to tell you something. No more have I ever played."

"I was *sure* of it," she said calmly, "and I thought it was so fine and strong and brave and noble of you to go in and try to do it—when papa made the mistake about the letter—for my sake."

I had been thinking all the time that it was rather a mean and sneaking performance, but of course if she looked at it in that way! And it is curious how a woman will look at a thing when the man happens to be the right man.

"It has been an awful experience," I said boldly.

"Poor dear!" she whispered tenderly. "I am so sorry!"

Of course we told her father, when we told him the other news, that Emily had consented to marry me. He was so pleased with my having won the match that he did not seem to mind. Since then I have played the game with such diligence and enthusiasm that he is now entirely contented. Indeed, the day when I beat him four up and three to play, I could feel that he was perfectly satisfied with me as a son-in-law. I do not abuse golf any more. I won too much in my first game ever to do that. Moreover, I am quite as mad about it now as all the rest of the family.

34

Golf in Colorado

CHEYENNE MOUNTAIN COUNTRY CLUB, FROM THE EAST.

GOLF IN COLORADO

By S. H. Thompson, Jr.

GOLF from its very inception has occupied a unique position in its environment in Colorado. An apparently unsoluble enigma presented itself to the pioneers of the game, who were confronted with inaccessible mountain sides and arid plains. But the enthusiasts in the vicinity of Denver were determined to conquer these conditions. Practical minds soon concluded that the only feasible method to pursue was to lay the course out on the plains and follow the irrigating system of the farmers—ditch the streams of melting snow from off the mountain sides and guide water down over the prairie. Much money and time was consumed in this task, but as a monument of their labor, the Overland Club now occupies a picturesque oasis in a sandy desert. The site selected, near the Platte River and the foot-hills of the Rockies, is within a few minutes' 'bus ride to the electric car, and a half hour's journey from the center of the business portion of Denver. The grounds are used conjointly by the Overland Driving Club, which originally occupied the entire place, and the Overland Golf Club. A pleasant shade is spread over the approach to the club-house by tall cottonwood trees, while the road winding through this grove, presents the first introduction to the main irrigating ditch, a tortuous canal, some twelve feet in width, and filled in season with a swift flowing stream. From the driveway one may obtain a panoramic view of the grounds, and especially the two fenced racing tracks, one within the other. Occupying the inclosure of the interior track as a center, the golf course radiates in all directions beyond the exterior track. High above the latter and on the opposite side from the river there is a bend in the great irrigating ditch, which offers an exceedingly difficult bunker. This stream upon the crest of an elevation fifteen feet above, and a hundred yards in front of the third tee, has brought so many players to grief, that it has been aptly termed "hell's hole." By means of pipes the water is gravitated down under the tracks and out into a network of small waterways, whose banks form bunkers. But there is no uniform hight in them, it is unnecessary to have the ditches which fringe the border of the greens, as large or deep as the one which is used as a reservoir. These obstacles are so numerous that they become quite formidable pitfalls, and make the course sufficiently difficult.

Eastern players who visit the club in the morning with the intention of playing later, must experience a feeling of despair as they watch the ground keepers calmly perforate the canals in numerous places, till the links becomes a veritable swamp. But that thirsty soil, which does not get more than a month of natural moisture during the entire year, drinks up the water with the voracity of a sponge, leaving the turf in excellent condition for the afternoon play. At the present time the course consists of nine holes, though one of eighteen will soon be completed. The distances between the greens vary greatly, the longest being five hundred and fifteen yards and the shortest but one hundred and thirty. Aside from "hell's hole" there are two other parts of the course which demand the most accurate playing. One of these is from the fourth to the fifth green, known as "Waterloo." Here the player has an opportunity for an unobstructed drive of two hundred yards before he again encounters the main irrigating ditch. To get over this and avoid the clumps of trees which flank both sides of the direction to the next green, which is obscured by a descent, is considered a difficult feat. But perhaps the most deceptive hole is the shortest one. With accuracy one may reach the green in a single stroke, yet the slightest ill luck will land the ball in one of the ditches, or carry it over the fence on to the race track, and give probably a score of four.

A comparative idea of the course and the skill of some of the members may be drawn from the scores made by champion Vardon and the leading players of the club. H. Vardon accomplished the round twice in thirty-four strokes, with a general average of several points higher. Russell, the late instructor of the club, had a record of thirty-five, while the most meritorious performance among the amateurs is that of Mr. Fairbanks, who has made it in thirty-six. He is an Englishman by birth and learned the game in the old country. Lately he has added to his list of victories by winning the championship of California. Following close upon him is the record of thirty-seven, made by Mr. Woodward, a native of Colorado, who learned the game at Overland Park. The skill of Mr. Hall, a youth of seventeen, who has been playing but a short time, augurs well for a brilliant career. This lad has finished a round in thirty-nine strokes. Aside from a number of "comers," who are hovering close to the forty mark, there is the usual crowd of mediocres, who either for the pure sport of the game, or because of its health producing results, are found going over the course with indefatigable constancy. Colorado's climate is proverbial for its mildness and the persistency with which the sun shines. With the exception of the last two weeks in March and the first two in April, there is almost continuous golf weather. Such an environment has produced its logical results in the number of players, who, though neophytes, have shown really excellent form.

The home built by the members, situated under the shadows of the Rockies and yet on a flat plain, is the center of the society life of Denver, the Mecca of temporary

EAST PARK GOLF COURSE.
LONG'S PEAK, 14,900 FEET HIGH, IN THE DISTANCE.

THE GLENWOOD SPRINGS COURSE.
MT. SOPRIS IN THE DISTANCE.

sojourners and of an extensive leisure class. To drive out in the afternoon, play a round or two, partake of supper on the spacious veranda, and enjoy the gentle snow-cooled breezes, which float down from the peaks, is sufficiently alluring to have built up a club of three hundred members, with a discouragingly long waiting list. Tennis, which is rapidly regaining its pristine vigor in the West, has compelled recognition in the home of its present victorious rival, and the club has constructed two fairly fast courts, which were the scene of an interesting tournament last autumn. The bowling alleys have also drawn about them a crowd of devotees. These adjuncts, together with a small but suitable ballroom lend additional charm, and make the place a well-equipped country club.

But golf enthusiasts, not satisfied with surmounting the difficulties of the plains, have introduced the game in Estes Park, a stretch of land covering ten thousand acres, and completely invested by mountains, some of which are fourteen thousand feet high. The park itself is eight thousand feet above sea level, an elevation which guarantees protection from heat. Two turbulent mountain streams sweep down through the valleys, giving a green touch to nature, which contrasts pleasantly with the usual sombreness of the Rockies. It so fascinated Lord Dunraven and a party accompanying him, years ago, that they bought up a great tract and erected a hotel upon it. Perhaps an additional charm lies in the fact that after traveling by rail fifty miles from Denver, one has a further trip of twenty-five more upon a stage coach from which is revealed some of the most enchanting vistas in Colorado. Such enticing opportunities for sport are offered, as mountain climbing, trout fishing, hunting in season, and games of every description on horseback, that each summer there is quite an exodus from Denver to the ranches

FIRST TEE—OVERLAND PARK.

scattered through the Park. After wandering over the hills for some time in quest of a location, a course was finally agreed upon near Elkhorn Lodge, within easy access of the log casino of that ranch. It was out of the question to construct grass greens at a hight where it was not possible to pipe water, so the players were compelled to use sand, and for cups resorted to tin cans. Interest in the sport has steadily increased in the Park, so much so that near the English hotel, on Lord Dunraven's property, a rival course has been laid out. Contests are held several times during the season, in which as many as thirty have participated.

ELKHORN LODGE GOLF COURSE, ESTES PARK—THE LOG CASINO.

It is difficult to draw a comprehensive picture of these courses, without laying oneself open to the charge of gross exaggeration, so that it is perhaps safest to merely hint at a few of the difficulties, unvarnished by adjectives. On the way to the first hole of the Elkhorn Lodge links there is a hazard about one hundred feet wide and thirty deep, the ground rising from the further side of this ravine, in a difficult angle to the green. No obstacle of note, obstructs the direction to the second hole except a row of pine trees, located a few feet off the direct line. The next drive is so short that it is necessary to use an iron and woe to the unfortunate who goes to the farther side of the green, for his ball will tumble down an incline a hundred feet or more, unless a lucky stone bars it. From this tee to the fourth the player should summon all his skill and call the fates to his assistance. A hundred yards beyond the ground rises to an eminence, which compared to the ordinary artificial bunker on an eastern course is a Pike's Peak. At the very apex of this hill there are clumps of pines, fifty feet apart, through which one must guide the ball, and at the same time must measure with exact precision the force which he puts in his drive, or run the risk of again encountering one of these temper destroying inclines. To play the next hole properly requires the ready use of the lofter to carry the ball over the top of a granite wall, lying directly in front of the tee, not over fifty feet away, and in some places twelve feet high. Should the player be unfortunate enough not to get a sufficient rise, he might as well give up the score for that hole, as the ball will rebound from the rock and tumble down a hill. Finally when it stops, the wall will still confront it. Gigantic trees, felled in prehistoric times, are strewn over the entire course, but these cause little worry to the player who has been circumventing boulders and living pines. Yet with all these difficulties, it is a curious fact, that those who have gone over this and the Overland courses, vary but a few points in their respective scores. While it is true that the Elkhorn Lodge course is shorter, this advantage is far outweighed by the obstacles one has to contend with on its sand greens. A most convincing illustration of this is revealed at the approach to the seventh hole. There are few impediments to overcome and the green in plain view from the sixth tee looks easy; the deception lies in the fact that the green is located upon the side of a hill, at an angle of descent parallel to it. The green may be made in two strokes, but if perchance the ball has any extra momentum it is sure to roll to the lower end of the scraped place, and then it is in the realm of chance as to the number of strokes it will require to climb up to the hole. On such a course skill with the lofter is the greatest essential, while the only clubs one need carry are a driver, putter, and lofter, there is no opportunity for a brassie.

Near the entrance to these links there is a structure, built of unhewn logs, and dignified by the name Casino, which though it lacks some of the modern conveniences, serves its purpose well in such a "roughing country" being fitted up with a bath-room, billiard tables and a dancing hall.

Golf has become a thoroughly established game in Colorado, competing against many popular outdoor sports, and perhaps contending with greater difficulties than are found in any other State. Clubs are springing up in all the outlying towns, building their links with more or less care. The Overland Club grounds show unquestionably the highest state of man's handiwork, while on the other hand the Elkhorn presents perhaps the most natural and least cared for course in the State.

Between these extremes, the flourishing Town and Gown Club of Colorado Springs occupies a secure position of prosperity. Though it has a membership of two hundred and fifty, drawn from a city of twenty-five thousand inhabitants, still the enthusiasm has not reached its zenith. The club has been content with a course laid out on a rolling prairie, which knows not the benefits of irrigation. There are some extenuating circumstances which might be presented as an excuse for the club, namely that the grounds are some distance from the city waterworks and the plane of the course is above the level of the irrigating ditches. It should not be long however, till the pecuniary strength of the club will become such as to permit an outlay sufficient to cover the cost of carrying water over the links. As in all games the number of star players bears a low ratio to the total participants, in so far the number of superior players of eastern States will continue greater than in Colorado, but this supremacy in numbers may perhaps be offset in part by the almost uninterrupted practice, obtainable in such a balmy climate.

THE MAIN IRRIGATING DITCH, OVERLAND PARK, DENVER.

Colorado Springs has still another club of which its members may be justly proud. The Cheyenne Mountain Country Club, located at the mouth of the famous Cheyenne Canyon, takes its name from the mountain on whose slopes its course is situated, a peak whose beauty assumes a variety of unexpected charms with each change of view. For ten years the original mem-

TOWN AND GOWN GOLF CLUB, COLORADO SPRINGS.

bers struggled to establish themselves as a permanent club. At first, being without a house, they played only in summer, though the winter climate is not more rigorous than in Denver. But since a first-class hotel has been erected and the members of the club have ensconced themselves in a pretty well-equipped house, the struggle for existence has become past history, while the club has formed itself into an exclusive close corporation with a limited membership of one hundred. Now, on this course of nine holes, relieved of the mountain barrenness by small oak trees and a gentle flowing stream, the game is indulged in both winter and summer.

The influence of golf has reached even the confines of the western part of the State. Glenwood Springs, celebrated for its hot sulphur baths and mountain scenery, is still in its infancy with respect to the sport. The hotel has a course laid out in the valley below it and commanding an excellent view of Mt. Sopris. Fortunately two of the holes are on one end of the polo grounds, which are sown in grass and thus make this part of the course very acceptable. But Glenwood has a bugbear to deal with, which

THE SIXTH HOLE ON THE CHEYENNE MOUNTAIN GOLF COURSE.

is more difficult to overcome than the aridness of the plains. Once the player has left the polo grounds his steps will stir up clouds of red dust, which become of such density that he is completely enveloped and the ball lost from view every time the lofter is used. Until this disagreeable obstacle is removed by irrigating, golf will not come to its full popularity in Glenwood.

35

Golf and the American Girl

MISS UNDERHILL AND MISS BOARDMAN ON THE 18TH GREEN.

GOLF AND THE AMERICAN GIRL.

BY H. L. FITZ PATRICK.

THE COX CUP.
omen's Championship Trophy.

WITH a swiftness that is truly characteristic of her race, the American golf girl has arrived! Not merely in the thousands who play a fair game on the hundred and one links that dot our broad domain from sea to sea, but in a small army who can, at a moment's notice, equal in the highest skill the product of the lands where golf is a plant of centuries of growth, and a select band who could be pitted against the pick of the golfing women of the rest of the world, and win!

Yet it is but nine years this month since one of your valued contributors ventured to lay before your readers a plea of "Golf for Women" and to fortify his plea with hope—for there was not then a link in the United States.

The next summer heard for the first time the swish of the club and the whir of the golf ball over the hills of Shinnecock, and the club was formed which has produced, besides many another, the peerless champion, Beatrix Hoyt.

It is a great achievement in these scant years of preliminary play, but the end is not yet; for, as clever in skill and sound in golfing tactics as the Ardsley players proved themselves, there was in the watchful "gallery" each day some little maids hardly out of the nursery, with hair in braids and simple frocks, who already are noted as players in junior matches on their home links and who may be relied on to show strong and capable golf whenever they enter for national honors. The appearance of these embryo golf girls from Wee Burn or Westbrook, Tuxedo or Morristown, under convoy of parents or big brothers, was a most interesting aspect of the competition and a most cheering one to those who would see golf "do well and prosper" under our flag.

The taking up of golf has a deep significance. There is nothing of the craze about it, as time will prove, for, while now, with the exception of Van Cortlandt Park, New York, Franklin Park, Boston, and similar public links at Cincinnati, Philadelphia and Providence, it is a sport restricted to the richer classes in this country, the next progress of the game will be the general establishment of village links, virtually free, throughout the length and breadth of the land; and, once the pastime broadens from a class pursuit, on these lines, it will never die out. "We Scots do not call golf a sport," said Willie Parks, Jr., to me once; "we regard it as an institution like the auld kirk."

One thing is certain, frills and finery will never smother golf, for in this sport women insist on thick boots, stout and untearable frocks, and the comfortable shirt-waists, jerseys and hats. In the name of golf, too, often they brave the weather bare-headed and bare-armed, careless of tan, freckles or sun-striped hair; but this does not mar the effectiveness of a state toilet, as all men who attended the golf balls at Ardsley or Morris County will swear with hand on heart. Beauty lies in the beholder, and it may be that the young women of our day are playing to the masculine "gallery," formed of the athletic youth of their "set." Golf will not tolerate the fripperies. No sight more odd may be conceived than the women at a certain seaside links last summer who wrapped bandages of veiling about their chin, nose and cheeks for the complexion's sake, while leaving the eyes and the rest of the face to be protected only by the hat. One thought of the veiled women of the harem in the Cairo market place, or, if of frivolous mind, of the half-masks of a fancy-dress ball.

It must not be supposed, however, that the golf woman makes no distinction in what she wears. She has an array of colors on which to base her costumes—the reds and greens and blues of golfing clubs—which, with the whites of summer and the tweeds of colder seasons, give an ample opportunity for changes and rearrangements of the feminine golfing garb. An appearance of the careless and unstudied is the way it seems to a man amazed to see for once comfort and fashion united in the attire of the sex.

Our men had been yearning for championship honors at golf for nearly two years before the golfers feminine aspired to such laurels. The first links to be graced by the women on such a mission were Meadowbrook, where, on a misty, drizzling morning in the late fall of 1895, a baker's dozen met to compete for the title and a cup presented by R. D. Winthrop and W. H. Sands.

Photo by T. C. Turner.

MISS HOYT DRIVING FROM THE 2D TEE.

The favorites, who had all been winning cups on their home links, were Miss Nina Sargent, of the Essex County Club, Manchester-by-the-Sea; Miss Anna Sands, Newport; Miss Anna Howland Ford, Morris County; Mrs. W. Fellowes Morgan, Baltimore, and Mrs. Arthur W. Turnure, Shinnecock Hills. The course is one of the longest of nine holes in the country, and was quite unsuited to test the skill, at least in an eighteen-hole medal play round, of the competitors, who had learned on much easier links. The winner proved to be Mrs. Charles S. Brown, Shinnecock Hills, while Miss Sargent, who had luck on one or two holes, was second.

By the time the next meeting came due, the United States Golf Association had formally assumed charge of the fixture, an action undoubtedly stimulated by the gift from Robert Cox, a Member of Parliament from Edinburgh, of a very valuable trophy to be the perpetual emblem of the championship. It was one of the generous acts in the cause of golf that Scots have a way of perpetrating the world over. The only condition of the donor was that the first contest, at least, should be played at the Morris County links, where he had played during the summer of 1895.

This second meeting was national from every point of view, and since then the championship has maintained the high standard then established. There were twenty-five starters, seven less than faced the tee the previous year, when the meeting was held at the Essex County Club, Manchester-by-the-Sea, and thirty-six less than the sixty-one who started at Ardsley last October.

So much for statistics, except that it is interesting to note the four best medal-play scores in each of the contests to date:

MISS HOYT PLAYS ROUND THE ALPS.

Meadowbrook, 1895—Mrs. Charles S. Brown, Shinnecock Hills, 132; Miss Nina C. Sargent, Essex County, 134; Mrs. W. B. Thomas, Essex County, 141; Mrs. William Shippen, Morris County, 145.

Morris County, 1896—Miss Beatrix Hoyt, Shinnecock Hills, 95; Miss F. C. Griscom, Philadelphia, 102; Mrs. William Shippen, Morris County, 102; Miss Anna Sands, Newport, 103.

Essex County, 1897 (stormy day)—Miss Beatrix Hoyt, Shinnecock Hills, 108; Miss Nina C. Sargent, Essex County, 114; Mrs. R. C. Hooper, Essex County, 121; Miss Margaret Curtis, Essex County, 122.

Ardsley Club, 1898—Miss Beatrix Hoyt, Shinnecock Hills, 92; Miss Edith B. Burt, Philadelphia, 100; Miss Madeline Boardman, Essex, 102; Miss Grace B. Keyes, Concord, 102.

At Meadowbrook, in 1895, the medal play settled the issue, but in the next two contests the first eight, and this year the first sixteen, had to fight it out at match play. With these details in mind some comparisons and deductions may be made on the play of the past and present.

Miss Hoyt who has held the center of the stage for three seasons must be mentioned first of all. The high position she has gained is the reward of intelligent practice backed by an aptitude for golf and a genuine fondness for the links. Her friends whom she has beaten have practiced as much, and, no doubt, love the game as well, but it has been Miss Hoyt's good fortune, as well as good play, to reach the winning line first, and to retain the lead for three meetings, as Lady Margaret Scott did at the start of the Ladies' Golf Union of Great Britain.

Miss Hoyt owes her series of triumphs primarily to her natural aptitude for golf and in the second place to the spur of success which changed a natural gift to a finished game. Her first golfing was under the coaching of Willie Dunn, the Shinnecock Hills professional, in 1895; and, prior to the woman's championship in 1896, the next professional there, R. B. Wilson, one of the best players with the iron clubs ever seen in this country, had a hand in framing Miss Hoyt's style. Her 95 was good golf, for the time and it can be ascribed only to good coaching and the zest with which she played. Her best playing then was with the iron clubs. In driving, nearly all of those who qualified could surpass her, but in the short game Miss Hoyt was quite unsurpassed.

This championship marked the turning point in Miss Hoyt's style. Throughout that autumn and in the following season until the '97 meeting at the Essex County Club those who saw her play noticed that her aim was to obtain a full, clean swing with driver and brassy and to follow through with the ball until, at the end of the stroke, she would often move on a step with the force of her finish. It was an exaggeration in style, but it gave to her both distance and greater accuracy in the tee shots and with the brassy.

After her second victory, Miss Hoyt labored to tone down what had been shown to be extravagant in her swing and follow-through, and, when she stepped on the tee at Ardsley this year, her style would have been pronounced most finished and effective by the most captious critic of old St. Andrew's.

MISS KEYES DRIVING ACROSS THE POND.

Miss Hoyt in driving has a low, round swing, and the most beautiful follow-through to be imagined. In four days of eighteen-hole matches she made but one bad drive, a topped ball from the ninth tee in the finals with Miss Wetmore, which, as luck would have it, carried the brook on the bound and reached a safe lie, from which she carried to the green with a cleek. In short mashie approach shots, or in playing out of a difficult lie, Miss Hoyt is absolutely deadly; and, as this effectiveness is shown not only in the use of the other clubs, but also in judgment of the time and place to use each club, one can see that it is hard to beat her.

Miss Hoyt's nerve is simply superb. At the tenth hole in the finals she and Miss Wetmore were square. No Park nor Vardon could have shown more serenity in the trying situation, yet, for the next four holes, Miss Hoyt ceased to chat with her brother, who was her caddie, and to exchange smiles with the girls she knew in the "gallery;" she trudged along as if the game alone was the thing. She won out in 4, 3, 5, 4—all good holes—and won the title by 5 up and 3 to play, neither player holing out on the fifteenth green.

A knowledge of the technique of the game, of the uses for all the clubs as well as how to use them, would seem to be the only advice worth imparting to the girls and wives whom Miss Hoyt defeated at Ardsley. Both in the first sixteen and in the unqualified fifty were girls and matrons who played certain holes as well as Miss Hoyt could have done, and who had certain shots down very fine, but there was not one who possessed her all-around style.

Practice and a competent coach are all that is needed in most cases to conquer the existing faults.

The American girl is seductive, but King Golf can neither be coaxed nor scolded, for he is a master to be served submissively before the jewel chests will be opened. A daily lesson on the links would soon bring the monarch to terms.

Unexampled was the widespread interest in the championship. There were competitors on the links who had journeyed one thousand five hundred miles or more to play, some of the travelers still schoolgirls under charge of their parents. Chicago, Pittsburg, Baltimore, Cincinnati, St. Paul and Scranton each sent starters, not to speak of the numerous clubs represented from the Boston, Newport, Philadelphia and New York groups.

In its lighter side the whole meeting was one grand success. The "gallery," walking at times in a solid line along the rope that extended clear across the fair green, in which the red of golfing coats added color to the panorama of gown and bonnets, made a brilliant picture; and, in the lulls of the game, there were whispers, tenderly or jestingly, that contained no golfing lore. In the grandeur of Nature's part, the glory of the turning leaves, the drifting clouds, the gloomy ravines that divide the sun-kissed putting greens on the Hudson's bank, true fairy rings, the magnificent sweep of wooded hills backed by the gray Palisades and distant mountains, viewed from the highland greens and tees, those were joyous days indeed. May our ladies who golf have always such blissful weather!

THE HALF-WAY HOUSE AND QUARRY.

36

Golf

GOLF

By H. J. Whigham

It is natural that a game which has formed the chief recreation of the Scottish people for several centuries should have by this time acquired a large literature of its own, so much so that two of the best volumes in the whole domain of sporting history are devoted to this subject. It will be unnecessary and superfluous therefore to enter upon a full description of the game's development in the remote past, for are not its annals written in the pages of the Badminton book upon golf and did not Sir Walter Simpson go back farther yet and invent a pretty legend to explain the origin of the pastime? All this has been done for us already. It is needless to recount how the popularity of the game began in the seventeenth century seriously to menace the profession of the soldier and the pursuit of religion; how the great Montrose preferred a friendly contest at Musselburgh to raiding the base Lowlander, or how Charles I. forfeited his crown and his life because he allowed the Irish Rebellion to break out while he was sacrificing his royal duties to indulgence in this ancient sport. More recent passages in history tell the same tale. The one fact of importance which has been related of the predecessor of Queen Victoria on the throne of England is that he was elected captain of the St. Andrews Golf Club, and it is certain to-day that Mr. A. J. Balfour would refuse the premiership of the British Government if he could by so doing become the amateur golf champion of Scotland and England.

In order, then, to avoid returning over ground that has been so often trodden before, it will be well to confine ourselves to the more recent incidents in the growth of the game, more especially those which have to do with its spread in this country. For even Mr. Horace Hutchinson's excellent work in the Badminton series was contributed before England became thoroughly converted. Nine years ago, at the English universities, not only was the game played by a very small body of undergraduates over the half-inundated cricket fields during the winter months, but the ignorance displayed by all who did not belong to this devoted band was simply appalling to one who had been born and educated north of the Tweed. The point of view taken by most Englishmen was well expressed when it was proposed about a year later that the members of the team selected to represent Oxford in the inter-university golf match should be allowed the privilege of wearing a "half-blue"—the full "blue" being the reward for services in the Rowing Eight, Cricket Eleven, or football teams. The president of the "blues" committee was at that time one of the best all-round athletes in Oxford, and he very strongly objected to extending any university recognition to the exponents of a game which—as he put it—did not induce perspiration. In other words, he confirmed the general opinion of outsiders that golf is not an athletic pursuit at all, but merely a mild recreation for old men.

Now, although it is perfectly true that children of ten and octogenarians can trudge round the links and enjoy the fresh air and the mild exercise involved in tapping the ball, it is entirely wrong to suppose that the game when properly played does not require the same muscular strength, skill, and endurance which are requisite for pre-eminence in all the higher branches of sport. Golf was never intended to be a game for team matches, and for that reason it is probably right to leave it out of the reckoning in university athletics. On the other hand we need only look for a moment at the career of the best amateur players in the world to see the truth of the assertion upon which I should like to lay some stress that strength, skill, and training are absolutely necessary for success in the royal and ancient game; for if it were really a pastime for old men, women, and children, as so many seem to imagine, or if it were simply a society fad, as it would appear to a large section of the American public, who have been unaccustomed in the past to any form of athletics which can be indulged in by a man after he has left college, then the best players would be drawn indifferently from the ranks of the strong and the weak, the young and the aged. This, however, is not the case. Every prominent golfer whose name comes readily to mind has achieved success in other branches of sport. Mr. F. G. Tait, the amateur champion of Great Britain for 1896, was a fair cricketer at school and a first-rate football player. He did not go through a university career, and so his prowess on the football field was not widely known; but he was one of the strongest players at Sandhurst, the training school for the army, where strong men are rife. His predecessor, Mr. Leslie Balfour-Melville, whose record as a golfer is a long and glorious one, was for years the best all-round athlete in Scotland. He was one of the few cricketers from the North who could ever rank with the English exponents of the game; at school he was one of the most brilliant football players in the country; his skill at lawn-tennis was far above the average, and it may be remarked in passing that he is a billiard-player of no mean ability, for curiously enough, accuracy in billiards and golf seem to go together in a great many cases.

Then, again, we are not surprised to find that Mr. J. E. Laidlay, who is without doubt the most brilliant match player of all the first class amateurs, was one of the most remarkable school cricketers when he was a boy at Loretto; and so instances might be multiplied. Mr. Horace Hutchinson was a good cricketer in his college days, Mr. Mure Fergusson, the Blackwells, and Mr. John Ball, are all men of great physical strength and muscular activity. The last named player had the distinction of being the first amateur to win the open championship, and although there are others who in the last two or three years have met him on even terms, he was for a short time quite unique in the power and accuracy of his play, and it is certain that he could never have reached such perfection if it had not been for the country life which allowed him constant practice and plenty of hard physical exercise.

It may be taken for granted then, that although a man can play the game as long as he can walk or even ride round the links on a pony, the real science of golf can only be acquired by men of athletic capacity. To saunter round the eighteen holes on a summer afternoon, with intervals for tobacco and conversation, is one thing. It is another and a very different undertaking to go through a championship tournament, playing thirty-six holes a day, when every drive must be hit hard and clean, every approach must be accurate, every put must be true to a hair's breadth. A football match is a matter of less than two hours; from the instant the ball is in play, the nervous strain is removed and the constant action requires a sound wind and fleetness of foot, but not the absolute freedom and yet control of the muscles which is requisite for steady driving, nor anything like the strain on the nerves which is kept up from the start to the finish of a close encounter at golf.

It was probably an awakening to the fact that golf was, after all, a real branch of athletics that brought about its sudden and extraordinary popularity in England eight or nine years ago. The conversion of the South began when many of the prominent cricketers discarded the bat to take up the golf club. Having for many years dismissed the Scotch game with various disparaging terms, such as "parlor skittles" or "Scotch croquet," they at length discovered that it only required a single trial to enamour them of this much despised pastime. Moreover, it became apparent that for those who had left college and settled down to a regular profession cricket was a vain and elusive pursuit, making far too strenuous demands upon the time and purse to come within the reach of any but the rich and idle. Golf, on the other hand, could be freely enjoyed by all who were able to spare an afternoon a week. No sooner, therefore, were the floodgates opened than the new waters threatened to inundate the whole field of English sport. The stanchest cricketers were found among the proselytes, lawn-tennis became a thing of the past, the crack shots from the midland counties would tarry on the links of St. Andrews late in the year when the partridges and pheasants were waiting to be killed at home; even the rabid fox-hunter found himself wasting whole days when the frost was out of the ground, chasing the gutta-percha instead of the brush. Heretofore in Scotland inland links were exceedingly rare; but now they sprang up in every county of Great Britain. Old lawns, on whose immemorial turf it had been reckoned a sin even to walk, were ruthlessly hacked to pieces by the iron of the golfing tyro; the cattle were robbed of their pasturelands in order that the putting-greens should not be disturbed; and last but not least the Sabbath was freely violated by men and women who had never before missed a morning service in church.

Needless to say, this sudden enthusiasm was regarded with supreme distrust by the conservative Scotchman. New elements were introduced into the game which he could least endure. Formerly the only prizes in the year had been the autumn and spring medals at the leading clubs, and these were coveted for glory and not for their intrinsic value, which amounted to less than that of the expense in clubs and balls which it cost to win them. The real game of golf was to be found only in match play, and the counting of scores was regarded with the utmost abhorrence except on those rare occasions, twice in the year, when it was absolutely necessary. The Englishman, however, looked upon the matter in a very different light. Long practice in lawn-tennis tournaments had inured him to the vicious habit of pot-hunting, so that golf for him was a new and unending source of joy. Tournaments and sweepstakes were matters of weekly occurrence, a system of handicapping was instituted, and the young golfer was chiefly engaged not so much in improving his game as in defeating the vigilance of the green-committee; nor was it at all rare to find a veritable duffer in possession of many valuable trophies, any one of which would have bought up all the medals in the keeping of the best first-class player in Scotland.

It can hardly be wondered then that the term "English golfer" became one of reproach upon the Northern courses. The pilgrims from the South were in fact a terrible nuisance. They had no respect for the sacred traditions of the game; they appeared on the classic heath of St. Andrews adorned in flaring "blazers," which filled the mind of the orthodox Scot with loathing, they never played a match, but toiled round the links with pencil and card, intent on deceiving themselves into the belief that they were daily lowering their record. A famous old caddie at North Berwick expressed the general feeling of his outspoken class when he pointed to one of these misguided individuals busily engaged with his card on one of the putting-greens, utterly oblivious to the fact that he was delaying the field while he worked in the higher branches of arithmetic, and remarked, in a loud tone of contempt to one of his party, "D'ye see yon man? D'ye ken the best club in his set—it's his pencil."

This was only one aspect of the movement, however, and now that the pencilling disease has more or less abated, it is only fair to admit that the new impetus given to the game by its sudden popularity outside of Scotland has been in the long run most beneficial. The competition has of course become far greater, and as young athletes have taken up the sport more and more, the standard of excellence has proportionately increased. I am quite willing to believe that "Young Tom" Morris was one of the greatest golfers that ever lived, but I am equally convinced that there were no amateurs in his time who could compare with the players of to-day. The conditions are certainly in our favor. Not only have the greens become easier, and straight driving less essential, but the implements of war are far more efficacious. The quality of the balls has greatly improved, and the introduction of the "bulger" has revolutionized the art of driving. With the old-fashioned long-headed club it was practically impossible to hit hard with any accuracy, the slightest deviation in aim involving a terrific slice or pull. Nowadays the curve on the face of the club, and the more compact volume of weight, makes the matter of direction so much easier that a far greater force can be given to the stroke. Twenty years ago a man who was a long driver was at once stamped as an erratic player, not to be relied upon. Now, unless a certain average of distance is maintained no one can rank as a first-class player.

But it was not merely the old-fashioned weapons which handicapped the amateurs of the past generation. We have only to consider who they were to see that, other things being equal, they could not possibly have competed with the best players of today. In the first place, they were far behind the professionals, which is not the case at present. Secondly, they were for the most part middle-aged men; so much so that it was considered an impertinence for any youngster to play against them. They kept up the pleasing fiction for a long time that at golf, as at whist, the ripeness of long experience was necessary for success, and it required many expositions of the game to persuade them that the cracks of the younger generation, men like Mr. J. E. Laidlay and the Blackwells, were introducing a new and superior kind of play. When, for instance, Mr. Ted Blackwell used to drive across the corner of the railway at St. Andrews—a carry of about one hundred and seventy yards—his feat was regarded as a sort of circus trick, wonderful to look at, but quite outside the true sphere of golf. After awhile, however, it became apparent that not only could the trick be repeated, but what was more important, Mr. Blackwell almost invariably beat his opponent, and gradually the old order began to change, making way for the new, which was hastened in its coming by the fresh impulse from athletes in England. In other words, the kind of golf which could be played by an elderly Scotch judge on Monday afternoon at Musselburgh in a stiff collar and a high silk hat ceased to be regarded as the best standard of excellence which could be reached by the amateur. It was recognized now that to play the game to its full advantage a man must be in good health and training, with muscle and eye in perfect accord; and we must thank the English cricketer for helping to impress this fact upon the hardy but conservative Northerner.

It is now time to turn to the growth of the game in this country, which is the main theme of the present article. We have seen that the sudden spread of golf in England was almost contemporaneous with a new development in the evolution of the sport. It remains to inquire how far that development has been appreciated in America. The particular genius of the American has a tendency to reduce sports of all kinds to a scientific basis, and therefore it is to be expected that sooner or later the lovers of the game in this country will be able to throw some new light not only upon the methods of play, but upon the interpretation of the rules, which has always been a difficulty since golf passed out of the hands of the few into the possession of the many who cannot be controlled by tradition alone, but need the assistance of hard and fast laws. It seems to me that so far the players in this country have been more exercised over the proper reading of the regulations than they have over the development of the game itself. And since it is extremely important that no radical changes should be made in the rules, which long experience has proved to be best adapted to the government of the game before, at least, it is definitely understood what the game is, it may be well to point out a few of the main shortcomings of the golf that is played on this side of the Atlantic.

You cannot play golf without links, any more than you can make bricks without straw, so that the first consideration is that your links should be as good as possible. It is five or six years since the game was introduced into the United States, and yet the fact remains that there is hardly a course in the country that in any way approximates a first-class links in the proper sense of the term. Of course allowances must be made for the many drawbacks which have to be overcome in the way of climate and soil, but there are so many errors in the best courses in the country which might easily be remedied, that it seems necessary to indicate exactly what are the features of the best courses in England and Scotland, and what is the standard at which we have to aim. To put it as shortly as possible: Great Britain is encircled for the most part by a belt of sandy soil from half a mile to a mile in breadth, which has been formed by the receding of the ocean. This belt of land is of an undulating character, with occasional abrupt sand-hills, and the whole surface is covered with a short velvety turf which stands a great deal of wear and tear, but is always smooth and soft; even in the rainiest summer the grass seldom grows long enough on the regular course to conceal a golf-ball from sight, while the climate of the British Isles is such that a drought seldom comes to parch the young blades, or scorch the putting greens. Such a thing as a stone or a tree is practically unknown on the best courses; good play will always secure good lies on perfect turf, while the putting greens are simply part of the regular course, not laid out with a spirit level, but taken as they come with the natural roll of the land, which greatly increases the necessity of skill and accuracy in negotiating the finer part of the game. The only hazards admissible are sand-bunkers, which occur naturally at irregular intervals, the long grass which on the seashore is called "bent," and which generally bounds the edge of the course to prevent wild driving, the gorse which is an incident of most Scotch links, and, if nature happens to supply it, a water hazard in the shape of a pond or stream. There are cases of stone-walls on Prestwick and North Berwick, two of the finest courses in Scotland, but they are there of necessity and not by choice, and to imagine that they are proper adjuncts, would be equivalent to considering that every racket-court must have a cracked wall, because there happens to be a slight fissure in the best court at Lords.

Now the courses which are laid out on this sand-belt of Great Britain are not held to be best because they are recommended by custom, but because it only requires a single day upon any one of them to find that the game takes on new features of interest which it has never possessed before. A man who has once ridden upon a modern safety with pneumatic tires would never go back to the old-fashioned high bicycle with thin cushions; so one who has played golf at Prestwick or St. Andrews knows at once what are the possibilities of the game. Imagine, therefore, the astonishment of a Scotch golfer upon reading the accounts of some of the prominent courses in this country. Here are a few examples: "It is an inland course of stone-wall hazards, rocky pastures bordered by ploughed fields and woods, and is prolific in those little hollows known as cuppy lies;" or this: "The hazards are mainly artificial; there are some stretches of sand, railroad embankment, and deep roads that are tests of skill and temper;" or this: "There are nine holes in the course which furnishes great variety in its hazards of hills, stone-walls, railroad embankments lined with blast furnace slag, apple-trees, and a combination of terrors in front of what is known as the Devil's Hole, consisting of brook, bowlders, and road, which has spoiled many a score;" or, best of all: "A player who has done a round at the Country Club will have passed over various points of avenue, steeple-chase course, race-track, polo-fields, and pigeon-shooting grounds; he will have come triumphantly through a purgatorial stone-wall jump, a sand-bunker and bastion, a water jump and finally a vast gravel pit or crater. . . . Stone-walls, trees, ploughed fields, fences, and chasms present excellent sporting requirements on a course."

Many more instances might be quoted, but these are quite sufficient to explain exactly what a golf-links ought *not* to be. A golfer is not a quarryman that he should go down into a gravel-pit to extricate his ball from the midst of bowlders; nor is he one of the hewers of wood or drawers of water that he should slash the trees with his niblick like a modern Don Quixote, or cover himself with mire from a muddy ditch. It is understood, of course, that Nature cannot entirely be overcome. The coast of Maine, where there is enough moisture in the air to keep the greens in good condition, is too rocky, while the summer climate of Long Island prevents the courses there from being kept in first-class condition, although the quality of soil is equal to anything in Scotland or England. Still, even if the ideal links can never be quite attainable, it is possible, by aiming in the right direction, to get a course which shall be for all practical purposes a perfect test of golf. To arrive at such a consummation, it is necessary always to keep the ideal in view; and the first object, therefore, should be to procure the best possible turf all through the course and on the putting greens. Next it should be remembered that, if possible, all the hazards, with the exception of a stream or a pond, should be sand-bunkers. Long grass is admissible, but should be avoided in the direct line of play, because it leads to so much waste of time in hunting for lost balls. Every single tree on the links should be ruthlessly cut down. If a picturesque landscape is insisted upon it is easy enough to leave the woods which may happen to lie on the confines, but they should be regarded as out of bounds and never played through. Every bowlder and stone should be removed with assiduous care, for they are merely responsible for broken clubs and loss of temper, and have nothing in the world to do with the game. Finally the putting greens should be left as Nature made them, except in so far as they are kept in perfect condition by rolling and mowing. They ought not to be laid out on a dead level so as to preclude any nicety in the judgment of curves, but should be gently undulating and always guarded in some way by a hazard. In this country it is generally necessary to water them, that they may not become parched and inordinately keen; on the other hand it must be remembered that the smoother and keener they are up to a certain point, the greater will be the skill called into play both in putting and approaching. A man who has been accustomed to pitch the ball boldly on to a slow level-putting green with fair accuracy, will find himself hopelessly at sea when he has to contend with a keen slope where a hair's breadth deviation from the true direction will lead to instant perdition. To take cases in point, the putting greens at Shinnecock, where the championship meeting was held last year, were far too small and keen, although they were beautifully true. Those at Meadowbrook, on the contrary, are perfect in condition, but they are for the most part so level and slow, that approach play is rendered comparatively easy.

So much for the nature of the ground. A word or two remains to be said upon the laying out of the eighteen holes. I say eighteen advisedly, because a course of half the distance can never be placed in the first class. The expenses incurred in laying out golf-links in this country are generally so great, that it has been deemed best in most cases to get nine good holes rather that eighteen of an inferior nature. But this should always be regarded as a temporary measure. It is not merely a matter of convenience in tournaments which can only be held with any satisfaction on a full course; but in every-day play a nine-hole round becomes very monotonous and does not allow sufficient scope for versatility in the game.

As far as I am able to judge there are many nine-hole courses in the East which are admirably constructed — Meadowbrook, for instance, being very well laid out —but there is not one of the eighteen-hole rounds that approaches perfection. Take Shinnecock, for instance, which, from the nature of its soil, ought to be an almost ideal field for play, there is hardly a single hole of a good length; that is to say, the distances are so arranged that not only is the prowess of the good golfer seldom brought into evidence, but the chances of good and bad are in a fair way of being equalized. The chief thing to aim at in distributing the holes is to arrange them in such a way that each can be reached from the tee by one or two or three *full* shots, as the case may be. That is practically the whole gist of the matter. For it is obvious that, under such conditions, a player cannot miss a single shot, cannot even play an indifferent stroke without being penalized. If, on the other hand, the length of a hole is such that it cannot be covered in one shot, and yet if the drive off the tee goes only a hundred yards or so, it can still be covered in two, by the aid of a good second; then it is evident that one drive is, for all practical purposes, as good as another. When there are many holes of such a description, a player may make a bad drive off every tee and yet defeat an opponent who never misses a single shot in the round. A careful study of the best courses in Great Britain will show that the number of holes measuring from two hundred and forty to three hundred yards is exceedingly rare; in other words, the rule referred to above is the one essential toward excellence.

As for the hazards, they should be sand bunkers, as far as possible. Sand should be procured, even at a considerable cost, because there is no other kind of hazard which answers the purpose so well. They should be of such a nature that a good player can always extricate himself from the difficulty in one stroke, and they should, above all things, be varied in their construction.

The everlasting line of cops seen on so many of our inland courses are both an offence to the eye and to the intelligence. The difficulties thrown in the path of a discriminating golfer should be of a far more subtile nature. In driving off the tee it is generally well to have something in front to catch a missed ball, and the hazard ought to be large and well defined; a little ditch, at one hundred and twenty yards distance, is not nearly sufficient because it punishes only a few out of the many bad shots. If possible, the hazard should extend in many cases over the whole distance between the tee and the carry of a moderate drive. Then, as regards the hazards near the putting green, particular care should be taken to have them placed in various shapes and positions. A single bastion in front of every hole is more often an aid to success than a ground for misfortune; it is an easy guide to the eye, and induces a player to be bold in his approach, a quality in which he is often deficient. Hazards should be placed on every side of the hole, more especially beyond it, so that every approach may call for careful calculation. Finally let me repeat that trees and stones must, at all costs, be removed; and the requirements of a good golf course will have been fairly stated.

When we have arrived at such a measure of excellence as this, the difficulties of the rules and regulations of the game will begin to solve themselves. The United States Golf Association, for instance, passed a rule permitting a player in a match to lift his ball out of any difficulty at the penalty of two strokes. Now this was in direct opposition to the original idea of the game that the ball should always be played under any circumstances, or else the hole should be given up. The excuse for the change made by the Executive Committee was that there were many courses in the country where conditions were different, and where it would often be impossible to hit the ball at all. The answer to such an argument is apparent. Such a course is not fit for the proper exercise of the game and ought not to be admitted to membership in the Association. Although it is impossible always to reproduce the perfect turf and bracing sea-air of the Scotch links, it is quite feasible to lay out a course in such a way that it may be as good a test as possible of proficiency in the game. Take, for instance, the Chicago Golf Club links at Wheaton. The course has been in existence only two years, and yet, when a few additional bunkers are finished, which are at present under construction, it will present as fair a field for the settling of rival claims as any links outside of the first half dozen or so in Great Britain. Of course the quality of soil is different from that of St. Andrews or Prestwick, but the turf is excellent; a good drive is hardly ever punished by a bad lie; the hazards are of the proper sort, chiefly consisting of sand bunkers, with an occasional water-jump, and above all there are no trees, stones, or buildings on the course. The holes are laid out in such a way as to eliminate, as far as possible, the element of chance; and taking it all in all it is probably the only eighteen-hole course in the country which can compare with the best links abroad. I state this, not as a matter of prejudice, but because it is an incontrovertible fact, and one which should be taken into consideration by all green-committees; for it is a simple proof that nearly all the Eastern courses could be improved to a similar extent by keeping the true ideal constantly in view.

The rules of golf have always presented a difficulty to those who are entrusted with the care of framing them, and since there are many points under discussion at the present moment of writing it will be well to take only a general view of the case. It is quite certain that many of the existing regulations as they stand are faulty, chiefly because while they have the right aim in view, they leave so much ground for argument and discussion; and it is equally certain that before long the American golfers, who are not bound hand and foot by tradition, will introduce one or two remedial measures which will incense the conservative Briton but will probably aid the true development of the game. Already an excellent innovation, for which the United States Association is responsible, is the method of deciding the Amateur Championship. It was considered a great step in the right direction when the competition by holes was first introduced into Great Britain, not by a Scotch club but by the green-committee of Hoylake in England. Since the hole game is the only true golf, it seemed a pity that the Amateur Championship should not be decided in any other way. A difficulty, however, has since arisen on account of the unwieldy size of the field which threatens to make the tournament a very protracted affair. It remained for American golfers to solve the problem by inventing the dual method of play; first weeding out the poorer players by two rounds of medal play, and then selecting the champion by several rounds of hole play—a plan which sounds very obvious and satisfactory as soon as it is suggested; for it cuts down the list of entries very quickly, and also necessitates excellence in both branches of the game; and after all the patience and accuracy brought out in medal play ought to count for something. Now, however, there is a proposal to go still farther into the weeding out process by fixing a definite scratch score for every links based upon the distances of the holes, and accepting no entry from anyone whose handicap at his home club is above a certain limit. Whether this suggestion should be carried out or not is entirely a matter of expediency. If it is found that so many entries are made as to seriously militate against the success of the tournament, it will be necessary to adopt some such scheme for keeping out all those who have really no chance of winning, but merely enter for practice or amusement. The national tournament is not a nursery for embryo golfers, nor is it fair that a good player should be handicapped by having to go through the preliminary rounds with a duffer who has not the ghost of a chance of winning. One of the arguments against the acceptance of a definite scratch based on distance, is that it can be so easily obviated by a slight alteration of tees so as to make the score as high as possible and include a number of players who would not otherwise have qualified. Still it must be remembered that it is always easy to defeat the ends of any government for the time being, and a certain reliance must be placed upon green-committees to do their best, not only for the interests of their respective clubs, but for the future of the game itself. In this matter of qualification experience alone will show whether a new regulation is necessary or not; but as a general principle it ought to be remembered that golf is still a very new game in the country, and the would-be iconoclasts should be discouraged from taking any premature action which would alienate us from golfers on the other side of the Atlantic in the meantime, and in the long run prove to be quite unnecessary.

Those who look for instruction in the science of golf must turn to the pages of the Badminton book which is still the highest authority on the subject; but it may not be out of place to throw out a few suggestions as to the spirit in which the book should be read. It must be remembered in the first place, that nearly all the men who have taken up the game in America of recent years, have reached an age when it is impossible to acquire the easy suppleness of youth. They ought accordingly to modify the instructions which come to them, not only from the literature upon the subject, but from many of the professional teachers who always seem to forget that their pupils have not had the same advantages in early youth as themselves. It is nearly always wrong for a grown man to attempt a full swing to start with. I have so constantly heard the most promising beginners reproached for what the conventional book-learned player calls a lack of form, that it seems very necessary to point out that a short clean sweep at the ball is not only far more effective, but far better form than the angular contortions which go to make up what many beginners are pleased to call a full swing. In driving the ball the main object is to keep the head of the club travelling as long as possible in the direct line of flight, and this must be achieved, at first, by letting the club go back only so far as is possible without making an angular bend in the swing. If this steady sweep is constantly kept in view, the beginner will find that gradually he is able to swing farther and farther back as the muscles become more accustomed to the motion, until finally he attains the proud distinction of possessing a real St.

Andrew's swing. In all other things, moreover, he should exercise his common sense and make up his mind that it is his duty to hit the ball clean every time, even if in so doing he sacrifices a good many yards in distance. Above all let him watch the best players and get into their style by unconscious imitation. If our beginners would only walk round with their professional teachers, and feel, as it were, the easy method of sweeping away the ball, they would learn far more than they do in a hundred verbal lessons ; and when they play they should always play matches and not trudge round the links with a pencil and score-card—trying to lower a record of their own which is absolutely meaningless. The young player who can take odds from his elders and betters, and compete with them more or less successfully, is far nearer the road to grace, although his total score should mount up ever so much higher than the record of the solitary and introspective knight of the pencil. Life would be far more worth living on a golf links if there were a rule in every club forbidding a member to mention his score or talk at length about the lowering of a record which nobody but himself cares about, and even he himself only half believes in. The game was originally intended to be a friendly contest of skill; the middle-aged beginner has made it a fruitful source of lying and self-deception, and a very scourge to his friends.

One word should be said about the courtesies of the game. There is no pursuit in life which exhibits the best and the worst of a man so freely as the game of golf. That a control of the temper is absolutely essential for success goes without saying, and there are many little points which suggest a loss of that control if certain rules of etiquette are not strictly observed. The most important of these is the way in which the rules are interpreted, and there seems to be only one way of dealing with the matter. First of all, if a penalty is incurred for any reason, the player should at once admit it without waiting for his opponent to call his attention to it, and no matter how trifling the breach of rule, or how unimportant the game, the full penalty should be conceded whether the opponent desires it or not. On the other hand, if the opponent should move his ball, for instance, in addressing it, it is his business to count the stroke, for stroke it is just as much as the longest drive that was ever struck from the tee ; and except when playing for a medal he should be left entirely to himself in the matter. To put it shortly, the word " claim " has no place in the golfer's vocabulary. It may be argued, of course, that your opponent may then take advantage of you. If he does, your remedy is simple—never to play with him again. In the meantime, if every golfer were intent upon acting up to the very letter of the law, there could never be any possibility of dispute. After all it is a game for gentlemen, and unless that is kept in mind, unpleasantness becomes endless. Perhaps it is this very fact which has made it so popular in this country, where the other great games are in danger of getting entirely into the hands of professionals. That being the case, it is most important that the tendency to multiply tournaments and lavish handsome trophies on indifferent players should be checked at the outset of our golfing history. Ten years ago the best players in the world were content with the custody of one or two small medals which they could not even keep, and I confess that in the best interests of the game, I wish the same state of things existed now. Possibly we shall have a revulsion of feeling in a short time, and golf will take on again its garb of Caledonian simplicity.

37

The Development of Golf in the West

Photo by R. Capes, Chicago.

Wheaton—A Drive for the Tenth Hole.

THE DEVELOPMENT OF GOLF IN THE WEST.

By H. C. Chatfield-Taylor.

A CLUB whizzed through the air—a sharp click—and Charles B. Macdonald drove the little sphere of gutta percha far over the water of Lake Michigan in approved St. Andrews fashion. I looked at Macdonald in amazement, and then followed his eyes in the direction of the Lake. He may have seen the ball, but I would have to take his word for it. That drive, however, started the golf craze in the West.

Macdonald teed another ball and handed his driver to me. I attempted to imitate his actions, and after a series of contortions which would have done honor to the rubber-man in Barnum's side-show, tore up a foot of turf without in any way disturbing the equanimity of the little white object I had striven so viciously to hit. Macdonald laughed, and I said "damn." That was in April, 1892—and I have been saying it ever since.

Macdonald had come up to Lake Forest to lay out a golf course. With supreme contempt he eyed the trees and flower beds, and said the ground would never do. Finally he decided it was worth while trying—if only to give the game a start—and after a few glances about the place, he started out to pace off the holes. And what a course it was! The first hole was eighty yards in length, the longest a hundred and seventy-five. Part of the course was amongst the trees and flower-beds of the adjoining places of Mr. C. B. Farwell and Mr. John Dwight, and the rest in a small park by the shore of the lake, where a sliced ball invariably went over the bluff and fell some two hundred feet to the beach below; but, such as it was, it had the honor of being the first golf course west of the Allegheny Mountains.

Macdonald did not play that first day. He merely drove a few balls to show me how the trick was done, and drove stakes in the ground to show where the holes were to be. When he went back to town, he left behind a collection of ancient Scottish clubs—relics of his college days at St. Andrews—and a few old balls.

On the following Saturday, Urban H. Broughton, an English resident of Chicago, came up for a visit. He had played—at Sandwich, or some such place—and was keen to have a go at the game. The hole-cups were not yet in place, and it was raining torrents—but that did not dampen our ardor. In a blinding storm, we waded around the nine holes, losing most of Macdonald's balls, and playing the game with the singular modification that holing out meant hitting the stake in the fewest number of strokes.

I have heard vague rumors of some Scotchmen driving balls in Jackson Park, at an earlier date, until stopped by the police—but they were Scotchmen, and they were only driving balls, so I believe that that attempt in the rain was the first authentic golf game ever played in the West.

A short time after, six sets of clubs and the other paraphernalia of the game arrived from Hoylake, and golf in earnest was inaugurated. But all during that summer of '92, the Americans held aloof from the game. It was left to a few stray Englishmen—enticed to Lake Forest for the purpose—and myself, to uphold the traditions of the game. We played persistently, and the Americans who chanced to pass the little links by the lake, stared in amazement, or, as was more often the case, laughed derisively at our antics.

In '93 it was a little better. But the coming of Sir Henry Wood, the British Commissioner General, to the Exposition, lent a certain dignity to the game—and during that year the Chicago Golf Club was conceived.

Macdonald, who had never thoroughly approved of the unassuming efforts of the Lake Forest golfers, had been casting about for a place where it would be possible to take a full swing without over driving the hole. Finally he discovered an Englishman with a farm of meadowland. The Englishman was J. Haddon Smith, the step-father of Miss "Johnny" Carpenter—the well-known player—and the farm was at Belmont, a suburban way-station, about twenty miles from the city.

Meantime, people had begun to hear of golf, so, with the assistance of such Scottish experts as James B. Forgan and Herbert and Lawrence Tweedie, a few Americans who were bold enough to try the experiment were "corralled" by Mr. Macdonald, and the Chicago Golf Club sprang into being. This was in the autumn of '93—too late for the effort to bear visible fruits that year.

Photo by O. B. Brand.

Exmoor Country Club.

After two seasons of ridicule and stray Englishmen, I became quite convinced that something must be done to lure the Americans of Lake Forest into the game. Early in the spring of '94, I developed a deep-laid plan to encompass their ruin. Lake Forest was a temperance town, and Scotch whiskey was an unknown quantity. So, with malice aforethought, I invited some ten or a dozen of the younger residents for a game of golf, one Saturday afternoon. They came—scornful, of course, but well-mannered enough to conceal their contempt. Golf clubs and balls were deftly distributed by Broughton and myself, and they were started to their doom in pairs. When they came in, hot and tired, I lured them to the dining-room, where decanters of Scotch whiskey were placed enticingly before their innocent eyes. Alas! they fell, to a man. Whether it was owing to the game or the whiskey I would not venture a guess—but on the following Saturday the number had doubled, and from that day to this, except on Sunday, golf has flourished at Lake Forest.

On the Fourth of July, 1894, we held our first handicap. Reginald de Koven won it, playing with a metal putter. He is left-handed, and we had no left-handed clubs. The putter faced both ways—so, nothing daunted, he ventured forth with that. While others tore up the turf in vain efforts to drive, or sliced their balls in the lake, he putted persistently, and, tortoise-like, distanced the hares of cleek and driver. A novel feature of this day was Major-General Nelson A. Miles and his staff, in full uniform, following the players on horseback. Even in those days we drew a distinguished gallery.

Meanwhile, the rival community at Belmont, with Macdonald and the Tweedies as preceptors, had been learning a thing or two, and as they had the advantage of Sunday play, a course which at least had distance, and real Scotchmen to spur them on, they thought the Puritans of Lake Forest would prove easy marks, so Lake Forest was invited to Belmont for a team match—the Scotchmen, of course, being *hors concours*. We played four men a side. Lake Forest was represented by F. C. Farwell, H. N. Tuttle, Scott Durand and F. C. Aldrich, the Chicago Golf Club by E. I. Frost, E. W. Cramer, Gustav Wilmerding and Stuyvesant Le Roy, Jr. Alas! for the vagaries of golf. Are any of either team in the first flight to-day? But it was a glorious match—the first three pairs all even, and the match won by the Chicago man of the last pair. The reason for the loss of the match was again Scotch whiskey. The wily Chicago men, thinking to entice their Puritan brethren from the straight and narrow path, and thus encompass their ruin, placed Scotch whiskey before them at luncheon. Three fell from grace, and they halved their matches; one remained faithful to his principles, and lacking the true inspiration of the game, he lost his match, and brought defeat to his club. Since that day there has never been any Scotch question at Lake Forest, except as to quantity.

For the return match Lake Forest was confident it had the easy end. Flower-beds and trees would be certain to ensnare the Belmontites—but, over-confidence has been the ruin of many a sportsman, and when the score was figured the Chicago Golf Club was so many up that an adding machine was brought into use. Tuttle being the only winner for Lake Forest.

One result of these team matches was to wean the Lake Foresters from their trees and flower-beds—the private course, and, it might also be added, the private bar were no longer sufficient to satisfy the cravings of the town for golf. So the following year saw the formation of the Lake Forest Golf Club, with a membership of a hundred and fifty, and a good, nine-hole course, on the farm of the late Leander J. McCormick, where the holes were of sufficient length to call for an occasional brassie stroke.

The same year ('95) the Chicago Golf Club moved to its present home at Wheaton, Ill. The first open tournament was held. Willie Dunne, Lloyd, Tucker, and other professionals, were brought on from

Photo by Chas. Allgeier, Chicago.

Midlothian Country Club House.

the East, to show how the game should be played, and last, but not least, Charles B. Macdonald brought back the Havemeyer cup from Newport—thus winning for the West the first American championship held under the auspices of the U. S. G. A. It was Wheaton's year, but Lake Forest was not to be outdone so easily. The nine-hole course and the two-room club-house of the Lake Forest Golf Club were but stepping-stones.

During the winter the Onwentsia Club was formed, and in '96 Lake Forest boasted of a full-grown country club, with golf, polo, tennis, and a membership of three hundred. The days of the flower-beds were over, and the quiet, Puritanic village had become a community of sportsmen. That year of '96 was, in the parlance of the streets, the "fiercest" year golf has known in the West. Chicago society was divided by the rival camps of "Wheaton" and "Onwentsia." The Red and White of Wheaton, and the Blue and Yellow of Onwentsia were worn as hat-bands and ties, and the feeling ran so high that families were divided, and the members of the rival clubs were scarcely on speaking terms.

When H. J. Whigham joined Onwentsia, and became its Captain, thus giving Lake Forest a champion to rival Macdonald, open war was declared, and the team matches between the two clubs became bitter contests, watched with breathless anxiety by partisans of both sexes. When Onwentsia won the series, and Whigham won the Amateur Championship at Shinnecock, it was not safe for a Lake Forester to venture in the wilds of Wheaton unarmed.

But those days of rivalry are over. Wheaton and Lake Forest are now the best of friends, standing together against all comers. Nobody knows and nobody cares who wins the team matches, except the players themselves, and the membership of the two clubs is so interwoven that it is only a question of convenience where a man plays. When there were but two clubs, the rivalry was natural and beneficial, but in recent years golf courses have sprung up so fast in the West that it would require a feat of memory to even record the names. Every station, nearly, on the Northwestern Railway, has its golf course, and the last is yet to come.

Photo by R. Capes, Chicago.

Glenview Club House.

In '96 the Illinois Golf Club, under the captaincy of Herbert Tweedie, was formen and took possession of the old Belmont course. In '97 the Exmoor Club was organized at Highland Park, as a neighbor of Onwentsia. In that year the Amateur Championship was played at Wheaton, and entries were received from but three Chicago clubs. Last year, at Onwentsia, six clubs were represented by thirty-four players, and seven Western clubs outside Chicago by twenty-three players, while at Newport in '95 Charles B. Macdonald was the only Western representative. In '95 there were but three golf courses near Chicago, with but one eighteen-hole course. Now — but five years later—there are twenty-two clubs, and six eighteen-hole courses within thirty miles of the city. The Chicago Golf Club, Onwentsia, Glenview and Midlothian, all have memberships exceeding two hundred and fifty, while each maintain an eighteen-hole course, fully six thousand yards in length, and a club-house comparable to the best of the Eastern golf clubs.

Chicago has, of course, been the centre of Western golf, and golf was played here several years before it was known elsewhere in the West. Milwaukee was the first city to fall in line, but now the golf craze has extended, not only to the large cities, but the smaller towns as well, and there is almost a continuous succession of golf courses from Pittsburg to Seattle. The Western Golf Association, formed last year, membership in which is confined to clubs in the U. S. G. A., situated within 500 miles of Chicago, musters nearly thirty clubs, and at its first tournament boasted an entry list of eighty-seven players, representing fourteen clubs.

But all this is merely dry statistics. It is sufficient to state that golf has conquered the West as has no other game. Western men are business men, who have not the time or energy to devote to tennis, racquets, hunting, polo, or other games requiring athletic training. Golf appeals to them as does nothing else. They can play one day a week, or seven, and take just as much, or just as little, exercise at the game as their tastes dictate. If one might venture a prophesy, it is that the golf craze will last in the West longer than in the East, as golf fills here a distinct requirement, in many ways peculiar to the community. It has been the means of getting Western men in the open air, for the first time in the lives of most of them, and they are going to keep on golfing until somebody invents a better game which does not demand greater activity or more endurance.

With the exception of the Scotchmen and the college boys, the average Western golfer is less adept than his Eastern contemporary—not from lack of incentive or skill, but from lack of time in which to practice. Owing to climatic conditions, the courses open later and close earlier than in the East, and the average golfer can get in but two or three rounds a week. If the average skill in the West is not equal to that of the East, the enthusiasm of the Westerners for the sport excels that to be found elsewhere, and golf has come to occupy in the West a place which has never been equaled, or even approached, by any other amateur game.

Onwentsia Club House.

38

The Golf of the New School

THE GOLF OF THE NEW SCHOOL.

By Horace Hutchinson.

THERE has been a great deal of spring ferment, so to speak, in British golfing circles. The working up of the younger element proving yet again the truth of the proverb that "youth will be served." The strange thing in golf is that youth has not sooner insisted with emphasis on its rights.

Mr. H. H. Hilton, Amateur Champion, Great Britain.

Hitherto the younger school has been kept under with some success by the seniors. This year, for the first time, it has asserted itself, in something like its true force. The latest accession to the ranks of the older school, latest to be admitted into the rather select circle of the very best, was poor Mr. F. G. Tait, who was killed by a Boer bullet in South Africa. Mr. John Ball also went to the war, we hope, with better auspices, and his absence, too, gives another opening that would not have been if war could have been averted.

The opportunity has not been neglected. Here and there in the list of the year's chief competitions we read, at the head, one of the old, well-known names; but for the most part the names are new, even if they do not always belong to the younger school.

The first intimation, to a slightly startled world, of the force of the younger school, was given by the performance of the Oxford University team in their annual match against Cambridge University, on the links of Sandwich. Not only did they beat their Light Blue rivals very severely, every member of the Oxford team beating his individual opponent, but every member was out, the first half of the round, under 40 strokes.

The uniform excellence of this play is obvious by the consideration that when the St. George's Vase was played for over the same course a few weeks later, and also the Amateur Championship Tournament, in no instance did a single competitor go out these nine in less than 36 strokes; and all the best of the amateur talent was there and on its mettle. The man that had the greatest reputation of these undergraduate players was Mr. H. C. Ellis. One, Mr. Bramston, at that time but little regarded, and actually playing no higher than fifth in the Dark Blue team, was also in the field, and beat his individual opponent very severely, holing the full course in 78 strokes.

Perhaps the next meeting of note was at Westward Ho, where the Kashmir Cup is given annually for competition open to all amateurs, over two rounds, scoring play, of the green. The result of the play for this cup was that the writer, a very old-time golfer, as will be admitted, was the winner, with Mr. Hilton and Mr. Osmund Scott, the latter quite one of the newest school, only a stroke behind.

It was the team matches of the week following the competition for the Kashmir Cup, however, that revealed the existence of a new golfing force of the first calibre in Mr. J. Bramston. He began the week by catching the writer badly off his game, and inflicting on him a defeat of which the memory still stings, and subsequently defeated Mr. Hilton and Mr. J. L. Low, successively, by a sufficient margin in each case.

This was, indeed, very fine work, and what made the last victory seem more im-

Jack Morris Ball. Robb. "Old Tom" and Richardson.

to be rather wanting.

At Muirfield, on the occasion of the medal meeting of the Honorable Company of Edinburgh Golfers (time-honored institution of a fine-sounding name) the winner was again one of those under-graduates of the Dark Blue persuasion, Mr. Mansfield Hunter, with Mr. C. Dalziel, also one of the younger school, second to him, while behind them in the list were such gallant players of the older type as Mr. J. E. Laidlay and Mr. Balfour-Melville, ex-champions both.

portant, was the circumstance that a few weeks later Mr. J. L. Low won the spring medal of the Royal and Ancient Club of St. Andrews. On this occasion there was but a poor representation of the younger school, so the result was not as interesting for the purpose of estimating the relative merits of the two schools as some others. Other competitions in Scotland tested the older players shrewdly, and it cannot be denied that they were found

But the most emphatic assertion of the power of the younger men was given at the competition for the Tantallon Cup, at North Berwick, where Mr. R. Maxwell, a notable player of the younger men, won, in a gale of wind, with a score of 85, which

Mr. C. Hutchings, Driving.

Taylor, the British Open Champion, in a Bunker.

was actually eleven strokes better than the next return, although the field included such fine players as Mr. J. E. Laidlay and other men of mark. This Mr. Maxwell is a young player of great power, who first won his spurs, while little more than a boy, by defeating Mr. John Ball and Mr. Hilton in successive rounds at Muirfield on the occasion of the amateur championship being played there. Subsequently he succumbed to the eventual winner of that year's championship, Dr. Allen.

The meeting for the amateur championship of the present year fell by rotation to be played on the green of the St. George's Club, at Sandwich. With the exception of Mr. Ball, holder of the title, who was out of the kingdom, no amateur golfer of any great repute was absent. On the day preceding the tournament there was a competition for the St. George's Cup on exactly the same lines, two scoring rounds of the green, as in the competition for the Kashmir Cup at Westward Ho. Mr. Maxwell sent in, for the St. George's Cup, the best round, a 77, in the morning, and following it up well with 78 in the afternoon, won the cup, with several strokes to spare.

The next to him in the returns was Mr. J. Bramston, who had made his name at Westward Ho a week or two before, and in the afternoon had a round that equaled Mr. Maxwell's morning return, though in the morning he had scored 82. Here was a very decided triumph for the new school, who thus returned both first and second in a field that could not be excelled for the quality of the amateur talent represented. Mr. Hilton, Mr. C. Hutchings and Mr. H. C. Ellis, a mingling of the old and the new, were equal third at two strokes more than Mr. Bramston. Thereafter the big event of our amateur golfing year commenced.

By the fortune of the draw, it happened that unless things went contrary to expectation (as they are apt to go in this royal and ancient, but gloriously uncertain game) Mr. Hilton and Mr. Maxwell would meet in an early heat, and it was thought by a good many that these two were fighting out between them the eventual holding of the amateur championship. Fortune is more fickle than golf itself, and awards to some a series of hard matches, to others a fairly easy succession until the final heats. In a tournament of this kind it is inevitably thus. No conspicuous acts of injustice were apparent in the present case.

Mr. Hilton did, as appeared likely, meet Mr. Maxwell. The latter was not quite at his best, and showed the weakness of the younger school as compared with the more wily seniors in not correcting, by head work, any lack of perfect harmony

Vardon, Defeated by Taylor, Approaching.

between hand and eye that his game suffered under, Mr. Hilton, with less driving power, was a deal wiser, and very steady and accurate. He picked up a hole whenever Mr. Maxwell gave him a chance to pick it back again. There is only one result of that kind of golf. He won by four up and three to play. Then in the final Mr. Hilton beat Mr. Robb, the latter not driving at all well, but making something like a fight with the winner by his excellent putting, which alone brought him into the final heat. Mr. Robb had played hard matches. He had knocked out Mr. Laidlay, the ex-amateur champion, by a single hole, and he had played a very hard match with Mr. Bramston—all even at the fifteenth hole, after saving himself by good putting at the thirteenth and fourteenth holes. This was in the semi-final heat, so it was as far as the semi-final that the younger school survived in the tournament, its representative being Mr. Bramston.

Taylor, Approaching.

Probably Mr. Bramston is the most promising of all the younger school. He has the inestimable merit of being very young. He is but nineteen. He has good nerve, drives a very long ball, and though he has not nearly as many strokes as, Mr. Hilton say, he yet has enough resource for the ordinary exigencies, and a deal more power, a deal longer ball, than Mr. Hilton.

Mr. J. Ball, Jr., Driving.

Mr. Maxwell is very possibly a better player for the moment than Mr. Bramston, though that is by no means demonstrated; but Mr. Maxwell has some five or six years advantage (at that blessed time of life it is an advantage) of Mr. Bramston in age, and more than corresponding advantage in golfing experience, for he has had better chances of playing against the best at North Berwick and in its neighborhood than Mr. Bramston in the few years of his golfing life at Westward Ho.

The final of the amateur tournament is hardly to be regarded as a test match between the old school and the new, Mr. Robb being hardly of the new school, although a younger man that Mr. Hilton.

Though the new school is thus asserting itself, still it is not to be denied that the amateur champion deserved the title thoroughly, by playing the best golf played in the competition. How good it was may be gauged by the fact that four up

Mr. H. H. Hilton, Driving.

and three to play was the smallest balance by which he beat any of his opponents. It was by this balance that he beat Mr. Maxwell, who gave him his hardest match, and who was really his most formidable foe. Mr. Graham might have been dangerous, but he was in no form. The only hard matches that Mr. Hilton had were against Mr. Maxwell and against Mr. Mr. Robb, and, as a matter of fact, they were only hard at the beginning, before his steadiness had broken the back of their defence.

So that is how we in Great Britain stand at present. Mr. Hilton is probably the best of our amateurs, with a younger man or two treading dangerously close on his heels, he is able thoroughly well to stave them off at present by his greater knowledge and steadiness, but they, with greater power, are bound to assert, very soon, the advantage of their blessed youth.

39

Holes by Accident in Golf

HOLES BY ACCIDENT IN GOLF

By GEORGE HIBBARD

ANY golfer playing the average amount, "in his time plays many" shots. He might wish that they were fewer, and the barometer of the score card did not mount so often toward the hundred point—so often run into a fever heat of disaster above it. But with the best of scores, playing constantly, each player drives, and approaches, and putts a goodly number of times. And when the thousands, and almost hundreds of thousands of present-day golfers are taken into account, the strange tales that are told are more readily credible—and golf stories need not necessarily be set down as "fish stories."

In speaking of curious golfing accidents, I have not the intention of speaking of remarkably skilful shots—of the shots that a man remembers with pride for years. I do not wish to say anything of the marvelously accurate work with the lofter, or the putter. These are matters in a certain degree of skill, though in their rarity they might appear matters of accident, or, at least, to be under the control of that tutelar deity of the links—Luck. They are not to be classed with the curious things which happen without the intention of the player.

The following story, which is well-known upon the other side, might be called an example of luck—as it is. Still it is something more, for what happened was not the result of intention, but directly contrary to it. Two golfers in an important match were playing up toward one of the last holes of the course. The man whose turn it was to approach made his shot, and played his ball as near to where the flag was as possible. The ball struck the flag, and bounded off at an angle. When the players came up to the green, they found that the flag was not in the hole, but the ball, in bounding off, had rolled in the direction of the hole and actually rolled into it.

An accident quite as remarkable, and with a touch of that humor which is showing itself ever in this wonderful game, took place in this country. Two well-known players were engaged in a close contest. One of these, at an advanced hole of the match, was a little down. Both had made equally good drives, but a poor second shot had put the player who was behind with a high board fence between him and the hole. The other man played, and placed his ball neatly on the green. He walked onward with all the confidence which comes from lying almost dead, while one's opponent is playing one more in a less advantageous position. Suddenly he saw the other ball roll across the grass, and come to rest within a foot of the flag. To play over the fence was almost impossible to do with any accuracy, but his opponent had played and made a poor shot. His ball, however, instead of striking the fence, had passed neatly through a knot hole, and come to rest in a position which enabled him to putt out, winning the hole.

For a long time I believed that the tale of a bird killed by a golf ball, was apocryphal.

The first convincing testimony came from the loser of the match last mentioned. A bird had been killed by a golf ball—to his knowledge. And, most remarkable of all, a flying bird by a golf ball also soaring through the air. The driven ball struck the bird fairly, and it fell dead. That there can be no doubt about this, I hasten to give the reasons for my confidence. The fact is attested by a distinguished divine of the Presbyterian Church, and a Judge of the Court of Appeals of the State of New York, than which, as any one must admit, there could not be better testimony. Usually an historical occurrence does not take place under such fortunate conditions.

Upon the principle of a deluge following a downpour, the writer's mind had no sooner been set at rest upon this hitherto doubtful point, than new proof was added to what was already so satisfactorily proven. With his own eyes he was witness of a golfing accident almost as singular. He was playing a short hole of three hundred and fifteen yards, with the green in a "punch bowl," the hole being in the center of the depression, surrounded by circular inclosing banks. His opponent played with the intention of dropping his ball in the hollow. He topped it, however, and it ran briskly along the ground. As it bounded onward, a number of birds which had been resting in the grass, rose and fluttered upward. At that moment the ball was stopped. The players thought that it had struck a piece of wood, as a dark object was seen to move. Coming up they found, however, that a bird had been hit. The ball had evidently struck the bird on the head, breaking its neck and killing it instantly. The player whose ball had brought down the bird sitting, in this unexpected manner, gave it into the hands of a taxidermist. Now in his house it stands to point and adorn another golfing tale.

Speaking of the bird killed on the wing—in a somewhat long golfing experience—the writer has only once seen two balls hit each other in the air. On the links where this happened, the First Hole was parallel with the Home Hole. A ball, sliced by an outgoing player, was hit in mid air by a ball pulled by a player coming in. Both balls broke in wildly different directions, and fell directly to the ground. Fortunately, the matches were not important, or the state of the game critical; as, in spite of the players being friends, the ire which seems so readily excited upon the links might have been aroused, and the eloquence of language, for which golfers are justly celebrated, have quickly followed.

A golfer once met with a singular piece of ill luck when playing the North Berwick Links. He tells the story himself, and even in his own club, where he is known as a most truthful and upright person it was not at first received with the entire confidence which he claimed for it. Knowing the narrator as I do, I have no doubt as to the accuracy and take this occasion to say that I am prepared to believe even a steeper yarn from the same source. As happened, this golfer playing a hole of the famous old Scottish links, and coming up to the place where he thought his ball was, could not find it. He and his caddy searched for some time. Near the line of the course was an excavation; into this they looked, but could not find what they sought. Looking closer, he saw that a large drain pipe led from the hole. Investigating still more, he discovered, at the opening of the pipe, a trap set to catch some small animal. Examining further, he found that his ball had rolled into the trap, sprung it, and was safely held there. Of course he lost the hole.

This might appear to be the "Ultima Thule" of golfing credulity—the outer limit to which belief cannot reach. Some might consider it the last straw to break the back of confidence. But as has been said before, the golfer who tells it has never been found wanting.

The present writer and golfer has seen a ball, played out of bounds, fall in a large tin can. The player was obliged to play the tin can. To write that the can was played to the green, and that the ball then fell in the hole would be pleasant. As was the fact, however, the ball, when the can was hit, bounded out of it, and was then played in the regular manner.

There are many legends of the links—as mythical as the old Greek Legends, and as wonderful. Perhaps, as was possibly the case with the Greek Legends, there was once in the dim past some foundation of fact, but there has been so much added to the original material, that the facts of the case can no longer be recognized. The story of the man who played a ball into the wool of a sheep on the course, may be true. Things quite as remarkable have happened. That the sheep walked to the green, and shook the ball off on it, must be, however, doubted. That something the same story is told of a mythical raven, which picked up the ball and deposited it in the hole, gives the tale more of the true mythical character; the same story often appearing in various changing forms. However, at the risk of having his own word doubted, the present scribe must relate something which actually happened to himself. He was playing on the private links in the extensive property surrounding one of the famous country houses of the East. In one of the fields through which the course passed, some cows were pastured. Driving from the tee, he saw his ball carry a respectable distance—roll on a little farther—only to be caught up in the mouth of a small calf, which had been feeding a short way off. If he could say that the animal carried the ball on, and dropped it near the flag, the story would be better. Alas, truth compels the statement that the calf, after curveting along for at most a hundred yards, let it fall. Even in its incomplete state—lacking finish and climax—there would be hesitation in advancing this tale if there were not three witnesses whose testimony could be produced on occasion.

Indeed, "the queer things we do, and the queer things we see,"—to quote from the popular song once so well-known—in golf are very numerous. A ball that has dropped directly from the tee shot into the four and a quarter inch orifice of an eighty-yard hole, only, however, to bound out again, is a minor happening that may be attested from personal knowledge. And at the same hole—a short shot across an old disused quarry—a strange golfing incident occurred, which, if not an accident, was singular enough to merit narration.

A man who was a scratch player, was giving another man a stroke a hole. The man who was receiving these heavy odds, having won the preceding hole, had the honor and played first. As happened, by wonderful fortune—and this was a curious accident—his ball rolled into the hole in one. The other man had lost the hole before he had played a shot.

The rolling of a ball into a hole in one is not an uncommon enough thing to need particular mention. There are, however, records of such very long holes made in one, that a list of such happenings might very well be placed among curious golfing accidents. But every golfer knows of such, or has heard of such.

There is another golfing story having something of the mythical tone, which is yet so possible as to be almost credible. On a very rainy day—upon a very soft and clay-covered course—a golfer swung his club down on a ball resting on the side of a bunker. Watching to see the flight of the ball, he saw nothing. Looking at the ground, he could not see it. But, happening to notice the head of his club, he saw a large clot of clay clinging to it, in which the ball was imbedded. The story goes on to say that he walked up to the hole, shook the ball out of the clay into it, claimed the hole, and it was given to him. That the first could happen is highly probable, but the climax may be questioned. Still, this is not beyond the bounds of possibility, as far as the Rules are concerned, and with such strange things occurring, if not true, it is *ben trovato*

As the writer remembers what he has written, he is suddenly assailed with certain doubts. Either he may seem a person of quite wonderful credulity himself, or else one who seeks to make great demands upon the credulity of others. But, indeed, neither one nor the other is the case. Truth is, in fact, often stranger than fiction, and there is no place where this is more clearly shown than on the golf links.

The illustration which sneers a little at the head of this article may seem to be looking in cynical doubt. But even the illustration itself is a case of a singular accident, the proof of what curious things can happen.

In a mixed foursome, a ball was driven with a top from the tee by a fair but inexperienced golfer. Her partner made a clean shot. Again the lady topped the ball. Her partner played once more, hitting the ball fairly. Once more the lady made a poor shot, the ball, however, rolling on the green. After holing out, the ball was found in the state presented in this illustration, which is a direct photographic reproduction. The three strokes of the fair performer had neatly cut eyes and mouth as well as if it had been done on purpose. That this happened the writer knows, for he was of the foursome. He picked up the ball. He had kept it, and he has it now.

He who has penned these lines asks for charity. That he has not allowed himself to be misled, he hopes. That he has no intention to mislead, he is sure. Indeed, he assures the reader that the most of what he has said may be accepted unquestionably. However, he gives his assurance on his word and honor—and he believes that what he has said proves it—that many strange golfing accidents have happened, and will continue to happen to give even more interest to what is one of the best of honest old games.

40
The Golf Clubs of Long Island

Photos by T. C. Turner.

THE SHINNECOCK HILLS GOLF CLUB HOUSE.

THE GOLF CLUBS OF LONG ISLAND,

BEYOND THE CITY LIMITS.

BY CHARLES TURNER.

WHEN the great ice-cap, which ends now with the everlasting snows that feed the glaciers of Alaska, set out on its mighty trail southward, over the great Northwest, and covered with its gripping hood the Adirondacks and the Valley of the Hudson, it met its Canute in the warm waters swirling out of the Caribbean Sea, northward and eastward by Sandy Hook. Thus far shalt thou go, and no farther! was their behest, and the ponderous march of its central glacier was stayed. Laden with the spoil which it had wrenched and filed off a thousand peaks, submerged beneath its giant mantle, it crumbled into the semi-tropical sea, and deposited, through centuries, in the ocean's bosom, its freight of fragmentary rocks, until by slow degrees was built up from beneath the sea, the hundred miles of breakwater, which, to-day, we call Long Island. The Atlantic, robbed of its aforetime sea-line on the coast of Connecticut, lashed and tumbled in its fury against this new encroachment, and ground its outlying components into minute fragments. The storms and tides, in their everlasting see-saw, cast up the resulting impalpable grit. The winds blew it inland with every blast, and thus, slowly and surely, covered the rugged outlines with silvery dunes; and the giant playground was ready in time for the needs of the giant city, to which it now ministers.

ONE OF THE NATURAL BUNKERS AT EAST HAMPTON.

Nature did her work to perfection, and except where Long Island is given up to the market gardener and truck farmer, it is a playground of unequaled possibilities.

The winding horn and baying hound make merry music after sly Reynard among the sloping pastures of Cedarhurst and Meadowbrook, rivaling the far-famed dumpling hills of Melton Mowbray and Belvoir. The click of the polo-stick and the wild rush of the native bronco are heard and seen far and wide over the flats of Hempstead, outrivaling Hurlingham and equaling the native heaths of the home of polo on its Indian plateaus. The cyclist finds on its billiard-table roads the Merrick course, celebrated in song and verse, with almost classic antiquity and the century rides dear to the heart and ambition of the knights of the silent steed. The fame of the long ranges of Creedmoor has been carried round the world by the skill of the marksmen they have produced.

The sea fisherman and the fowler yearly bless its thousand inlets and land-locked waters, for sport beyond compare. Yachtsmen, the summer through, waft hither and thither in the safe protection of its bulwark against the raging Atlantic. Sportsmen after the higher game find in the wilder haunts of remote Montauk the seclusion their quarry demands. The summer girl, the summer hotel, and the family cottage dot its margins with evidences of happiness and prosperity that cheer the heart to look upon; and to crown its triumphs it is, without exception, the ideal spot of the United States to delight the heart of the golfer. Did claimants for links, each perfect in its conditions and environment, come "not single spies but in battalions," every claimant could be supplied with an ideally perfect ground, and leave yet others in countless profusion. On the coast alone, where the waves of the ocean, or the Sound, or one of the thousand bays of the island lave and lap the sand dunes dear to the golfer's heart, there are literally hundreds of square miles waiting for the arrival of golfers for whom it is no stretch of imagination to say it was made; to say nothing of the inland courses which other hundreds of square miles of unredeemed nature render possible.

ELEVENTH TEE, MAIDSTONE CLUB, EAST HAMPTON.

THE EIGHTH TEE, NASSAU COUNTRY CLUB, GLEN COVE.

See, ye golfers, what this profusion means, and how all your initial difficulties disappear! Here is no need to hunt for sites, no crushing debt to be incurred, to lay on the game its incubus; no heavy expense to create the needful bunkers. Nature has done that. No haunting fear that there lurks in the nearby village the speculating builder to oust you and forfeit your hard-spent capital; for you can draw stakes and move on to probably a better pitch to the right or left or forward or backward. And hereby comes in another advantage which will tell year by year the more in favor of Long Island courses. Having no drain on capital for site or bunkers, the greens can be the more lavishly provided for from the first, instead of having to wait, as in so many other districts, till the last. What this means to the golfer needs no comment.

That golfers early recognized the particular advantages which Long Island presented was partly made manifest in

OVER THE BROOK TO THE SECOND GREEN, MEADOWBROOK.

the article which I had the pleasure to contribute to OUTING last month on "Golf in Gotham," within the city limits. Over those arbitrary lines the march of the games continues uninterrupted from Garden City to Shelter Island.

One is scarcely over the border before the first evidence of the superior facilities for golf are evident in the course of Garden City, where, whilst winter is lingering in the lap of spring on all the nearby grounds, the perfect natural drainage of this somewhat thirsty land drinks up to the dregs winter's overflowing cup, and presents, ere March be well past, a condition well-nigh perfect for the golfer eager to flash his new-born zeal. It is not surprising, therefore, that Garden City's links should provide the first championship tournaments of the legitimate summer season, and that as early as April it should be ready for the championship contest of the Metropolitan League. It owes its existence to the zeal of Devereux Emmett, who, having played on most of the links at home and abroad, laid out the course over nigh faultless prairie pasture, and welcomed all the world and his uncle to enjoy its golfing excellence.

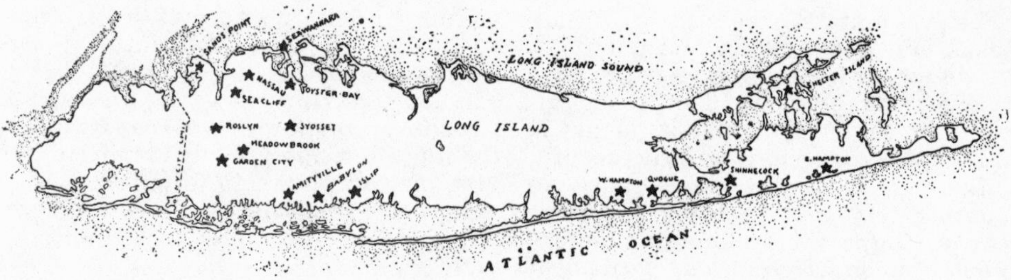

The beginnings of this course were peculiar in that, although they were not public links, in the sense of being made and maintained at the city's expense, they were open to the public under conditions. It is only within the past few weeks that they have come under the exclusive jurisdiction of the Island Golf Club.

The course is one of the longest in the country, measuring over its 18 holes, 5,651 yards; and is, through all its length, over a sandy, tough sod, covered with a red-top grass which gives, when mown, natural greens of unlimited extent, and of a texture to make envious the heart of a disciple of old Scotia. The pride of the course, which often goeth before a ball, is the bottomless pit between the second tee and hole, an old gravel pit, forty feet deep and seventy-five yards wide, which has to be carried, or woe betide the hapless player.

It was on this course, on the 15th and 16th of April, that Findlay Douglas and H. M. Harriman, who met in final play, at Chicago, had their preliminary skirmish, and Harriman gave the world notice that its golfing David had appeared, for he then won from the doughty Scotchman, the Metropolitan Championship.

Again, only just over the border of the city limits, but slightly further south than Garden City, is the links of the Meadowbrook Club, the home club of H. M. Harriman who, at the contest now just closed at Chicago, carried the scarlet coat, so familiar to the members of the Meadowbrook, to final victory in the contest for the amateur championship of the United States. The scarlet coat may be said to be the ancestral livery of the Meadowbrook, for the club has its roots far away in the seventies, when F. Gray Griswold hunted a pack of hounds hereabout, and was followed by a bevy of the best horsemen and women the metropolis ever boasted. The club is still the crack hunt club, with a side ally in polo that naturally suggested the conjunction of golf; for the swish of the polo mallet is akin to the swish of the golf club, and each may be made helpful to the other. That there should arise a demand for a golf course amongst such a set, was the most natural of evolutions. The kindred spirits had a common object; the country which presented the best features for the mounted scarlet coat was just the country for the scarlet-coated golfer afoot, and over its nine-hole course society disports itself each spring and autumn in numbers unsurpassed by any suburban club. The position of the links, lying on the yonder border of Hempstead Heath, over two miles from the station of that name, and the somewhat exclusive nature of the club tend to a limitation of their use; but, as in everything the club undertakes, the course receives the best of attention and well repays it, and golfers over the Meadowbrook links may well become accomplished players. The whole of the surroundings bespeak the enthusiastic sportsmen, and it is not surprising that Harriman should there have, quietly and almost unnoticed, prepared himself for the final efforts which this year first made him metropolitan champion, and now have crowned him with national honors.

The Nassau Country Club, the next nearest important club to the city limits, has no impulse behind it but golf. In its present location on its own 105 acres of splendid meadow and upland, immediately adjacent to Nassau railroad station, it may be in one sense considered the latest and most ambitious of the Long Island clubs; but in reality it traces its lineage back to a more remote period, for it is an outgrowth of the old Queens County Club whose links lay over on Oyster Bay, inconvenient to the bulk of those who through its medium became inoculated with the virus of the game. The extent of their enthusiasm may be measured by the outlay they incurred to secure and insure for years to come the exercise of the game in the uncontaminated country where, secure in their own possession and surrounded in every direction by estates which are not and are not likely to be in the market, they are intrenched against the probabilities of disturbance and enjoy a sylvan prospect, uninterrupted and unmarred. The 18-hole course of 6,102 yards length they are preparing here is commensurate with all the other preparations of the club, not the least of which is the magnificent collection of buildings which will make the Nassau Country Club a home and rendezvous worthy of the splendid residential district in which it is so happily placed.

ON THE RACE TRACK, FOURTH GREEN, WESTBROOK, ISLIP.

On the Berry Hills, a mile and a half from Oyster Bay station, is a links that finds excellent sport over its nine holes and 5,400 yards for the Oyster Bay colony, amongst whom the honored name of Havemeyer stands deservedly high.

FROM THE CLUB-HOUSE, NASSAU COUNTRY CLUB, NASSAU STATION.

Its proximity to the home of Governor Roosevelt connects it naturally with his family, and to give even a sprinkling of its most devoted players would be to cull the names of several of New York's best-known families. It is a typical club of the overflow of the golfers of the great city in their summer homes.

A near neighbor of the Oyster Bay Club, but on the hither side of the bay, is another organization maintaining a golf course, which shows how kindly golf affiliates itself to every class of outdoor life, and how necessary it has become to provide for it wherever that life is at its healthiest, or the cup of joy is not overflowing; and so that enterprising organization, the Seawanhaka Corinthian Yacht Club, has added to its Oyster Bay home a nine-hole golf course, on which those who are not actively engaged in the pursuit of the chief object of the club, yachting, can turn to that never-failing diversion, golf. That such a provision is wise and needful is attested by the patronage bestowed

THE CLUB-HOUSE, WESTBROOK, ISLIP.

FROM THE PIAZZA, SOUTH SHORE COUNTRY CLUB, BABYLON.

upon the links. We cannot all be Corinthians, and there be times and seasons when the weaker brethren and their fair charges show the better part of valor, "prudence," by stopping on land. 'Tis then that the wise providence of a healthy and invigorating land pastime justifies itself; and the parties thereto of the first, as well as of the second part, end a day of mutual satisfaction, and foregather in the evening to extol their chosen sports.

It will not be profitable to linger longer on the Sound shore of the island more than to mention the existence of links at Sands Point, over whose nine holes near-by visitors will have more than their dues by paying the merely nominal fee of $1 per day; and of another useful addition to the really pleasant life of Roslyn, in a course upon which it would be a libel to say that good practice could not be had, and no one who uses it will ever complain that

FIRST TEE, SEAWANHAKA.

they have not had experience and diversion for their money. Indeed, *en passant*, I am not quite sure whether learners are gainers or losers by the perfection of some of the classic courses, where everything is reduced to the theoretical "as it should be." A little of the rough-and-tumble often opens the eyes of the amateur to the possibilities and saves the subsequent adept from what might otherwise be very sudden and discomforting surprises.

When we don again the seven-league boots of imagination and skip-jack from the Sound shore to the Atlantic, and along that coast, we come to a new set of conditions, or, rather, to two new sets of conditions, the one the tidal inlets which thrust their thousand fingers into and through the soft marshes that marge them in the nearer parts of the coast by Great South Bay and its maze of waters. Then, further onward we come to the rugged sand dunes which live by the devouring wind and thrive on the hardy coast line in the yonder end of the island, toward Montauk.

A fair specimen of a marsh land course is the South Shore Country Club of Babylon, an old association, as becomes so ancient an assemblage, which aforetime made merry, and very merry, with lawn tennis. To Babylon golf has come, not like a devouring monster, but like a fairy godmother with magic in its wand, and lo! the expiring flame of outdoor life has revived under its benign influence. The old club-house has been floated to new quarters on the Santapogue River; the metes and bounds have been extended by the acquisition of the necessary acres of the McCue estate and forests; the old life has returned rejuvenated and lawn tennis is preening its feathers with the really well-deserved unction, "we told you so!" We are only too grateful to the pioneers who sowed the good seed and broke down the first barricades, which had too long divided the sports of the field from business and from sweet woman; and lawn tennis did that! So much, therefore, to Babylon's credit.

THE MAIDSTONE CLUB-HOUSE, EAST HAMPTON.

The next link in the chain of the seaside courses is Islip, or rather, to give its full official title, the Westbrook Golf Club at East Islip, within a quarter of a mile from Great River depot on the Long Island Railroad. The course is not ambitious in the number of its holes or its length, yet its nine holes give to the golfer some of the best of sport. It is an excellently kept course, too, and the turf is good, nigh on all the year round. It is intersected by two hazards of a somewhat unusual nature, a railroad and a race track, to say nothing of a perfect network of split rail fences that have the most exasperating habit of seeming to rise out of the pasture several inches higher whenever a ball has the right direction, but is pitched *just a trifle too low*. The race track is in reality the private training track of that old-time sportsman Pierre Lorillard, whose colors on Iroquois first carried America's thorougbred to the winning post in Great Britain, and not even the golfer, who most devoutly wishes his fences were twelve inches lower, will ever say so.

Eastward from Islip it is a long cry by the coast before the familiar tokens of golf in practice are again seen, but the possibilities, the unused and available thousands of acres, the miles on miles to which the golfer is the natural heir, pass under the tire of his wheel as he spins on and on, sometimes on good roads, and sometimes along the hardened line of sand which threads betwixt the passing and the coming of the tide, towards the little colony of four clubs which minister to the end of the island, lying between West Hampton and Montauk.

Of these, the first in point of age, honor and golfing importance, is beyond peradventure "The Shinnecock Hills Golf Club," of Southampton. Indeed, the claim of the Shinnecock Club to a premier position is by no means to be measured by comparisons with its three near neighbors. It may be compared in any of its characteristics with any club in the United States, and still maintain its right. No other club, for instance, can show on its charter a date at all comparable to that inscribed on Shinnecock —*September 22, 1891*. That alone would entitle the organization to preëminence; but it rests its right on no such a technicality. Over and beyond that, it has been the foster-mother of a colony of golfing missionaries who have year by year carried the faith back from its sandy and sea-washed home, to the remotest inlands, and produced as the practical outcome of the doctrine it has preached the incomparable and unconquered championess (whom it is still impossible to call *women*), Beatrix Hoyt.

Shinnecock is, strictly speaking, the one real link in the Scottish acceptance of the word that I have yet discovered, and I am familiar with many. Its every tee and green is within sight of the sea or bay; its base is the sand; it is, in fact, nature's handiwork.

THE TENTH TEE, MAIDSTONE CLUB, EAST HAMPTON.

Golfers therefore who know the links at Shinnecock, their natural attributes, their grand position between the bays and the Atlantic, the charm of the society which has so long gathered round Southampton, the zeal with which the game is played, the general and intimate knowledge of it, and the care with which nature has been improved on, will not be the least surprised that "Shinnecock" is a name to conjure with; and that the opportunity of its annual tournament draws with magnetic force the faithful from many points of the compass to do battle, and mainly meet defeat at the hands of "the knights and dames of the red course

ON THE FIFTH GREEN, SHINNECOCK.

and the white." For Shinnecock boasts two complete and separate courses, "the red course" of nine holes, being 2,642 yards in length, mainly devoted to women and lads, and the "white course" of eighteen holes, 5,369 yards in length, mainly devoted to the use of the sturdier section.

In point of picturesqueness neither of the courses has much to boast of over the other; both are beautiful. If anything the smaller course carries the palm for position, lying compactly in the undulating valley to the north of the club-house, and between it and the great Peconic Bay.

Nothing which suggests Scotland seems to be out of place at Shinnecock; yet I must own to a shock of surprise at finding in several places a plant of the real genuine Scotch thistle. Now I am satisfied these were not planted, the impalpable gossamer seeds of the thistle, so light as to rise in the air on the lightest breeze, almost forbids that theory. They were not planted by the hand of man, but may have been by his feet; for golfers in Scotland, as elsewhere, often wear

hob-nailed soles to their shoes (Findlay Douglas did last week at Chicago) and

A FOURSOME, LEAVING THE TENTH TEE, SHINNECOCK.

the soil in the interstices between the nails may well have brought over the seed imbedded in the hard mud, and when their wearers were playing at Shinnecock small fragments would here and there work out and plant the handsome emblem of old Scotia.

Away beyond Southampton lies the farthest outpost of golf on Long Island, "The Maidstone Club of East Hampton," whose eighteen holes lie picturesquely dispersed among the dunes skirting the Atlantic ; seven of them on the very margin of its waves, and the remainder surrounding, on either side. "Hook Pond," though why it should be called "Pond" is one of those things, as the late Lord Dundreary used to say, "no fellow can understand;" at least no fellow who has the spirit of outdoors in him, and the ozone, and the sweet-scented air, and the glorious sea and cloud scape of East Hampton, in all its summer glory around him, wants to understand. It is sufficient for him that pond, or inlet, or whatever its strictly correct definition, it is there to help his game, and by it to be transformed from a stumbling-block to an accessory. Not that it is altogether removed from the category of stumbling-blocks, as those who bemoan the balls buried beneath its placid bosom will be ready to attest by "appy-davit." Fortunately, the pond is not alone among sinners on the sporty links of East Hampton. It divides honors with other ponds of dry ancient sand, lacking nothing but water to add to their terrors, and with patches in a state of transition betwixt water and sand, which will be the more readily recognized if I called them young swamps ; whilst rank and sturdy botanical specimens of hardy grasses, which the proverbial donkey would lose patience in masticating, even though thistles trouble him not, are guilty of a capacity to entrap and secrete balls which might almost be mistaken for a guilty combination to promote trade. Yet, with all its sins of omission and commission upon its head, no course on Long Island yielded me the infinite delight of "Maidstone-in-the-Dunes," and that I am not alone in my tastes is attested by the loyal devotion of those who, through it, have made this remote corner of the wilderness blossom with the virtues that are the outcome of the health-promoting tramper after golf.

Yet one other course, one I have not personally seen by the bye, is reported to me to be worthy of a few lines, and I doubt it not; for the reputation of the Manhanset House on Shelter Island as a summer resort would indicate it to be one of those favored hostelries whose guests came from just the social strata to whom golf has become a necessity. For where youth and beauty and wealth and leisure are, and *health* is the supreme desire, there will golf flourish like a green bay tree ; and nowhere in surroundings more natural and appreciated than in "Long Island beyond the city limits."

THE SAND PIT, GARDEN CITY.

41

The St. Andrew's Golf Club of America

ON THE FIRST GREEN.

THE ST. ANDREW'S GOLF CLUB OF AMERICA.

BY JOHN REID.

I DO not think there is any golfer in the land, certainly there is no golfer who has once seen the present links of the St. Andrew's Club, at Mount Hope, N. Y., who will not be prepared to apply the reasoning that Dr. Johnson applied to the strawberry when he said that, of course, the Almighty *might* have designed a better fruit than the strawberry, but that He never had! With equal truth it may be said that nature might have prepared a better site for an eighteen-hole golf course, but she never had!

Nature has indeed been lavish in the outpouring of her gifts on that favored section of Westchester county. Woodlands, bountiful and diversified, with foliage which in summer covers hillside upon hillside with billows of greens of every shade to the farthest sky-line, till lost in the blue haze of distance, and through winter still preserve enough of cedar to soften the barren outlines and checker the scene to its remotest limits. Orchards in the valleys that, in the springtime, become a veritable ocean of delicious pinks; and meadows where the iris weaves its ribbons of the tenderest blues and black-eyed Susans and Margarets fight a battle royal for the championships of gold and white.

Even the primeval forces that raised this outcrop of the Laurentian hills from the backbone of the world, and the mighty ice-plough that graved through centuries untold its winding valleys, could not have worked with better judgment had they been directed by a mind specially bent on preparing for the day

T. B. UPHAM, DRIVING.

JOHN REID, EX-PRESIDENT.

when the pioneers of golf, for its own sake, would be searching for their ideal playground.

Even social evolution aided in the cause, for there are but few places within twenty miles of the home of the insatiable metropolitan real-estate prospector where such an estate has been preserved in all its primitive glory, undefaced and undefiled, descending in two centuries through but two families, and those, by good fortune, conservative and nature-lovers.

What nature planned, the experience of those who have been entrusted with adapting it to the use of golf have improved upon; and now, crowned in the very center with a club-house that stands, fort-like and commanding, at the apex of its playground, the St. Andrew's Club is a thing of beauty, and will be a joy forever. The very sturdiness and imperishability of the walls of its club-house attest the faith that "they dreamt not of a perishable game who thus could build."

Perched on its coign of vantage and jutting out of the brow of a hill, its piazzas on the one side command an unbroken view of the play on nine of the consecutive greens, whilst from its front porch the hills, gently rising and falling, lift up to perfect view the first and last tees of the unequaled eighteen.

Nothing seems wanting in site or in design, and certainly nothing else is omitted, that can make the tees, greens and bunkers perfect, or nearly approaching perfection, for their various functions. The purr of the busy mower, softened by distance to the faintest trill, rises from far and near; and through all the panorama the warp and woof of the ceaseless machine is weaving the green cloths to the similitude and quality of billiard tables rather than lawns. Twenty-five horses and ten men, plying from dawn till dewy eve, attest the untiring labor and care that are bestowed upon this first essential for serious and successful golf.

And serious golf is the charter of the club, its aim and its end. Not serious in the puritanical sense of gloomy—far from that—but serious in the sense that golf to be felt, to have the core of it reached and the pith and marrow of it enjoyed, must be played under certain fixed conditions. Then, and then only, its influence slowly but surely masters the mind, and it becomes a pleasure, indeed a fascination, which custom stales not nor does age decay.

Is it to be wondered at that under these circumstances the influence of the St. Andrew's Club for good has been widespread, and lasting, through the length and breadth of the land, and that its principles have given happily a tone

WILLIE TUCKER, THE CLUB'S PRO', DRIVING FROM THE FIFTH TEE.

and permanence to the sport, from the farthest extremities of Maine to the Golden Gate, and from Lake Superior to the Gulf?

It follows, from what I have said of the earnestness of the object of the club, that its course is by no means a drawing-room course. It calls into play all the sturdy and sterling physical qualities, and into requisition the skill of the most exact, accurate, and faithful practitioner. In the round of its eighteen holes the player will find, indeed, that there is need of all the judgment, energy and craft that practice has accumulated.

It may not be amiss, and may indeed be helpful, to those who in the coming years, from far and near, will visit this ideal home of golf for its own sake, and try their fortune in friendly contest for honors or against the mythical, masterful, and almost unconquerable Colonel Bogie, if, in the language understood by the golfer, I describe in some detail the physical conditions and the kind of play which experience has proved to be those required for a successful negotiation of the greens, from the drive off the first tee to holing on the eighteenth green.

The first tee is about fifty yards north of the club-house, the drive being almost due west to a green on the very top of the hill. There is at least 175 yards of level sward before the rising ground is reached. A really fine drive will reach the rising ground, and an exceptionally strong second may reach the green, although most players will be contented if well on in three. The green is a natural plateau, and is well guarded by natural bunkers. This green is on the highest part of the club's property, and the view from this point is very fine and most extensive. The distance from tee to hole is about 340 yards, and is set down as Bogie five.

The next drive is almost due east, to a large green overlooking a glen. There is nothing on the way to penalize bad play excepting some rough cops about forty yards from the tee. This green is edged with trees, the various shades of green, with the luxuriant dogwood blossoms, making it a very lovely picture in the early part of the season, while in the fall it is still more beautiful. To this hole is about 270 yards. A good drive and an iron shot should get the ball well over the ground. The Bogie score for this hole is four, and, unless some bunker be placed to make it more difficult, it ought to be done in four quite often.

THE CLUB-HOUSE, DESIGNED BY R. H. ROBERTSON, VICE-PRESIDENT.

The third tee is about fifty or sixty yards to the south of the second green and is on the edge of the cliff. The drive is over a hillock about twenty or twenty-five feet high. A good long drive should enable the player with a cleek or brassey to get on the green, although, in view of the bunker that is staked out to protect the green, the approach will have to be a very clean carry. The distance is about 240 yards. The green is undulating and very fine. The Bogie for this hole is also four.

THE CLUB-HOUSE PIAZZA.

The next drive is from a tee thirty yards north of the third green to a green within thirty yards of the first tee. The drive is downhill, and if the player gets a good long carry a brassey or cleek will get the ball well on the green; but after the bunker, which is now staked out, is made to guard the green, we think Bogie five will be found none too many. The distance is about 350 yards. The illustration (p. 403) shows fourth green, with Mr. J. C. Ten Eyck, the St. Andrew's president, putting.

Now we come to the fifth tee, of which we give two cuts, one showing W. Tucker, the club's pro', driving (p. 400);

THE DINING-ROOM, LOOKING DOWN THE VALLEY.

the other (p. 404) showing Dr. Moffat driving, with Mr. J. C. Ten Eyck, the president, looking on. Although we have not the pleasure of seeing his face in the picture, yet his friends agree that it is a most expressive likeness.

The drive from this tee is not only a novel one, but, indeed, is quite sensational. We venture to say that nothing quite like it will be found on any other links in the country. The drive is into a valley 150 yards below. A good drive—and it must be practically all carry, for the ball, by the time it reaches the ground, is dropping so straight that there is little or no run—will get the ball within twenty or thirty yards of the brook that guards the green, when a fairly good iron will get it safely on the green, which is a very large natural one. Though perfectly level it is a most interesting hole to play. Not only is the drive a sensation, but the approach over the brook has to be well calculated, as an ill-judged shot is apt to get the ball into the brook in front of the green, or, if played too strong, it is apt to get in the second brook, which is just beyond. The distance from tee to hole is about 250 yards. The Bogie is four, and the Colonel will not be so very often beaten on this hole.

We are now in the valley, where are nine holes, all on perfectly level ground, in fact ideal, both from a sense and golfing point of view. This beautiful stretch of lawn, with its elm and chestnut trees (as shown by our illustration, p. 405), reminds one of some old English park.

The sixth tee is just by the brook, near the fifth green. Thirty yards ahead and extending to fifty or sixty yards toward the right is an old brook with some very rough ground, which means no end of trouble to a topped or sliced ball. This carried, however, by a good long drive, then a long brassey may reach the green, which is protected by an artificial bunker running obliquely from forty to twenty yards in front of it. The Bogie for this hole is five, and four would be exceptionally fine play, the distance being about 340 yards.

The drive to the seventh hole is from an elevation of about twenty feet, just alongside the road, and over 130 yards must be carried to clear the bunker; a good brassey will then lay the ball near the first brook; then a good, stiff iron will make the green. All must be perfect shots, however, otherwise a score can be badly mutilated. The first brook is about forty yards from the green, while the second one is immediately in front of it; the distance is over 400 yards, and the Bogie six strokes. To beat Bogie on this is exceptionally good golf.

The next hole is one of the shortest and most interesting on the course. The tee is from an elevation back of the seventh green. The distance being about 135 yards, the green can be reached with a good iron shot, although it must be played just right, as a short-driven ball is likely to be caught by the brook in front of the green, while an

PRESIDENT J. C. TEN EYCK PUTTING FOR THE FOURTH HOLE.

over-drive may reach the brook beyond. This hole is Bogie three, though a very lucky drive may often score it in two.

The ninth tee is about twenty yards back of the main brook, but about 100 yards have to be carried to get over the second brook, after which it is all fair going until the green is reached, which takes three good shots: a drive, a brassey, and a good strong iron; the distance is 390 odd yards. The green is natural and an exceptionally fine one. A proposal is under consideration to lengthen this hole by changing the green to the north side of the road, making the distance at least 500 yards. This will increase the Bogie score, probably, from five to seven.

a good long straight drive is made, however, an iron should reach the green, which is guarded immediately in front by a brook, so that a ball cannot be run up, but must be pitched on the green. This is Bogie four, which should, I imagine, be hard to beat.

The next hole, as at present played (for this, too, is, probably, going to be changed), is rather tame in character, being a straight drive, without anything whatever in the way, to a green about 190 yards off, the Bogie figure being three, which ought to be made without trouble.

To the next hole, which is the fourteenth, the drive is over a hillock, about thirty feet high and about thirty to

Dr. H. H. Curtis. Dr. H. Moffat. President J. C. Ten Eyck.
THE FIFTH TEE.

forty yards from the tee. A carry of 150 yards will avoid all trouble, and an iron shot will reach the green. The distance is 225 yards, and the Bogie for this hole is four, it being a blind hole.

The tenth hole, as now played (in the contemplated change this hole will be done away with), is a little over 200 yards. The tee is from an elevation twenty-five feet above the present ninth green or brook. About 130 yards from the tee has to be carried. This leaves three shots for the hole to make it in Bogie figures.

In driving for the eleventh hole a brook about a hundred yards from the tee must be carried; then a good brassey and an iron should get the ball well home and the hole in five.

No mistake must be made in driving for the twelfth, as a pulled or sliced ball is almost sure to find a bad lie. If

The drive to the fifteenth green is over quite a high ridge, but, the distance being only about 165 yards, a fairly good driver will generally make the green. This green, as our illustration (p. 405) shows, is most picturesque in character. It is situated in a glen surrounded by lovely trees; indeed, a most ideal spot. The green is called the horseshoe, because of its shape.

The tee to the sixteenth hole, as that illustration shows, is from an elevation

IN THE HORSESHOE, FIFTEENTH GREEN.

just behind the green. This hole is most interesting. It can be played in two ways, either in a straight line, which necessitates carrying a clump of trees on the second, or by carrying the ridge about 150 yards from the tee, which insures a roll downhill on the other side, where the green can be approached at right angles. A strong player may make the green in two, but three will not be considered amiss, and the hole in five is Bogie play. This green, which is on the crown of a knoll, is one of the best on the course, being the very finest kind of old turf. In a straight line from the tee the distance must be

THE VALLEY GREENS FROM THE CLUB PIAZZA.

W. H. SANDS PUTS FOR THE FINAL HOLE.

about 260 yards, but in the way the hole is usually played it must be over 300.

The next, *i. e.*, the seventeenth, is the longest hole of the course at present, being about 430 yards, and, unless on the drive, is mostly uphill; consequently, making it in Bogie figures, that is six strokes, is to most players very satisfactory.

Now we come to the last or home hole. The drive is from the edge of the seventeenth green across the ravine to a green quite near the club-house, as our illustration shows. A good long drive, if straight (for a sliced or pulled ball is fatal here), will enable the player to make the green with an easy approach and enable him to go down in four, Bogie figures. This is an ideal home green, as the finish of all matches can be watched from it, the drive-off and all the play to the last put.

Mr. Chas. F. McKim. Mr. J. Fisher. Mr. H. O. Tallmadge. Mr. Robert Lockhart. Dr. Moffat. Mr. J. C. Ten Eyck. Mr. John Reid. Mr. J. B. Upham. Mr. H. Holbrook.

Copyright by "Golfing."

AN OLD-TIME GATHERING AT THE OLD LINKS AT GREY OAKS.

42

Golf on the Seaboard

BY HUGH FITZ PATRICK.

APHRODITE, arising from the sea, perchance invented golf; at any rate, the theory is short and is as good as any yet propounded concerning the inception of the ancient game. No one will deny that the best sites are those bordered by the ocean. "Links," in themselves, reveal this pertinent truth, for the original meaning of the word in Scotland, as Robert Louis Stevenson defined it in his story, "The Pavilion on the Links," was a stretch of country by the sea, consisting of "sand that had ceased drifting and become more or less solidly covered with turf."

In these United States there is no condition of soil strictly analogous to the perfect golfing ground of Scotland, yet the lighter cohesion of the turf, due to the absence of clay in the earth and the infrequent presence of clover on the putting greens, at times permits a comparison between seaside links here with those on the far side of the Atlantic, while, in the further charm of the game on the borders of the multitudinous seas—the bracing breeze or gentle air from the ocean, the ceaseless echoes of billows breaking on the shore, the flight of distant seabirds, and the contrasting views of land and sea spreading out in panoramic variety—the golfers of the two lands may clasp hands in full fellowship.

Whatever may be said of the origin of golf in this country the right to claim the first fully completed links is the due of a seaside club, the Shinnecock Hills Golf Club, which, in 1892, began the task of transforming the bushy sand dunes of Southampton, where until then the mosquito had sounded undisturbed "the small horror of his bugle-horn,"

FIRST TEE, NINTH HOLE, AND CLUB-HOUSE—TARRATINE GOLF CLUB.

THE TARRATINE GOLF-CLUB LINKS.

into a nine-hole course, since extended to eighteen holes.

The Shinnecock Hills, it is true, are not on the actual margin of the ocean, but on either side are the waters of Shinnecock and Peconic bays, while from every crest of the hills the rolling Atlantic fills the eye, which, with the calmer waters inland and the ever-present sea-breeze, keep the marine world keenly in mind. The turf, too, recalls the grass of the Scotch sand dunes.

After Shinnecock the trend of golf was for a time inland, and near every city from New York to Chicago the zealots imbued with the witching fever of the game had taxed their skill and art in the construction of links, with lawn-like putting greens and long stretches of rolling grass for the fair green, cleared often by the sacrifice of groves of noble trees. Nearly every hunt and country club had soon its golfing course, in most cases amid picturesque

SHELTER ISLAND GOLF CLUB.

surroundings. The inland links are an added attraction to the clubs and a new and health-giving recreation to the members.

Now the trend of golf is again to the sea. The underlying motive in this movement is with the golfing masses the desire to flee for a few months from summer heat inland to the cool shores of the ocean, and, as they will not endure any deprivation from their favorite game, the seaside links have come as a necessity into existence.

Seaside golf is, of course, therefore at its height when inland links are mainly deserted. The wane of the season at St. Andrew's means the wax of the season at Newport, Narragansett, Shinnecock and many another breezy site. After the summer crowds have gone the links are too often neglected until the dawn of the following season. In Scotland the seaside links are usually playable even in midwinter, and, even when snowclad, the greenkeepers are kept at work.

The golf season is now at its height along the Eastern seaboard. The links will be thronged until the golden rods show their bloom in the late fall, when the players will leave for links inland or to wield driver and cleek in the South, for, from October to the early spring there are seaside golf courses from Old Point Comfort to Miami, almost at the extremity of the Florida peninsula, to be visited. From the palms of Florida to the pines of New Brunswick is, as the Scots say, "a far cry," but it must be made to begin even an informal catalogue of the links on which the golfers are now gathered.

To cross the border is, perhaps, not a diplomatic move in these days of complications by sea and land, but as the course in question, the Algonquin Club links, at St. Andrew's, N. B., is chiefly upheld by Americans, the excursion is justified. Moreover, it is an eighteen-hole course, a distinction shared among seaside links only by Newport, Shinnecock Hills and Easthampton. The course is on a peninsula lying between Passamaquoddy Bay and the St. Croix River, which separates it from Maine. Eastport, the northeastern point of the United States, is twelve miles away. The St Andrew's links, although resembling inland rather than sea-sand links, afford grand golf, while beyond the links is a picturesque amphitheatre of tree-clad hills overlooking the town, the coast of Maine and the island-studded bay.

The rock-bound coast of Maine is far from being a fine golf country, yet the shore has its quota of links spreading over the grassy hills and plains that border its famous harbors. One of the most northerly is at Isleboro, at Dark Harbor, the Tarratine Golf Club. The Tarratine is a very popular resort for Philadelphia golfers. In 1897 the record for the course, of 41, was held by J. Wilmer Biddle, of the Philadelphia Cricket Club, while this season it has been cut down to 39 by J. D. Winsor, of the University of Pennsylvania. The course overlooks the waters of Dark Harbor and St. Anne's Cove, and is always swept by a sea breeze. It is a short course, 1,939 yards, to be exact. As befitting a course for seaside sojourners, the holes bear such nautical names as "Porthole," "Wave Crest," "Hard-a-Lee" and "The Mooring," the latter is the last hole, usually known by the hackneyed and threadbare title of "home hole" on club cards, so that this variation is very welcome. The turf is firm, and not so long ago was farmland. The view brings out the characteristics of the links, which. but for the proximity of the sea, might be mistaken for an inland golfing ground. But in the presence of the sea lies the great charm which draws the Philadelphians and their followers season after season to Isleboro. The club-house has been transformed by verandas and awnings from a quaint old home long used by a fisherman, and from this vantage place the scene in its calm beauty is refreshing.

There are other links in Maine, notably at Portland, Old Orchard, York Harbor and at Bar Harbor. Golf has not had an altogether prosperous career at Bar Harbor, although the Kebo Valley links are the best known in the State. The principal players are recruits from the links near Boston and New York, who pay annual visits to Bar Harbor and Mount Desert. Last year an open tournament was held on the links, with a brilliant field of players, that included M. J. Wright, a Philadelphian, who had been abroad to learn the game; A. M. Robbins, J. Wilmer Biddle, N. C. Reynal and Paul Gibert Thebaud. The Kebo Valley Club links are now maintained by a committee of summer residents that includes Waldron Bates, Robert Amory, Miss Draper, Mrs. Charles Carroll Jackson, Mrs. Henry J. Biddle, Mrs. Pierrepont Edwards, J. Montgomery Sears, A. C. Barney, George S. Robbins, Edmund Pendleton and Mrs. Joseph T. Bowen. It is a course of about 2,400 yards, and as Acadia Park, on the Cromwell Harbor Road, and crosses and recrosses the Kebo Valley race-track. It is of course a sacrifice to keep so good a links in order for so short a season, and there would seem to be a brighter future for golf at Bar Harbor if its promoters would seek the seashore a site nearer.

In New Hampshire golf flourishes near the sea at Rye Beach and Portsmouth, the naval officers taking an active part on the latter links, while the shore of Massachusetts is fringed with links. To summarize the holes and hazards of each course with the fidelity of an almanac compiler would not be of interest, but something may be noted of the varied features of the better-known links. The Plymouth Golf Club, the Myles Standish, of Duxbury; the Essex County Club, of Manchester-by-the-Sea, and, down on Cape Cod, the Oysterville and Cummaquid Clubs, the latter at Great Yarmouth, are all well known. The Cape Cod links are of the sea; sand dunes and thin-bladed grass suggesting future golfing possibilities, while the Essex County links are almost park-like in point of cultivation.

Stone walls encircle the links and a brook flows through a country that suggests an English inland course. Yet, as persons go to Manchester to be within driving distance of the sea, the course by courtesy deserves a place in this roster. It is a links that demands good golfing, and one of the red-letter times in the club's history was on that memorable day last August, when, in the final round for the women's championship of the United States Golf Association, Miss Beatrix Hoyt, of the Shinnecock Hills Golf Club, won the title for the second time by defeating Miss Nina Sargent, the champion of the Essex County Club. Miss Hoyt's win was by 5 up and 4 to play, and, during the tournament, she made the women's record for the course:

Out—5 4 7 4 5 5 6 5 6—47
In —7 5 6 5 5 5 5 5 7—50—97

This card is nearly as good as the grass records made by the Class A players of the club in the men's handicap.

Although lying back from the harbor of Newport, the Golf Club links are in sight of blue water, and there is, on the hottest days, a fresh sea breeze to inspirit the players. On one side, the view commands Narragansett Bay, lively with yachts and steamboats, and on the other there is a glimpse of the ocean. In that resort of fashion golf is now the most fashionable of pastimes, its devotees ranging from the wights who play at the game for a mild recreation to men who are scratch players at the best clubs, meeting at Newport for their summer holidays. Consequently there are always large fields in the semi-weekly members' matches, and, when the annual open tournament is held, usually in the last week of August, there is an additional influx of players, and the golf is of the most brilliant class. The club-house is one of the grandest and most beautiful buildings for golfers in the world. Originally, as when Charles Blair MacDonald won the first amateur championship of the United States Golf Association there in 1895, a nine-hole links, the course has been extended to eighteen holes, and it is a very good one, natural and artificial hazards alternating in agreeable variety, while the putting greens are of remarkable extent and in splendid order.

Down the bay at Narragansett Pier, golf is acclimated, but, with the perversity that marks the Bar Harbor, the players have gone inland for their links. One course is at the Point Judith Country Club, and, on the well-kept greens, golf fairly rivals the older established sports of polo and tennis with the members. A second course is at the South Country Club, a decidedly sporty one of some 2,200 yards, especially under the changes in holes made by the new professionals this season. There are hills and hollows galore, with some deep sand pits to be carried and a water hazard or two in the way of ponds.

Still within the confines of "Little Rhody" is the nine-hole course of the Misquamicut Golf Club, at Watch Hill. It is nearer the sea than the links at Newport and Narragansett Pier, and from its elevation is a grand place for midsummer golfing under most picturesque surroundings by land and water. Much of the soil is like Shinnecock Hills, but on the holes further inland the turf is thicker and mostly old pasture land. An open tournament is to be a feature this season, and there are any number of members' competitions. Many of the players are residents of the Watch Hill colony. The Misquamicut links are kept "in commission," to use the yachting phrase, the year round.

From Newport, Narragansett Pier and Watch Hill, southward to Atlantic City and Cape May, one might go golfing on a yacht, stopping every few hours to visit a links contiguous to blue water. Passing down the Sound the yacht would find a harbor at New Haven, where the links of the home

ENTRANCE ATLANTIC CITY COUNTRY CLUB.

club, on which the Yale boys have the right to play, commands a view of the shipping, while at the old yachting rendezvous, Greenwich, the course of the Fairfield County Golf Club overlooks the haven.

Weighing anchor, golfers would find a welcome at the Larchmont Yacht Club, with the right to play on the nine-hole course on the banks of the Old Saugus River, and, in passing Pelham Bay, the first tee of the finely arranged links of the County Club of Westchester is within a stone's throw of the anchorage. Heading across the Sound, the yacht might stop at Centre Island, the home of the Seawanhaka Corinthian Yacht Club, where, when not on their "knockabout" fleet, the sailormen practise on a short links, visiting for formal matches the nearby courses of the Queens County Golf Club or the Oyster Bay Golf Club.

A run to another famous harbor for yachts, Shelter Island, affords a chance for seaside golfing under historical surroundings. The course, of nine holes, is laid out on pasture land a century old, which affords the best possible lies for the ball, and is maintained by the Shelter Island Golf Club, an organization of the summer residents with the nautical Latham A. Fish as President. From the high greens there is a view of Gardiner's Bay, now thronged by white-winged yachts, and, in the Revolutionary times, the wintering place of the British men-of-war Culloden, Royal George, Grand Duke, and six or seven more great ships. The golf house, rejuvenated and sumptuously furnished, is a quaint Colonial structure erected about 1770, and on its veranda the golfer may rest mind and body, after the strain of chasing after the little white ball, in the contemplation of the landscape, with Gardiner's Bay and the distant sea as the background.

The putting green of one hole is on the highest point on Shelter Island, called Mount Pleasant. Here, at the close of the Revolutionary war, a beacon was kindled by the ardent patriots to send the tidings of peace eastward. Another hole is dubbed "Kidd's Treasure," and the putting green is on one of the spots where in times past fortune-hunters had dug to find the plunder of the notorious pirate. The playing length of the course is 2,428 yards for the nine holes. The professional, Willie Hunter, a newly arrived scion of the Hunters of Prestwick, in passing judgment on the links, states that "the turf is of the best, being very old, and it grows nice and thick, but not long, giving fine lies through the course in the line of play, but off the line the player is punished badly among a lot of small trees and bushes." This opinion is of increased value in its casual mention of the difficulties just off the line of play. It is not good golf to permit a jungle-like growth of tangled weeds and bushes just off the direct line of play, and, when the golfing enthusiasts have their way, there will be no vexatious delays made by the proximity of such hazards on a golfing estate.

Golf has found a sea-surrounded resting-place this season also at Fisher's

Island, on the Sound, the greatest of game preserves near New York, and in other years the scene of famous field trials, ere yet dogs and handlers migrated to the South for their yearly contests. On Long Island, sharing with Shinnecock Hills in the boon of a thin sandy turf, and even closer to the ocean, are the links of the Quogue Field Club and the Westhampton Country Club, while near ancient East Hampton is the eighteen-hole course of the Maidstone Club, which extends for more than a mile on either side of Hook Pond, and reaches from the club-house lawn across to the ocean dunes and beach. But Shinnecock Hills must still be judged the most typical of our Northern seaside links, for its sand dunes, as that devoted golfer, the Honorable Henry E. Howland, has said, "since the resolution of matter from chaos, have been waiting for the spiked shoe of the golfer."

Around Montauk Point a night's run down the southern shore of Long Island, the Shinnecock and Fire Island lights serving as distance posts for the race through the Atlantic, will bring the yacht abreast of the double towers of the Highlands, and, entering the harbor of New York, past Sandy Hook, there are fine water-front links that may be visited.

On Staten Island, close to Fort Wadsworth, is the course of the Richmond County Country Club, essentially an inland course in its hills and glens, but glorying in a mansion-like club-house perched high above the water. The porch, graced by huge fluted pillars that support the projecting roof, was the favorite resting place of the former owner, a man of power in the world of shipping, who here would wait, telescope in hand, to catch the first glimpse of his returning cargoes or to signal farewell to his outward bound craft. Now, all unmindful of marine ventures or of the perils that await those who go down into the sea in ships, the porch is a grand lounging place.

Should the golfing yachtsmen cast anchor in Gravesend Bay, they would have choice of the Dyker Meadow Golf Club, which, with a playing length of 3,006 yards, has the distinction of being the longest nine-hole links in the United States. It is withal one of the best, for the turf has been common land since the days of the battle of Long Island, and crisp and sinewy as only such old pasture grass can be, the blades holding up the gutta ball in tempting fashion for the brassey shots. Just back of Dyker Meadow is the short but sporty links of the Marine and Field Club, and at Bath Beach the golfer would find a greeting and good cheer at the headquarters of the club, in other years the patron of many canoe regattas. Adjacent to the yachting anchorage off Bay Ridge, is the cozy and picturesque club-house of the Crescent Athletic Association, where a well-arranged eighteen-hole links tempts the athletes from lacrosse, baseball and the cinder path to the practice of the ancient game.

Before sailing seaward again the voyagers would turn their prow to the mouth of the Navesink River and a landing be made at Seabright. Here, like the adventurers in Cooper's novel, the "Water Witch," who had studied so well the shoals and changing channels of the Shrewsbury, the yachtsmen would board the gig and row up the river to the links of the Seabright Golf Club.

The course is an excellent one and is on the north bank of the estuary, near the Rumson Road, about a mile above Seabright's ocean-beaten front. The turf is grand, although the red soil of New Jersey predominates in the earth, and from every part the silver ripples of the Shrewsbury and the deeper-hued waters of the Atlantic meet the vision. Near one hole, aptly called the "Hawk's Nest," a pair of those rare birds, the sea falcons, have claimed for generations a home on a gnarled and leaf-denuded tree, soaring seaward to return laden with the spoils of their fishing excursions to feed their nestlings, in utter indifference to the gaudy red coats of the golfers who tramp beneath their aerie.

The faith in the golfers is well founded, for to protect the sea foragers there is an unwritten edict at the club that the kingbirds, the active and predatory foes of the fish-hawks, must be shot at sight.

Across the river are the links of the Monmouth Beach Club, started fifty years ago for fishing and duck shooting, but now surrounded by seaside villas, and in senior and junior divisions ardent supporters of cycling, catboat-racing and golf. To mention the cycle is a reminder that by a short run awheel from Monmouth Beach our summer yachtsmen golfer may visit the links at Norwood Park and Hollywood. On the first-named course, as at Seabright, there is annually an open tournament for amateurs, attended by golfers of repute from near and far. The two links are in well-ordered perfection.

With the Blue Peter flying, the yacht has now but Atlantic City and Cape May to gain as havens. At Cape May golf is still in its primary stages, but a good beginning has been made, while at Atlantic City the season has witnessed a vigorous golfing foray, and it is there the sport of all sports, even tempting the veterans from the delights of chumming for weakfish or trolling for bluefish to hazard their peace of mind on the links. The course is on a stretch of meadow-land washed by the waters of Little Egg Harbor, somewhat rough, but by next season it will be one of the best in the land for all-the-year-round golfing. The club-house is admirably appointed, and the Atlantic beach is within a short journey for a dip after the round of the links.

There are vast possibilities for seaside golfing along the Jersey coast, for the beginning has only been made. Point Pleasant, Deal Beach and Allendale, near Asbury Park, where some of the holes are within a drive of the breakers, have started golfing this season with some energy, and the outcome is sure to be a success.

ATLANTIC CITY COUNTRY CLUB.

43
The Golf Links of Paris

OUTING

Vol. XLIII NOVEMBER, 1903 No. 2

THE GOLF LINKS OF PARIS

By VANCE THOMPSON

PHOTOGRAPHS BY V. GRIBAYEDOFF

WHEN you go out in a red coat with clubs, the Parisian no longer looks upon you as a sumph. He, too, plays golf. To be sure he is no Scot at the game. Not for him is the keen, steady, canny, judgmatical play of the man in red who drives a ba' ower the whinny links o' St. Andrews; still he does his best. Last year two clubs were established within a near cry of Paris. Each of them is due to French enterprise, though probably half the members are English and American. The links at Compiègne are a bit too far from town for the man who does not live for golf alone. If one is willing to go a couple of hours out of town for his golf he might as well go further and reach the sandy knolls of Dieppe or the dunes of Boulogne-sur-Mer. He who has played on the dunes, stretchin' lan'art in frae by the sea, will find little to tempt him to Compiègne. And yet 'tis a good field, well-grassed, with eighteen holes in the three miles of it, by the race-track. It was there they brought off the International Championship of France, which was won, you may remember, by Charles Sands, the historic tennis champion. The nine-hole course at Boulogne is about a mile and three-quarters, but it is admirably laid out, and the natural difficulties of sand, furze, and water are made the most of. It is on the race-grounds at Aubergues, within a short tram-ride from the sea-town.

For the Parisian the most accessible is the Golf Club of L'Ermitage. There, too, the casual visitor—wayfaring Scot or Yankee—finds the frankest welcome. And so, if you please, 'tis there we shall go first.

The Hermitage is a picturesque old farm lying between the Seine and the lift of windy hills on which Saint-Germain is built. It is the property of Monsieur Jean Boussod. He has bred many a good horse there—Kaiser, who won the Hundred Thousand, and that slim, gray beauty, Zodiac, among them. The links have been laid out in a straggling course round the paddock and pasture. They are new yet; indeed, there has been only six-months' play on them. You might describe it as a ladies' course—nine holes in a hazardless sward, without what Tom Maguire calls prime natural difficulties. The play, however, by reason of the narrowness of the course, is by no means easy. Unless you go very straight you are bound to get into the heavy grass or—heaven help you!—into the paddock or the Seine. The bogie is 37. So far the record is 33, made by the professional instructor, while Mr. Daunt has gone round in 34.

In addition to the breezy, poplar-shaded links there is a good tennis court. The club occupies three or four old-fashioned cottages, clambered over with vines and roses, which have been modernized into comfort. The decorations and furnish-

In Heavy Grass at L'Ermitage.

ings are summery and sportsmanlike. Withal there is a good table and a capital cellar. The best of it all is that "Golf de L'Ermitage" has been organized for golfers. One does not need a modern burglar's kit in order to break into the club. So broad is the hospitality that the member of any American or British club is admitted upon the presentation of his card. In fact, any one who is decently introduced may take out a subscription and play golf. The conditions are not onerous. You may subscribe for a year—men pay $24, women $12, and youngsters $8 for an annual subscription—for a month or a week. And then again the passing tourist or the lukewarm golfer may play for a single day by securing one of the special cards, which cost eighty cents. The gentle spirit of clubism, I fancy, can no further go. 'Tis an old true saying that no golfer ever committed suicide. That is well enough in its way, and the timid man might take to it as a kind of insurance, but the best of it is that it makes every man feel toward his fellow in a red coat like a verra brither. And this golfy, fraternal feeling the Hermitage Club carries a bit further than any club I have ever known. There is a teahouse out under the apricot trees where every one foregathers at five o'clock. Casual girls filch fruit and flowers. Men and women in flannel confront each other with score-books of more or less veracity, and though you may be an unmitigable stranger from what Chicago I know not, you will find yourself quite at home—all on the strength of the long drive you made for the seven, that famous blind hole. Thursdays and Sundays are the notable days at the Hermitage. The great courtyard is crowded with automobiles and cars and carts. The breezy links are speckled with women in white and men in red, working round, while the caddies shout "Fore!" to the amazed brood-mares in the pasture. And the folk who golf not may play tennis or Badminton or ping-pong—all pastimes in their way. 'Tis pleasant, too, to lunch in the raftered dining-room of the old farmhouse or to dine there as the night comes down into the valley and the lights begin to flare out along the heights of Saint-Germain. This is the sort of thing that decorates life.

Golfers who are serving time as exiles in Paris owe the Hermitage a heavy debt of gratitude. The verra place is health, and beauty, and freedom, a' in ane, no' to speak o' the blind-hole where you are aye playing "two mair." With all this, the club is not quite content. Mr. Boussod owns a big, wooded island, midway in the Seine, and opposite the five-hole. Next year the island will be included in the links, and a very pretty drive a man may make over the river. Whether the golfer is to swim across or take a boat I know not.

The young woman who went out in white upon the links of La Boulie said: "We are unduly tamed by civilization. There is pleasure even in being turned out on the grass. Parisian life is limited to two or three strong sensations: love, gambling, and the divorce court; golf combines them all."

Nor was she far from right, if by golf she meant the game described by a French writer as an amiable *promenade à deux à travers les sites vallonnés et changeants.*

Around the Farmhouse of La Boulie.

In the Tea Arbor.

The smart set goes to La Boulie because it is convinced that golf is elegant, *chic*, and a trifle wicked; *c'est le flirt*—by which they would intimate that the honest Scotch game is a mere roguish excuse for talking nonsense to a woman. 'Tis the French way of looking at things. Nine Frenchmen out of ten who play at the game take this view of it. Did they not see it in this light they would play not at all. And so the crowd that streams out to La Boulie, along the old Picardy highway—in automobiles, and breaks, and dog-carts—any fine day in the season, is largely made up of folk who do not know a tee from a hole in the ground. Princes and dukes and minor counts, a dowager marchioness or two, the Grand Duke Michael, Prince Orloff, the Marquess of Anglesey, counts of Montebello and Moltke-Hvitfeld, a half-dozen de Rothschilds, a few fashionable Americans give La Boulie a social weight and dignity to which the Hermitage does not aspire. This set forms the fringe and decoration of the "Société de Golf de Paris." It has given the game its vogue, and made possible the splendid links out there by Versailles—all of which may be accounted to it for a sort of righteousness. Steady players like Ridgeway, Pell, Haggarty, Daunt, Harrison, Barnard, Froment-Meurice, and Jacques de Pourtalés rise up and call them blessed—these scented girls and smiling Parisians who discovered that golf is merely a new form of *le flirt*.

La Boulie is a bit over a mile from the Gare de Chantiers at Versailles. It is the best inland course in France, and I fancy there are few better in England. Any one who knows the new course at St. Andrews, which lies between the old course and the sea, will have a fair idea of it; the lift of the hills is about the same, and, as at St. Andrews, the grass is new. In fact the links were only finished in May. In the 5,897 yards of it there is plenty of diversity. The fourth hole—a splendid rise of steep hill with two great bunkers in it—is as difficult as any. They have a pretty way of calling it the Himalayas, which is perhaps exaggerative. Still "No. 4" does crane himself notably above his seventeen brethren.

As I have intimated there is no difficulty in getting to La Boulie; it lies on the rim of Versailles. A long-legged man might walk out from Paris and take no harm. Leaving Versailles, you rattle over a cobbled street into a country road, mount a gradual

A Small but Attentive Gallery.

hill, and find yourself in a huge, square stable-yard. From unseen corners yelping dogs and yelping caddies swarm out on you. Odd enough is it to hear the French youngsters howling "Chances!" with good Scotch accent. (Come to think of it there was not quite that fine roll of the "a" that maks oor native Doric seem sae like to that o' auncient Greece, but for puir Frenchers 'twasna sae bad.) You drive out of the stable-yard and along a graveled road to the clubhouse, which is a bungalow on the crest of a hill. Comes to you there the secretary, a slim, bearded, amiable man, whose one defect is that he does not smoke tobacco. In precise and rhythmic French he tells you many things; among others: The membership of the club is now nearly four hundred—that fatal number! Of more interest to the wayfarer, keen for golf, is the fact that temporary membership is within reach of any one who is vouched for by two of that four hundred. Thus introduced one may play for one dollar a day, for five dollars a week, or fifteen dollars a month—a half off for the lucky folk who do not have to shave and may legally wear petticoats. Having learned these things, I said:

"I refer you to the Grand Duke Michael and James Gordon Bennett."

"Excellent," said the secretary; he summoned Higbee with a bag of clubs.

"But how do you know they'll vouch for me?" I asked.

The secretary bowed: 'twas as fine a bow as I ever saw: the secretary smiled: 'twas worth coming over sea to be smiled at that way; he said: "The Grand Duke is our honorary president, and I am sure he would be delighted, while Monsieur Gordong Bennett is the most amiable of men."

The first hole should be done in five; what I did it in doesn't matter—he was scant o' news that tauld his gran'faither was hangit. Then the girl tried; there was almost spiritual significance in the way she swung round on her dainty heel, as she sliced the ball out into the wilderness. What she said was "Dame!" a genteel French expletive which has nothing at all to do with your horrid English dash-blank. She is tamed by civilization and "Dame!" sufficed her. A wheen o' lean caddies went looking for the ball and we continued. I might remark—not that it is necessary, but merely that I happen

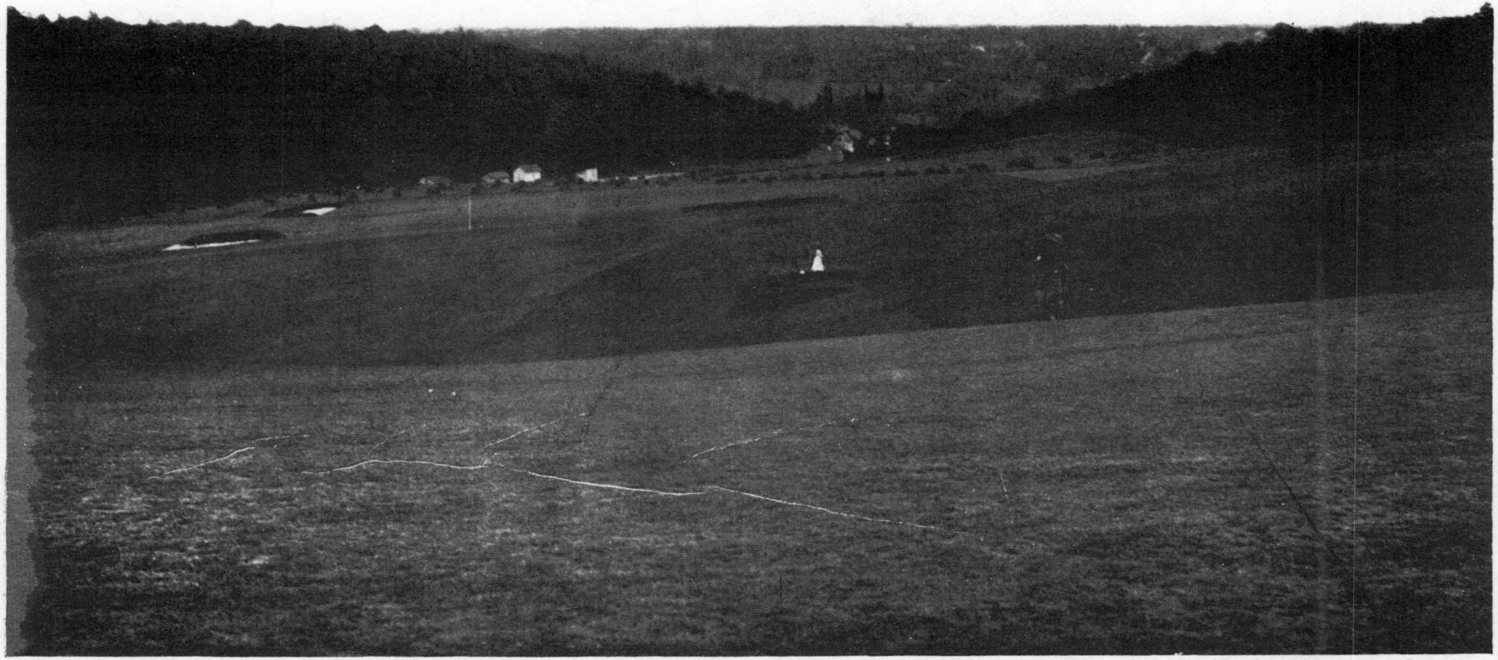

"No. 4," the Himalayas, at La Boulie.

to think of it—that even as the lady sliced the ball, a fat photographer dancing to and fro in the background and squinting through his finder, did ignobly snap-shot her.

The two-hole in five; "Verra guid," said Higbee, but it wasn't. The three-hole in four; "Verra guid," said Higbee, and it was. Then we went up against the Himalayas and played two more in the hollow, and then watched the ball come back from the rise at the top, as one might watch Santos-Dumont. There are maniacs who say the par value of the hole is five—instead of eight or ten or fifteen, as it should rightfully be. The nine-hole brought us back to the bungalow, and we set out in the other direction, down the lawny slope of hillocks toward the Versailles road. It was a sylvan scene—

Made green by the sprinkling of hoses,
And gracious with temperate hills.

New grass, quoth 'a? It was smug as a cricket-field. There were eight horses there pulling grass-clippers, and twenty men in blouses were picking up grass blades. Do you remember the story of the Archbishop and the Duchesse de Lesdiguières? 'Tis not so good as the story of the Grouse in the Gunroom, but that is older. The Duchesse really had no right to visit the Archbishop and philander with him, strolling to and fro in his garden of Conflans. They both realized it. Therefore, as they strolled, gardeners followed with rakes and effaced their footsteps. So, if there was any sin in it (I sincerely hope there was none) there was no scandal. It was the same thing with the half-price, skirted thing who sliced and topped and holed her ball round the links of La Boulie. Eight horse-drawn machines and twenty diligent men effaced her traces; sin there may have been, scandal there was none. As one scratches the head of a hawk to please him, one pays uncostly compliments to half-price folk.

"Golf were nothing without women," said I, "and it was well said by the Frenchman: '*Golf—c'est le flirt.*'"

The half-priced thing stared with angry, honest eyes and spoke with decisive lips—she was a Yankee, and looked upon love as a four-square ring wherein one should wrestle in a spirit of unself-sacrificing vehemence—and she said: "Oh, I do hate a fool!"

There are politer ways of acknowledging that one can't play golf.

It was an August afternoon; golfing Parisians were at Deauville or Dieppe, Pau or Boulogne, or on the tolerable links of Compiègne. Still as we daundered up to the bungalow we found nearly three dozen enthusiastic French golfers. Magnificent in red or white, beribboned with the club colors, were these native French golfers. Some of them were playing tennis; some were playing Badminton; some were playing ping-pong; some were playing croquet; the rest—who really had got close to the auncient game—were drinking Scotch whisky and water. Thin silhouettes in the distance, a half-score Yanks and Britishers were whanging invisible balls. I said to Higbee: "Higbee, have a cigar?" Higbee had the cigar.

"And tell me," I said, "what do you think of the French as golfers?"

Like Balaam (that unwilling prophet) he spoke under compulsion and in spite of himself, and he said: "The fact is the Frenchmen dinna and *canna* understan' games. I'm no meanin' cairds or billiards and sic risky things as you lose money by, but neeborly oot-o'-door games. I think it maun be allooed that a native like mysel kens mair aboot the thing than a foriner."

"Native o' what, Higbee?"

"O' St. Andra's. Na, the Frenchmen are na preceesely adapted for gawf. They are an even-forrit, playfu' people, wi' exuberant speerits, but they are na canny and judgmatical as the gawfer maun be."

I am very much afraid that Higbee is right. Shall I tell you a true thing—once will hardly fasten the habit on me—this, then: Four men I saw and they were golfers; the grassy knolls lay before them a picture and an incentive and an unco' temptation; and they sat around a table under the trees and played what game of cards I know not. They were counts and dukes, perhaps, and one of them might have been a Rothschild. Men, men, dinna ye ken how it gars me grue? Ye, who micht be whanging the ba' ower the breezy knowes! And there ye sit, bitten by the black, vermeellion-spotted spider o' the cairds, wastin' siller at a thowless game! Well, 'tis by ordinair, the French callant's way—puir daft loon that he is in maiters he dinna and canna understan'.

The sweep of the view was before us as we sat in front of the bungalow and drank tea. The evening fell. From some village church among the hills the Angelus rang, faint and thin as a skeptic's prayer. A flight of startled rooks streamed overhead, shrieking like lost souls. It was the melancholy hour, neither night nor day. The very tea tasted bitter. The cigarettes smelt of hay. The half-price thing, I was persuaded, should be marked down to a quarter. Neither golf nor girls are tolerable at twilight. Golf belongs to the windy day, when there is a veil across the sun. Women should come in with the lamps and the moths. Something of this sort you said to the skirted Yankee, and she retorted, properly enough, that there were lights in Paris. Therefore, you drove away from La Boulie and out of Versailles and through Ville d'Avray and down the steep, stony road of Sèvres, and so on into the big city, violently lighted now, and clanging with life and laughter. Thus you rounded up the day with lamps and moths. And between the salad and the cheese you read the rules of the Société de Golf de Paris and learned:

"Les enfants de membres âgés de moins de 18 ans, sont admis à jouer au Golf, *sur la demande écrite de leurs parents*. Ils paient un droit de 50 francs par an, ou de 10 francs par mois."

It occurred to you that the eighteen-year-old infants of America should know of this. Lest they forget!

A Bit of the Club House at L'Ermitage.

44

Golf for Women

GOLF FOR WOMEN.

BY "ALBION."

ARCHERY and croquet were the pioneers that made a breach in the walls which that awful personage Mrs. Grundy had raised up to separate the sexes in outdoor games; lawn tennis came with a rush, and, taking the fortress by storm, the colors of the stern and gentle sex now mingle in friendly contests on the netted courts and tented fields. The advent of this popular and health-giving pastime has created a new era in the lives of "our girls," and certainly has done "our boys" no harm. Baseball, cricket, and even football, have been lately tried by the fair sex, but never can become popular with womenly women. For those who object to the "slowness" of archery or croquet, or the fatigue which a hard-fought tennis battle entails, a splendid medium will be found in the grand old game of golf. Like the thistle, golf was but a few years ago considered indigenous to the soil of Scotland, but, thistle-like, the "down" has been wafted to many a fresh field and has opened up pastures new.

The main point which distinguishes golf from all other outdoor games is that it is a game of competition only and not of antagonism. Each player's object is to reach the goal with fewer strokes than the other competitors, and no effort is made to balk or delay them. It is a race of skill, in fact, and not an antagonistic struggle. The means of indulgence in golf are quite easily available in most parts of the United States.

The only condition which may in some cases create a difficulty is the extent of the field of operations, known to the golfer as the "links," for these fields must be of considerable area. In England the provision near most large cities and villages of commons or greens obviates this difficulty in inland cities, while the sea side in both countries affords an easy way of overcoming it for all the great centres of population bordering it. Indeed the broad beach is a favorite resort of the golfer.

If the site selected be on the level sands of the sea shore, which in a natural state presents too even a surface, and consequently few or no obstacles to the ball when traversing from one hole to another, it will be necessary to create artificial obstructions by placing between at least some of the holes banks of sand, technically known to golfers as "bunkers." This has been done to very great advantage in some of the links in England, notably on those which have been created on the level sand sea beach at Sandwich and on the chalk beach at Cromer. These bunkers soon get covered with vegetation, mostly of a coarse nature, and thus make excellent obstructions.

In the neighborhood of a city there are, however, pretty sure to be available rough pastures which, with little alteration, will make capital links. With such a ground provided all the golfer's real difficulties have disappeared. The remainder is but to learn the few simple rules which govern the game, or better still, secure the co-operation and instruction of some son of Scotia, of whom there must be many who possess at least an elementary knowledge of a pastime so common in the land of their birth. These secured, a little ball for each player, and a few light, easily handled clubs, and the golfer's outfit and field of operations are complete.

The game is to send a ball set on a slight elevation in such a direction and with such force and judgment as will best enable you by following it up and striking it again and again to take it, in the fewest strokes, into each of a circle of holes cut entirely round the links, as the playing grounds are called, and finally home into the last hole. The holes, which vary in number from seven to eighteen, according to the capaciousness of the ground, are about four hundred yards apart and are two or three inches in diameter; the ball is of hard, compressed gutta percha, about half the size of an ordinary lawn-tennis ball; the clubs are of ash, about three and a half feet long, tapering from the handle down very fine to the club head, which forms an obtuse handle and is weighted with lead and faced with horn. There is great elasticity in one of those "drivers," and a ball can be sent a long distance by an expert. "Cleeks" and "irons" are used if the ball gets into sand or scrub, and the "putter" when making fine strokes near the holes. The object is to go from hole to hole with the smallest number of strokes, and the party who makes the round with the lowest score is the victor.

It will naturally occur to the mind of the novice that in traversing the complete round of the links a ball, hit even with the best judgment, must, of necessity, meet with numberless obstructions, and at times get into difficult positions, from which it must be extricated by the blow of the club alone. These varying circumstances call for the use of clubs of differing shapes and fashioned for different effects. To go backward and forward to a given point for the particular club required would entail an endless tramp, and to obviate this a lad, technically called a caddy, follows each player with the reserve clubs.

When the intervening obstructions between each hole have been successfully overcome and the ball is brought into position near a hole, the interest in the game intensifies. To facilitate the play at these points the ground has, for a certain distance round each hole, been artificially or by the aggregation of footsteps leveled. This area is "the putting green," and it is here, simple though it seems, the greatest nicety in play is requisite. Too little momentum and the ball is still short; too much momentum and it skips the hole and, like vaulting ambition, "falls o' the other side."

At last the joyful moment of success is reached; the little ball disappears and a "hole" is scored. Then the struggle begins again; the ball is taken out and mounted on a slight artificial elevation; a driving club is again selected, and with a swish away it flies on its course toward the next hole, and so on and on until the whole round is successfully accomplished. And all this time the zest of rivalry animates the players. Sometimes one's opponent has forged far ahead; sometimes a few fortunate strokes have left him, or her, far behind, and over all blows the health-giving breeze and through all there is just that moderate exercise and play of wit and judgment which enervates without exhaustion and distracts the mind without absorbing it.

That the game is admirably adapted for a ladies' pastime there can be no doubt, and it has the advantage of being an amusement in which the fair sex are not so heavily handicapped as in other games.

Lady golfers are taking quite a prominent part in the game both in England and Scotland. Warwickshire, in the former country, and North Berwick and St. Andrews, in the latter, have ladies' clubs which have lately held very successful meetings, as many as forty competitors taking part in some of the contests.

At the West Cornwall meeting we find two ladies competing in the handicap, and one of them, Mrs. W. N. Harvey, made an excellent score, beating a number of her male competitors. At many of the summer resorts, and in close proximity to great cities, excellent fields for the game, which would bear favorable comparison with the famous Scottish "links," are in daily use. As a game for ladies there can be no doubt that it must become a favorite and popular one. It has the advantage of giving plenty of moderate and healthful exercise, without any of that over exertion that tennis may call forth and which every young lady is not equal to.

Even if the fair golfer does not become very expert, the mere indulgence in the game will ensure a return more commensurate with the effect than almost any other pastime. It will ensure at least one health-giving exertion of the most valuable nature, for the necessities of the locality will, in most cases, ensure the links being placed at a distance from the residential centres.

A pastime that proves an incentive to taking a brisk walk of a mile or two, over the fine breezy "downs," cannot be over estimated, while the pleasurable excitement of the changes and chances of the game keeps the mind from every thought of fatigue, and it is a game which can be very quickly learned.

LADY PLAYING GOLF.

45

The Giant's Golf

THE GIANT'S GOLF

By Henry Wallace Phillips

"YOU gintilmin think youse play a heavy game iv gawf, an' so, fur the koind of game it is, you do," announced Jerry, the club steward, softening criticism with discretion, a habit sometimes seen in loftier spheres, the idea being that if you knock a man down six inches with the right hand, and up the same distance with the left, his position is left undisturbed, although his feelings may be injured.

"Why, what's the matter with our golf, Jerry?" asked a young member, seating himself for the benefit of enlightenment.

"Nought, as I say, fur th' *koind* of game it is, but it ain't the only koind," answered Jerry, setting the lamp on the table so that he could speak with freedom. "Toime was when theyre was a diffrunt koind. Now jus' tek th' game th' Joint Shaugn played wid th' little man: that was sum'thin' loike; it had feachures to it, you moight say."

"I remember the Giant Shaugn very well, but I didn't know he played golf, Jerry; tell us about it."

"Oh, I d'n' know as 'tis so much iv a story," said Jerry, with a smile of conscious modesty, "but," he added hastily, before his hearers could come to the same opinion, "'twas loike this: Yer see th' Joint Shaugn was th' koind iv man you cuddent hardly say was a man at all.

"They'll show yer th' place back home, where he sat on Shaugn's Rock, an' washed his feet in th' Tiffy Brook, forty foot below. That 'ud mek him nointy foot hoigh, at the least calkilashun.

"Now, whoile Shaugn wasn't an aisy man, still he wasn't all bad; he was loike a ditch iv water wid a barrel of whiskey in it—there was plenty iv good in him, if only y' cud get at it.

"An' dear Mother! but wasn't he th' lad fur gawf! He had th' troonk iv a tree fur a droiver, which he'd put his foot on th' end of it whoile 'twas green, an' bent it round for a crook.

"As fur 'brassie bulgers,' an' 'baps,' an' 'niblicks,' an' 'baffy spoons,' an' 'taffy spoons,' an' the rest iv it, he made no use iv them at all.

"Wan club was enough fur him—an' truth! had ye seen th' ball he played wid, you'd know th' reason why.

"'Twas made iv the hoides iv three cows an' a calf, stuffed wid corn-straw an' fedders; ag'in, 'twas as big around as a steeple-clock. Sure, if it sat on the flure theyre, ye'd hafter get on th' chayre t' look over it.

"Much use theyre was fur a 'baffy spoon' wid a ball loike that!

"Well, one toime Shaugn went down to Galway, an' played the Joints theyre a match iv forty holes, an' he fair bruised the eart' wid 'em.

"Thin he showed 'em a trick. He ran around th' links foive toimes, keepin' th' ball in ther air th' whoile—that is, he'd hit her wan, an' thin get under it before't cud fall, an' whale her ag'in. A loively lad was Shaugn, fur his soize.

"That noight comin' home he thought well iv himself. The Joints had stood a bite iv supper an' more'n a swaller iv the rale ol' brew, an' Shaugn stepped hoigh an' woide, wid mebbe a swing soideways here an' theyre, as he went sloshin' across th' country.

"Now an' ag'in he'd let go iv a yell that made the grass stand up on th' mountain tops, an' if ever he saw a shanty, he sent a rock through th' windy.

"So he was havin' a great toime, when all iv a suddent, a tiny man, not over three foot hoigh, pops up in the road in front iv him. This man had a little, quick face like a monkey, an' 'Hillo, Shaugn!' ses he.

"An' Shaugn looks all around from th' hoight wheyre his oyes were ter see wheyre the sound kem from, feelin' very unkoind at bein' stopped in his woild career.

"'Th' divvel tek you!' ses he. 'Wheyre are ye hid?'

"'Here am I, at your feet, Shaugn,' ses th' little man,—sure, it was a fairy he was,—'an' I stopped yer t' see if you'd loike t' play a round with me in the moonlight.'

"'Er-hoo-hoo-hoo!' laughs Shaugn, when he sees him. 'G'way!' ses he. 'Git out iv me way!' ses he, 'or I moight step on ye an' spoil me clogs.' He ses this t' show his contimpt.

"''Tis a large cam-stick ye have theyre, Shaugn, me buck,' answers the fairy-man, 'an' it's loike you're good at th' play—you're big enough. Still, if ye feel that your hand's strong, an' your eye's stiddy, I'd loike to try ye wan,' ses he.

"Shaugn gits mad at that.

"'What d'ye mane by me oye bein' stiddy?' he ses.

"'Oh, nought at all,' ses th' fairy-man, 'only I saw by your gait you'd been havin' a sosherbul toime, an' mayhap you're not fit fur th' game—it takes a moighty clear eye,' ses he.

" 'Arragh!' yells Shaugn, twirlin' th' troonk iv the tree aroun' his head. 'Come along, ye gill iv nuthin! I'm the lad fur enny man that's under noine or over nointy!'

" He meant it t'other way round, but he was too excoited t' think.

" 'Come along, I say,' ses Shaugn. 'We'll play the Drood's Cave yonder fur the fust hole.'

" Wid that he goes an' picks up a rock half th' soize of a house t' use fur a tee.

" Now, whoile he was doin' that, th' fairy-man charmed both th' tee an' th' ball, so's he'd only t' wish, an' they'd do what he wanted.

" So when Shaugn, after teeterin' an' tiltin' t' git th' range, comes down fit t' droive a moile or more, the fairy-man just makes the ball hop fifteen foot t' th' front, an' old Shaugn's club whistles through th' air an' nigh dis-locates his shoulder in th' bargain.

" 'Well struck, Shaugn!' yells the fairy-man, 'but ye see I was roight in havin' me doubts about your eye!'

" Shaugn says nuthin', though, man! his thoughts was black, but at it ag'in goes he, an' ag'in he hits nuthin' harder than wind; now this would try th' timper iv a blessed angil, let alone a joint, so th' next toime Shaugn hammers away woild, blind, an' crazy, an' he foozled! Sure he knocked a hole in the eart' you could hide a horse an' cart in; the gravel an' rocks flew tremenjus, but theyre sat the ball on its tee as quoit an' easy as moight be; it didn't even trimble.

" 'Agh! Agh!' ses th' fairy-man, shakin' his finger at him, 'them eyes of yours, them eyes of yours, Shaugn!' ses he.

" 'An you say that ag'in,' roars Shaugn, shakin' his fist in answer, 'Oi'll smash you flat, as sure as O'im a joint!'

" 'Dawn't let the whiskey spoil your timper, as well as your eye,' ses th' fairy-man. 'Do you go on an' play till you're toired, an' then I'll show ye the game,' ses he, 'for, faix, I dawn't believe y' can hit the ball at all, at all,' he ses.

" If Shaugn was mad before, he was loony now. He welted an' he lammed an' whaled at it; he hit up an' down an' soideways an' cross-ways an' every way, but the ball always quoietly slid just out iv his reach.

" Th' way he stirred up the air made th' wind blow a gale; the sweat dropped off iv him in drops as big as a water-bucket, as he footed it around theyre swearin' the most awful that was ever heard—not little ord-nary remarks like youse gintilmin drop when you're caught in the bunker, but great big joint curses, that rumbled loike thunder in a cave.

" At last he was done entoirely, joint though he was, an' he couldn't so much as raise his club, so he lays down wid th' foam on his black beard as thick as suds in a washtub.

"'Are you through, Shaugn?' asks th' fairy-man.

"Shaugn nods his head 'Yis.'

"'Thin pay attinshun,' ses th' fairy-man as he cloimed up a tree to where he could hit th' ball. 'Now you see this,' ses he, holdin' out a mashie about twicet the soize iv a lid-pincil. 'Well, wid this small insthrument I will illusthrate th' foine points iv th' game fur ye. Are you lookin', Shaugn?'

"'I am,' grunts Shaugn. 'What will yez do wid th' tooth-pick?'

"'Watch close,' ses th' little man, 'an' make no remarks. I raise it so—d'ye see? an' I bring it down so—d'ye see? an' away goes th' ball,' ses he, 'straight fur th' Drood's Cave.'

"An' iv coorse it was so, fur the fairy-man had th' ball charmed, an' up it wint, an' down it came—bang! into th' cave.

"Theyre sat old Shaugn wid eyes th' soize iv cart-wheels, watchin' it.

"'Now, Shaugn,' ses th' fairy-man, 'I've shown ye th' art iv it, an' th' sun's 'most risin'. I'll give yer th' good advice not to play this game ag'in whin ye're in strong liquor—an' good-by to ye!'

"He jukked out iv th' way before Shaugn could get a crack at him, an' disappeared. Then up gits Shaugn, an' he goes to wheyre th' was a flock iv illyphants in Oireland at th' toime, an' he bate an' basted an' kicked illyphants till he took the edge off his timper—sure he broke th' backs iv fifteen before he could see straight, he was that mad.

"Thin he wint home an' built a big foire, an' he put th' cam-stick on th' very top iv it; an' after, he took th' ashes an' scattered thim to all th' winds that blow.

"An' that was th' last iv gawf, as you call it, fur th' Joint Shaugn."

46

The Why and Wherefore of Golf Rules

THE WHY AND WHEREFORE OF GOLF RULES.

Charles B. Macdonald,

Member of the U. S. G. A. Rules Committee.

IN America every person is comparatively a beginner at golf. For a beginner to comprehensively and intelligently understand and apply the rules of golf he should acquire some knowledge of the history of the game from which the rules have evolved.

A golfer born and bred in St. Andrews, Scotland, intuitively absorbs the spirit and traditions of the game, though he may know really little about the letter of the law. Custom made the law, and so St. Andrews has ever been a law unto itself in golf. When the myriad of golf clubs sprang up throughout the world, with every variety of golf course, some laid out in the Garden of the Gods in Colorado, others on the torrid lands about Aden, in Arabia, by the rocks, rills, ravines, and woods of Ardsley-on-the-Hudson, or in the cotton fields amidst the piny woods of Georgia, with their clay and sand putting greens, the custom at St. Andrews did not satisfy, nor could it meet the emergencies arising from the new conditions.

The original rules were drafted to apply to golf courses laid out on links, and later to apply to lands where it was reasonable to suppose it was possible to lay out a first-class golf-course. It was left to green committees to content themselves by making local rules to govern the exigencies of unusual courses. Nevertheless, the pressure eventually became so great by the mass of golfers that the premier club, the Royal and Ancient Golf Glub of St. Andrews, consented to a revision of the rules, appointing from its own members a committee known as the Rules of Golf Committee, to revise the rules, and to stand in future as the final court in all matters concerning the rules, their interpretation and their application.

As a matter of fact, this committee has scarcely made any changes in the actual play of the game; they have simply altered the wording of the old rules, and tried to arrange and state simply the many unwritten laws, that is, customs which have obtained in playing the game on the ancient links of Scotland.

The particular phases of the history of golf which should be thoroughly understood by anyone trying to master the rules, are the character of the ground, or links, golf was anciently played over, and an understanding of the early codes. Knowledge on these two points will materially assist one in imbibing the true spirit of the game in conjunction with the letter of the law.

Turning to the old Scottish dictionaries, we learn from Jamieson's Scottish Dictionary (Edinburgh, 1803) that links were originally the windings of a river. The word also meant the rich ground lying among the windings of a river. Later it also meant the sandy flat ground on the seashore covered with bent-grass, furze, etc. It was on such ground the ancient game was first played, so far as history harks back, that is, on links at the mouths of the Eden, the Tay, and the Forth.

Jamieson says: "In time the name was transferred, but improperly, to ground not contiguous to the sea." "The most probable reason of the designation is, that it having been customary to play golf on the links of Leith, when the ground in the vicinity of Bruntsfield came to be used in the same way, it was in like manner called links."

The student will at once realize that the original rules of golf were made to apply to links proper: low and slightly undulating sandy soil, well covered with whins, bent-grass, etc.

Where there was no turf the wind blew the sand so as to make hollows or bunkers. The old dialect dictionaries give the definition of a bunker as "A small sand-pit," or "A sandy hollow formed by the wearing away of the turf on the links."

The two original fundamental laws of golf embodying the true underlying principle and spirit of the game are:

The ball must be played from wherever it lies.

Nothing shall be done to improve the lie of the ball.

Given links and these two rules, surely the spirit of the game will be better understood by every sportsman.

The revised rules as they stand to-day have been evolved from the above conditions; and the extension of the code has been sanctioned gradually by the Royal and Ancient Golf Club of St. Andrews, a ruling body which has ever been in touch with the ancient traditions and customs of the game, handed down as they have been from generation to generation, from century to century. That is why the club is recognized as the ruling golfing body.

In reviewing the revised rules I shall endeavor to show wherein the alterations affect the game as it has been customary to play it in America, and to draw attention to some points that will probably cause discussion. The definitions are now grouped under rule 1 instead of being embodied in the different rules. I will touch only upon the principal changes or alterations.

The putting green now comprises the green beyond a hazard, if within twenty yards of the hole; formerly it did not.

What a hazard is, is now definitely stated. The phrase in the old rule "anything which is not the ordinary green of the course" is omitted. Golf clubs having quarries, ash, stone, or rubbish heaps, pigeon traps, woods, gopher holes, wood-piles, and other obstructions in their links must legislate for them if they desire them to be treated as hazards.

Bunker and hazard are not synonymous terms. On many courses in this country the writer is aware the term bunker is indiscriminately applied to all kinds of hazards, doubtless growing out of the loosely worded old hazard rule 15. A bunker is a distinct kind of hazard, viz.: A sandy hollow, whether natural or artificial.

The dictum that "Permanent grass within a hazard shall not be considered part of the hazard," has already caused an interpretation to be asked for. The ruling of the U. S. G. A. by the old rule 14, "That turf in a hazard or surrounded by a hazard shall be considered part of the fair green," the writer thinks was much clearer than the new law.

Straggling or scattered grass is not permanent grass, though it possibly might be considered permanent where the green committee has neglected the upkeep of the green. The spirit of the game would dictate to a player that the club should not be soled if it was possible to make an impression on the soil where there was any question as to the grass coming under the rule.

Further referring to this definition the writer notes his confrère, Mr. Laurence Curtis, in his article in New York *Golf* for April, asks the following question:

"Does this mean when the ball lies on such permanent grass that then loose impediments lying within a club-length of it in the hazard may be removed, whether they lie on or beside permanent grass?"

Mr. Curtis thinks the grounding of the club *only* should be allowed, and that loose impediments must not be removed on the permanent grass. A ball in play must be in one of three places: in or touching a hazard (e), through the green (f), or on the putting green which is being played to. (Def. d and f.)

Permanent grass not being a hazard it evidently then must be a part of "through the green" or the putting green being played to (which is not impossible). Consequently rule 10 governs the question, and any loose impediment (not being in or touching a hazard) which is within a club length of the ball, may be remov

Definitions (f) (g) and (h) are all new. That of "through the green" (f) is excellent and simplifies the interpretation of the rules. It has been customary to consider "out of bounds" (g) and "casual water" (h) as the committee has defined them.

In definition (i) [A ball shall be "in play" as soon as the player has made a stroke at the teeing-ground in each hole, and shall remain in play until hand out, except when lifted in accordance with the rules.] it is the opinion of the writer that the committee makes its only serious blunder. It undoubtedly was an oversight, when it added to the definition of a ball "in play," "except when lifted in accordance with the rules." This technically would practically permit a player to do what he pleased when his ball was lifted and in hand; clean the mud off, break or bend anything fixed, and take other liberties contrary to the spirit of the game.

Rules 9, 12, and 14 apply to a ball "in play." Rule 9, [. . . . . . . A ball in play shall not be moved nor touched before the hole is played out, under penalty of one stroke. . . . .] Rule 12, [Before striking at a ball in play the player shall not move, bend nor break anything fixed or growing near the ball. . . .] Rule 14, [A player or caddie shall not press down nor move away any irregularities of surface near a ball in play, etc. . . .] Rule 20 applies to a ball on the putting green. Rule 20, [When a ball is on the putting green, no mark shall be placed nor line drawn as a guide . . . etc.] According to the definition as it now reads, if the ball is lifted and in hand it clearly is not "in play" nor "on the putting green," consequently these rules technically are ineffective until the ball is replaced.

London *Golf Illustrated*, March 30th, says: "Mr. Curtis' proposed ruling was, 'A ball when lifted is not in play, and may be cleaned or another ball substituted for it.'" *Golf* commends the committee as acting wisely in rejecting this rule, adding "it would never do to allow a muddy ball lifted on the putting green —to be cleaned."

The writer was uncompromisingly opposed to Mr. Curtis' ruling as being in violation of the spirit of the game as expressed by the two original laws above given. Assume two competitors, each having an almost unplayable ball owing to adhering mud lying on the putting green, one ball stymies the other within six inches; the nearer competitor lifts and cleans his ball, while the other must play penalized by his muddy ball. Any golfer must see this would be unfair to the field as well as to the player's fellow-competitor. The letter of the law as it reads now might justify the player, but the spirit of the game—never. Many such instances might be cited.

Old rule 13, "A ball stuck fast in wet ground or sand may be taken out and replaced loosely in the hole which it has made," has been omitted, undoubtedly because it is against the true principle of the game to change, touch, or move a ball once driven from the tee if it possibly can be avoided. On first-class links it can be avoided, and why legislate for second or third rate courses? Local rules can cover their deficiencies without burdening the whole world of golf.

Regarding rule 33 [A player shall not ask for advice from anyone except his own caddie, his partner, or his partner's caddie, nor shall he willingly be otherwise advised in any way whatever, under penalty of the loss of the hole.], the question has arisen, Can an outsider looking and finding a lost ball be considered as giving advice in violation of the rule? Technically, it is an open question, but the spirit of the game has made it not customary to so consider it.

Another question sometimes asked is, At what time are competitors to assume new holes have been made under U. S. G. A. interpretation of special rule 3? It has been ruled that the Green Committee should decide this when giving notice of competition; in event of their failing to do so, competitors must assume new holes to have been made the morning of competition.

There will always be ingenious minds who will be forever proposing problematical questions as to the application of the rules of golf. Most of these persons are entirely ignorant of the fact that golf legislators have always recognized there are many questions that can be decided only by equity. Note old rule 40, or new rule 35: "If the point in dispute be not covered by the Rules of Golf, the arbiters must decide it by equity."

Only the other day an official of the U. S. G. A. read the writer the following query: What is the penalty when a player's opponent steps in the line of his (the player's) putt and increases the difficulty of the putt? The reply was, The rules provide no penalty, and the dispute not being covered by any of the Rules of Golf, arbiters must decide by equity.

This reminds one of the following story, which is quite apropos, for it shows the spirit versus the letter of the law:

In England, five-and-twenty years ago, during the infancy of lawn tennis, a heated discussion raged among the wise ones as to whether or no a player was justified in letting his racquet go over the net when rokeying. The wording of the rule was ambiguous on the point, and the disputants referred the reading of the rule to a well-known sporting barrister. His answer was: "I don't know any rule at cricket that will prevent the batsman leaving his wicket and hitting the bowler over the head with his bat; *but it isn't usually done*."

In like manner, in golf a player can step and mar the line of his adversary's putt. A player can also hit his adversary or his caddy intentionally with his ball and claim the hole; *but it isn't usually done.*

47

Theory and Practice in Golf

THEORY AND PRACTICE IN GOLF

By James A. Tyng

I AM firmly convinced of the desirability of the beginner in golf starting with a theory the mandates of which should be accepted without question; but the point to be determined is, whose theory, or what theory is to be recommended?

There are theories and theories. There are, for instance, the theories which are the exclusive property of the individual or class, such as the theory which induces Vardon to use his peculiar grip; the theory that advises Laidlaw to play all his shots off of his left leg; the theories that advocate respectively short swings and long swings, short shafts and long shafts, light heads and heavy heads, and so on *ad* (almost) *infinitum*. The family being such a large and prolific one, it would be quite impossible for the incipient golfer to determine for himself beforehand, which theory or how many theories it would be wise for him to adopt, for the reason that they are largely founded on the peculiar mental and physical characteristics of the individual.

Distinguished, however, from these theories of the individual or class, is what might be called the general theory of the game, which is the common property of all, and, consequently, is limited in its application to general principles, is concerned only with fundamentals, and has nothing to do with the thousand and one variations of form and style, the development of which is due to the special peculiarities of the individual player or class. If we accept this definition, the importance of adopting theory as a preliminary to practice is too obvious to need argument. It becomes at once a necessary part of our equipment. It is our helmet of faith. In every stroke there are certain elementary principles that are essential to a successful result. However widely they may vary in their methods, every successful player, consciously or unconsciously, is governed by them. Even the most "practical" player, who may think that he is bound by no rules, will find in the end that he is dependent upon them for whatever success he may attain. His struggle may be long and arduous before he comes to a realization of this, but sooner or later he will be driven to it; and when we hear of the trials and tribulations, the gropings in the dark to which he has subjected himself, we cannot but think how much mental anguish might have been saved him if only he had had a chart and had not tried to steer his bark by guesswork: for, even if, after many shipwrecks, he finally reaches port, he will inevitably think with regret of the rocks and shoals so needlessly encountered. His course at best is bound to be a stormy one; the hand of success is stretched out to him over no summer sea—and yet, others have navigated those seas successfully, and from their experiences have been able to draw a rough map of the route which, however imperfect, at least shows the principal dangers to be avoided.

I think it more than probable that I have been asked to write this article with the idea, that being generally considered a self-made "swatter," I would devote the space allotted to me to a presentation of the claims of practice as being alone worthy of recognition; but I must confess, that if in my early experience with the game I adopted the Dotheboys principle of "going out and doing it," it was only because I did not have the advantage of professional or other competent assistance, and was obliged to rely entirely on my own efforts for advancement. If the lamp of experience did not illumine my pathway it was only because I did not happen to have a match about me. I believe I found about all the bogs and pitfalls there were on the way, and have not yet been able to get the mud out of my eyes.

Casting aside, however, these beautiful rhetorical bouquets, we may come down to the plain categorical statement of fact: that the experience of others ought to be worth something to us, and when that experience results in a general agreement as to what are the essentials of success, we are taking a gambler's chance in seeking a better way. Now it may be asked, what are these essentials, and how are they to be recognized? The answer to this is, that an observation of the methods of the best players and a careful study of the various works on golf will give us the desired information; will reveal to us those basic principles from which each particular variety of play is evolved. And as we are concerned only with that part of the varying methods of play on which there is a general agreement, we need not be surprised to find how limited the field or how few the rules which govern it. Six of these rules I call to mind as I write. There are others, no doubt, though maybe not of equal importance, but the following will serve as illustration:

(1). Keep your eye on the ball.

(2). Don't hit; sweep the ball away.

(3). Don't sway your body.

(4). Let your club be moving at its fastest pace when striking the ball.

(5). Don't press—and last but not least

(6). Follow through with your stroke.

The correctness of the theory which embodies the above rules, and others of a similar character, which can be easily ascertained by observation and reading, must be accepted without question. To allow practice to swerve us from a rigid adherence to them would be to court immediate disaster. This caution should always be borne in mind and engraven on the tablets of our memory.

When, however, we have so assimilated the doctrines of this general theory of the game that they have become a part of our very being, we are then, and then only, it seems to me, at liberty to examine the credentials of the various other members of the theory family.

In the solution of the problem, if our bump of going to extremes is highly developed, we shall be likely to adopt one of two alternatives. If, on the one hand, we are not on speaking terms with precedent, we will reject all theories and rely on practice exclusively. If, on the other hand, we are theorists pure and simple, we will make a sort of a grab-bag selection of one or more and stick to them through thick and thin, regardless of all consequences—and whether the state of the last man will be worse than that of the first is a question that would furnish fine mental exercise for a Philadelphia lawyer. Still, on the whole, I rather think that the devotee of practice would have the better of the argument. Practice, unaided by theory, may stumble on a good form, but all the practice in the world under the guidance of a defective theory will never produce blue-ribbon results. Of course, there might be a chance of our theoretical friend stumbling on a proper selection of a complete set of preconceived theories, but the odds against this are too long and life is too short to figure it otherwise than as impossible.

If, however, we are not looking for trouble, and do not wish to play "fantastic tricks to make the angels weep," we will adopt neither of these alternatives: will neither cling irrevocably to any theory, which, however admirably adapted to the wants of others, is worse than useless to ourselves; nor refuse to take advantage of the discoveries of those who have already trod the path that lies before us: will neither persist in a style of play, which, however highly it may have recommended itself to us at first, is entirely unsuited to our particular physical and mental make-up; nor, rejecting the "glad hand" of experience, and walling up every avenue leading to success, except that of practice, endeavor to work out our salvation by our own unaided efforts.

We should fully realize, and never forget, what an important part these physical and mental peculiarities should play in governing our choice of methods, and have a keen appreciation of the fact that a vicious style once acquired is a very hard fiend to get rid of. As we ourselves are the only ones concerned, except in so far as the development of an evil temper consequent upon our failures and disappointments may react on others, we should be governed entirely by expediency. We have no commission that I know of, from either theory or practice, to preach the narrow gospel of exclusiveness. If we are thrown in contact with a likely looking member of the theory family, the forming of whose acquaintance would seem to promise advantage to us, let us cultivate him by all means, but let us remember that there is no mutuality about this friendship. He is our friend only for what we can make out of him. "Is there anything in it for me?" should be our constant query. Let us give him a thorough test, and if we find we are not receiving any benefit from his acquaintance, let us have no hesitation in throwing him over. We must never let sentiment or obstinacy enter into the case for a minute.

48

The Year in Golf

THE YEAR IN GOLF

A RETROSPECT AND SOME PRESENT-DAY CONSIDERATIONS

BY VAN TASSEL SUTPHEN

TEN years ago a beginner at the Royal and Ancient game borrowed a nice new ball of the professional and started out to learn golf. At the second stroke the ball went off the course and diligent search failed to discover its whereabouts. Sorrowfully the duffer returned to the club house and signed a voucher for fifty cents, the price of the lost gutta, according to the schedule then prevailing. To-day, in the window of a sporting goods shop, may be read the following legend: "Closing-out sale of gutta-percha balls, finest quality, $1.50 a dozen."

There is a gulf other than financial between 1895 and 1905. Golf is no longer a merely fashionable amusement, or a source of income to professional newspaper humorists; and secondly, an American invention, that of the rubber-cored ball, has marked a distinct epoch in its development as a game of skill. To consider the first proposition.

A decade ago there were but two prime essentials to the peace of mind of the American golfer, a red coat and local rules. The game could not be played at all without the former, and of the latter he must have as many as possible. To-day both red coat and local rules are as extinct as is the five-toed horse. The modern golfer prefers to distinguish himself by his deeds rather than by his apparel, and as for local rules, they have disappeared together with the freak courses that gave them birth. The following from my scrap-book reads oddly enough in this year of grace:

"A player who has done a round at the —— club will have passed over various points of avenue, steeple-chase course, race-track, polo-field and pigeon-shooting grounds; he will have come triumphantly through a purgatorial stone wall jump, a sand bunker and bastion, and finally, a vast gravel pit or crater. Rock piles, plowed fields, quarries, fences and chasms are among the other excellent sporting requirements of the course."

What a catalogue of horrors. But the adjective "sporting" was supposed to stand for every possible golfing virtue, and it was left for Mr. H. J. Whigham, our first real champion, to puncture the bubble. Commenting upon the above description he was moved to remark sorrowfully, "This sort of thing is exactly what a golf course ought not to be, since a golfer is neither a jockey nor a quarryman."

Fortunately his admonitions were heeded, and green committees began to realize that terraced teeing grounds, pocket-handkerchief putting greens, and an endless succession of cross cop-bunkers were not the whole of golf. Wheaton and Garden City were evolved and became the models for the new order of things. Golfers of the old guard will remember when the championship was first held over the Garden City course, and the astonishment with which they perused the simple statement printed on the score cards: "No Local Rules."

The rubber-cored ball. Volumes have been written about it pro and con, and it has been the endless theme of every golfing smoke-room. The first occasion upon which Mr. Travis experimented with the rubbered ball he condemned it utterly, on the ground that it could not be putted with any degree of consistency. A few months later he played with it at Atlantic City and won the championship. Since then it has been the subject of equally extravagant praise and denunciation; legislative aid has been invoked to bring about its suppression; numberless attempts have been made to improve upon its basic principles of construction. Yet it continues to maintain its premiership, a notable example of the survival of the fittest. Let us now consider its present and future influence upon the game.

Undoubtedly, the first and immediate effect has been to make golf easier. Men who could not possibly get more than one hundred and seventy yards with the "gutta" now drive their rubber-cored balls a full two hundred, and with less exertion; sheer physical strength has been very properly discounted. Unquestionably again, the crack player, as compared to the duffer, has failed to reap a proportional advantage from its use; the scratch man still drives a longer ball off the tee; but the iron shots through the green have become infinitely easier for the ordinary player to negotiate. When this became apparent a remedy was sought; the simple and direct one seemed to be the lengthening out of the holes. It is human nature to over apply a corrective principle, and, accordingly, the pet idea among green-committee men during the past three years has been to get the tees moved back farther and farther. As a consequence we began to hear of golf courses composed entirely of magnificent distances, of single holes eight hundred yards and upward in length, and of numberless kindred monstrosities. But for all that the goats refused to be separated from the sheep; the long handicap players, with irritating persistency, continued to keep themselves in evidence. It is only of late that we have begun to realize that the initial mistake has been the deification of the long driver and the consequent conversion of golf courses into mere slogging arenas, as an English expert puts it.

What then is the remedy if mediocrity is to be forced back to its proper level and golfing genius is to receive its meet reward? What sort of premium is to be placed upon skill as opposed to brute force and blind luck?

Obviously the play must be made more difficult, and we have already determined that this end cannot be achieved by indefinitely stretching out the linear measurement of the course. Neither is it advisable to pinch it in beyond certain recognized limits; there must be a reasonable allowance for human frailty in the matter of pulls and slices. The only expedient left is the judicious multiplication of the hazards.

During the past two seasons we have seen some interesting experiments in the placing of new side hazards along the line of play, and when these changes have been made with judgment they have worked invariably for better and most interesting golf. The man who prides himself upon his long, albeit erratic, driving is apt to think himself badly treated if a long pulled ball finds itself safely tucked away in a pot-bunker. Nevertheless, his grounds of complaint are untenable. Golf is a game in which brains should play a part at least equally important with that of the physical organization. In the old days, if a player happened to strike an unusually clean hit ball, with a following wind, and so reached a cross-bunker intended, under ordinary circumstances, for the second shot, he then considered that he had the right to drop back without penalty; generally there was a local rule that allowed him to do so. Now we realize that a true golfer adapts his game to changing conditions, and avoids the penalty of overplay by using a less powerful club. The same principle holds good for all hazards that lie within range of practical politics—keep out of them. All that a player can ask is that he be allowed a reasonable margin for safety.

It is upon the guarding of the greens that we must particularly depend as a basis of differentiation between the scratch man and his long handicap brother. The real art of golf lies in the approach shot (including of course the approach putt), and herein is made evident the slight but constant percentage that skill holds over luck; it is the distinguishing mark of such first flight professionals as J. H. Taylor. We must, therefore, make the approach to the hole as difficult and yet as varied as possible, and in so doing we shall also eliminate that old-time bugbear the leveler. It used to be contended that all holes should be laid out as even multiples of the full shot, so that the duffer should not be able to make up for a poor stroke by using a more powerful club for his second or third. In practice, this principle was found to be fallacious, since, granting a fair degree of steadiness, the class player must always reach the green in one or more perfect full strokes, and the approach shot proper was virtually eliminated. The man who could really handle his irons had no opportunity to show his skill, and everybody knows that free swiping is the easiest part of the game. Now, by the proper disposition of hazards, we may make a hole interesting and golfy (to coin a needed adjective), no matter what its measurements may be in linear yards. This great truth has been long in dawning upon our green committees, but it has arrived at last, and its fruits may be observed in the gradual evolution of old established links toward the higher standard. It should be noted in passing that club committee men are entirely justified in placing the holes for tournament play in difficult positions, so far as the side and back hazards are concerned. The long drivers consider themselves ill used if the flag is not in the exact center of a half acre of putting green; whereas, if it is golf that is being played, the delicate and well-judged approach ought to be as necessary as the screamer off the tee. But remember that variety of play is also desirable. To compel a lofted approach at every hole tends to monotony of play quite as effectually as the running up to the hole with a "Musselburg iron" on an open course. The prime essential is to place a premium on real iron play.

Inventive interest, in the past three years, has been so closely centered upon the improvement of the cored ball that the number of golf club patents has sensibly decreased. The use of aluminum as a material for club heads has had its little boom, and the clump form of putter still holds a good lead. Mr. Travis's fifty-inch driver is about the only innovation of note this season, and its novelty is more apparent than real. Clubs of abnormal length have been tried time and again in the past, and the pendulum is continually oscillating between the two extremes. Another year and we may all be experimenting with slugger clubs as short as a base-ball bat. In the long clubs the increased leverage does bring off a longer ball—that is a simple mechanical proposition. But if greater accuracy in hitting be also involved, how shall it profit a man who is wild with the ordinary clubs?

When the rubber-cored ball was first brought out it was thought that in time its use might do away with wooden clubs, for it goes proportionately farther off iron, and there are plenty of players who can drive a longer ball with a cleek than with a driver. But the real reason is that they are not so accurate with a wooden club, and are consequently afraid to let themselves out. The class man still gets his best results from the orthodox instrument, and this is as it should be. A year or so ago there was a movement to return to the old scarehead type of wooden club, but the reaction was too feeble to produce appreciable results, and the socket driver and brassey are still pre-eminent. Finally, the ball filled with compressed air instead of rubber windings seems to suit a certain class of players and is growing in popularity abroad. It all depends upon the style of a man's stroke whether he can get as far or farther with this type of ball; it is especially adapted to the heavy hitter.

It really appears as though golf had reached its bearings in this country, and we have only to wait for the more general elevation of standards in the lay-out of courses to see the establishment of a respectably large class of scratch players. Class A men cannot be turned out on Class B courses, and it is very doubtful if Mr. Travis could ever have done what he has without Garden City to try him out. Several years ago the proposition was made by some New England golfers to construct a so-called classic course, but the movement never came to anything. The idea has been revived by Mr. Charles MacDonald, and it was announced not long ago that the money had been subscribed to lay out a course which should not only be perfect in itself, but should contain as many reproductions as possible of famous holes on Scottish and English links. Certainly an interesting proposition, although, as a British authority remarks, it will be difficult to see how it can be carried out unless a combined attack be made some dark night on Great Britain's golfing territory, and the coveted hazards and putting greens be lifted bodily. Fancy the celestial wraths of the old-world golfers at being thus bereft of the Himalayas, the Redan and the Maiden! Seriously, the classic course is an admirable idea, and no one would be better qualified to work it out than Mr. MacDonald. May the required $100,000 and the suitable ground be speedily secured.

So far as the actual play of 1905 is concerned there is nothing sensational to record, no *tour de force* that is comparable to Mr. Travis's win of the British Amateur event the year before. Perhaps the most interesting happening of the season was the presence of nine American women in the Ladies' championship of Great Britain, the party including Miss Bishop, the then holder of the United States title, Miss Griscom, champion in 1900, and the Misses Curtis and Miss Adams of Boston. From the tone of the British golfing press before the event it was evident that the American invasion was to receive most respectful attention; there was even a hint that a feminine replica of Mr. Travis's success of Sandwich might be on the cards.

As it turned out, our representatives acquitted themselves creditably if not impressively, Miss Bishop losing a close match to Miss Roberts, and Miss Adams lasting until the sixth round. But even if victory was not to perch on our banners, it is gratifying to note the opinion of a well-known English critic to the effect that the play of the Americans averaged well up. To quote the exact words: "Their long game can be taught nothing more, but as yet they are not steady with their short irons or putting."

Miss Bishop was generally acknowledged to be the strongest of the American contingent, and Miss Margaret Curtis's long driving attracted comment. Best of all, to quote again from an English contemporary: "They won golden opinions from every one for their splendid grit and sportsmanlike spirit, accepting defeat as cheerily as victory. 'Real good sorts' was the general verdict."

The results of our national competitions reveal nothing that calls for special comment. The Amateur event went for the second time to Mr. H. Chandler Egan. Mr. Travis was a factor, as always, but his game this season has lost the consistency of former years, and it was no great surprise that the ex-champion failed to get even a bronze medal. But he may be well content to rest on his past laurels.

Unquestionably Mr. Egan is our premier native player, and he is the only college golfer who has consistently maintained his place in the larger golfing world. Wild as he often is off the tee, his wonderful powers of recovery are always in evidence, and he seems to need an occasional bad or heavy lie to keep him up in the collar. Dr. Fredericks' performance in winning the low score prize deserves a word of hearty commendation.

The Open event was again fought out between Willie Anderson and Alexander Smith, the former retaining his title by the margin of two strokes. The score of the winner was 314, which is eleven strokes worse than his card at Glenview last year. Mr. Egan did not play, and it is a pity that the old-world convention that the Amateur Champion of the year should enter the Open should not be observed here. It was Mr. Travis who first broke through the old established custom. As was also the case in the British Open, none of the amateurs at Myopia came within hailing distance of the honors. The score game continues to be the strong card of the professional. It may be noted that both Anderson and Smith were contestants in the British event, but their performance did not land them in the money. As neither man is a native

American born player their showing could have but a secondary interest in any event. It is somewhat discouraging that after ten years of active play no American professional has been turned out who can hold his own with the imported men. But there are some possibilities in view, notably young O'Loughlin of the Plainfield (New Jersey) Country Club.

Mrs. Stout was confidently picked to win the Woman's Championship, but her play was a disappointment all through and she lost to Miss Margaret Curtis in the third round. After being three down at the turn she made the match square on the fourteenth green, and seemed likely to duplicate her old-time specialty of winning journey home. But her tee shot on the next hole was bunkered, an inexcusable foozle, since the trap is barely one hundred yards from the tee. Another mess of the sixteenth hole followed and her chance was gone.

Miss Mackay, who finally won the title, is a veteran player and steadiness is the feature of her game. She made one score below 90 in the course of the week's play, but she never even approached the brilliancy displayed by Miss Margaret Curtis. The latter indeed should have won easily, but her old weakness in the short game cropped out at the critical moment. During the tournament Miss Curtis twice made the outward journey in 41 and once in 40. Considering the fact that the greens were not at all good, such scoring is simply remarkable. If she could only acquire a consistent quarter game and keep from going into the air on the greens she would be a champion indeed. On the whole, the general average of feminine golf has risen, and the tie at 87 in the qualifying round was very creditable considering the state of the greens. It is in the long game that the most improvement is noticeable.

The one important feature in the world of golf for 1905 has been the revival in Great Britain of foursome play. The four green match between Vardon and Taylor and Braid and Herd attracted an enormous deal of interest, and the galleries were said to run as high as fifteen thousand spectators. The English pair won by a large margin, but the interest was nevertheless maintained to the end, and there is every indication that the real foursome is again to have its rightful place on the golfing calendar. It is to be hoped that the fashion may reach our shores by next season, even if it results in nothing more than the dethronement of the cumbrous and tiresome four ball hybrid. The legitimate foursome is an ancient and most honorable variation of the Royal game, and it is an exceedingly useful discipline for the man who aspires to the scratch mark. There are arguments against it of course. It is annoying to be put into a bunker by your partner, and, as one eminent player has remarked, you only get fifty cents on the dollar in playing the round. On the other hand, there is a keen pleasure to be realized in making up for a mistake of your other self, and a crack player is sure to find many new and interesting problems in the negotiation of a foursome round. He gets a chance for brilliant recoveries and for the bringing off of strokes that might never come in the course of his ordinary play, and in the overcoming of unexpected difficulties there lies a rare and subtle charm. Moreover, one's morale may be infinitely strengthened by participation in an occasional foursome. The ethical objection has been urged against golf that it is essentially a selfish game, and the partnership interest is an excellent antidote. To bear with reverses that come not only with one's own failures but on account of another's shortcomings is excellent discipline for the soul, and may bring forth harvest on other fields of endeavor. Defeat is not so bitter when it is shared, and any victory is big enough to divide. Above all the foursome does not clog the green.

And now a final word. Golf is a good game, as we who love it know full well. But it has its active annoyances, and the chief of these, so far as our own country is concerned, is the caddie. Indeed, it is not too much to say that the American caddie is the worst in the world; every golfer knows what it is to have his day at the game literally poisoned by the laziness, the ignorance and the insolence of the average club carrier. But let us be fair to the boys, for it is entirely our own fault. For example, in Great Britain a player never touches his ball from the beginning to the end of the round. The caddie tees it (and tees it properly), picks it out of the cup, cleans it and indeed does everything but hit it. When golf began in this country our players were too impatient to train the caddies in their appropriate duties; the golfer wanted to do everything himself, and he never dreamed of enlisting the active interest of the boy in his play. The caddie was treated as a mere beast of burden, and such he remains today, an expensive and intolerable nuisance.

Now it is perfectly possible to make a decent caddie even out of unpromising material. It simply depends upon the establishment of friendly relations between the employer and the employed. Our American boys are quicker and sharper-witted than their English and Scottish cousins, and all they need is training to make them the best caddies in the world instead of the worst. The man who treats his caddie as a human being, who speaks to him in a friendly and kindly fashion, who makes of him a confidant and a mentor on doubtful points of play, is sure to get a response more or less promising. The boy must be made to feel that he is a partner in your business if he is to take a vital interest in it.

This is the theory, but in practice it is virtually impossible owing to the rule prevailing at nearly every club, under which the boys are sent out in rotation and the player is obliged to accept the caddie assigned to him. It is obviously impracticable for a golfer to train thirty or forty boys to his requirements, and he soon abandons the task. The player treats the boy as a mere machine and possibly never speaks to him except by way of correction; the caddie regards his work as a dull exercise on the treadmill and consequently shirks it as much as he dares. The result is mutual dissatisfaction.

At some clubs an attempt has been made to minimize the evil by dividing the boys into two divisions: Class A and Class B. The Class A caddies are supposed to be more efficient and better behaved, and get a slightly higher wage in recognition of their superior qualities. Promotion and degradation follow for cause.

This plan is only a makeshift, not a remedy. The boys are still sent out in rotation, the argument being that to keep a full corps on duty it is necessary to guarantee an equal amount of employment. As a consequent the standard of efficiency is fixed by the work of the poorest boy of the lot instead of by the best. There is still no incentive for individual improvement.

Now there is a remedy, and it is offered in the hope that some progressive club may see fit to give it a fair trial. Let the club guarantee to all the boys employed a minimum wage for the week—enough to secure their regular attendance even if there be no play at all: (Indeed, this is the custom now in force at most of the leading clubs.) Then let the players who care to do so be allowed to choose their own caddies, paying a small sum for the privilege, the extra compensation going to the caddie himself. Five cents would be enough or, if the premium be fixed at ten cents, then the caddie should be expected to clean the player's clubs without further charge. To adopt such a plan will cost the club nothing, the regular golfers will be only too glad to pay a small fee for really satisfactory service, and the boys themselves will have something to work for, a definite incentive to make themselves of value to the player. Under the laws of the game the player and his caddie are nominally one entity and they should be so in reality. A good caddie! If only American golfers knew what the word might and should mean!

The U. S. G. A. should be congratulated upon the fact that Mr. Ransom H. Thomas is to take a second term as president. He has made an admirable executive, and it was largely through his tactful handling of the problem that a growing scandal at the Open meeting was finally squelched. I refer, of course, to the action of certain golf-ball manufacturers in offering pecuniary inducements to professionals for exploiting their goods. The preliminary bidding was so spirited that the contest threatened to degenerate into a duel between the ball and the ball instead of being an exhibition of golf playing. It was proposed that the U. S. G. A. should bar all balls boomed after this fashion, but such discrimination would have been neither wise nor fair. Mr. Thomas communicated with the manufacturers, and at his suggestion all offers of extra prize money were withdrawn and the contest again became the Open championship. Otherwise we might have been treated to such a spectacle as was presented at a recent tournament in the Metropolitan circuit, when a certain manufacturer had the effrontery to enter as a contestant. He was attended by a scorer, a caddy and a negro carrying a large suit case filled with balls, to be distributed where they would do the most good. This sort of thing is trade, not sport.

The selection of Mr. H. Chandler Egan as one of the new committee men was an excellent move. Mr. Egan's popularity in the west is unbounded, and the fact that he is serving in the national organization will put a stopper on the plans of certain western secessionists who annually threaten the establishment of a western golfing empire. Nevertheless if the U. S. G. A. is to hold its premiership it must be truly national in its attitude, and legislate only for the broad and general interests of the game.